What Readers Are Saying About *INSIDE MicroStation...*

"[This book] is an invaluable resource for thousands of MicroStation users... [The author's] understanding of MicroStation is paralleled by only a few in this industry."

From the Foreword by David Dadoly, Vice President, Bentley Systems, Inc.

"...an outstanding job of presenting MicroStation CADD concepts to the user. The examples are real life ones that a user can relate to. The user is gently guided through a lesson and is shown more than one method or com - mand by which to complete a task. There are many helpful hints, tips and much practical advice on stand - ards that a user should consider."

Randall Damron, Manager of CADD Services, Eichleay Engineers, Inc., Peter F. Loftus Division

"I love [the author's] writing style—very readable. Good coverage of MicroStation."

Mac Otis, Manager of MicroStation Technical Marketing Group, Intergraph Corporation

INSIDE
MicroStation®

Fourth Edition

**Ranjit S. Sahai
and the
OnWord Press Development Team**

INSIDE MicroStation®
By Ranjit S. Sahai and the OnWord Press Development Team

Published by:
OnWord Press
2530 Camino Entrada
Santa Fe, NM 87505-4835 USA

SAN 694-0269

Fourth Edition, 1996

10 9 8 7 6 5 4 3 2

Printed in the United States of America

Library of Congress Cataloging-in-Publication Data

Ranjit S. Sahai and the OnWord Press Development Team
INSIDE MicroStation®

Includes index.

1. MicroStation (computer software)
2. Computer-aided design I. Title

ISBN 1-56690-099-9

Trademarks

MicroStation, I/RAS B, and InterPlot are trademarks or registered trademarks of Intergraph Corporation. OnWord Press is a registered trademark of High Mountain Press, Inc. Other products and services are mentioned in this book that are either trademarks or registered trademarks of their respective companies. OnWord Press and the author make no claim to these marks.

Warning and Disclaimer

This book is designed to provide information about MicroStation. Every effort has been made to make this book complete and as accurate as possible; however, no warranty or fitness is implied.

The information is provided on an "as-is" basis. OnWord Press shall have neither liability or responsibility to any person or entity with respect to any loss or damages in connection with or rising from the information contained in this book.

About the Author

Ranjit S. Sahai is a practicing professional engineer. He is employed by Alpha Corporation, a multidisciplinary consulting engineering firm based in Sterling, VA. He has worked on a wide variety of projects, including bridges, commercial buildings, waste water structures, airports, inspections, estimates, and construction management. Drawings for most of his projects are done in MicroStation.

Ranjit earned his Bachelor's in Civil Engineering and Master's in Structural Engineering from the prestigious Indian Institute of Technology in New Delhi, India. He then went on to earn another Master's in Mechanical Engineering from the University of Houston. Personal computers in general, and CAD in particular are a passionate hobby with him.

He was first introduced to CAD in 1987 when he joined Alpha, where all drawing production was done on a DEC VAX 750-based Intergraph system running IGDS, MicroStation's precursor. Of course, the original computer hardware at Alpha has long since been replaced. In its place are two RISC-processor-based systems running Windows NT Server providing print and file-sharing services to personal computers running a mix of Windows NT Workstation, Windows for Workgroups 3.11, and Windows 95.

Ranjit brought this best-selling book on MicroStation up to date for the fourth edition.

Ranjit conducted workshops on Windows 95/NT and the benefits of running MicroStation under that environment at the 1995 and 1996 MicroStation Exhibition and FORUM events. He actively writes for several magazines. His articles frequently appear in TMC's *MicroStation Manager* magazine, a monthly resource of MicroStation-specific information; and occasionally in *CADalyst* and *CADENCE,* both AutoCAD-specific magazines. He also reviews a variety of CAD software packages for CMP's *Windows Magazine* and writes a monthly column, "Ranjit's CAD Corner," for the Capital PC User Group's *Monitor* magazine. CPCUG is the third-largest PC user group in the country.

In his spare time Ranjit dabbles in photography. He also enjoys reading and listening to music.

Acknowledgments

I would like to take this opportunity to thank Bentley Systems, Inc., and their MicroStation Synergy Program for authors that kept me current on the evolving MicroStation 95, and provided me access to help during the course of writing this book and other magazine articles spanning the last few years. Special thanks go to the Bentley brothers, and to Phil Chouinard for always following up on my e-mail requests for information.

Intergraph Corporation deserves a special thank-you for letting me hang on to the dual Pentium Pro-based TDZ-400 I was reviewing for *Windows Magazine* just a little bit longer so I could get this book completed. Most of the screen shots you see in this book were captured on it. I would also like to thank my two contacts at Intergraph: Dorseda Wegert and Clive Maxfield.

Although I have not met any of the folks at OnWord Press who were responsible for getting this book in your hands, they deserve my thanks for their part. I would also like to thank Daril Bentley, also at HMP, who served as my project editor and kept the schedule for this book on track.

Essentially, I have revised the materials to bring them up to date with MicroStation 95. Dave Talbott at HMP asked me if I would take on this project. I am glad I said yes. I have enjoyed working on this book. Thank you for seeking me out, Dave.

And finally, a word to my wonderful wife, Manjit, and to our preschool-going son Amrinder. Without your support and tolerance for the time I have spent in my office at home, I could never have written this book. My heartfelt appreciation.

Ranjit S. Sahai
Sterling, VA
March 1996

Book Production

This book was produced in Corel Ventura for Windows by Patrice Werner and Michelle Mann. The cover design is by Lynne Egensteiner, using QuarkXpress 3.2 and Aldus Freehand 3.0. Additional software used during the creation of this book includes MicroStation, Hijaak Pro Windows, Corel Draw 3, and Novell Netware 3.11.

OnWord Press

OnWord Press is dedicated to the fine art of professional documentation.

In addition to the author, other members of the OnWord Press team contributed to making this book. Thanks to Ed Lorusso, Barbara Kohl, Suzanne Henry, Dwight Chase, Randall Mix, Roxsan Meyer, Michael Polera, Zeke Olguin, and Debora Willford, who contributed to the production and distribution of this book.

Dan Raker, Publisher and President
Gary Lange, Vice President, Finance and Administration
Janet Leigh Dick, Associate Publisher
David Talbott, Director of Acquisitions
Daniel Clavio, Director of Market Development
Rena Rully, Senior Manager, Editoral and Production
Daril Bentley, Project Editor
Carol Leyba, Production Manager
Michelle Mann, Production Editor
Patrice Werner, Production Editor
Lynne Egensteiner, Cover Designer

I dedicate this book to my loving wife Manjit, and to our son Amrinder. This book would not have been possible without your support and love. Thank you for the gift of time.

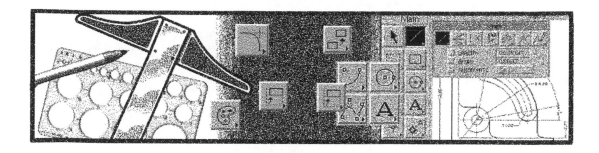

Contents

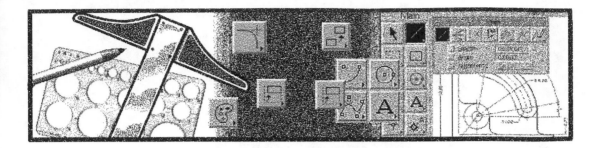

List of Exercises

From the Foreword to the Third Edition

Most experienced users of MicroStation agree that it is an amazing product. It has a limitless number of application areas it is used for and it is generally accepted that no single CAD product is as versatile.

Here's the problem: How can you become experienced with it? Where should you place your priorities on learning? When I need to learn a product quickly, I constantly find myself asking, "How can I get as high up the learning curve as possible, in the shortest amount of time?" While MicroStation's documentation is excellent, it may not provide you with the results you need. Sometimes you need to look at things from a different perspective before you can make sense of them. This book gives you that opportunity.

INSIDE MicroStation unleashes many important concepts and features of MicroStation. It is an invaluable resource for thousands of MicroStation users. It does not dwell on concepts used by a minority of our users. However, there are some lesser known goodies in here as well. Many of the topics covered are funda-mental to MicroStation, while integrating the latest technology and features of version 5.

.

.

.

As always, thanks for choosing MicroStation.

David Dadoly
Vice-President, Technical Services
Bentley Systems, Inc.
Exton, Pennsylvania, March 1994

Preface

Two years have gone by since April of 1994, the date of the Preface to the third edition of this book. I am pleased to once again have the opportunity to extol its virtues. This fourth edition of *INSIDE MicroStation* has undergone some significant and exciting changes. Its new title reflects the book's incorporation of MicroStation 95, including Windows 95/NT's new interface, AccuDraw, and MicroStation BASIC.

Ranjit Sahai and the OnWord Press Development Team have done a remarkable job of updating existing text and incorporating new material to make the latest advancements and features of MicroStation eminently accessible. They have also succeeded in preserving and improving on the best of previous editions.

MicroStation has grown with the needs of its users, and *INSIDE MicroStation 95* is right in step. Breadth of coverage, intuitive organization, and lucid text supported by illustrations, exercises, and examples throughout remain hallmarks of this perennial classic. Simply stated, it remains the finest professional MicroStation training tool on the market.

Dan Raker
Author, INSIDE AutoCAD
Publisher, INSIDE MicroStation 95
Santa Fe, New Mexico, April 1996

From the Preface to the Third Edition

Well it's ten years since we started writing CAD books and four years since the first edition of *INSIDE MicroStation* hit the streets.

I'm convinced that writing the third edition of a book is the hardest task an author can go through. With the first edition you pour your heart and soul into a book. In the second edition you clarify or fix problems you or others found with the first edition, while adding changes about new software features.

Then the third edition hits. The software you're writing about is probably 50% or more updated. The user interface is completely different. Even the way one thinks about CAD is different.

What to do? Do you keep the examples that worked so well in earlier editions or scrap them for new ones? Will thousands of new readers still appreciate the humor or do new levity's need be added to entertain loyal readers.

.

.

.

This book is nearly 90% rewritten: new pictures; new examples; and vastly improved type, images, and layout. But most important, this book covers MicroStation 5.0 like no other.

.

.

.

Without hesitation I reaffirm my statement from the second edition: "Congratulations! You have purchased the finest profes-sional MicroStation training tool on the market today."

Dan Raker
Author, INSIDE AutoCAD
Publisher, INSIDE MicroStation
Santa Fe, New Mexico, April 1994

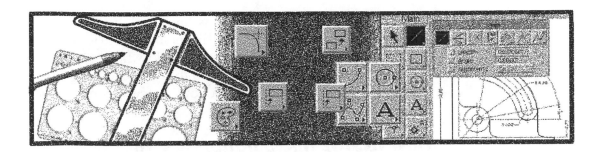

Introduction

How to Read This Book

Congratulations on purchasing one of the best-selling MicroStation books available. This isn't mentioned lightly. There are over 200,000 copies of OnWord Press' entire line of MicroStation books in print, *INSIDE MicroStation* being one of the cornerstones of the MicroStation line. What this means to you is at the conclusion of this book, if you have followed the exercises, you will understand MicroStation.

As MicroStation has evolved to become more mature, so has this book. The fourth edition has been updated to reflect not only the new interface in MicroStation 95 with its lessened emphasis on keying in commands, but updates you on the momentous changes that have taken place in 1995 at Bentley. An entire chapter covers AccuDraw, MicroStation's new tool designed to help you create accurate geometry with the speed and actions associated with quick and dirty sketches. There is also coverage of MicroStation BASIC, an easy-to-use macro language.

INSIDE MicroStation is written to guide you through the intricacies of the MicroStation CAD software package. During the course of reading this book you will learn how to use MicroStation in your design process.

As with any complex system it is impossible to cover every aspect of the program in one book. The intention then is to expose you to as much of MicroStation as possible while guiding you through the individual commands and their uses. Along the way, tips, tricks, and traps are pointed out as new concepts and commands are introduced.

How *INSIDE MicroStation* Is Organized

INSIDE MicroStation is organized by subject matter, starting with the basics and working through to the complex issues. *INSIDE MicroStation* roughly follows the design process, starting with simple drawing placement, moving through construction and manipulation commands. Along the way you will get hands-on experience with illustrations of various commands and detailed exercises that take you through the design process one step at a time.

Illustrations, Exercises, and Typographical Conventions

In the course of reading this book you will find a number of exercises, illustrations, and notes. These are all designed to clearly illustrate concepts discussed in the text. In fact, a lot can be learned about MicroStation by simply studying the illustrations and exercises.

To make them as clear as possible, they are presented to you in a standard format. These are some of the things you will find in this book:

Command Illustrations

To help orient you to MicroStation, a "standard" illustration of individual commands was developed. In keeping with MicroStation's cross-platform strategy, command selection is nearly identical on all platforms. The following diagram shows a typical tool illustration from this book.

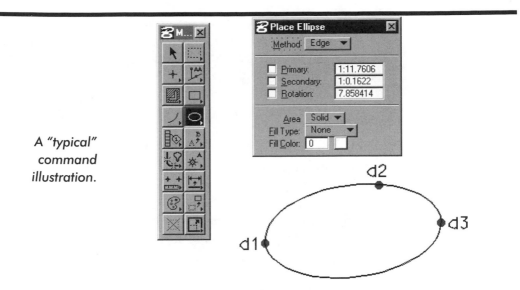

A *"typical"* command illustration.

Each illustration contains specific information on how the tool operates. First, you are shown its location on the toolbox. The option fields associated with the tool are always shown on the Tool Settings window. Next you are shown an example of the tool in action. Each step of using the tool is labeled with sequential labels starting with "d." For instance, if a tool requires three inputs from the user, the steps are labeled "d1," "d2," and "d3." The result of using the tool is also shown.

In the previous edition, greater emphasis was placed on using key-ins for commands. In this edition, however, the emphasis is on invoking commands from toolboxes and view control icons on the view window border.

Exercises

Each exercise is designed to illustrate one aspect of MicroStation. Step-by-step instructions are given, showing you how to use MicroStation to solve a problem. You can work through these exercises and create design files as you go. The companion disk contains the referenced design files for use with these exercises.

If you installed the companion disk, you will find a text file called EXERFILE.LST. This file provides additional information about the files on the disk. In addition, you should read the README.TXT file if one is present on the disk.

Each exercise contains a number of important features. Each step is individually numbered and contains a text narrative on performing one aspect of the exercise. Important information within the narrative such as user-entered data or tool names are shown in italic or a special font. Furthermore, in the case of specific commands or tools, the path to the tool is always given in bold (e.g., **Settings ➡ Design File...**). Tool names are shown in italics (e.g., *Place Arc by Center*).

Where appropriate, an illustration is provided, highlighting the portion of the exercise under discussion. Whenever possible, these illustrations are used to clarify potentially confusing directives within the narrative. The following example is a portion of such an exercise.

Exercise: Creating a Flower Vase

In this exercise, the flower vase presents the designer with the challenge of locating the two tangent curves.

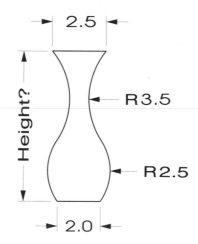

2.5

Height?

R3.5

R2.5

2.0

1. Open the design file VASE.DGN. Essentially an empty design file, you will need to establish a starting point for this project. We suggest the origin point (x0y0) as the bottom center point of the vase.

.

.

.

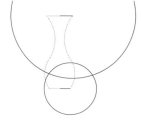

4. Set the *Circle by Center Radius* option value to 6.0" (that's 2.5 + 3.5). Again, using the endpoint tentative snap, tentative point to the right end of the vase's mouth. The result should be two circles that intersect, as shown in the figure.

You've now overcome the hardest part of this exercise, that of locating the base arc's center point. Let's place the circle.

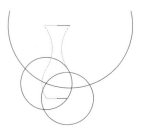

5. With the *Place Circle by Center Radius* tool active, set the Radius value to 2.5 (remember to select the Radius option). Next, we need to override the default snap (Keypoint) with the Intersection snap. Choose **Settings ➡ Snaps ➡ Intersection** and tentative point/data point at the leftmost inter-section of the two arcs. A circle of the desired radius should now touch the endpoint of the bottom line. This will later be trimmed into the correct arc using the *Delete Partial* tool.

Special Icons

Several other typographical features you will find in this book are notes, warnings, timeouts, tips, and metric issues.

 NOTE: *Notes present important information or concepts that might otherwise be overlooked.*

 WARNING: *Warnings point out functions and procedures that could get you in trouble if you are not careful.*

 TIMEOUT: *This is used to elaborate on a fact that may not be germane to the discussion in progress but is nonetheless important.*

 TIP: *Tips show short-cuts and hints that help you to be more productive.*

 METRIC: *Metric icons note issues of special interest to metric users.*

Special Notes to Metric Users

One of the strengths of MicroStation is its support of practically all measurement systems known to humanity. For this reason, it is a great tool for people who must work in English, metric, or both units of measure. A concerted effort was made to keep this book as "neutral" as possible. This means whenever units are discussed, a neutral term such as *unit* is used instead of *feet* or *meters*.

There are times, however, when you must take the particular measurement unit into consideration. In these cases, the author has chosen English units. The reasons for this are simple. First, English units are what he learned and uses on a daily basis.

Second, where English units are used in the discussion, a special note has been created to flag metric issues. This note will provide additional information for the metric user.

An example of a Metric note.

This note is also of interest to English unit users as well because it points out key differences in the two types of measurement and even includes a discussion on how to convert from one to the other.

How to Use This Book

INSIDE MicroStation is an introductory-level book designed primarily for users new to MicroStation. Nevertheless, there is information here for more advanced users as well.

The key to this book is the way the material is presented and indexed. Fully indexed illustrations, tutorials, and exercises provide a quick way of finding graphic representations of commands and concepts. This suggests several ways of using the book.

The New User: Reading from Beginning to End

This is highly recommended for those who are new to MicroStation. *INSIDE MicroStation* is an accessible introduction to CAD. More than just a compendium of command descriptions, it shows how to work through a design, from where to place the first point, to detailing, and finally to plotting. Reading this book will turn the complete beginner into a real MicroStation user.

The Intermediate User: Looking Up Commands

Not only are most of MicroStation's tools and commands in this book indexed, but exercises and illustrations are indexed by the tools they represent. This makes *INSIDE MicroStation* a powerful reference for the intermediate user who still needs to look up facts about MicroStation's operation. In that tool illustrations cover all MicroStation platforms, this book will be useful to anyone working in a multiplatform environment.

The Advanced User: A Training Guide

The advanced user who has any responsibility for training others will find *INSIDE MicroStation* an excellent training guide, especially when used in conjunction with the companion *INSIDE MicroStation Exercise Book*. Its practical, "working design" will help you instill good working habits from the outset.

What Is Not Covered in This Book

Because *INSIDE MicroStation* is an introductory-level book, some important concepts have necessarily been covered only lightly. The focus of this book has been to show new users how to start with a blank screen and complete a usable drawing.

If you find yourself wanting to know more about certain functions and the reasons behind them, it is time to consider a more advanced book, such as the *MicroStation Productivity Book,* the *MicroStation Reference Guide,* and the *MicroStation Bible.* These books show those familiar with MicroStation how to get more out of it and how to customize MicroStation. They also contain a lot of valuable reference material never before published.

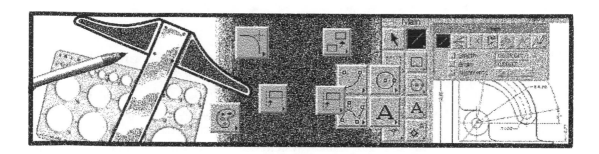

Installing the Companion Disk

A companion disk is delivered with *INSIDE MicroStation* (found inside the back cover). This disk contains all of the exercises shown in this book in both the "before" and "after" conditions.

There are two ways to use this disk. One is to load the files relevant to particular exercises and see how the exercises work. The other is to try to work through the exercise, and if you get "stuck," you can call up the appropriate file and see how it was done.

The EXERFILE.TXT file is a simple ASCII text file that explains which disk files belong to which exercises. You can read this file with any word processor or ASCII text editor.

 NOTE: *All the exercises are indexed, and there is a table in the front of the book that lists all the exercises.*

Installing the Companion Disk

Installing the companion disk is easy. Using a simple procedure you copy the contents of the companion disk into a specified directory. We recommend the directory "ISMS" (or "isms" for you UNIX users).

The files are actually stored on an MS-DOS-formatted disk. This is done to ensure data integrity during the disk duplication process (most high-speed disk duplicators perform better on DOS disks than other formats). For this reason, the procedure for copying the companion files requires the use of native DOS-to-whatever system utilities. Most systems are equipped with such utilities. You may want to review these procedures with your system administrator if you are unsure about anything.

Installation on an MS-DOS-Equipped PC

Place the disk in your A: drive and perform the following steps:

1. Insert the diskette into your floppy drive.

2. Create a directory named "ISMS."

3. Copy the contents of the diskette into this directory (e.g., COPY A:*.* C:\ISMS).

Installation on an Apple Macintosh Running System 7

To read this disk your Mac must be able to read a DOS format diskette. Prior to System 7.1, this required a separate utility (Insignia Solutions AccessPC, etc.) or use of the Apple File Transfer application. With System 7.2 Apple incorporated the ability to read and write MS-DOS-formatted diskettes using the SuperDrive (Apple's name for the 1.44MB 3.5" floppy).

To copy the files from the floppy from the desktop do the following:

1. Insert the diskette into your floppy drive.

2. Create a folder on your hard drive called "isms."

3. Open the diskette by double-clicking on its icon.

4. Drag the contents of the disk except for the TEXT folder to the isms directory.

5. Open and drag the contents of the TEXT folder to the isms folder.

You may have to convert the text files (extension.TXT) to native Macintosh text file format. Use Apple's File Transfer application to perform this function. However, keep in mind that many word processor applications can read DOS text with no problem, so before performing this additional step, open the file with your favorite word processor and see if the text appears normal.

Installation on an Interpro CLIX Workstation

This procedure assumes you are installing the optional disk files into your present directory. If this is not the case, you need to first create a new directory to hold the files.

1. Insert the diskette into your floppy drive.

2. Create a subdirectory named "isms" under your home directory (e.g., mkdir isms).

3. Copy the files from the floppy drive's root directory (e.g., $dtu -p *.* /usrX/newdir). Make sure you use the "-p" option. This copies the binary-compatible files with no modification.

4. Copy the files from the floppy drive's TEXT subdirectory (e.g., $dtu \text*.* /usrX/newdir). This automatically converts the DOS-formatted text to UNIX-formatted text.

Installation on a Windows NT or Windows 95 Workstation

Follow these steps to install the files:

1. Insert the diskette into your floppy drive.

2. Using *File Manager* or the *Windows Explorer,* create a directory called "isms" on your hard drive.

3. Copy all of the files from the diskette to the new directory. Be sure to copy the files found in the subdirectory TEXT as well as the design files and cell library files in the floppy's root directory.

Installation on a UNIX Workstation That Directly Reads a DOS Diskette

Some UNIX workstations have floppy drives that can read DOS diskettes. To install on these systems, follow these steps:

1. Insert the diskette into your floppy drive.
2. Mount the floppy drive if it is not already mounted.
3. Create a directory called "isms" in your home directory.
4. Using a "dos2unix" transfer method, copy the files from the diskette to the new directory.

Installation on a UNIX Workstation Networked to an MS-DOS System

If you have a workstation that cannot read DOS diskettes but is connected to a network with a PC, you can transfer the files from the PC to the workstation.

1. Insert the diskette into your floppy drive on the PC.
2. Copy the files from the diskette to a temporary directory on the PC.
3. If using PC-NFS or an equivalent, mount the UNIX workstation drive to the MS-DOS system.
4. Create a directory called "isms" in your home directory on the workstation.
5. Transfer the files to the workstation via TCP/IP connection, network mail, copy command (PC-NFS mounted drive), or any other method available.
6. Convert the text files (.TXT extension) from the DOS format ASCII to UNIX format ASCII if necessary. Other files that were transferred are binary-compatible from platform to platform so no further action is needed.

PART ONE

1

GETTING STARTED

Introducing MicroStation

Its History and Its Interface

Welcome to MicroStation, the most functional and usable CAD (computer-aided design) software you can buy at any price. It is no wonder that tens of thousands of engineering design firms, both large and small—such as Alpha, Bechtel, Brown and Root, CH2M Hill, Fluor Daniel, and Sverdrup—across the world, have standardized on MicroStation as their CAD software of choice. Additionally, scores of government agencies—such as the U.S.

Army Corps of Engineers, state departments of transportation, and Finland's Civil Aviation Administration—also use MicroStation.

No matter what your field of work—whether 2D, 3D, architecture, civil, facilities management, electrical, mapping, mechanical, industrial plant design, or another—MicroStation packs the power to meet your needs. If you have a vision, MicroStation can help you give it reality. And, as you will discover during the course of reading this book, all this power is not difficult to master. MicroStation offers a breadth of features and is at the same time extremely usable.

Some of the key features that have made MicroStation so popular are the flexibility provided in attaching, manipulating, and displaying reference files; the implementation of drawing, editing, and viewing commands to maximize user productivity; and the most comprehensive set of customization tools for both end users and developers of third-party add-on products.

Such functionality does not come overnight. Behind the birth of MicroStation there is indeed a very interesting story.

A Brief History of MicroStation

Intergraph: Turnkey CAD to Technical Desktop

The origin of MicroStation dates back to the late 1960s, when Intergraph, then known as M&S Computing, got its start during the Apollo moon mission years, developing real-time software for the space program. During its early days, the company developed, among other things, a printed circuit board software package for NASA, and a mapping graphics package that would later evolve into IGDS, their most successful product.

IGDS, an acronym for Interactive Graphics Design System, was a minicomputer-based turnkey CAD system. "Turnkey" refers to the fact that you purchase the entire system—software, support, and associated hardware (such as graphics terminals, computer, disk drives, digitizing tablets, and plotters)—as a value-added bundle from the same vendor.

Although initially concentrating on the mapping and geophysical sciences market (e.g., oil companies), IGDS became a general-purpose CAD system capable of supporting almost any engineering discipline. From electronic and mechanical design through architectural and civil engineering, Intergraph's IGDS clientele represented the total spectrum of engineering world-wide. Originally, IGDS ran on Digital Equipment Corporation's 16-bit PDP11 minicomputer souped up for graphics performance by Intergraph. Then came the migration to the 32-bit VAX super minicomputer. Intergraph's systems became known for their ergonomic design and support of dual graphics terminals.

Dual graphics terminals, such as on this Interact workstation, were the hallmark of Intergraph's turnkey systems from their early days.

It goes without saying that Intergraph's systems, at $75,000 a seat, were expensive. Only large firms could afford them. It was quite common to run them around the clock so as to maximize the return on investment in them.

As computer hardware and operating systems evolved, so did Intergraph's workstations. From the VAX super minicomputer, Intergraph moved to its own RISC chip, named Clipper, running a variant of the UNIX operating system called CLIX. And now, Intergraph's workstations, called technical desktops (TDs), are based on the Intel line of processors that use both single-processor and multiprocessor designs. As always, these TDs are tuned for graphics performance. For instance, Intergraph's TDZ-400, a dual Intel PentiumPro-based computer running Windows NT, is powered by its own 3D OpenGL graphics accelerator card that outperforms many RISC processor-based workstations.

Today, Intergraph is the largest MicroStation reseller that also bundles this software with its line of graphics workstations. This billion-dollar company has two primary divisions. Intergraph Computer Systems (ICS) builds high-performance computer hardware systems and scanners designed for the technical graphics industry. Intergraph Software Solutions (ISS) develops a wide range of discipline-specific MicroStation-based add-ons, such as Project Architect, PipeGen, InRoads, InSewer, InSitu, CogoWorks, and others. ISS also develops other independent and non-MicroStation-based software applications. Without a doubt, Intel processors and Windows NT are a large part of Intergraph's future strategy.

How does this all relate to MicroStation? Read on to find out!

Bentley Develops MicroStation

DuPont has been a large Intergraph customer, and during 1981-82, Keith Bentley was employed with its CAD support group. Noticing that not all who needed access to IGDS files could get near a CAD station, he developed a software that ran on inexpensive VT-100 VAX terminals equipped with a graphics card to let users call up design files.

This design file access software, called PseudoStation, marked the birth of MicroStation. Acquiring the sales rights to PseudoStation, having developed it in his spare time, Keith left his employer in 1982 in search of greener pastures. He soon found more than a hundred customers who would pay $7,500 for a copy of PseudoStation.

With the early success of PseudoStation, and the popularity of the IBM PC at that time and a growing interest in a powerful CAD software for it, Keith Bentley decided to port the VAX-based PseudoStation to the microcomputer. Thus the name, MicroStation. It is a powerful CAD station running on a microcomputer.

Keith Bentley, the creator of MicroStation software.

Considering that the IGDS design file format had been fine-tuned for the 32-bit minicomputer environment, porting MicroStation to the PC of 1986, an 8-bit environment, was no mean task. That Bentley Systems was able to create a software program that not only could read and write IGDS-compatible files but would act and feel like IGDS (with its rich feature set intact) while running on an IBM PC is a testimony to Bentley's genius.

Without a doubt, the PseudoStation project had given Bentley good insight into the workings of IGDS and prepared them for the task of creating MicroStation 1.0, which was never commercially released. It was a read-only IGDS emulator that ran on an

IBM PC. This effort was followed quickly by MicroStation 2.0, the first fully IGDS-compatible CAD program for the IBM PC.

As opposed to other CAD packages that originated on the PC with 2D capabilities and gradually added more powerful features, MicroStation has had high-end features from the start. When released in 1986 as MicroStation 2 running on PCs, it supported reference files for workgroup computing on a network, external database manipulation for managing associated nongraphic data, and 3D graphics for sophisticated modeling.

MicroStation evolved quickly, from version 3, which introduced screen menus in 1987, to version 4, which gave MicroStation an entirely new graphical interface and the MDL programming environment on all supported platforms in February of 1991. The release of version 5 in 1993 greatly enhanced the software, with special emphasis on usability with a host of new features, such as multilines, custom line styles, workspaces, and realistic render-ing with material mapping capabilities. MicroStation 95, released in 1995, continues the trend of improved functionality and usability. New to this version are features such as SmartLine for composite shapes, *AccuDraw* for faster drafting production, and MicroStation Basic macro language for easier end-user customi-zation. Indeed, MicroStation 95 sets the standard for usability in CAD software.

In MicroStation 2, released in 1986, the user interaction was bare, with only status messages and no menus.

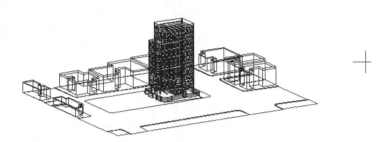

```
Locks=GR,SN,                    LVL=1,SOLID,WT=0,LC=SOL,PRI,CO=0
(1) uSTN> _
```

MicroStation 4 was a dramatic change in the look and feel of MicroStation when it gained a true motif-based graphical interface on all supported platforms.

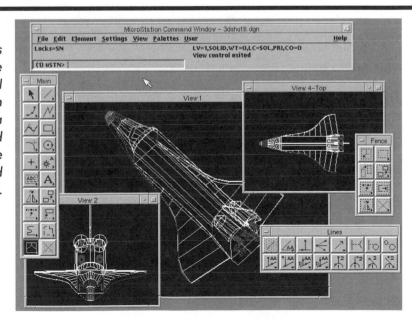

MicroStation 5 enhanced usability by consolidating command palettes and increasing functionality by adding multi-lines, workspaces, and custom line styles.

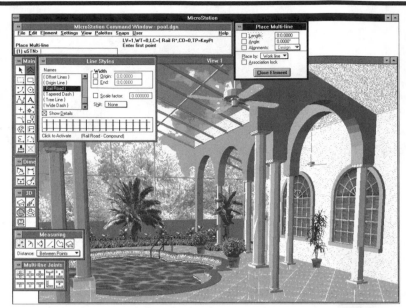

MicroStation 95 adheres to version 5's file format, adopts the popular Windows interface, and improves usability through innovative tools such as AccuDraw.

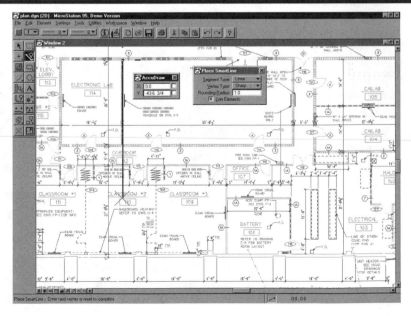

Despite its evolution over the years, MicroStation has not forgotten its roots. It continues to include features to allow the interchange of design data with the older IGDS system. This point is crucial to understanding the MicroStation philosophy. Bentley has gone through great pains to maintain software as well as graphics file compatibility across all computer platforms. Platform compatibility now extends to everything from the old VAX systems, to PC compatibles, to modern workstations.

When Bentley Systems, Inc., or simply Bentley, as it is now known, finished work on MicroStation in 1986, its founders, the Bentley brothers, got in touch with Intergraph for support. Intergraph bought half the shares in the company, and entered into an exclusive distribution agreement with Bentley. MicroStation would be developed and enhanced by Bentley, and Intergraph would market it. This arrangement remained in place until December of 1994.

1995: A Watershed Year

Bentley underwent a major transition in 1995. Intergraph would continue to own half of Bentley, but Bentley assumed complete control over MicroStation. Rather than just being the MicroStation software development wing of Intergraph, Bentley now markets the CAD package as well. The software is no longer Intergraph MicroStation, but Bentley MicroStation.

From its humble beginnings, Bentley has come a long way. Whereas the company was founded by Keith with his brother Barry in California, the company moved shortly to their home-town in Pennsylvania, and now employs all of the five Bentley brothers (Barry, Greg, Keith, Ray, and Scott). From just a handful of employees in 1984, Bentley had, at the end of 1995, an employee base of over 400 and annual revenues that are expected to be nearly $100 million.

The year 1995 also marked the year Bentley shed its image as a single-product vendor. There is now a line of MicroStation products.

❑ *MicroStation:* Comprehensive drafting and design package for the professional who depends on CAD as a key aspect of his or her work. The software runs under 14 different operating system platforms.

❑ *MicroStation CSP:* An annual subscription support program for MicroStation designed to provide comprehensive technical support, quarterly updates (including minor upgrades and major releases) to the software, and other benefits.

❑ *MicroStation Field:* Designed to work on a portable pen-based computer for use in the construction field, MicroStation Field provides access to design files and associated databases for markup and data collection.

❑ *MicroStation GeoGraphics:* An add-on environment that provides basic GIS (geographic information system) capabilities to MicroStation.

❑ *MicroStation Masterpiece:* An add-on application to MicroStation that extends its already powerful rendering capabilities by providing ray tracing, radiosity, and automated animation-scene transition facilities for 3D models.

❑ *MicroStation Modeler:* Geared to the mechanical designer, Modeler provides sophisticated feature-based, parametric solids modeling capabilities.

❑ *MicroStation PowerDraft:* A half-price version of MicroStation that incorporates its most used features in a simpler interface but excludes support for user commands, external databases, digitizers, and rendering. It supports both 2D and 3D drafting, and can run MDL applications. It includes AccuDraw, SmartLine, and MicroStation Basic.

❑ *MicroStation PowerTools:* A line of discipline-specific add-on products designed to be run on PowerDraft. Products available under this category include CivilDraft, DRAFTPAK Mechanical, PowerArchitect, PowerScape, and PipeMaster, with additional products under way.

❑ *MicroStation Review:* For viewing, plotting, and red-lining MicroStation design files, Review offers the same look and feel of MicroStation. Additionally, it features the ability to run MDL applications that do not alter the design file.

❑ *MicroStation TeamMate:* A network document management system, initially released for the 32-bit Windows environment on Intel processors, designed to work in conjunction with MicroStation for maintaining file integrity and controlling access.

What does this all mean to you? By selecting MicroStation, you have joined illustrious company. Its comprehensive feature set and thoughtful implementation will let you tackle your drafting needs with aplomb. And if you need to undertake engineering design within MicroStation, you have access to a broad array of discipline-specific add-on software packages from several independent vendors.

A final note about 95. Although Bentley decided to call it MicroStation 95, probably in honor of the year the company went through such significant changes, the software is designed to run on over a dozen operating system platforms, including Microsoft Windows 95. The following are the 17 platforms Bentley has committed to port MicroStation 95 to:

❑ DOS

❑ Windows 3.1

❑ Windows 95

❑ Windows NT on Intel processors

❑ Windows NT on Alpha AXP processors

❑ Windows NT on PowerPC processors

❑ Intergraph Clipper

❑ Sun SPARC

❑ Sun Solaris

❑ Hewlett Packard PA-RISC

❑ Silicon Graphics

❑ IBM RS/6000

❑ Digital UNIX

❑ OS/2 Warp

❑ Macintosh

❑ Power Macintosh

With that said, let's take a look at the MicroStation environment—both hardware and software.

A Look at the Computer

As noted earlier in this chapter, MicroStation runs on a wide array of operating systems. Whether you use DOS, Windows 3.1, Windows 95, Windows NT, a UNIX version for your workstation, Macintosh, or OS/2 Warp, you can run MicroStation on your computer. As today's computer hardware has progressed, so has MicroStation. Because we will not be discussing hardware issues in the remainder of the book, let us take a moment to review some hardware aspects of your MicroStation-equipped system.

No matter which computer system you use, we can make certain minimal assumptions about its configuration. It is sure to have one, or even two, video monitors capable of displaying graphics, a mouse or other pointing device, a keyboard, the main computer unit, and some sort of hard-copy device (a plotter or printer). Within the main computer system unit, you'll need memory (8 to 32 Mb minimum, depending on the operating system), hard disk space (40 to 80 Mb for installation, depending on components installed), math co-processor (may be integrated into the processor), and system processor (single or multiple).

The Video Screen

One aspect of a MicroStation workstation that dates back to the IGDS days is the use of dual video graphics monitors. Although this is by no means required, the fact that MicroStation provides you with twice the virtual drafting table of other products leads many companies to take advantage of this capability.

MicroStation is a very visual product. This makes sense, as it is a computer graphics program. Over the years, MicroStation has kept abreast of the progress in human engineering, and thus presents a lot of visual material to the user via the video monitor (in the past, the graphics tablet was more central to the operation of MicroStation).

Of Mice and Tablets

 If video is how MicroStation communicates with you, then the mouse is the main method by which you communicate with it. There is still the ever-present keyboard, where you may enter commands and parameters, but the fun stuff is done with the mouse and cursor.

Mice come with differing numbers of buttons. Choosing be-tween the three-button and the two-button variety can be tricky. Because MicroStation assigns a number of functions to the mouse buttons, you may find yourself "chording" (pressing two mouse buttons at once) a lot with the two-button variety. If you find chording a little difficult to master, you may want to consider a three-button mouse. In the case of the Macintosh, a one-button mouse is standard. MicroStation Mac knows this and compensates by offering keyboard mouse-button functions.

Trackball

One mouse alternative that has become very popular is the trackball. Identical to the mouse in function, this device consists of a large ball you roll with your fingertips. Picture it as an upside-down mouse and you get an idea of how it works. Most laptop systems come equipped with trackballs as an alternative to a mouse. In all of the important aspects of operation, the trackball functions just like a mouse.

Graphics Tablet

The same cannot be said for the other major input device, the graphics tablet. Also known as the digitizer—a reference to its use to convert drawings into a digital format—the graphics tablet differs slightly from the mouse in its use and operation with MicroStation.

The graphics tablet consists of a flat, book-like (thus the term *tablet*) box and a mouse-like "puck." Electronic circuitry in the tablet senses the location of this puck as it is moved over the tablet's surface, and transmits it to the computer. Whereas a mouse is a relative pointing device, the digitizer is an absolute device.

What this means is that you can pick up the mouse from the table you glide it on and place it at another location without affecting the relative screen location of the mouse pointer. On a tablet, however, there is an absolute correspondence between the location of the puck on the tablet and the location of the cursor on the screen. It is worth noting that tablets can also be configured as relative pointing devices.

An example of a graphics tablet you might use with MicroStation. (Courtesy of Intergraph Corp.)

On the puck there is a series of buttons. The use of these buttons plays an important role in how MicroStation interprets your input. For this reason, MicroStation requires the use of a puck with a minimum of four buttons. Because there are other pucks with fewer buttons (and indeed one style of puck that looks like a pen or pencil), you should read the instructions about which graphics tablets are supported by MicroStation.

There are two major advantages to tablets over mice. One, you can use a tablet to trace an existing drawing into your MicroStation design. Two, because of its puck location technique (it absolutely knows where the puck is at all times), a graphics tablet can be used with tablet menus.

The major disadvantage of the tablet is its size and cost. Even a small tablet takes up significant space on your desk and costs many times more than a mouse. It should also be noted that in certain configurations you may actually desire both devices; for instance, a mouse for use with Windows and a tablet for use with MicroStation.

Keyboards

Yes, MicroStation uses the dreaded QWERTY keyboard found on every computer system. You can enter most commands via this stalwart of I/O operations. However, MicroStation's extensive use of "heads up" tool selection has relegated the status of the keyboard to that of a secondary input device. That's not to say that MicroStation ignores the keyboard. In fact, MicroStation provides support for keyboard shortcut keys to the most popular commands, as well as programmable function keys and keyboard navigation of dialog boxes. Because keyboards vary greatly in layout from machine to machine, MicroStation uses the basic features of the "standard" keyboard: function keys, arrow keys, and the QWERTY keys.

Plotters

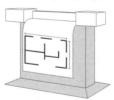

Just as every office has a photocopier, all MicroStation installations include some sort of plotting device. This is necessary to get that all-important paper copy of your design information to the client. Plotters come in all sizes and varieties. In fact, you may have more than one. It is not uncommon to have laser printers serving both as document printers and plotters for smaller drawings.

Larger-format drawings are usually created on dedicated plotting devices. A discussion on the variety and capabilities of plotters can, and does, take up an entire chapter later in the book; just keep in mind that MicroStation supports all of the industry standard plotters available today. In other words, if you can draw it, MicroStation can plot it.

Starting MicroStation

We took a quick tour of the computer hardware you use to work with MicroStation. The next logical step is installation. However, because installation is usually only done once, and in a typical business setting, more likely than not, will already have been done for you by your computer support group, we will not discuss it. Suffice it to say, MicroStation includes an install program that copies all program files and relevant support files into a directory of your choice on your local hard disk, or on your network file server's hard disk. And if your operating system—such as the Macintosh, OS/2 Warp, or Windows—includes a graphical inter- face, the install program will also create an icon to start MicroStation.

There are many ways you can start MicroStation on your computer. All methods, however, can be grouped in two. Only some of the procedures described in the following material may be relevant for your operating system environment. For instance, if your operating system, like DOS, offers just a text mode interface, only the methods described in From the Command Line will be applicable.

From the Command Line

❑ On many of the systems supported by MicroStation, you can launch it by keying in its executable file name. At the system prompt, whether in a terminal session (UNIX, Windows NT, OS/2 Warp, Windows 95) or dedicated video (MS-DOS), you type in:

```
ustation
```

This starts MicroStation with default settings.

❑ On many systems—such as UNIX, OS/2 Warp, Windows NT, and Windows 95—that support preemptive multitasking, there is a command to invoke a separate process from within one terminal session. From Windows NT, Windows 95, or OS/2 Warp you would key in:

```
start ustation
```

This method invokes a second system process to run MicroStation and keeps your current terminal session still available for additional tasks.

❑ The two methods previously discussed start MicroStation with default settings. However, if you are familiar with MicroStation's workspaces (a feature introduced in version 5 and something we will discuss a little later in this chapter), you may have a custom workspace you wish to use. In this case, you would type in:

```
ustation -wuworkspace
```

The workspace name is preceded by "-wu" and passed as a command line option while starting MicroStation. Many application vendors, such as IdeaGraphix (a division of Softdesk) and Jacobus Technology, provide separate workspaces for their applications.

❑ MicroStation supports script files at start-up. Script files are plain text files containing a sequence of MicroStation commands. If you have a script file you want to run when you open a MicroStation design file, you would key in:

```
ustation -sscript
```

The complete script filename, including its extension, if any, must be preceded by "-s" and passed as a command line option while starting MicroStation.

❑ If you have access to MicroStation design files you should not modify, you can start MicroStation so it opens files in read-only mode. For this, you would key in:

```
ustation -r
```

When MicroStation opens files in read-only mode, it displays a red icon on the lower right corner of the status bar.

NOTE: *To start MicroStation from the command line, as previously described, you must either switch to the MicroStation product directory (normally USTN55) or have the directory on your path statement.*

No matter which of the foregoing options you use to start MicroStation, your terminal session will switch to graphics mode and bring up the MicroStation Manager dialog box. (We will discuss this dialog box a little later.) The only exceptions are either when your system has not been properly configured, in which case MicroStation will exit with an error message, or when you supply the name of a design file as a command line option, in which case MicroStation will bypass the MicroStation Manager dialog box and take you directly to the specified design file.

From the Graphical Environment

❑ Launching MicroStation from an operating system that provides a graphical environment (such as Windows, OS/2 Warp, or MacOS) is very similar: you launch MicroStation by selecting its program icon. Usually found in a related program group or the Start menu (but not always), you double-click on the icon. This brings up the default MicroStation Manager environment, which awaits your next command.

*To launch
MicroStation,
double-click its
program icon.*

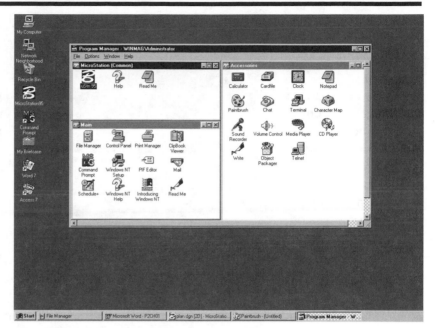

What about the various command line options previously discussed? Are they not available under the graphical environment?
Yes, they are. Most graphical environments allow you to edit the
command line associated with an icon, giving you the same
flexibility in starting MicroStation as does the command line. For
instance, to incorporate the workspace command line option into
the MicroStation icon under Windows 95, you would click the
right mouse button on the icon and select the Properties pop-up
menu option to bring up the Properties dialog box. You would
then edit the Target field under the Shortcut tab to include the
"-wu*workspace*" option.

*You may edit the
Target field under
the Shortcut tab in
the Properties dialog
box to incorporate
command line
options into the
MicroStation icon.*

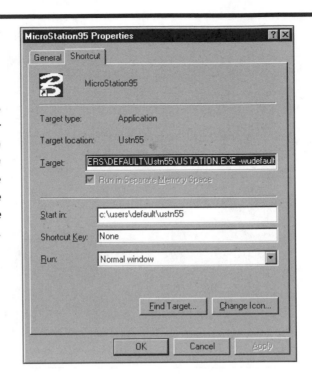

❏ You can also launch MicroStation from the Windows File Manager or the Windows 95 Explorer. To do this, navigate your computer or network server's hard disk to locate the MicroStation executable file "ustation.exe" and double-click it.

❏ Another way to launch MicroStation from the Windows File Manager or the Windows 95 Explorer is to double-click a design file with the dgn filename extension. Optionally, you could drag a design file icon with the mouse and drop it on the MicroStation icon. This latter technique is known as Windows' drag-and-drop facility.

MicroStation Manager Dialog Box

However you activate MicroStation, unless you specify a filename at the time you launch, you will encounter MicroStation Manager. Much like the familiar Windows File Manager, the MicroStation Manager is a tool to manage your design files. With it you can create new files, or copy, rename, delete, merge, or compress existing files. You can also manage directories, select the type of supported file to open, and specify the workspace you wish to use when opening a file.

NOTE: *If your software hasn't been properly registered, you will be presented with the Registration Information dialog box to complete the registration process. If you opt not to register your copy, you can choose the "15 min. tryout" button. This allows you to enter MicroStation, but the software will terminate after 15 minutes.*

If you see this dialog box, your software has not been properly registered.

Registration Information	☒
Your Name:	
Organization:	
Serial:	

[Continue]   [15 min. tryout]   [Quit]

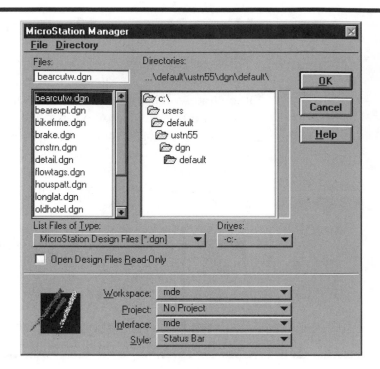

The MicroStation Manager dialog box is your gateway to MicroStation's drawing environment.

Think of the MicroStation Manager dialog box as the entrance door to MicroStation. Its primary function is to let you select a design file (a name given to drawing files you create with MicroStation) and present it on screen for viewing, editing, or printing. Before we actually open a file, let's take a moment to examine the facilities offered in the MicroStation Manager dialog box.

The File and Directory Pull-down Menus

Directly under the MicroStation Manager dialog box title bar is a menu bar with the words *File* and *Directory*. Upon clicking either of these a pull-down menu will appear. This menu lists numerous commands you can execute. The File menu lets you manage design files, and the Directory menu offers directory management functions. The following is an overview of what each available command does.

❑ *File | New:* Select this command to create a new design file. This is the first of two commands under the File menu that do not require you to first select a file in the Files listbox.

❑ *File | Copy:* Select this command to copy the highlighted file to another location. If copying the file to the same directory, you must specify a different name for the file. However, if you copy it to another location, such as another drive or directory, you can maintain the same name. If no file is selected in the Files listbox, this option will be grayed.

❑ *File | Rename:* Use this command to give another name to an existing design file. You may choose to change just its file name extension, or the entire file name. If no file is selected in the Files listbox, this option will be grayed.

❑ *File | Delete:* Use this command with caution, as a file once deleted is difficult to recover. If no file is selected in the Files listbox, this option will be grayed.

❑ *File | Info:* Select this command to display the size of the highlighted file and the time of its last modification. If no file is selected in the Files listbox, this option will be grayed.

❑ *File | Merge:* This command lets you select several design files and merge their contents into an existing design file. Of course, you can only merge 3D files into an existing 3D file. This is the second of the two commands under the File menu that do not require you to first select a file in the Files listbox.

❑ *File | Compress:* As you edit elements in a design file, a copy of the edited elements is maintained for the purpose of undoing edits if necessary. The more editing you do, the larger this base of reserve elements. The Compress option under the File menu, like the pack operation in a database software, actually re-moves elements that had been marked earlier for deletion. If no file is selected in the Files listbox, this option will be grayed.

❑ *Directory | New:* Use this command to create a new subdirectory under the current directory.

❑ *Directory | Copy:* This command copies all dgn files in the current directory to another location you type in.

❏ *Directory | Compress:* You can compress all dgn files in the current directory with this option.

❏ *Directory | Select Configuration Variable:* Use this command to set the current directory to the value specified by a MicroStation configuration variable.

In addition to the foregoing commands, a list of your four most recently accessed files and directories is maintained under the pull-down menu. This is in recognition of the fact that most projects are ongoing and that you are likely to work on the same files again. By making them available in the menu, you gain quick access to them.

The Files and Directories listboxes under the pull-down menus are standard directory navigation and file selection tools you are likely familiar with in the File Open dialog box found in most applications. Also, the List Files of Type field in the dialog box acts as a file list display filter. You can choose to display files of a given type; for instance, dwg. The Drives field lets you select the drive, local or on a network, you wish to navigate.

 NOTE: *MicroStation can directly open several vector file formats, such as IGES, CGM, and DWG/DXF. DGN is MicroStation's own file format, and GRD is the file format used by MicroStation Field. When MicroStation opens a foreign file format, it keeps the original file intact while creating on the fly a new translated copy in its native file format.*

The only checkbox in the MicroStation Manager dialog box is labeled Open Design Files Read Only. Much like the -r command line option discussed under the Starting MicroStation section, if this checkbox is enabled, files you open will be read-only.

Introducing Workspaces

All MicroStation Manager dialog box options and commands we have so far reviewed are pretty straightforward and easy to understand for even a novice MicroStation user. Workspaces, on the other hand, are a more advanced feature that are likely to be created by the CAD manager at your firm. Whereas creating new workspaces requires an understanding of how MicroStation accesses its various features and commands, using available workspaces is simply a matter of selecting the one desired during start-up.

We discussed the -wu command line option earlier. The Workspace option list in the MicroStation Manager dialog box is another method of selecting the desired user workspace when opening a design file. What then, you might ask, is a workspace?

A workspace is essentially a customized MicroStation environment for a particular user, project, site, or application. Suppose you need to work on two projects today, the first architectural and the second civil. When creating the architectural drawing, you need access to your company's architectural fonts, line styles, and symbol library. For the civil drawing, you need the Civil Symbols and Settings groups. By implementing two workspaces, one architectural and the other civil, you can simplify the selection of various workspace modules (a term that refers to various MicroStation support files such as fonts, cells, seed, data, glossary, and others) as easily as selecting a menu option.

To better understand workspaces, you might want to take a look at the contents of the "config" subdirectory under the MicroStation base directory. It contains several additional subdirectories. All user configuration files (files with the UCF extension) under the "config\user" subdirectory appear as options on the Workspace option list in the MicroStation Manager dialog box.

Much like the Workspace option list provides access to user configuration files, the Project option list provides access to project configuration files (files with the PCF extension) under the "config\project" subdirectory under the MicroStation base directory.

The Interface option list under Project provides access to customized interface components such as menus, dialog boxes, and palettes. The choices available on this option list correspond to the names of subdirectories under the wsui (workspace user interface) subdirectory in the MicroStation base directory.

NOTE: *If you do not yet follow the concept and implementation of workspaces, worry not! You can safely ignore the various options related to them and yet become a proficient MicroStation user. This discussion is merely offered for the sake of completeness. You might want to come back to read this section again after you have become more familiar with MicroStation and have a better understanding of its configuration variables.*

The final workspace parameter presented by the MicroStation Manager dialog box is the Style option list. It offers two choices: Status Bar and Command Window. If you are familiar with version 4 or 5 of MicroStation, you know the Command Window. It used to be the command center offering pull-down menus, a key-in field, and message fields. If you needed to see what MicroStation was telling you, or wanted to determine MicroStation's active settings, you would glance at the Command Window. With MicroStation 95, you have a choice. You can have MicroStation display its messages on a status bar along the bottom edge of the screen, or use the Command Window of old, minus the menu bar. The status bar, new to this version, was implemented for better conformance to Microsoft Windows interface standards.

The Command Window.

Command Window	☒
Locks=BS,GG,SN	LV=11,WT=0,LC=SOL,CO=0,TP=KeyPt
Element Selection	
	Display complete

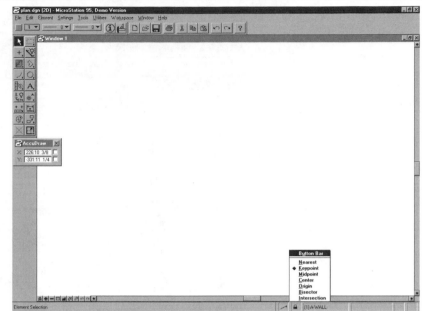

The status bar is located along the bottom edge of the screen, shown here with the Snaps pop-up menu invoked.

Opening a Design File

By now you should have a good understanding of the various commands and options found in the MicroStation Manager dialog box. As noted earlier, its primary purpose is to let you select a design file to open in MicroStation.

Once you have selected a supported file type, or created a new design file, and made sure the other available options reflect your needs, you can choose to go to MicroStation's drawing environment, or you can exit out of MicroStation entirely. If you look at the right edge of the box, you'll notice three buttons: OK, Cancel, and Help.

MicroStation Manager

File   Directory

Files:
bearcutw.dgn

Directories:
...\default\ustn55\dgn\default\

Choose OK to open the highlighted file in MicroStation's drawing environment, or choose Cancel to exit.

bearcutw.dgn
bearexpl.dgn
bikefrme.dgn
brake.dgn
cnstrn.dgn
detail.dgn
flowtags.dgn
houspatt.dgn
longlat.dgn
oldhotel.dgn

c:\
users
default
ustn55
dgn
default

OK
Cancel
Help

List Files of Type:
MicroStation Design Files [*.dgn]

Drives:
-c:-

☐ Open Design Files Read-Only

Workspace: mde
Project: No Project
Interface: mde
Style: Status Bar

TIP: *In lieu of clicking a file name and then selecting the OK button, you will find it quicker to double-click the file name to open it in MicroStation.*

Before we move on, let's take a moment to distinguish between a dialog box and a settings box. As far as MicroStation is concerned, a dialog box is always "in your face," meaning that before you can proceed to another task in the software you must respond to its request. That is, you must either accept or cancel the dialog function. This is the distinguishing feature of all dialog boxes. In contrast, a settings box, though similar in appearance to a dialog box, does not require you to interrupt your system's operation. That is, you can leave a settings box open while you attend to other operations.

Understanding MicroStation's Interface

Finally, it's time to enter MicroStation's drawing environment. Just call up any design file from any directory where you can find one (they're identified by the DGN name extension), or create a new one if you so desire. For the purpose of this tour of MicroStation's interface, the file chosen isn't critical.

MicroStation's various interface elements.

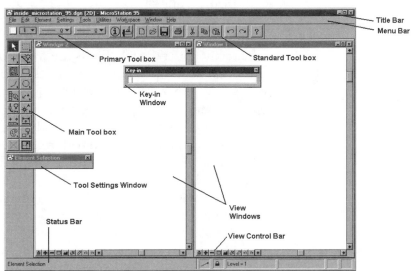

In an effort to conform to your preferences, MicroStation remembers, between sessions, several settings about your display, such as the location of toolboxes and the key-in window. If your screen does not exactly match the one shown here, this may be the reason why. In any case, let's take a few minutes to explore MicroStation's interface components, some of which convey information to you, and others of which do your bidding.

Title Bar and Menu Bar

Along the top edge of the MicroStation application window is the title bar. It displays the name of your active design file, the type of file it is (2D or 3D), and the name of the software, MicroStation 95. Additionally, it contains a few icons. If you are running Windows 95 or Windows NT 4.0, to the left of the title bar text is the Application icon. On other platforms, it is the Control menu. To the right there are the Minimize, Maximize/Restore, and Exit buttons. You click the Control menu to activate commands that control the application window. The buttons to the right offer one-click access to the most frequently used control menu commands.

Directly under the title bar is the menu bar. It is from here you get access to file operations, toolboxes not already on your screen, views, and other settings that let you control your MicroStation environment. You can click an item on the menu bar, or press the Alt key in conjunction with the underlined menu letter, to pull down the menu of commands offered. Selecting an item from this menu will in turn either perform an action or pull down yet another submenu. Several commands also have shortcut key-strokes shown next to them. You can invoke these commands by pressing the shortcut key to save yourself a trip to the menus.

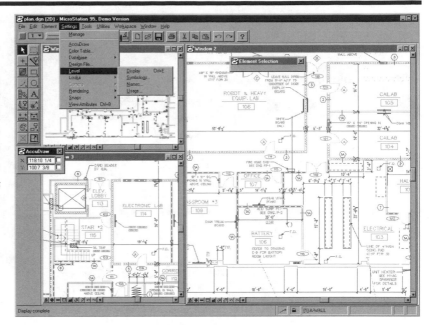

Click an item on the menu bar, or press the Alt key in conjunction with the underlined menu letter, to pull down MicroStation's menus.

A menu option with a small arrowhead next to it denotes a submenu. Menu options that have an ellipsis next to them denote dialog boxes. Other menu options either invoke a command or denote a settings box. See the Opening a Design File section earlier in this chapter for a distinction between dialog boxes and settings boxes.

On some platforms, depending on the amount of memory your computer has, you can run multiple instances of MicroStation 95. When you reduce the size of the MicroStation application window on your graphical environment's desktop, the title bar shrinks in size and therefore the text area becomes smaller, but the title bar icons always remain visible. No matter how narrow you make the application window, the menu bar wraps to occupy additional lines as needed so that you have all options visible.

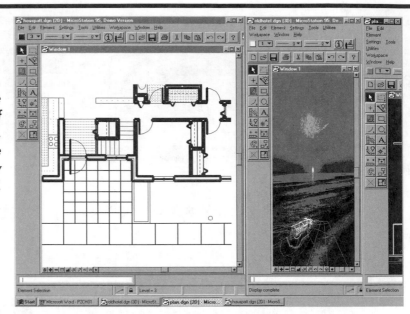

On some platforms, you can run multiple instances of MicroStation, depending on the amount of memory your computer has.

NOTE: *You can customize MicroStation's menus, toolboxes, tool frames (toolboxes that contain other tear-off toolboxes), and icons along the bottom edge of view windows. Tools to accomplish this in an interactive, point-and-click manner are available under the Workspace menu.*

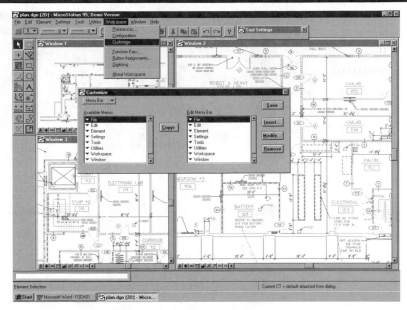

The Customize option under the Workspace menu allows you to customize MicroStation's menu and other interface components.

Toolboxes

As important as the menu bar is for the settings and commands it provides access to, you may have noticed it does not incorporate drawing or entity modification tools. These commands, vital to creating drawings, are tucked away in MicroStation's toolboxes or palettes. The Main toolbox is home to most of MicroStation's drawing, modification, and annotation commands. For a default configuration, it is docked along the left edge of your screen. If you don't see it, don't worry. All you have to do is go to the menu bar and select the Tools menu, followed by Main, followed by Main again (**Tools ➡ Main ➡ Main**). This will bring up the Main toolbox on your desktop. If you click one of the icons on this palette (go ahead, we'll wait...) you will activate that particular tool. This is noted by the tool name in the status line along the bottom edge of your screen, along with feedback on what the command expects next.

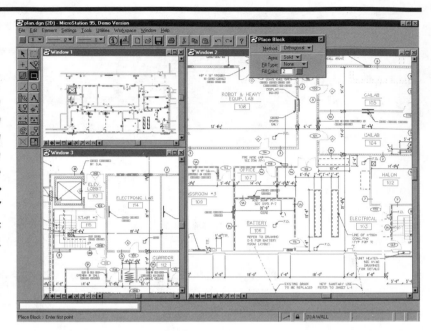

Upon clicking a tool, its name, along with feedback on sequence of data input, appears on the status bar. Note the "Place Block ➡ Enter first point" prompt on the status bar.

Tool tips, a feature to help you decipher what an icon stands for, is new to MicroStation 95. Simply pause your cursor on an icon, and a tool tip (name of the command that would be invoked by that icon, enclosed in a rectangle) will appear on screen. This lets you determine the command associated with an icon without first invoking it.

Go ahead, feel free to explore the various commands on the Main toolbox. You may have noticed that all but two of these icons have a small arrowhead at their lower right corner. This arrowhead implies that additional icons will pop up if you click and hold your cursor on an icon. These additional icons are actually a part of another toolbox you can drag away, or tear off, to float on your screen at another location. A toolbox, such as Main, that is a collection of other toolboxes is referred to by MicroStation as a tool frame.

NOTE: *Most MicroStation 95 toolboxes, when floating, can be resized, much like other windows. Tool frames, on the other hand, have a fixed size.*

Before we move away to examine other interface elements, let's look at three other important toolboxes: Primary, Standard, and Tool Settings.

Primary Tools

As you draw various elements—such as lines, circles, and arcs—you will want to assign them a certain symbology, depending on your needs to organize and differentiate real-world objects they represent. For instance, on a site layout plan, existing buildings may be shown red, and new buildings may be shown yellow and with a thicker line style. The Primary toolbox is designed to let you easily switch active symbology settings. It also includes the *Analyze Element* and *Start AccuDraw* tools.

NOTE: *Symbology refers to attributes, such as color, style, weight, and level of a drawing element.*

NOTE: AccuDraw *is new to MicroStation 95. See the Key-in Window section that follows for additional information on it.*

As a default, the Primary toolbox comes up to the left and docked under the menu bar. If it is not there on your screen, you can activate it from the Tools menu.

Use the Primary toolbox to easily switch between active symbology settings.

Standard Toolbox

No matter what software packages you use, regardless of their category—such as word processing, spreadsheet, database, or CAD—they all share many standard functions. Each will offer a command to create a new file, open an existing file, or call up help. MicroStation organizes commands for standard file and clipboard operations in its Standard toolbox.

The ten icons on the Standard toolbox are very similar to the icons found on most Windows applications. You may recognize them right away. In any case, from left to right, the icons represent these commands: New File, Open File, Save Design, Print, Cut, Copy, Paste, Undo, Redo, and Help.

As a default, the Standard toolbox comes up docked to the right of the Primary toolbox under the menu bar. If it is not there on your screen, you can activate it from the Tools menu.

Tools on the Standard toolbox cater to standard file and clipboard operations.

Tool Setting Box

One of the key reasons for MicroStation's popularity is the breadth of its command set. Virtually all elements you draw can be placed in not just one but several ways. Thus, if you place an arc, you can specify three points along its perimeter, or specify its radius and start and sweep angles, and merely pick its location. True to MicroStation's interactive, graphical nature, it implements variations to its commands as option buttons and drop-down lists in the Tool Settings box.

In addition to looking at the status bar for feedback on what MicroStation expects by way of data input, you will always want to keep an eye on the Tool Settings box. Here you will be able to select from among the variety of settings a tool might provide.

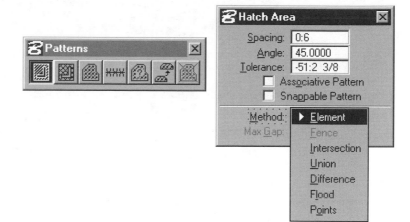

The title of the Tool Settings box, shown to the right of the Patterns toolbox, changes to reflect the name of the active command (Hatch Area) and displays available command options.

Unlike prior versions, in which you had to make sure the Tool Settings box was open, MicroStation 95 automatically opens the Tool Settings box when you invoke a command.

Key-in Window

Now, what about precision data input, you might ask? How do I key in exact coordinates for elements I wish to draw, or invoke commands by typing them in rather than getting them from toolboxes? Is the trusty old command line no longer provided? In an effort to deemphasize the command line, MicroStation 95 does not automatically bring it up. However, it is still there and has actually been enhanced. *AccuDraw,* a new tool, is a well-implemented drafting aid that will further reduce the need to use traditional MicroStation key-ins.

Select the Key-in option under the Utilities menu to display the Key-in window. You will notice that it is very similar to the Key-in Browser window in version 5. Also, the Key-in window can be docked by dragging its title bar close to the screen edge you wish to dock it along.

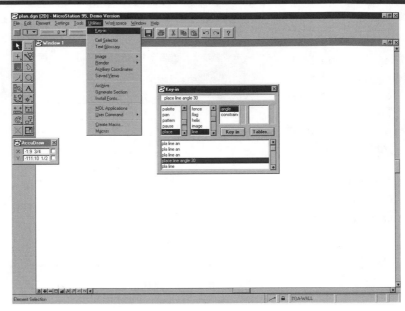

The Key-in option under the Utilities menu brings up MicroStation's Key-in window.

NOTE: *MicroStation 95 has an intelligent assistant,* AccuDraw, *designed to speed up precision data input. You will find it a more convenient tool for supplying input coordinates than the DL and DX key-ins you used in prior versions. You will also find* AccuDraw *to be a handy helper for most drafting tasks, both 2D and 3D. We will cover* AccuDraw *later.*

Status Bar

In prior MicroStation versions, the Command Window was used to display all messages and active settings. With the 95 version, all of its functionality has been moved to three interface elements: the Primary toolbox, the status bar, and the Key-in window. The Primary toolbox displays active settings, the Key-in window accepts keyboard input, and the status bar displays messages MicroStation conveys to you. The status bar is located along the bottom edge of the MicroStation screen.

NOTE: *If you do not see the status bar on your screen, you probably selected Command Window under the Style field in the MicroStation Manager dialog box when invoking MicroStation.*

In addition to displaying messages, the status bar also displays your current snap mode, level names, and status of toggles. In fact, the status display fields also act as hot-spots to invoke pop-up menus to let you change these settings.

Clicking the snap display filed on the status bar invokes a pop-up menu to let you change your active snap mode.

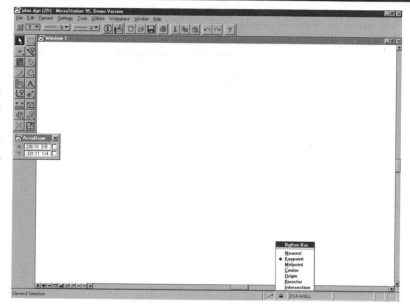

View Windows

Thus far we have looked at all interface components on your screen, except windows labeled Window followed by a number. Called a view window, this is where you do your actual design work. MicroStation supports up to eight of these windows and uses them to display the contents of your drawing. Commands—

such as open, close, tile, and cascade—that operate on view windows are located under the Window menu.

Within the view windows, all of the various instructions you enter will construct your design. As it progresses, this design will start to fill up the window and eventually you will need to "zoom" out to get a better view of it. In fact, the commands associated with this and other screen control commands are collectively known as the view control commands. Most of the common *view control* commands are located to the left and along the horizontal scroll bar for the view window. They may also be invoked from a separate toolbox. See the option View Control under the Tools menu.

Most frequently used view control commands are located to the left of the horizontal scroll bar of a view window.

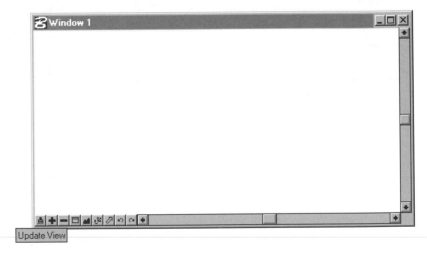

Each view can be resized by clicking on and dragging its surrounding border. In addition, you can move, minimize, or maximize it. Located along the top edge of all view windows is a series of push buttons that control these functions. The upper left corner of each view window also includes the window control menu for access to these and other functions.

The title bar that contains the name of the window is used to move that window. What each view displays (or doesn't display) is controlled by various "view-dependent" commands. Note the View Attributes option under the Window Control menu. This option will be discussed at length in later chapters.

MicroStation and the Mouse

No discussion of MicroStation would be complete without talking about pointing-device functions. As previously mentioned, there are a number of buttons found on a mouse. Each of these buttons serves very specific and important purposes.

Whether the mouse is used with a graphics tablet (where it is commonly referred to as a "puck") or not, the standard configuration for the buttons is Datapoint, Tentative Point, and Reset. If you have a two-button mouse, simultaneous clicking of the two buttons performs the tentative point function.

Mouse Buttons

What's this *datapoint* thing? you ask. Each button on your mouse is given a specific function to perform. The three functions normally assigned to your mouse buttons are as follows.

Mouse Button Assignments	
Mouse Button	**Description**
Datapoint	Used to select tools, pull-down menus, and buttons, and to identify coordinate locations in your active-design place and manipulate elements
Tentative Point	Used to temporarily locate a point in space or an element of a drawing in your design file
Reset	Releases the current operation or rejects a highlighted element

Confusing? Don't worry, as we get into coordinates and elements we'll revisit these definitions. For now, just remember the datapoint is the button you use to select a command, tool, or option. So, which button on your mouse performs this very important function? Good question. The answer is…it depends. It depends on what type of workstation you are using and whether anyone has changed the button assignments. If you think some-one has changed button assignments, check with your system administrator. The following illustration points out the default assignments.

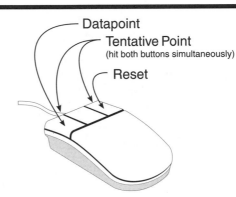

The mouse button assignments.

Puck Buttons

In addition to the three mouse button functions, the graphics tablet puck also has a Command Point button. With this button a command can be selected from the tablet menu attached to the graphics tablet.

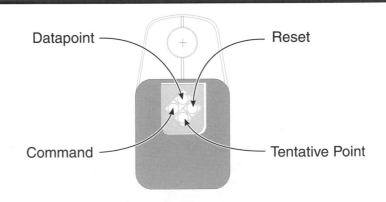

A typical four-button puck showing the Datapoint, Reset, Tentative, and Command buttons.

The Datapoint Function

As you have already discovered, this button is used to select commands and tools from within MicroStation. In addition, the datapoint is used to identify coordinate locations on the screen. When you press this button with the cursor over one of the view windows, you pass the present coordinates of the screen's cursor to MicroStation. These coordinates are used by the active tool or command to perform an operation. Quite often, the act of datapointing on a view tells MicroStation which view you want a particular operation to work on (view commands are typical of this type of operation).

The Reset Function

After the datapoint, this is the most used button on either the keyboard or mouse. This function tells MicroStation either to release the present element selected or to exit out of the active operation. With one exception, this is the only function provided that does not alter the design file when activated.

The Tentative Point Function

The tentative point is one of MicroStation's most powerful features. Likened to the old "blue pencil" that doesn't reproduce when copied, the tentative point allows you to select a point in space for use as a datapoint prior to actually datapointing. In other words, the tentative point lets you try a couple of places before actually selecting the final spot for the datapoint.

Tentative points also have the ability to "snap" to other elements for selecting that location as a datapoint. This snap-to feature is really the strength of the tentative point, and is always available, regardless of which command is active. There's even a separate button bar, invoked from the Snaps option under the Settings menu, to let you modify the behavior of this button.

The Command Point Function

This button is found only on graphics tablet pucks. It is used to identify commands on the graphics tablet menu.

This button is necessary because of the dual nature of most graphics tablets, sharing the same area for menus and on-screen cursor control. The Command button tells MicroStation to select a command at the puck location.

By using the tablet in this way you are assured maximum control of the cursor, and the convenience of a printed menu. Most first-time users of MicroStation will find themselves inadvertently selecting a command from the tablet, instead of placing a datapoint, because they put their finger on the Command button.

A good rule of thumb to remember is that the Command button only works when you are looking "down" at the graphics tablet, and the datapoint only works when you are looking "up" at the screen.

And Finally...

Exiting MicroStation

To exit MicroStation, go to the File pull-down menu and select the Exit command. You can also key in EXIT or QUIT in the Key-in window. Other ways to exit? Double-click the control menu, or press Alt-F4.

With this introduction out of the way, we can begin the journey toward understanding how MicroStation works, and more importantly, how to make it work for you. In the following chapters you will learn all of the aspects of MicroStation's very powerful tools and commands, as well as how to apply them to your design situation. By now, you must be itching to get at using MicroStation to "build something." That's precisely the purpose of the next chapter, where you'll actually draw something with MicroStation. After that, each chapter will take you through specific concepts and features of MicroStation, building on the knowledge of the previous chapters. Good luck!

A Sample Design Session

Layout of a Kitchen

Enough with the introductions! Let's try our hand at designing a kitchen. In this exercise you are given a space 10′-4″ by 7′-11″ to lay out an L-shaped kitchen. Start by launching MicroStation. We will be going through the exercise very quickly, and using several MicroStation tools you are not familiar with. Do not let this alarm you. Once we have completed this fast-paced exercise, we will begin the process of covering MicroStation's tools and features in detail.

METRIC: *This particular exercise involves the use of the English measurement system. If you wish to work in the metric equivalent, the exercise will involve a space 2.4 m by 3.15 m where possible.*

Creating a New Design File

The first step in beginning a new project is to create a design file. The following diagrams show how to start MicroStation and use a seed file to make a new design file called KITCHEN.DGN.

TIP: *You will find a completed version of this exercise on the enclosed disk.*

A complete listing of the files found on the disk can be found in a file called EXERFILE.LST. You can also use the listing in the List of Exercises at the beginning of the book to match the disk's design files with exercises.

Exercise: Creating and Activating a New Drawing

To get started we need to "launch" MicroStation. This is accomplished in a variety of ways, depending on the computer system you are sitting in front of. This is one of the few places where procedures differ, depending on whether you are running MicroStation on a PC or on a UNIX workstation.

From the Graphic User Environment

MicroStation
95

1. If you are running under a windowing environment, whether it is Apple Computer's Finder, Microsoft's Windows, IBM's OS/2 Warp, or CLIX's Looking Glass, you can execute MicroStation by double-clicking on the icon that represents it.

From the Command Line or System Prompt

1. From the more traditional system prompt, key in USTATION.

2. Whether you double-click an icon or key in MicroStation's name, the result is the activation of MicroStation proper. After a few seconds of preparation, MicroStation presents you with your first dialog box: MicroStation Manager.

3. The text field under the label Files may or may not contain a filename. If you have not previously operated MicroStation, the field will be empty. If a filename is displayed in the field, it will be the name of the last design file opened. MicroStation remembers this filename between design sessions and assumes you want to reenter the previously opened file. In addition to the text field, there are several items on the dialog box you should note.

Files   This field displays a list of files in the current directory.

Directories   This listbox is used to navigate through your system's directory structure.

Type   This field displays a list of file types MicroStation can read.

Drives   This field displays the list of available drives, both local and network.

NOTE: *If a filename was displayed in the Files listbox, and you wanted to reenter the previously opened design file, you would simply select the desired file and then click on the OK button. However, since we want to create a new design file, we will need to take a few extra steps.*

4. Select the New command from the File pull-down menu. This is done by first clicking on the File option on the MicroStation Manager menu bar. Follow this by clicking on the New option. For the rest of this book the operation of selecting a menu option like this will be presented like so: (**MicroStation Manager ➤ File ➤ New**).

Another dialog box, Create Design File, similar in appearance to the MicroStation Manager dialog box, appears. You create new design files here.

5. In the text field under the label Files, key in KITCHEN.DGN. Wait! Before you click the OK button, look at the Seed File section. MicroStation creates new design files by making a copy of an existing file. Several seed files are delivered with MicroStation. Before you create your new design file, you must specify which seed file to use. For this exercise we will use the default seed file SEED2D.DGN.

6. Click the OK button on the Create Design File dialog box, and the SEED2D.DGN file will be copied into your working directory with the name KITCHEN.DGN.

7. Once the new file is created, you will be returned to the MicroStation Manager dialog box. Click on the OK button to activate MicroStation and open the new design file.

You have now successfully created and activated a new design file for your kitchen project. Although you copied a seed file to create KITCHEN.DGN, some preparation must be done before the design work can begin. The most important preparation is to tell MicroStation what units of measure you will be using. You do this by changing the working units in the Design File Settings dialog box as illustrated in the following exercise.

NOTE: *The working units of your new file will be the same as those of the seed file you initially selected. You will want to maintain a library of seed files with appropriate working units for the types of drawings you expect to create.*

Exercise: Changing Working Units

NOTE: *If you are interrupted at any time during this exercise or otherwise get dumped out of the design session, you can return to your work by opening the KITCHEN.DGN file.*

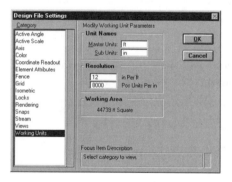

1. Select *Design File* from the Settings pull-down menu (**Settings ➡ Design File**).

2. This activates the Design File Settings dialog box. Under the Category listbox on the left, highlight Working Units. Because SEED2D.DGN is a generic seed file, its working units are set to a generic value. Master Units (the largest unit of measure) are currently set to *mu*, and the Sub Units (the second largest unit of measure) are currently set to *su*. You will learn all about working units and their unit names later. For now, let's concentrate on modifying this file to work in the more traditional units of feet and inches.

3. Replace the current Master Units unit name (mu) with the initials ft (abbreviation for *feet*) by clicking in the descriptor field and keying in the initials, and then pressing the Tab key.

4. Replace the current Sub Units unit name (su) with the initials in (abbreviation for *inch*) by clicking in the descriptor field and keying in the initials, and then pressing the Tab key.

5. We will tackle the Resolution section on the dialog box next. The first field specifies the numeric relationship between Sub Units and Master Units. In our case, we know that there are 12 inches in a foot. So, you click the text field next to the "in per ft" label, enter the number 12 with the keyboard, and press Tab.

6. The second field in the Resolution section of the dialog box specifies the relationship between the Sub Unit and MicroStation's smallest unit of measure, called the Positional Unit. If we were manually drafting we would typically be working with fractions no smaller than 1/32 of an inch. Since we are using a computer, however, we can greatly increase the accuracy of our document. Rather than specifying that the Sub Unit (inches) be divided into only 32 equal parts, we will specify that each inch be divided into 8,000 equal parts by clicking on the "Pos Units Per in" field and keying in 8000.

METRIC: *Working units for metric should be set to: Master Units.*

7. Once you have changed all of the Working Units fields to their new values, click on the OK button. An alert box will appear on the screen, informing you that changes to the working units will alter the dimensions of any elements in your design file. Click the OK button to accept the changes.

NOTE: *To save your working unit changes, you must select the Save Settings command (**File ➡ Save Settings**).*

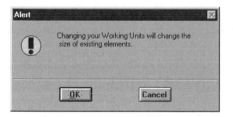

Now that you have modified your design file's units of measure to feet and inches, and you know that you have plenty of space in the MicroStation design plane (called the working area in the Working Units category of the Design File Settings dialog box), let's get back to work.

Placing Lines

Once your file is created and prepared, the next step in the design process is selecting a starting point. In this case we will start the design at X=0, Y=0. This is right in the middle of MicroStation's design plane.

If you don't have the Main toolbox and the Key-in window active on the screen, it is time to do so. Select Main from the Tools pull-down menu, followed by Main again (**Tools ➡ Main ➡ Main**). This activates the Main toolbar. Next, select Key-in from the Utilities pull-down menu (**Utilities ➡ Key-in**).

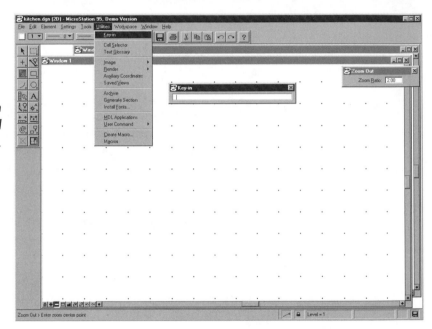

Activating the Key-in window is a good idea at this point.

The Main toolbox should already be docked along the left edge of your screen, as this is the default setting. The Key-in window can also be docked along an edge to save screen space. For the screen shots in this exercise, the Main toolbox is shown docked along the left edge of the screen, and the Key-in window is shown docked along the top, to the right of the Standard toolbox.

Exercise: Placing the Lines for Our Kitchen Extension

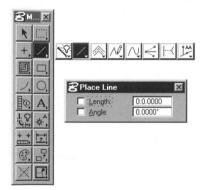

1. Activate the *Place Line* tool by selecting it from the Main toolbox.

2. The Place Line command prompts you to enter the first point. (See the status bar.) Rather than placing the datapoints interactively with a mouse, in this part of the exercise you will use the Key-in window to type them in.

NOTE: *Entering data from the keyboard is commonly referred to as "keying in." The noun equivalent is a "key-in." From this point on, we will refer to data entered via the keyboard as keyed in. Key-ins can be uppercase or lowercase.*

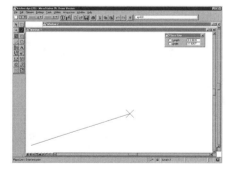

3. Now key in the coordinates that follow into the Key-in window for each line. If there is no blinking cursor in the Key-in window, MicroStation is "focused" elsewhere. Click anywhere on the Key-in window, or hit the Esc key. (Don't worry if you can't see the entire line, as your key-in is placing the element.)

> xy=0,0
> xy=7:11,0
> xy=7:11,10:4
> xy=0,10:4
> xy=0,0

METRIC: *Enter the following.*

```
xy=0,0
xy=2.4,0
xy=2.4,3.15
xy=0,3.15
xy=0,0
```

4. Hit the Reset button (rightmost on mouse or puck).

Now you have a box defining the limits of the kitchen design. Did you notice the dots and tic marks on your screen? This is a visual grid generated by MicroStation to aid you in placing elements. An alternative to typing in the XY values, or arbitrarily picking datapoints, is turning on the grid lock (key in: LOCK GRID) and mouse-clicking or *datapointing* at each location. Or, you could select the Grid option from the Locks submenu under the Settings menu item (**Settings ➡ Locks ➡ Grid**). Later you will learn how to specify the values that control the grid's appearance. Yet another alternative, new to Micro-Station 95, is the use of *AccuDraw*, MicroStation's drafting aid. If *AccuDraw* interests you, feel free to digress and read Chapter 15 at this point.

NOTE: *Mouse clicks are also known as datapoints.*

To display the full extent of the box we just drew on the screen, we need to use the Fit View command.

Exercise: Fitting the Design on the Screen

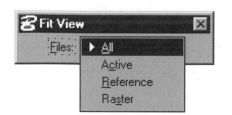

1. Click the Fit View icon located along the bottom border of the view window you wish to fit the design in. It is the fifteenth icon from the left that looks like a two-peak mountain.

Or, click the Fit View icon available on the View Control toolbox (**Tools ➡ View Control**). Or, type in FIT VIEW EXTENDED in the Key-in window.

However you activate Fit View, the Tool Settings box displays the choices available for the command. The default option All fits in the view window the active design and all of its reference files.

2. If you selected the Fit View command from the view window border, MicroStation fits the contents of the design file immediately.

3. If you have multiple views open and selected the command from the View Control toolbox or keyed it in the Key-in window, MicroStation prompts you to select the desired view. Enter a datapoint once in Window 1 and the contents of the active design file will fill the view window.

NOTE: *If you make a mistake placing the line, just type in Ctrl+Z, or select Undo from the Edit menu. This will reverse your last command. Consecutive undos reverse consecutive commands; a nice safety net for first-time users.*

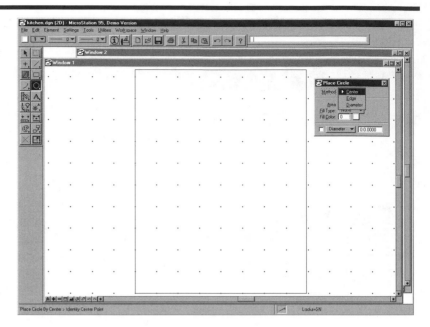

MicroStation displays options for the active command in the Tool Settings window.

As you will notice from the previous illustration, many Micro-Station commands require additional information to properly execute. As you activate a command by either selecting it from a toolbox or keying it in the Key-in window, the Tool Settings window dynamically changes to reflect available options for the active command.

Options on the Tool Settings window are implemented as either drop-down lists, checkboxes, key-in fields, or action buttons. The Tool Settings window is configured to automatically pop up on screen if needed by a command. However, if you accidentally closed it on your screen and wish to get it back, select Tool Settings from the Tools menu. Much like other toolboxes, the Tool Settings window may be positioned anywhere on the screen.

NOTE: *When first activated, the Tool Settings window may not show the current tool's options. To correct this, select an alternate tool and reselect the original tool. This action forces the Tool Settings box to select the correct options.*

Copying Lines

Now that you have defined the kitchen space, let's draw the kitchen counters. This way you can see if there is adequate space for small appliances. This part of the exercise constructs the countertops with the *Move Parallel* tool, using its Distance and Make Copy options in the Tool Settings window.

As you just saw with the Fit View command, MicroStation typically has at least two ways to activate a particular function: via key-in or a toolbox. Because of the graphical nature of MicroStation, and the strong possibility of misspelling the key-ins, the remainder of this lesson will use toolboxes for activating commands. With this method, MicroStation will offer command options in the Tool Settings window, and provide feedback through the status bar. Thus, you should get used to reading the information MicroStation displays in the status bar and glance at the Tool Settings window for available options. This is a good habit to develop and maintain.

Exercise: Placing the Kitchen Counters

NOTE: *If you are interrupted at any time during this exercise, or otherwise get dumped out of the design session, you can return to your work by opening the KITCHEN.DGN file.*

1. Activate the *Move Parallel* tool. The Tool Settings window provides options to key in a distance and to copy, rather than move, elements.

2. Enable both the Distance and Make Copy checkboxes in the Tool Settings window, and key in :25, for 25 inches, in the text field next to the Distance checkbox.

NOTE: *Be sure to enter the colon (:) before the number 25.*

METRIC: *Enter* : 635 *for 635 mm instead of* : 25.

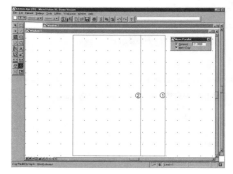

3. MicroStation prompts you to identify an element. On selecting the line on your screen, MicroStation responds by placing a line 25 inches away on the cursor side, and parallel to the selected line. If you move the cursor to the other side of the selected line, the new line will flip to that side.

> Select the far-right vertical line, labeled 1 in the diagram.

4. Next, copy the selected line.

> Place the cursor to the left of the selected line and click at the loca-tion labeled 2 in the diagram.

5. Hit Reset on your mouse or puck. This releases the selected element from further parallel copies.

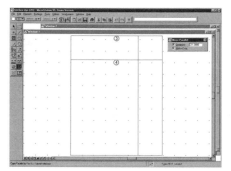

6. Select the topmost line, labeled 3, and place the cursor below it and click the location labeled 4 in the diagram, and hit Reset.

You have just taken an existing set of elements and constructed new lines from them. This is known as element manipulation. It is an important concept of CAD. Unlike the PAD (people-aided design) approach, you are assured that the resulting elements are accurate and available for further manipulation.

Trimming Lines

Now it's time to clean up the countertop lines. You can use one of the *Modify* tools (**Tools → Main → Modify**) for this. In this exercise you will use one of the element modification tools, called *Extend 2 Elements to Intersection*.

NOTE: *The current active command or tool is always shown in the status bar. Begin to develop the habit of reading the command and its prompt.*

The status bar shows that the Extend 2 Elements to Intersection command is active. Note that after you select the command, its name is followed by prompts for what the command expects as input.

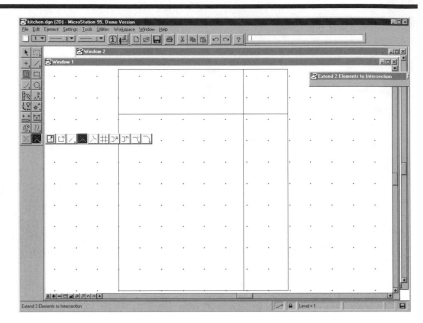

Exercise: Trimming Up the Countertops

The balloons identify the sequence of mouse clicks for the following exercise.

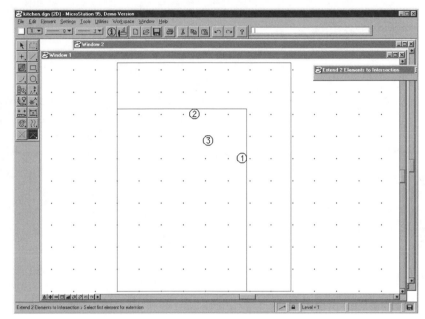

1. Select the Extend Elements to Intersection icon from the Main toolbox.

NOTE: *The name of the icon as it appears in the tool tip box may not exactly match the name of the tool as it appears in the Tool Settings window.*

2. MicroStation responds by activating the Extend 2 Elements to Intersection command and prompting you to select the first line for extension. Using the mouse, click on the line labeled 1. Take care to datapoint on the part of the line you do not want erased.

3. MicroStation highlights your first element and prompts you to select the second one.

4. Select the horizontal line at the location marked 2. Upon selecting the second line, MicroStation displays how the command will affect the two existing lines and awaits your approval of the modification.

Note how the lines are trimmed to show how they will look if you accept them. Hit Reset now if the result is not what you expected and you wish to select the second element again. Or, hit another Reset to start the command over.

5. With the mouse, datapoint once anywhere in the view, such as the location marked 3 in the diagram on the previous page, to accept the modification.

6. The command now cycles back to the beginning, awaiting your next selection. Repeat steps 2 through 5, selecting the horizontal line labeled 4, and the vertical line labeled 5, and accept the modification with the datapoint at location 6.

Continue by trimming the two lines marked 4 and 5.

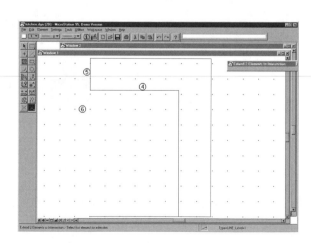

Because *Extend* tools use the datapoint to decide which segment of the line to keep, this exercise asked you to select lines at a specific location.

More Element Manipulation

Your kitchen is now ready to receive appliances. Let's say the refrigerator needs an opening of 33 inches. You can make this opening by shortening one end of the counter and capping it off. This uses an element manipulation tool.

Exercise: Making Room for the Refrigerator

The Extend Line *tool offers the Distance key-in option in the Tool Settings window.*

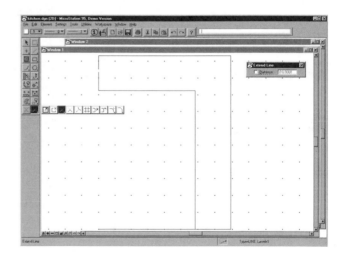

1. Select the Extend Element icon, which activates the Extend Line command.

2. Enable the Distance checkbox in the Tool Settings window and key in −:33. The minus symbol tells MicroStation to shorten (rather than lengthen) the soon-to-be-selected element by 33 inches.

METRIC: *Enter* −:838 *instead of* −:33.

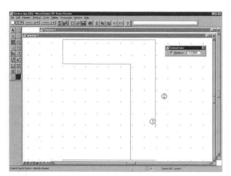

3. Place a datapoint at location 1 in the diagram. Note how MicroStation shows you how the change will look if accepted.

4. Datapoint at point 2 in the diagram to accept the modification. Be careful not to accidentally select another line you do not want to change. Hit Reset after the datapoint to make sure the Extend Line command releases the selected line.

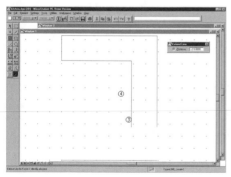

5. Repeat steps 3 and 4 for the vertical line shown by clicking at locations labeled 3 and 4.

Did you notice how Extend Line by Key-in continues to prompt you to select more elements? That is because the *Extend Line* tools remain active until you select another command.

Active commands are an important aspect of MicroStation. They conserve steps by allowing you to select the next element to be changed while accepting the last change. Most MicroStation commands work this way.

The Tentative Point

There are a lot of ways to cap off the end of your countertop. You could Copy Parallel the bottom line up 33 inches and trim it, but let's try something different to illustrate a useful concept: the *tentative point.*

In many instances it is necessary to place one element at the same point as another element. This is accomplished by using the tentative point. By identifying the keypoints of an element, the ends of a line, or the center of a circle, you can accurately place an additional element with respect to this coordinate. This important function is always available and is another strength of MicroStation.

Exercise: Cap Off the Counter

NOTE: *If you are interrupted at any time during this exercise, or otherwise get dumped out of the design session, you can return to your work by opening the KITCHEN.DGN file.*

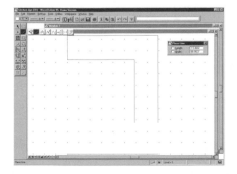

1. Select the *Place Line* tool from the Main toolbox.

2. MicroStation activates the Place Line command and prompts you for the first point. However, rather than specifying a datapoint, we will use the Perpendicular snap to construct a line perpendicular to the right vertical line. For this, click the active snap display box on the status bar.

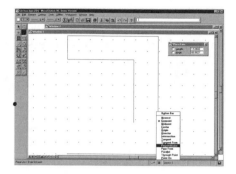

3. This activates the Snap pop-up menu. Select the Perpendicular option.

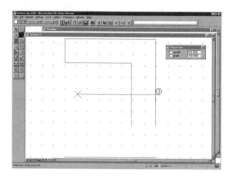

4. Place a tentative point (click both the left and the right buttons simultaneously) on line labeled 1 in the diagram. Notice how a large cross appears at that point. Now accept the tentative point with a datapoint, and a line perpendicular to the line will jump out attached to your cursor.

 NOTE: *If you are using a two-button mouse, the tentative function will be activated by simultaneously pressing both mouse buttons.*

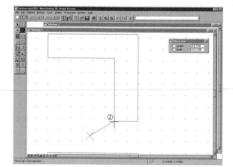

5. Tentative point at location 2 in the diagram and note how a large cross snaps to the end of the line. Datapoint anywhere to accept the tentative point.

6. Press the Reset button on your mouse or digitizer to cancel the placement of additional line segments.

 NOTE: *One feature of the tentative point not readily apparent in this exercise is that you can keep placing tentative points until you get the element or location you want. The tentative point will keep moving around without concluding the active command.*

Exercise: Deleting the Construction Line

The last thing we need to do before placing the kitchen appliances is to clean up any extra lines we used during the construction of the kitchen.

1. Select the Delete Element command from the Main toolbox.

2. MicroStation responds by requesting a datapoint on the element you wish to delete.

3. Datapoint on the horizontal line, labeled 1, at the bottom of the screen.

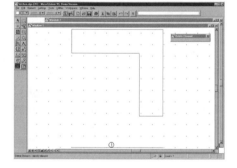

4. Datapoint *again* anywhere to accept the deletion of the selected element. It is also a good idea to hit the Reset button once after the conclusion of the deletion process. This releases any element you may have accidentally datapointed as a result of accepting the first deletion.

Building Appliances with the Place Block Tool

To complete this design you will need to build the refrigerator, stove, and sink. For this exercise we will keep these items simple. Using the *Place Block* tool and a precision input key-in, we will build the necessary appliances.

Exercise: Building the Refrigerator

1. Select the *Place Block* tool from the toolbox.

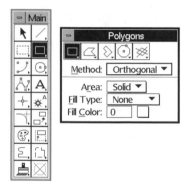

2. MicroStation responds by prompting you for the first corner of the new block.

3. If you do not have enough room, click the right arrow on the horizontal scroll bar to pan the drawing to the left.

NOTE: *The scroll bars on the view windows are one of MicroStation's many window manipulation commands. You may activate a view window control command in the middle of an active command without aborting the active command. Once the window has been changed, simply press the Reset button to resume the previously active command.*

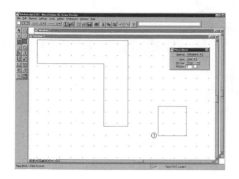

4. Click at the location labeled 1 on the diagram. A "rubber-banding" (dynamic) rectangle should appear, representing the refrigerator. To lock it to a precise size, key in the distance: DL=:30,:31. Be sure to hit the Enter key.

NOTE: *Again, don't forget to enter the colon (:).*

METRIC: *Enter* DL=:762,:787 *instead of* DL=:30,:31.

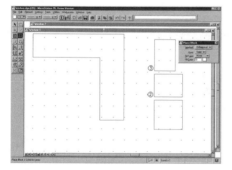

5. Now let's repeat this process two more times. Select a point just above the refrigerator block. Datapoint at location 2 (in the diagram) for the corner of the stove.

6. Key in 30 inches by 24 inches, the size of the stove.

DL=:30,:24

METRIC: *Enter* DL=:762,:610 *instead of* DL=:30,:24.

7. Now create the sink in a similar fashion, just above the stove. Datapoint at location 3 (in the diagram) for the corner of the sink.

8. Key in 22 inches by 33 inches, the size of your sink.

DL=:22,:33

METRIC: *Enter* DL=:559,:838 *instead of* DL=:22,:33.

This concludes the creation of the appliances.

Moving the Appliances into Place

Now that you have built these simple (an understatement) appliances, it's time to put them into the kitchen. By now you should be getting the hang of selecting commands and answering MicroStation's prompts. You have been paying attention to MicroStation's prompts in the status bar haven't you?

For the next part of the exercise, note that the steps described must be repeated for each appliance. Each should be moved to places shown in the next diagram.

Exercise: Moving the Appliances

A "roadmap" showing where the various appliances are going to be moved during this part of the exercise.

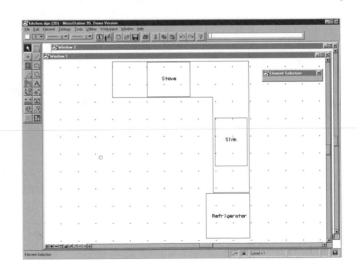

1. Select the Move command from the Main toolbox.

2. Now click the block representing the refrigerator. It gets attached to the cursor. Move the cursor until the refrigerator is in its proper place and hit a datapoint.

3. Hit the Reset button to release the refrigerator.

4. Move the stove and the sink in the same manner as the refrigerator. You can reposition the blocks until you are satisfied with the arrangement.

That concludes this exercise. By now you should have a feel for how MicroStation's basic drawing commands work.

You can continue to embellish the drawing by adding some burners and sink wells to the stove and sink. Try your hand at some of the Place Element commands. For illustration purposes, you can place any of these elements freehand and move them as you did the blocks in the previous exercise. Use the *Place Block* tool to make sink wells.

To dress up the stove, you can add some circles to represent the burners using the *Place Circle by Radius* (use a radius of :4) tool. If you don't like where you put the blocks and circles, move them the same way you moved the appliances in the previous exercise.

As the final touch to this kitchen layout, show an overhead cabinet in dashed-line relief. To do this, first Copy Parallel the walls by 12 inches (the typical depth of overhead cabinets).

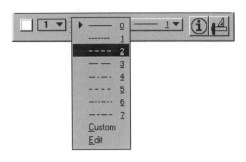

Next, change the line style of these overhead cabinet lines. To do this, first change the active line code to the medium dashed-line style by selecting it from the Primary toolbox. Then key in CHANGE STYLE and select the overhead cabinet lines you just created with a datapoint on each. If you followed these steps, you should see the results on your screen as they look in the following diagram.

If you want to continue embellishing this drawing, try to create a tile floor. The commands shown so far are all you need to finish the floor with, say, one-foot squares.

HINT: *Move Parallel and Extend....*

You can continue embellishing this kitchen plan by adding a pantry or a dishwasher. The commands given you during this short session can be used to modify this design any way imaginable.

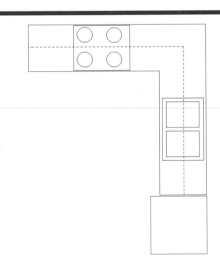

Conclusion

From this little exercise you can see there is a wealth of commands available to you for creating and manipulating objects. In fact, there are several hundred such commands in MicroStation.

You are probably becoming aware that there is more than one way to execute a design. With time, you will develop your own set of favorite commands that you will use more than others. This is natural and, in fact, encouraged. However, before developing that set, you should keep an open mind as this book shows you the rest of what MicroStation has to offer.

The Fundamentals

Basic Principles of Designing with MicroStation

When you sit down in front of a CAD system for the first time, chances are you feel a little intimidated and even a little nervous. Don't worry; this is natural. Unlike the pencil you have been using all of your life, the computer may seem an awkward tool for drawing pictures. Fear of the unknown may have something to do with this. After all, how many of us *really* know how a computer "thinks"?

The point is, with a little understanding of how MicroStation works, the mystique of CAD may be alleviated enough to allow you to go about your business designing things. Let's take a look at what's inside MicroStation.

First Things First

First and foremost, MicroStation is a computer program, and as a program it has limitations in how it does things. For one, it cannot resolve ambiguous information into usable drawings. A common phrase for this is "garbage in, garbage out."

This, however, may not be all bad. The information you provide to MicroStation will be remembered in exact detail. If you tell MicroStation to create a line 22 inches long, it will store that line as *exactly* 22 inches long. This is an important aspect—a law, as it were—of CAD.

 NOTE: *The First Law of CAD: All spatial data (coordinates) will be stored to the maximum accuracy possible.*

This differs from manual drafting. Even though we are taught in drafting classes to be as accurate as possible, there is no way we can be *absolutely* accurate. For this reason, when manually creating a drawing, all of the various drawing geometries you create are double-checked with a calculator.

This is not because there is something wrong with our ability to draw and work out problems. It is really due to the limitations of traditional drafting hardware.

Distilled to its most basic form, manual drafting consists of paper and pencil lead. If we were to think of manual drafting as people-aided design (PAD, for short), we would find there are only two commands at our disposal. We draw lines on the paper to represent a particular idea or concept using the Place Lead command. When we make changes to the drawing, we remove some of the pencil lead (the Erase Lead command), and replace it with some new lead (again, the Place Lead command).

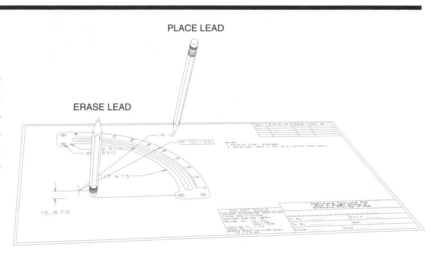

In people-aided design (i.e., manual drafting) the only two commands at your disposal are Place Lead and Erase Lead.

With CAD, on the other hand, you have literally hundreds of commands and functions to assist you in developing your idea into a final product. Unlike manual drafting, where you thought you were drawing a line 22 inches long, but were merely laying down graphite powder, CAD really does create a line 22 inches long.

"Aha!" you say. "But I can't really trust CAD any more than I can my trusty drafting board. How do I know the line is 22 inches long and not 21 and 63/64?" Easy! Ask MicroStation to measure its length and report it (the *Measure Distance* tool). MicroStation will report that the line is 22 inches long.

So what does this have to do with using CAD, and more specifically, MicroStation? Well, if you were just using MicroStation for creating a few lines and measuring their length, *overkill* would not be too harsh a term. In reality, you will do a lot more. MicroStation is ready with over a thousand commands at your disposal.

Modeling Versus Drawing

Whether it is the layout of a printed circuit board, or the plans for a new power plant, the drafting or designing process is used to convey an idea, or ideas. These ideas are expressed on paper as a series of diagrams with enough text annotation to eliminate any ambiguity in the design. This annotation usually takes the form of dimensions and various notes and callouts. The goal of the design, or drafting, process is a set of drawings used to guide the creation of the original idea.

The process of creating these drawings is commonly referred to as the "drawing process." In many instances, a CAD system is used as the primary tool in this process. The total focus of the CAD effort is to generate a finished set of plans. In most cases, CAD mimics the methodology used in traditional manual drafting, with a few additional functions. In this case, CAD stands for "computer-assisted drafting." Nowadays, however, many compa- nies have started to use CAD in computer modeling.

By modeling the underlying objects of the active design project, CAD has much more to offer to the design professional. Now, instead of relying on approximations of the design on paper, the engineer/designer can construct accurate, arithmetically driven models of a design within the computer's memory. The crux of all of this is that the CAD system becomes an active participant in the design process.

Most times when you think of modeling, some sort of physical scale model (such as a clay or foamcore model) comes to mind. When you use a CAD system to construct an idea, you are essentially creating an electronic model. This is an important aspect of CAD that forms the heart of more and more CAD operations.

Unlike manual drafting or physical modeling, where you are working at some sort of scale (i.e., 1 inch = x feet), CAD allows you to work at the full size of the product being designed. This is true if you are designing the longest bridge or the smallest electronic device.

This is not to say that scale plays no role in CAD. However, the only time scale comes into play is toward the end of a project, when you set the drawing scale for the plotter or printer. Otherwise, you are free to forget about such things as whether this is a 20-scale or 100-scale drawing.

 NOTE: *The Second Law of CAD: Work in real-world units and true size wherever possible.*

Measurement Systems and MicroStation

Of course, if you had to design a road exclusively in inches or create a printed circuit board using kilometers, you would probably consider CAD an expensive nuisance. In reality, any CAD system worth its salt must be able to work with the user in the measurement system he or she is most comfortable with. This leads to another "law."

 NOTE: *The Third Law of CAD: The user must be able to express his or her ideas in any measurement system available. In most cases, it should be possible to convert from one measurement system to another.*

To this end, MicroStation supports a variety of measurement systems. In fact, its method of defining units of measure is fully user-customizable. This means that if you were inclined to design a widget in rods and chains, MicroStation would be able to accommodate you. If, on the other hand, you decided to use feet and miles, you could do that as well. Or, meters and millimeters.

There is a minor cost to this flexibility. MicroStation provides user-selectable units of measure by fixing the size of the "design plane." Picture a sheet of blank paper. On this paper you can draw anything you like; however, you can *never* go beyond the edge of the paper. Does this sound a little like Columbus sailing west? It would be if it weren't for the sheer size of this paper.

If you were to set up MicroStation to work in miles and feet, for instance, the paper size would be large enough to map an *entire continent,* down to about a tenth of an inch!

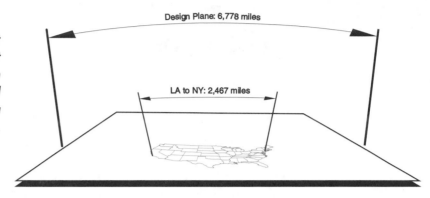

Using miles and feet for measurement units, you can "map" the United States down to a tenth of an inch.

A set of measurement units that allows you to map a continent to a tenth of an inch.

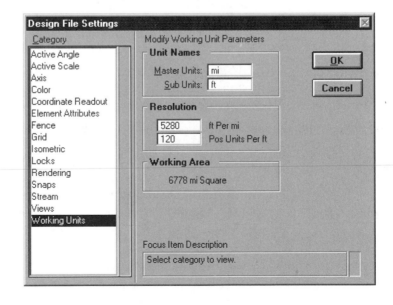

The Design Plane

This gigantic sheet of paper is referred to as the "design plane." This "space" in which you work consists of a network of absolute positional units. These units are indivisible, meaning they can't be split. This is also referred to as an integer coordinate database.

So, how limiting is this absoluteness of design size? In a word or two, not very! There are over 4.2 billion of these positional units (4,294,967,295 to be exact) in each direction of a 2D drawing, not to mention another 4.2 billion units along the Z axis of a 3D drawing.

This means you have a total of 4.2 billion^2 points with which to create your design; a truly awesome number. These "dots" are also referred to as "units of resolution," computerese for a unit of measure the computer understands. The following diagram illus-trates a design plane full of positional units.

An illustration of the design plane and its positional units.

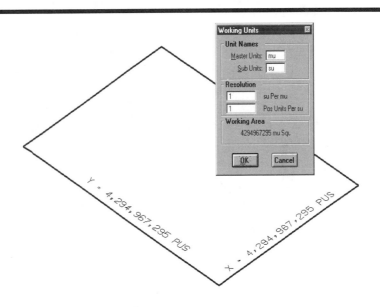

If you've ever attended an introductory data processing class, you probably remember that all computers think in binary, or base 2. The same is true for MicroStation. The 4.2 billion is not a random number somebody just thought up. It is the decimal (base 10) equivalent of 2^{32}. This is an especially significant number when you consider that the Macintosh, the Interpro32, and the latest Intel-based PCs are all considered 32-*bit* computers. Thus, each coordinate value takes up one computer storage location, or "word."

NOTE: *The binary nature of MicroStation is evident in other places. These include the number of standard line styles, eight (2^3); levels, 64 (2^6); reference files, 256 (2^8); and many others. MicroStation's internal design file structure has been fine-tuned over the years to maximize its capacity.*

As a mental exercise, you may want to keep your eye out for all of the places where this base 2 nature of MicroStation shows itself.

MicroStation's Working Units

How You Develop Your Units of Measure

If all measurement systems were decimal in nature, MicroStation's job would be a lot simpler. Unfortunately, this is not the case. You've got feet and inches, miles and feet, and meters and centimeters. Indeed, you even have microns and angstroms.

To accommodate these widely varying measurement systems, MicroStation supports the concept of "working units." By collecting equal numbers of units of resolution (UORs) into a single unit, and assigning that unit a name (say, an inch), then in turn collecting several of these inches together into a foot, you begin to see how the working unit system works.

The foot-to-inch relationship is a good example of how working units accommodate the designer's needs. There are times when a designer will want to work in feet (say, for the length of a wall), and other times when inches are more appropriate (as with the thickness of a wall). In either case, MicroStation keeps track of the relationship of feet to inches.

There are two relationships a user defines to create working units. These are the number of subunits in a master unit (the inch-to-foot relationship in the previous example) and the number of positional units in a subunit.

What's a Positional Unit?

Good question. The relationship of feet to inches as master units to subunits is relatively easy to follow. However, the positional unit is a little trickier to understand. The standard definition of a positional unit is that it is the smallest unit of measure you can use to accurately describe a distance in your design. In other words, you cannot split a positional unit into finer units of resolution. As with the master unit-to-subunit relationship, the positional unit is defined as a fraction of a subunit. Or better, a subunit consists of a set number of positional units. The relationship of master units, subunits, and positional units collectively defines MicroStation's working units.

Thinking back to the 4.2 billion-unit limitation of the design plane, there must be somewhere you "add up the leftovers and divide evenly." That is the primary purpose of the SU (subunit)-to-PU (positional units) definition.

You must keep in mind that as you increase the number of positional units each subunit contains, the overall "size" of the design plane shrinks. This is an unequivocal fact. The relationship among the three parts of the working unit can be expressed mathematically.

#master units × #subunits per master unit × #pos units per subunit = 4,294,967,295 (4.2 billion).

Rearranged, the formula makes more sense.

4.2 billion ÷ #subunits per master unit ÷ #pos units per subunit = total number of master units available.

This representation is how MicroStation displays its working units. The following exercise acquaints you with MicroStation's working units.

Exercise: Setting Your Working Units

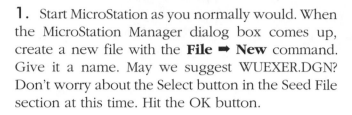

1. Start MicroStation as you normally would. When the MicroStation Manager dialog box comes up, create a new file with the **File ➡ New** command. Give it a name. May we suggest WUEXER.DGN? Don't worry about the Select button in the Seed File section at this time. Hit the OK button.

2. Select your just-created design file and hit the OK button. This takes you into MicroStation and presents you with your newly created drawing. Next, select the Design File option from the Settings pull-down menu (**Settings ➡ Design File**).

In the Design File Settings dialog box that comes up, select Working Units from the Category list on the left. Looking on the right of the dialog box, you should note the three sections Unit Names, Resolution, and Working Area. The Unit Names and Resolution sections contain data fields where you adjust the various parameters associated with working units. The Working Area contains the calculated size of your design plane.

3. Let's change Unit Names to something we can relate to (FT for feet and IN for inches). Enter the label value for the Master Units and Sub Units. Note that the Tab key or arrow key can be used to move from field to field.

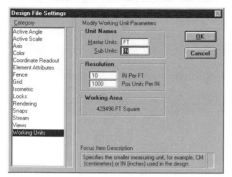

4. You should now be in the Resolution section of the dialog box. The first field sets the subunit-to-master unit relationship. In this case you want to select 12 INches Per FooT. Key in 12 and hit the Tab key. This sets your master unit-to-subunit relationship to 1:12. The total working area should have changed as a result of hitting the Tab key. If your Pos Units Per IN is 1000, the Working Area should now read "357,913 FT Square."

5. Key in 8000. This sets the positional unit-to-subunit relationship. Note how the Working Area number has fallen to 44,739 feet.

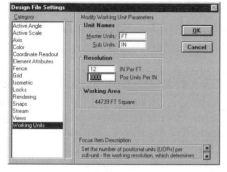

6. Click the OK button to close the Working Units dialog box. MicroStation warns you that changing the working units will change the size of any existing elements. In that we haven't placed any working units in the design file yet, it is safe to click OK.

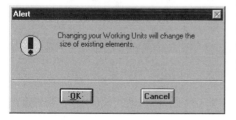

7. That's all there is to changing your working units. If you decide to change any value of the working units, you can go back and click on any of the fields and enter a new value.

NOTE: *Be sure to select Save Settings from the File menu to save your working units after you change them.*

A pictorial representation of the design plane showing the relationship among master units, subunits, and positional units.

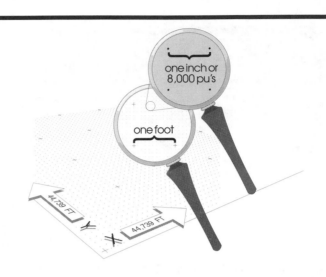

Balancing Units

Probably the most difficult part of setting the relationship of positional units to subunits is knowing when you have enough master units to perform your design, and conversely, when you have enough positional units per subunit to maintain the accuracy required.

Because the relationship among master units, subunits, and positional units is linear, you can increase the overall size of the design plane dramatically, with small changes in the positional unit-to-subunit relationship.

When you are deciding how many working units are enough for a particular design, a good rule of thumb is to multiply the proposed size of the project by a factor of four. For instance, if you are designing a building, an accuracy of 1/8,000 of an inch is more than adequate. Maintaining this degree of accuracy still gives you a working area capable of holding a building 44,739 feet, or 8.47 miles, on a side—more than adequate to build a new Pentagon!

Since most designs probably do not require a dimensional element finer than 1/32 of an inch, why set the accuracy so high? The answer is "tolerance buildup." When you lay your linework down, you can safely assume that MicroStation will record its coordinates accurately.

However, as you go through the design process, you will undoubtedly come across a variety of situations that involve irrational numbers. Remember them? The most famous one, of course, is pi, that most nasty and most common of irrational numbers. Every arc and circle you create must, by nature, include pi in its composition. Other instances are such things as dividing any given object by three (resulting in .3333333...).

On the surface this would not affect your design process. However, because you are *designing,* much of what you create will go through some sort of modification. As long as you maintain enough positional units to handle these odd calculations, any round-off error will be held in the inconsequential portion of the positional units, the 1/1,000 of an inch, for instance. If, on the other hand, you were to set your positional units to 1/10 of an inch, it is feasible that a round-off error might creep into your significant fractions category.

In most cases, if you carry one or two decimal places more than your most critical dimension, you should be safe from round-off errors. Just be aware of the situation. If while setting your units you find that you can add extra positional units, do it.

Prepackaged Working Units and Workspaces

On the plus side of all this discussion about working units and selecting the right relationship among MUs, SUs, and PUs (quaintly known as "MooSooPoos"), MicroStation provides a number of predefined seed files associated with design-specific "workspaces." These workspaces are designed to provide a customized MicroStation environment for the various design disciplines. This means that if you are an architect primarily concerned with building design, there is a workspace set up specifically for you. As part of the workspace facility, the drudgery of selecting working units for your design is greatly reduced. Although you can always change your working units, the default file setup associated with your workspace is predefined with the units most commonly used in your design community.

NOTE: *For purposes of addressing the concerns of as many users as possible with this book, the default workspace is used throughout. In Chapter 1 we discussed how to select a specific workspace from the MicroStation Manager dialog box.*

Converting Between Metric and English Measurements

A Special Consideration

In these days of international cooperation, one area of special concern is the reconciliation of the metric and English measurement systems. Due to the odd conversion factor (1 inch is approximately 25.4 millimeters), it's a good idea to preserve this ratio in your positional unit-to-subunit relationship to prevent round-off errors.

In most cases, maintaining this ratio will not affect your design process. In the event you should need to convert between the metric and English measurement systems, the incorporation of the 25.4:1 relationship would ensure no loss of resolution. The following exercise shows how to incorporate the English/metric conversion constant into your design file and how to convert from English to metric.

Exercise: Converting Between English and Metric Measuring Systems

1. Using the WUEXER.DGN design file from the previous exercise, let's bring up the Design File Settings dialog box (**Settings ➡ Design File**).

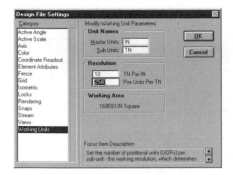

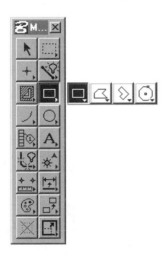

2. Enter the following settings for the Master Units and Sub Units values:

Key in IN<Tab> for the Master Units label.

Key in TN<Tab> for the Sub Units label (TN for tenths of an inch).

Key in 10<Tab> for the subunit-to-master unit relationship.

Key in 2540<Tab> for the Pos Units Per TN.

3. Click the OK button to exit the Design File Settings dialog box.

4. Select the Place Block command from the Main toolbox, or key in PLACE BLOCK in the Key-in window.

5. In the Command Window, key in XY=0,0↵.

6. Key in XY=10,5↵. You just used two precision key-ins to create a rectangle 10 inches long by 5 inches high. If no rectangle appeared on your screen, don't worry; the next step will bring it into focus.

7. To fit the view, use the *Fit View* tool found on the View Control bar located to the left of the horizontal scroll bars along the lower border of a view.

The Fit View icon on the View Control bar along the lower border of a view window to the left of the horizontal scroll bar.

8. To check your work, we need to measure the corners of the box. Select the *Measure Distance* tool from the Main toolbox and make sure you have the Between Points option in the Tool Settings window.

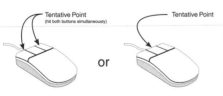

9. Place a tentative point followed by a datapoint on the lower left corner of the box. Place a second tentative point followed by a datapoint on the lower right corner of the box. The distance shown in the right corner of the status bar should be 10IN 0.000TN. Remember, a tentative point uses the middle button of a three-button mouse, or the simultaneous pressing of the left and right mouse buttons of a two-button mouse.

10. Reactivate the Design File Settings dialog box and select the Working Units category as before. Change the values as shown. Click OK on both the dialog box and the warning box. You want the element size to change.

11. Measure the distance between the lower left and lower right corners again, as in steps 8 and 9. This time the measurement should show 25cm 4.000mm, the correct conversion.

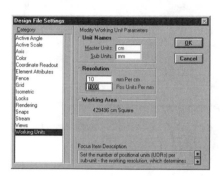

By setting up your working units as shown in the previous exercise, you can easily switch back and forth from metric to English. A neat feature of this approach is seen when you begin dimensioning your design. By selecting the appropriate working units, you can set up a complete set of dimensions in both English and metric units.

The Design File as a List File

So, how does MicroStation store all of the lines and circles you see in your drawing? Knowing a little something about this will help take some of the "fear of the unknown" out of working with MicroStation. A convenient metaphor to think of when visualizing MicroStation's design file (your drawing as stored on the computer's hard disk) is a grocery shopping list. As you add elements to the design, you are in essence adding items to this list. As a result, the list continues to grow, taking up more space on your disk. This is illustrated in the following diagram.

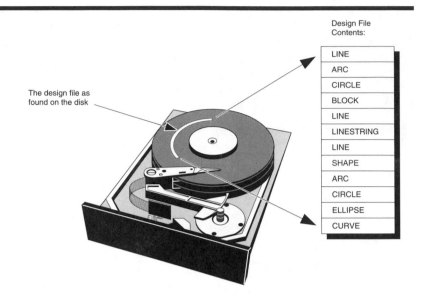

If you lifted the computer file off the disk, it would look like a shopping list with each element you placed in the design file in consecutive order.

The design file as found on the disk

Design File Contents:

LINE
ARC
CIRCLE
BLOCK
LINE
LINESTRING
LINE
SHAPE
ARC
CIRCLE
ELLIPSE
CURVE

When MicroStation needs to locate a specific element, say at the location of your cursor, it scans this list for an element matching the cursor's coordinates. As you create your design, MicroStation is constantly working through the list, looking for elements, modifying elements, and yes, even deleting them.

Part of the information that MicroStation stores with each element is its coordinates. Without them, MicroStation wouldn't be a CAD system, would it? These coordinate numbers are always stored as a count of positional units. During the discussion about setting working units, you recall there was a warning whenever you exited the Working Units dialog box. This was to alert you that you may have redefined how the positional units are divided up, but the actual numbers stored with each element stayed the same. Thus, an element may appear to grow or shrink after you change the working units, but in fact, it remains the same in the design file.

Some of the commands you use can dramatically increase the length of the design file, and, as a result, the amount of space it takes up on the disk. On the other hand, some commands only affect the individual items without changing the overall list. Such commands usually change some portion of an element, such as its coordinates or display characteristics.

 NOTE: *Although MicroStation is considered a CAD program, it is in fact a highly sophisticated database manager, not unlike Borland's dBASE or Microsoft's Access. The internal structure of its design files are organized in a manner that allows fast search and retrieval of a drawing's individual elements.*

As you continue using MicroStation, you will begin to see how it stores information. When you select elements for modification, watch how it always selects the elements in the order in which they were inserted into the design file. With a little practice you will be able to select a specific element, even if it shares its location with other elements.

2D Versus 3D: A Prime Consideration

MicroStation is a fully 3D design tool capable of creating just about any object imaginable. In this power there lies a danger. Unless you've used other CAD systems, or, you are a natural 3D thinker (a rare person), you should start out using MicroStation in its 2D mode. Working in 3D "virtual" space can be very confusing for the first-time CAD user. To keep you out of trouble when starting off with MicroStation, there is an option to work in 2D only, thus avoiding some of the pitfalls associated with 3D. As you become more comfortable, the 3D aspects of MicroStation will be presented. In the meantime, this book introduces basic design concepts in a 2D environment. However, most of the commands discussed here work in 3D files as well. 3D will be discussed in a later chapter.

Conclusion

Understanding these fundamental functions of MicroStation is very important to your success in using it as a design tool. Although on the surface things sound a bit complicated, in actuality MicroStation is very easy to learn. However, as with any complex and powerful tool, there is an absolute need for you to understand the fundamentals before venturing further.

The good news is that Bentley supplies you with a variety of predefined seed files that already have the units set up for most design situations. Just keep in mind that there will be times when none of the supplied templates will be just right. At these times you should have an understanding of these parameters so that you can modify them to get the results you desire.

2D Basics: Part 1

Learning the "Tools of the Trade"

You've done the exercises. You've slogged through the "concepts," and now you are ready for the real thing. Welcome to the tools chapter.

Here you are introduced to MicroStation's basic drawing commands. This chapter shows you how to create a drawing. It shows how to place elements graphically using the mouse, and with the keyboard using precision key-ins. All along the way you will see how MicroStation solves real problems.

Setting Your Drawing's Working Units

There is one major decision to make before you can begin your design: the working units of the drawing. As discussed in the previous chapter, MicroStation supports just about any measurement system you can think of.

In a previous exercise, wherein you created your first design file, one of the steps involved picking a seed file. One of the functions of this seed file is to provide the measurement system associated with the design discipline you are working in.

Workspaces and Your Design File's Working Units

With version 5, a new facility called Workspaces was incorporated into MicroStation. Among its many functions—of which there are more than can be discussed here—the workspace provides a simplified approach to setting up your drawing. Later in this book you will find a more in-depth discussion of the workspace, but for now just think of it as a way to quickly get your drawing up and ready for design.

 NOTE: *Concerning Workspaces: When MicroStation is installed, a number of default workspaces are provided. Each workspace is oriented around a specific design discipline, such as architecture, mapping, mechanical and civil engineering, and learning. Obviously, to address each of these disciplines and all of their nuances is beyond the scope of this book. For this reason, the default workspace is assumed in all examples and discussions.*

With the default workspace, a number of standard seed files are provided to help you quickly establish your drawing's settings. Key among these settings is the working unit values. The working units associated with each of these seed files follow.

Seed Files and Their Working Units	
Seed File Name	**Unit Label**
2dm.dgn	meters
3dm.dgn	meters
schem2d.dgn	millimeters
schem3d.dgn	millimeters
sdsch2d.dgn	inches
sdsch3d.dgn	inches
seed2d.dgn	master units
seed3d.dgn	master units
seedz.dgn	master units
transeed.dgn	master units

Looking at this chart you'll notice that the last four files use a label called *master units*. Not a real measurement system, this refers to the fact that these seed files are neutral and waiting for you to select the measurement system for use with your drawing. In reality, the working units for these seed files are 10 subunits to each master unit and 1,000 positional units per subunit.

You create your new design file either from the **File ➡ New** command within MicroStation itself or MicroStation Manager. The seed file is selected via the Select button in the Seed File section of the dialog box, as shown in the following diagrams.

MicroStation's New option under the File menu is used to create a new design file...

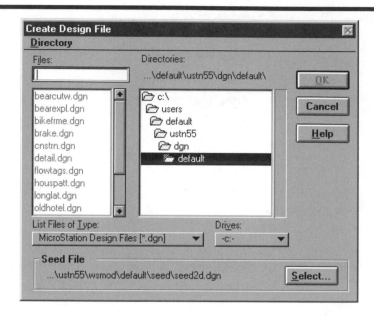

...and selecting the Seed button brings up this dialog box for selecting the seed file to merge into this new file.

If after you've created your drawing you want to change the working units, all is not lost. You can change them using the Design File Settings dialog box (see the next diagram) activated from the Settings pull-down menu.

You don't have to live with the working units provided with any seed file. By invoking the Design File Settings dialog box, you can change your drawing's default values.

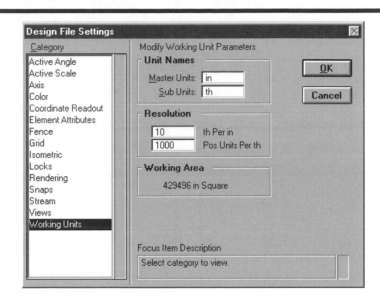

If you've been wondering what the significance of all of this unit selection is, remember, the design plane is *fixed* in size. If you change your working units, keep in mind that as you increase your accuracy (read: increase the number of positional units per subunit), the maximum size of your drawing will decrease exponentially.

The Primitive Elements

The Building Blocks of MicroStation

MicroStation is a full-function, full-featured CAD system. Just what does that mean? In a nutshell, MicroStation helps you tackle just about any design problem you can imagine. MicroStation is used to create everything from highly detailed maps to the smallest electrical components.

More importantly, when you arrive at your final design you will have full confidence in your results. By relying on MicroStation's intrinsic accuracy and profusion of tools and your design abilities, you will know the final design is *correct*.

If you were to dissect even the most complex CAD design, you might be surprised to find that it consists of no more than ten element types. Most of these are already familiar to you. Perhaps you recently worked with lines, arcs, and circles on a drafting table. In CAD, these same elements are also in heavy demand (why reinvent the wheel?). To get started, let's explore some of these basic elements.

The basic drawing elements of MicroStation.

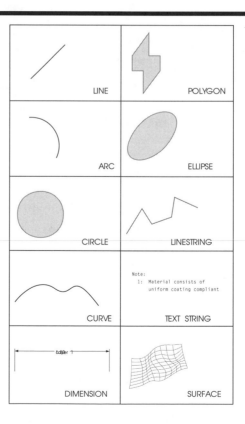

Drawing Lines

"A (straight) line is the shortest distance between two points."

This definition of a line is especially appropriate in CAD. You, the user, supply the two points, and MicroStation provides the line. In its most basic form, placing a line involves nothing more than selecting the appropriate tool, in this case the *Place Line* tool, and providing the endpoints. As with most of MicroStation's ample drawing tools, there are a number of associated options. We will discuss these in a moment.

But first, you need to know how to activate *Place Line*. Although there are various methods for activating this tool, most users will pick it from the Main toolbox. Of course, you have to have the Main toolbox active to select *Place Line*.

Activating the Main Tool Palette

From the menu bar, select the **Tools ➡ Main ➡ Main** command (yes, that's *two* Mains) to activate MicroStation's Main toolbox. You may have noticed the additional toolboxes available under the Main option on the Tools pull-down menu. These are, of course, the toolboxes associated with the Main tool frame. For now, we should concentrate on the Linear Elements toolbox.

Activating the Linear Elements Toolbox

With the Main toolbox active we need to invoke the Linear Elements toolbox. This is done by first locating the SmartLine icon and then tearing off the toolbox associated with this icon.

Select the Smart-Line icon on the Main toolbox to bring up the full array of linear element commands. Drag your cursor past the end of the nested toolbox to tell MicroStation you want to tear off this toolbox. The result is a free-standing toolbox.

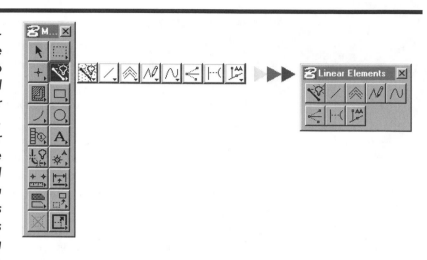

Although you can slide the cursor over the appropriate icon in the nested toolbox and release the mouse button when the appropriate command icon is highlighted, in many cases you may want to work with several related commands on the same toolbox. In such a case, you will find it more convenient to tear off the toolbox so that all of its command icons are visible at all times. To do this click over the SmartLine icon in the Main tool frame and drag the cursor past the toolbox outline that pops up. When you drag the cursor past the toolbox outline, you are telling MicroStation you wish the toolbox to be torn free of the Main tool frame and placed on your screen as a separate toolbox.

As mentioned in previous chapters, you will want to keep an eye on the Tool Settings window at all times to be aware of the options available to you for the selected command.

TIMEOUT: Activating the Tool Settings Window

*The default user-preference configuration is set to automatically open the Tool Settings window at the beginning of your MicroStation session. You can verify this by opening the Preferences dialog box (**Workspace ➡ Preferences**) and selecting Tools from the category list. You can identify the Tool Settings window on your screen by looking for a window with the name of the currently active tool in its title area. The Tool Settings window is something of a chameleon; it takes on the title of the active tool and dynamically changes to offer options for the active tool. If you look for a window titled Tool Settings, you will not find it.*

Believe it or not, the window to the right of the Main toolbox is Tool Settings. Activate various commands from the Main toolbox and notice how it changes to reflect options, or settings, for the active command.

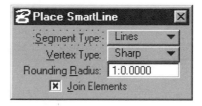

If you accidentally closed the floating Tool Settings window from your screen, don't despair. You can activate it easily enough from the menu bar. Simply select the **Tools ➡ Tool Settings** command.

Now, back to the *Place Line* command.

Place Line Continued

Now that you have your Main toolbox active, all that remains is activating the *Place Line* tool. This is done by clicking and holding the cursor on the second icon in the second row of the Main tool frame to open the Linear Elements toolbox. Place Line is the second icon on the toolbox. When you select this icon and release the cursor, the command name with available options appears in the Tool Settings window, and prompts to help you use the command appear in the status bar.

In its most basic form, the *Place Line* tool allows you to draw lines by specifying their endpoints. Once active, you must provide the first endpoint. This is where you want the line to start. The simplest way to do this is to use the mouse or puck to click somewhere in your active design file. As soon as you do, MicroStation establishes a rubber band, a line that is tacked down at this first point with the rubber part of the line attached to the cursor. Clicking a second time establishes the endpoint for the line.

With no options selected in the Tool Settings window, the Place Line command requires two datapoints to draw a line.

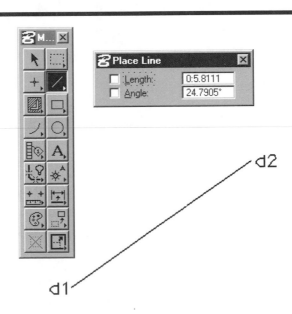

So much for placing your basic line. Let's look at the options associated with the *Place Line* tool.

Place Line Options

With the *Place Line* tool selected, you should see two tool options in the Tool Settings window. These options give you further control over what MicroStation will do with the *Place Line* tool.

Placing a line by clicking datapoints at various locations in your design is fine. However, in the real world, you will want more control over how MicroStation creates your lines. That's the purpose of the tool options. By selecting combinations of these options, you enhance the capabilities of the selected tool. Let's take a look at these options.

The Length Option

This is a very simple but capable option. When you click on the Length option and enter a value in the associated data field, you are telling MicroStation that all lines placed from this point forward will be of the length entered. For instance, if you want to create a 36-inch-wide door, entering 36 (for 36 inches) and clicking two datapoints will result in a line exactly 36 inches long.

The Angle Option

When you select the Angle option and enter the direction in degrees in the adjacent data field, you are telling MicroStation you want to restrict the line to a specific direction. Think of it as striking a line with your triangle or protractor. The length of the resulting line is not affected by this option. That's the job of the Length option.

While you are still reviewing the Place Line command, you may want to try out the Length and Angle options. Try setting various values and combinations for these two options.

While on the subject of lines, you may have noticed other tool icons on the Linear Elements toolbox. These icons represent related commands that help you activate variations of the basic *Place Line* tool, or related linear element creation tools. These are covered later on in the book. For now, just think of them as line-construction and special-duty line commands.

TIMEOUT: *Let's call this Teaching an Old Dog New Tricks. You may have noticed the interchanging use of the terms* tool *and* command. *In the "olden days" all of the commands you selected within MicroStation/IGDS were called "commands." With the introduction of MicroStation version 4, this changed. Instead of commands only, you now had commands and tools. Commands are actions you select from the pull-down menus, and tools are actions executed from a tool palette. However, the differences between these two terms are so minor that you may find yourself referring to tools as commands. Don't worry. Where it is important to make the distinction, the author will refer to tools as tools and commands as commands.*

Drawing Circles

When you first learned drafting techniques, one of the instruments you mastered after the straightedge was the compass. This handy device aided you in constructing those tricky circles and arcs.

MicroStation also has its compass. Better known as the *Place Circle* tool, this compass-like apparatus helps you to draw circles from various sets of datapoints and to key in data in the following ways:

❑ By clicking a datapoint to define its center, and another on its circumference

❑ By predefining its radius and clicking a datapoint for its center

❑ By setting three datapoints on its circumference

❑ By predefining its radius and setting two datapoints on its circumference

❑ By setting two datapoints representing its diameter

The order of these circle methods is not an accident. When you activate the *Place Circle* tool, this is the order in which the various options appear on the Tool Settings window.

The Ellipses toolbox provides access to MicroStation's "compass."

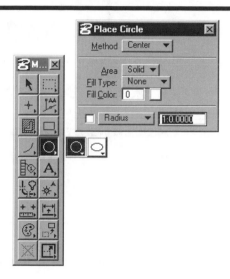

NOTE: *Beneath MicroStation's friendly graphics interface there lies a monstrous arithmetic engine. To give you the accuracy and graphics performance necessary for CAD operations, all of the various elements are constructed using basic geometric formulas such as those you learned (and probably forgot) in high school geometry class. This is important because just as there is a minimum number of variables that must be supplied to solve a geometric problem, so must MicroStation be supplied with key pieces of information before it can perform its task.*

NOTE: *When MicroStation asks for certain information, you can be certain that it is important in solving the problem. The Place Circle command is an example. When the result of a given command does not appear correct to you, it's a good bet the information you supplied was either incorrect or in the wrong order.*

MicroStation provides various circle placement commands to meet the constraints of various drawing problems. The following sections look at some of the ways you can place circles.

Place Circle by Center

Place Circle by Center is the most basic of the circle commands. It is familiar because it most closely mimics the compass instru-ment. Ensure that the Method option in the Tool Settings window has Center selected, and that the Radius checkbox is turned off. By setting a center point and selecting a corresponding point on the proposed circle's circumference, you generate a circle. Just as with the Place Line command, MicroStation responds to your center point selection with a rubber-banding circle.

NOTE: *The Radius data field in the Tool Settings window dynamically indicates the radius after the first datapoint for the circle's center is placed.*

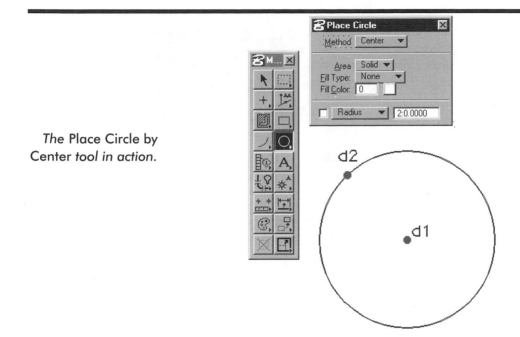

The Place Circle by Center *tool in action.*

The Key-in Radius Option

In addition to freehand selection of your circle's proposed radius, you can also preset the radius value. This is done by turning the Radius checkbox on in Tool Settings. You supply a value for the radius in the Radius key-in field, and a datapoint for the center point, and MicroStation draws the circle.

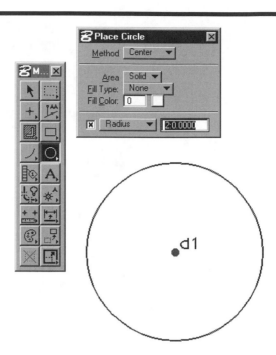

The Radius option associated with the Place Circle by Center command controls the size of the resulting circle.

NOTE: *A holdover from previous versions of MicroStation is the Place Circle by Keyed-in Radius. If you key in* PLACE CIRCLE RADIUS *in the Key-in window, you activate this close cousin of the* Place Circle *tool just discussed. However, this command gives you the option of entering the radius directly in the Key-in window. On the surface, these two commands appear to be the same, but they are in fact different. You should be aware of this, as you may one day find yourself working with a tablet menu or an older sidebar menu that invokes this command instead of the new* Place Circle by Center *tool.*

Place Circle by Edge

One of the more confusing circle tools is *Place Circle by Edge*. Simply put, this tool places a circle through three given datapoints. The trouble lies in how these three points are entered. Remembering that MicroStation is an arithmetic engine, and that there is but one solution to a circle intersecting three points, the result will always be the same. This is true no matter which order you give the points.

The same icon on the Main toolbox that activated the *Place Circle by Center* tool activates this command. All you need to activate this command is to select Edge from the Method drop-down list in the Tool Settings window.

Place Circle by Edge. Note how the rubber-band circle displayed at step 2 (d2) follows your cursor until you click the third point. MicroStation is constantly recalculating the circle through the first two points and the mouse position. The radius is continually displayed in the Radius data field.

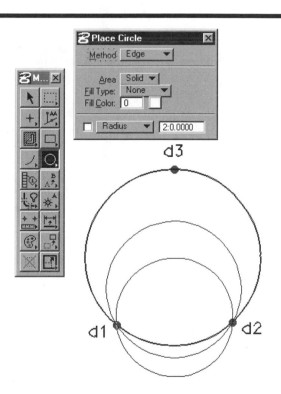

First-time users of CAD are sometimes confused by this. They frequently make an enormous circle that usually goes off the screen. To understand this variation of the Place Circle command, try it a few times. To better understand how this command works, let's draw some circles.

Exercise: Placing a Circle by Edge

1. Open a new 2D design file. If you've installed the companion disk, open the CIRCLE.DGN file.

2. Select the *Place Circle by Center* tool from the Ellipses toolbox and make sure the Edge method is selected and that the Radius option is turned OFF.

3. Place a datapoint anywhere in view window 1. A small filled box appears on the screen at the location you just selected as a datapoint. This is a nice touch. It gives you a visual reference for your next point.

4. Place another datapoint in view window 1.

5. This time you should see a dynamic (read: "rubber-band") circle attached to your cursor. As you move it about the screen, this circle will change in accordance with the location of your first two datapoints and the current location of the cursor.

6. To finish the placement of your new circle, place a datapoint somewhere in view window 1.

The use of the markers for your datapoints has "tamed" this command considerably over versions 4 and earlier of MicroStation. Because you can tell what points the circle is drawn through, you can predict how your final circle will appear. Try placing a few more circles in this manner.

A variation of this command is to predefine the radius of the circle. In this case you would only need to locate two datapoints, and a circle with the radius specified will be drawn.

With the radius defined, the Place Circle by Edge command only needs two datapoints to draw the circle.

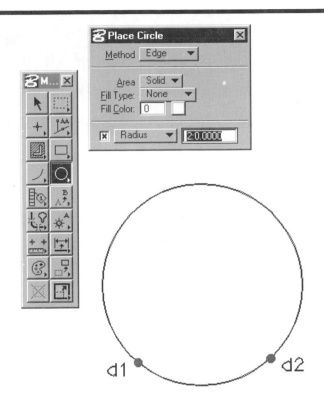

Place Circle by Diameter

Another great tool for creating circles is *Place Circle by Diameter*. With this tool you select two points on the circle's circumference. MicroStation assumes that the two points given are diametrically opposed (in other words, on opposite sides of the circle). The result is a circle fitted between the given points. Of course, the midpoint of the invisible "line" between these two points would be the circle's center.

The Place Circle by Diameter tool lets you draw a circle by clicking two points that define its diameter. Note the lack of the Radius option for this tool.

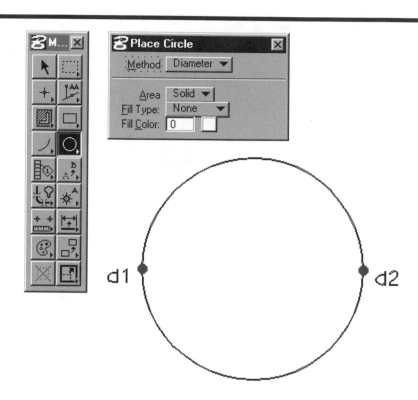

The Art of Deleting Elements

If your screen is now full of "bubbles" (i.e., circles), you are ready to perform your first element manipulation with the *Delete Element* tool. This is one of the most popular tools known to MicroStation users, ranking right up there with its close cousin the pencil eraser. Essentially it serves the same purpose as the eraser, removing unwanted graphic elements. The *Delete Element* tool also holds the distinction of being only one of two tools always available from the Main tool palette (the *Selection* tool is the other one).

One basic difference between the Delete Element command and the eraser is the Delete command's ability to remove the entire element in one quick operation. Because every element is a complete object unto itself, the Delete command can differentiate it from surrounding elements and completely remove it from the drawing without affecting the other parts of the drawing. This is true even when elements overlap each other.

The Delete Element

 You activate Delete Element either by keying in DE-LETE↵ in the Command window or by selecting the *Delete* tool from the Main tool palette. You then select the element to be deleted by placing a datapoint on it. Once highlighted, the chosen element's demise is only a second datapoint away.

If the element you selected was not the one you wanted to delete, you can hit the Reset button to release the selected element. Selecting the wrong element happens most often when two or more elements are very close together. As you hit Reset, MicroStation searches for the next element in the vicinity of your datapoint and highlights it.

Once you've highlighted the element you want to delete, just hit another datapoint to accept the deletion. If your selection command was near another element, it will then highlight, waiting again for your next datapoint.

 TIMEOUT: *This "accept/reject" (select next element) process is common throughout MicroStation and is meant to minimize the number of datapoints needed to perform your task. Although very efficient in the hands of an experienced user, this method will cause you some consternation, and yes, inadvertent loss of elements, until you get used to it.*

To minimize unwanted deletions, always place a datapoint away from all surrounding elements (in a relatively empty part of the design) for the accept point. As you become more experienced with MicroStation, you will begin to conserve these acceptance datapoints and use them for the next selection.

TIP: *When you have finished with the* Delete *command, another good habit is to choose another command to deactivate the delete function. This will keep you from inadvertently causing havoc by accidental deletions. A "safe" command to select is the* Element Selection *tool or the* Place Fence Block *tool.*

Go ahead and delete the circles you created in the last exercise. Deleting elements is always fun!

TIP: *If you inadvertently delete an element, select Undo from the Edit menu. You can also key in* UNDO *in the Key-in window.*

Ellipse, the Circle's "Cousin"

You may have noticed the *Circle* tool was in the Ellipses toolbox. The other tool in the toolbox is the ellipse. From MicroStation's point of view, these two element types share much in common. Both are nonlinear, both have a center point, and both use radius information.

The major difference between the circle and the ellipse is in the latter's treatment of the radial dimension. Unlike the circle, which has only one radial component, the ellipse has two. The ellipse consists of a single center point with a primary radius length and a secondary radius length. In addition, the ellipse has an axis along which these two radii are situated (the two radii are always perpendicular to each other).

Sound complicated? It does at first. However, if you think of an ellipse as a "squashed" circle, where the long side of the ellipse is the axis, you can picture how MicroStation treats the action of the Ellipse commands.

Place Ellipse by Center and Edge

Similar to the *Place Circle by Center* tool in its default condition (no options selected), this tool creates an ellipse from three datapoints. The first datapoint defines the all-important center point, the second locates a point on the ellipse itself, and the third locates another point on the ellipse. Thankfully, there is a mathematical formula for interpreting this data into one, and only one, ellipse.

The Place Ellipse by Center and Edge command provides the fastest method for creating an ellipse.

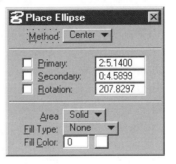
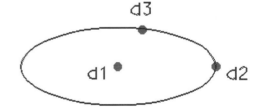

As with the circle, there is only one solution for creating an ellipse from three points. As a result, you don't have to know precisely where the "axis of rotation" is prior to creating an ellipse. However, there are times when you will want to specify this and other key data about your ellipse. This is done with option fields in the Tool Settings window.

With the Place Ellipse by Center and Edge command you can control the two radii values and the rotation of the primary axis with respect to the X axis. If you specify all three values, you only need identify the location of the center to draw the ellipse. If you select the angle of rotation and the primary radius value, you will need to provide the center point and the secondary radius via another datapoint.

Why would you want to control your ellipse axis? Simply put, to get the results you are looking for. For instance, you may be creating an isometric drawing for which "traditional" circles won't work. But knowing that all circles in an isometric diagram fall on either a 30-, 60- or 90-degree axis means that you can control the direction of the resulting ellipse.

Place Ellipse by Edge Points

When you need to position an ellipse by identifying three points along its perimeter, the tool for you is *Place Ellipse by Edge Points*. Similar in operation to the *Place Circle by Edge* tool, this tool requires two datapoints that serve to define the major axis of the ellipse, as well as the primary radius. A third datapoint generates the secondary axis. As with the previous ellipse tool, you have options to control all three aspects of the ellipse process.

The Place Ellipse by Edge Points *tool. Note how datapoints 1 and 3 lie along the major axis of the ellipse.*

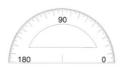

TIMEOUT: A Bit of Trivia

MicroStation treats the circle and ellipse as something closer to identical twins than cousins. Internally, MicroStation stores the information about these elements in exactly the same manner. If you stop and think about it, a circle is nothing more than an ellipse with equal primary and secondary radii. Later on, you will find this relationship is a key consideration in how a command such as Scale Element performs its job.

Drawing Arcs

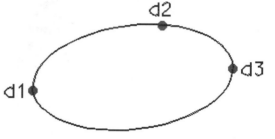

Another close cousin to the circle is the arc. Sharing the same traits as the circle (a radius and a center point), the arc has one additional characteristic: *endpoints.*

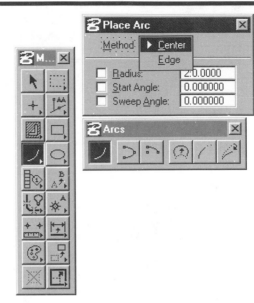

The Arcs toolbox and its settings.

As mentioned earlier, the formula for a circle has but one solution for three given points. This is not true for arcs. For three given points you have two possible arcs. The trick is telling MicroStation which arc segment you want. So, how do you tell MicroStation which piece of the circle you want? Through a little trick called the *counterclockwise rule.*

For any given three points there are two arcs: the one you want and the one you don't.

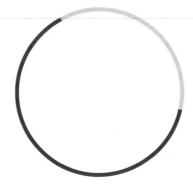

The Counterclockwise Rule

Just as no drafting tool set would be complete without a protractor, MicroStation must also be able to handle angular data. Arcs by their very nature use angular information. The "length" of an arc is typically measured in degrees of sweep. The problem is that there are two possible sweeps: the actual arc and the portion of the circle not occupied by the arc.

MicroStation "solves" the problem by requiring you to enter all radial information in a counterclockwise direction. When you give the first endpoint, the center point, and the final endpoint of an arc, MicroStation automatically strikes the arc from the first point counterclockwise to the final endpoint. This can be confusing to the first-time CAD user. For now, just remember that *all radial input must be entered counterclockwise.*

A simple protractor showing how the counterclockwise rule should be envisioned. MicroStation supports the entry of negative degrees, which produces a clockwise or opposite sweep.

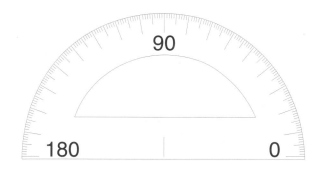

Place Arc by Center

Placing an arc with the *Place Arc by Center* tool is very straightforward. You select the first endpoint, the center point, and, following the counterclockwise rule, the final endpoint.

The radius distance of the arc is set by the distance from the first endpoint to the center point. The final endpoint only sets the "sweep" angle of the arc. This is shown in the following diagram.

The Place Arc by Center *tool relies on the counterclockwise rule.*

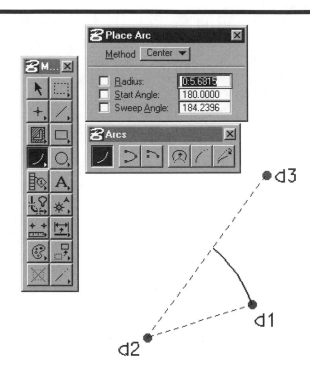

Place Arc by Edge

After all of this talk about the counterclockwise rule, along comes an arc placement command that doesn't follow it! Instead, *Place Arc by Edge* uses the order in which you place datapoints to determine the final arc.

The first and third points still define the ends of the arc; however, the second datapoint is used to compute the radius. Think of it as "From-Through-To," an idea that will reappear in other commands. When you specify an arc by edge, you start *from* point 1, pass *through* point 2, and go *to* point 3, as shown in the following diagram.

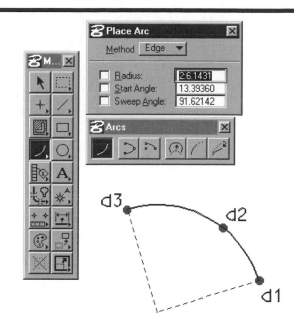

You switch the Method to Edge in the Tool Settings window to activate the Place Arc by Edge tool. An easy way to remember how the arc is drawn: From-Through-To.

Options When Placing Arcs

As with the *Circle* tools, the placement of arcs can be controlled by setting the appropriate options. With both of the standard arc tools there are three specific options. These three options match the three parts of an arc:

❑ Radius

❑ Start angle of the arc

❑ Sweep angle

The Radius option is easy to understand. With this option selected, you enter the radius you want the arc to have in the associated data field.

The Start Angle option, on the other hand, is tougher to understand. How the command operates depends on your selection of the drawing *method,* whether Center or Edge. Assuming you are placing the arc by center, and the start angle is 10 degrees, MicroStation locks your second datapoint to 10 degrees from your first datapoint.

MicroStation responds by drawing a dynamic dashed line from the datapoint (noted by a small filled box) at the angle specified in the Start Angle data field. This gives you a visual reference for selecting your second and third datapoints.

In a similar fashion, when you select the Sweep Angle option and enter a value, MicroStation responds by displaying a dynamic arc attached to your cursor at the center point and tied to your first datapoint.

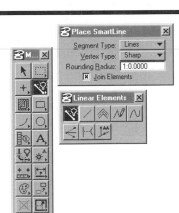

TIMEOUT: *One of the more powerful features of MicroStation is its integration of a tool's various options. For instance, with the arc tools just described, it is implied that you can turn on any combination of these options and MicroStation will respond accordingly. In fact, if you turn on all three of the options, a complete arc will be created, just waiting for you to select its new location. This "Chinese menu" approach to command selection results in very flexible drawing capabilities. Don't be afraid to try unusual combinations just to see what MicroStation can make of them.*

Drawing SmartLines, or Connected Strings of Lines and Arcs

The SmartLine tool on the Linear Elements toolbox.

The *SmartLine* tool, new to MicroStation 95, replaces the "line string" tool found in prior versions. Whereas the older tool was designed to let you place a string of connected lines that are treated as a single unit, the *SmartLine* tool lets you combine lines and arcs. It also adds the ability to automatically chamfer and fillet corners. In its simplest form, a series of lines placed with the *SmartLine* tool looks no different than those drawn with the *Place Line* tool. However, they do differ in how MicroStation treats them. For this reason, let us look at these two element types in closer detail.

A simple line consists of two coordinate pairs, period. No more, no less. However, there are times when you want to associate more than two pairs of coordinates with a particular design situation. For instance, you may want to connect two symbols on a wiring diagram with a multisegmented line (i.e., line string) so that, should you move the symbols around, the line string interconnection is maintained. Enter the line string. Although it looks like a series of connected lines, in reality it is a single entity containing a number of coordinate pairs known as *vertices*.

Place SmartLine

 Found on the Linear Elements toolbox, this tool is used to create line strings, complex chains, closed shapes, and even individual line segments. Although the proce-dure for creating SmartLines is fairly straightforward, its Tools Settings window offers a variety of options you will want to get familiar with. In its simplest form, you simply place datapoints at the vertices you want MicroStation to connect with a single line string. With each successive datapoint, MicroStation draws another line segment of your not-quite-finished line string. A final reset after you've placed a datapoint at the endpoint of your line string is needed to complete it.

*Place SmartLine.
Note the use of the
Reset command to
terminate the
construction of the
SmartLine.*

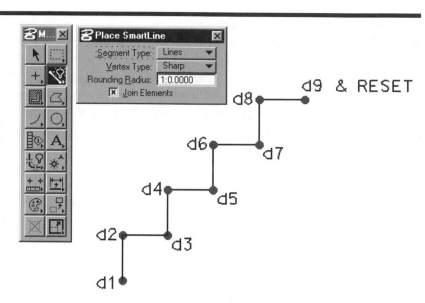

>
>
> **NOTE:** *The SmartLine and its cousins the curve and
> multi-line are the only elements that require the use of
> Reset as part of the element's creation process. Because
> MicroStation uses Reset to back out of most commands,
> this can be very disconcerting to the first-time CAD user.*

So, what do you do if you find yourself creating a SmartLine
you don't want? Easy, you just undo it! Either press Ctrl+Z on the
keyboard, or select **Edit ➡ Undo** from the menu bar. And if you
prefer keying in your commands, you can key in Undo in the
Key-in window.

The question is, where would you use a SmartLine? A good
example is an electrical schematic drawing such as the following.
A typical design would consist of various electrical symbols
interconnected with line strings, representing the logical connec-
tions or wires. Maintaining the sometimes convoluted pathways
of these wires is paramount to the process.

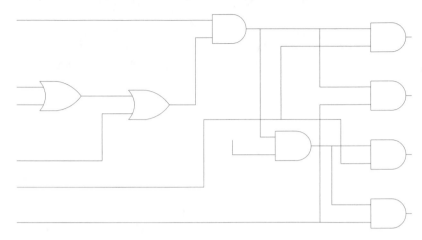

An electrical schematic diagram; a good example of SmartLines at work.

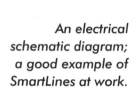

NOTE: *SmartLines drawn in the manner shown on this schematic would be tedious without the use of MicroStation's grid functions. By "locking" each vertex of the line string to a preset grid, the result is orthogonal linework. Grids will be discussed in detail later.*

If you were to use plain line elements in such a drawing, the chances of leaving a line segment floating (not connected to anything) are pretty good. Because a SmartLine's segments are by default joined, they serve the role of schematic wires perfectly. MicroStation also includes a set of editing tools specifically designed to add and subtract line segments. More on these later.

Options When Placing SmartLines

As with most other tools, you can control the parameters of SmartLines by using the options displayed in the Tool Settings window. If you glance at the Tool Settings window, you will notice the availability of four options. These options control whether or not you wish to have the SmartLine segments joined, whether segments should be lines or arcs, or whether you want corners automatically chamfered (beveled) or rounded. Let's look at them individually.

❑ *Segment Type:* You have a choice between drawing line segments or arc segments. Placement of arc segments is similar to the *Place Arc by Center* tool discussed earlier. Keep in mind that you can switch between line and arc segments at any time during the construction of a SmartLine while still keeping it all connected; just don't hit the Reset button.

❑ *Vertex Type:* The default option is Sharp, which means that corners of the SmartLine are sharp. Other options are Rounded and Chamfered. The former automatically fillets adjoining line segments with a tangential arc of radius specified in the Rounding Radius data field; and the latter automatically chamfers adjoining line segments with a value specified in the Chamfer Offset data field. Obviously, if the specified rounding radius value or the chamfer offset value is inappropriate for a particular vertex, the SmartLine tool will construct it sharp.

❑ *Rounding Radius/Chamfer Offset:* This field changes its name to either Rounding Radius or Chamfer Offset depending on whether the vertex type is selected as Rounded or Chamfered.

❑ *Join Elements:* This checkbox is turned ON as a default. If you turn it off, the SmartLine segments will not be joined and MicroStation will treat them as individual elements.

While constructing a SmartLine, if you snap to its beginning vertex, additional options appear in the Tool Settings window. These are shown in the following figure.

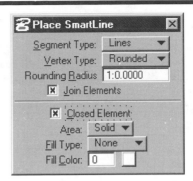

The Closed Element checkbox lets you decide whether or not to construct the SmartLine as a closed shape.

Drawing Curves

If we continue the drafting tool meta-phor, we have covered the triangle/T-square (*Place Line*), the compass (*Place Circle*), and the protractor (*Place Arc*). The next tool we'll cover is the equivalent to the French curve template found in almost every designer's template collection. MicroStation's French curve is the *curve string*.

Place B-spline Curve Through Points

The *Place B-spline Curve* tool works something like the *Place SmartLine* tool. You place datapoints to define the shape of the curve with a final Reset to accept the curve.

However, the B-spline curve tools are not found on the Main toolbox. You will need to invoke the Curves toolbox from the Tools menu to access them.

The result of the *Place B-spline Curve* tool with the Through Points method is a gentle curving element that passes through each datapoint. The degree of curve is established by the angle between the datapoints. The more acute the angle, the sharper the curve. By keeping the angle very shallow, the result is a gently undulating curve.

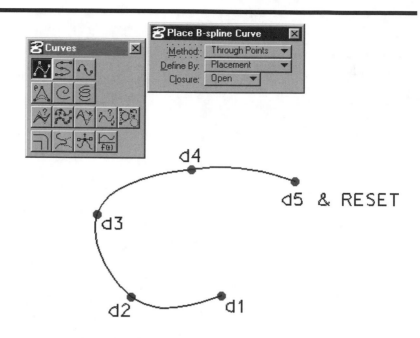

The Place B-spline Curve *tool can be found on the Curves toolbox. Note that you must hit the Reset button to complete the construction of the curve.*

Such curves constructed to pass through points are a favorite element for creating topographic contours on a site plan. As with SmartLines, you can modify the shape of your curves after you have placed them. More on this later.

Drawing Polygons

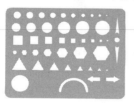

If you've ever used a general-purpose drafting template, you've no doubt drawn boxes, hexagons, and triangles. MicroStation, too, has its equivalent to these very useful shapes. Called polygons, these shapes share one important characteristic: area. All of these shapes are closed elements, in that they start and end on the same point. You've already seen one such element, the circle.

There are several tools to help you create polygons. Let's look at some of them. All of the Polygon tools are located on the Polygons toolbox. There are tools here to create everything from simple shapes to specialized isometric ones.

- *Place Block*
- *Place Shape*
- *Place Orthogonal Shape*
- *Place Regular Polygon*

Place Block

The simplest of the polygon tools is *Place Block*. This tool creates a four-sided rectangle based on the data-points you supply. When you select this tool, you have a choice of methods for placing the block: Orthogonal or Rotated.

Place Block has only one option: Method. Seen here, the Orthogonal method results in a block aligned with the view.

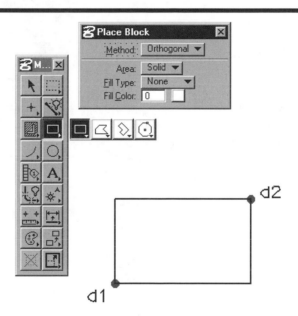

With the Orthogonal method chosen (the default), the block is aligned with your view. To place such a polygon, all you need to do is enter two datapoints for opposing corners of the box. It doesn't get much simpler than this.

With the Rotated method, you provide the axis along which the block will be placed. Your first two datapoints define this axis. A third datapoint provides the height and width of the new block.

Place Shape

There are, of course, other types of polygons. One of the more useful ones is the free-form shape, which you can make with the *Place Shape* tool. By specifying every vertex, you have full control over the final form of the shape.

The Place Shape tool in action. The shape will close itself when you click a datapoint at the beginning point or hit the Close Element button.

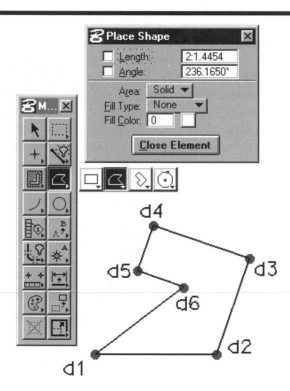

The one tricky aspect of the shape is closure. Unlike the SmartLine, which needs a Reset for completion, the *Place Shape* tool relies on your returning to the beginning point of the shape. MicroStation provides a button on the bottom of the Tool Settings window (Close Element button) that, when selected, forces closure of the shape. You can also key in C L in the Key-in window.

TIP: *If your shape is small, or has closely spaced vertices, MicroStation may suddenly close on the beginning point before you have finished drawing the shape. The best defense against premature closure is to select your starting point along the longest side of your intended shape.*

There are a number of options associated with the *Place Shape* tool. The Length option allows you to specify the length of each shape segment. Entering a value in the Length data field will result in a dynamic segment attached to your cursor for which you datapoint at a given angle. The Angle option allows you to provide the angle at which the current segment should be drawn. One note of caution about the Angle option: you *must* change the value for each segment, especially when used in conjunction with the Length option, or else you will end up with a very *flat* shape!

Place Orthogonal Shape

Related in function to the previous tool, *Place Orthogonal Shape* sets the axis of the shape with the first two datapoints. The shape created from this "baseline" will be orthogonal in nature (i.e., at right angles to it).

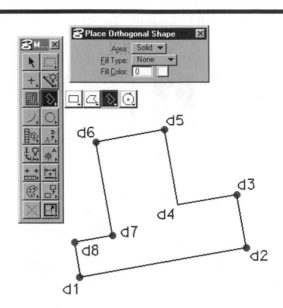

The Place Orthogonal Shape tool. Note the lack of a Close Element button on the Tool Settings window.

As each datapoint is entered, the resulting line will be set close to the datapoint. But, because it must be orthogonal to the axis set with the first two points, it will not be on the point itself. You close the shape by clicking a datapoint at its starting point.

NOTE: *Place Orthogonal Shape does* not *have a Close Element button, nor does it work with the* CL *key-in. If you do use the key-in, the shape is aborted.*

Place Polygon

The tool that most closely matches the function of the general-purpose template is the *Place Polygon* tool. A very powerful shape maker, this tool allows you to set the number of equal-length sides (the Edges option) you want on your polygon. In addition, you have control over how your multisided polygon will be placed (the Method option). Finally, you can control the overall size of the polygon via the Radius option.

One of the fun tools, Place Polygon gives you flexibility in creating your polygon.

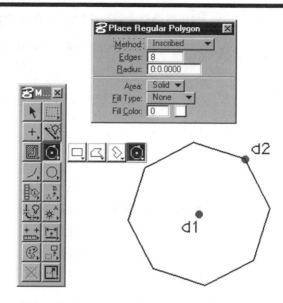

The most confusing aspect of this tool is the difference between the three methods of placement. The three options are:

❑ *Inscribed:* Placement of the shape is by a center point and a point on one of the polygon's vertices.

❑ *Circumscribed:* Placement of the shape is by a center point and the midpoint on one of the polygon's segments.

❑ *By Edge:* Placement of the shape is by two adjacent vertices of the polygon. Note that the radius value has no effect on this placement method.

The major difference between the Inscribed method and Circumscribed method has to do with how they relate to a circle of equivalent radius. With the Inscribed method, the vertices fall on the radius of the phantom circle, whereas the circumscribed polygon's segments are tangent to this radius.

Placing Isometric Elements

A common type of drawing used in many design disciplines is the isometric plan. This type of drawing consists of a pseudo-3D drawing of an object oriented in a specific rotation. Isometric drawings, whether they are plumbing riser diagrams or PID heat-trace illustrations, use the 30/60/90 degree isometric drawing to establish the location of key elements with respect to an entire system in a 3D space.

MicroStation supports isometric drawings with two special tools and specially designed text fonts. The two tools are:

❑ *Place Isometric Block*

❑ *Place Isometric Circle*

You access these tools from the Isometric toolbox activated by selecting **Tools ➡ Isometric** from the menu bar.

The two tools in the Isometric toolbox simplify the creation of isometric drawings.

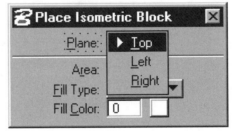

By selecting the particular plane you wish the element being created to reside on (top, left, or right), the result of using these tools matches the standard isometric orientation. The orientation of these elements falls along the 30-, 60-, or 90-degree axis of your 2D drawings. The plane is chosen from the Plane option field. The actual operation of these two specialty tools follows their normal brethren, *Place Block* and *Place Circle by Center*.

Isometric Text

Although we haven't yet discussed text, while we are talking about isometric drawings you should know that there are two text fonts delivered with MicroStation specifically designed to mimic the oriented text found on most isometric plans. These fonts are:

❏ Font 30: Iso_fontleft

❏ Font 31: Iso_fontright

Both fonts are stick-figure-like, but do serve the purpose of creating realistic isometric plans.

Selecting the Isometric Pointer

As a final aid in creating isometric drawings, MicroStation allows you to change the shape and orientation of the on-screen cursor or pointer. This is done via the Preferences dialog box (**Workspace ➡ Preferences**). Selecting the Operation category provides you with two options regarding the pointer: Pointer Size and Pointer Type.

The defaults are normally Pointer Size, Normal and Pointer Type, and Orthogonal, meaning the cursor/pointer is displayed as a small cross oriented along the X and Y axes. Changing the pointer size to Full View displays a large cursor that runs from one edge of your view to the other. Changing to Pointer Type/Iso-metric results in a skewed cursor that visually shows the orientation of the current isometric plane value (set with the Plane option on the appropriate Tool Settings window).

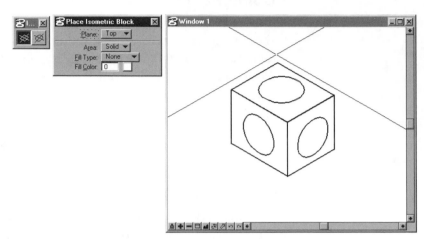

With the Pointer Size set to Full View and Pointer Type set to Isometric, this cursor is the result. Note how its orientation reflects the Plane setting shown in the Place Isometric Block tool.

Controlling Element Placement

If you have been following along with the examples and exercises presented in this chapter, you have placed all elements "free-hand." Freehand graphic input is not the only method of inserting elements in a design file. In fact, it is rarely used in real design work. More often, you create your drawings using very precise placement of the various elements that make up your drawing. In addition, you often place new graphics in precise relationship with other, previously placed elements. For instance, you nor-mally *fillet* (the act of placing an arc tangent to two lines) an existing pair of lines. Imagine trying to first place the fillet's arc and then the lines associated with the fillet. Not a very efficient method.

For precise control over your lines, arcs, circles, and so on, you can turn to two intrinsic features of MicroStation: *element snaps* and *precision input.* Although in the following discussion we are treating them as separate functions, in most day-to-day operations you will find yourself using snaps and precision input in unison. So, what are these features? Let's tackle element snaps first.

Snapping Along in Your Design

Let's look at how you normally create a drawing on the drafting board. You start with a drawing sheet, draw the major features of an object under design, and refine the image by placing other lines and erasing and otherwise changing the first lines you laid down on the paper. In CAD, you follow a similar approach. First, you strike the major lines of the object under design. Then, using an ability found only in a CAD program, you begin to construct other elements as they relate to these first lines. This ability to use the start-up lines as a jumping-off point is one of the major strengths of CAD.

In MicroStation, this ability to work from existing geometry is called *snapping to* an element. Being able to start an element by first selecting an existing one is the cornerstone of efficient CAD design. MicroStation's snaps have improved dramatically since the program's inception, and its current incarnation (version 95) contains no less than fourteen different snap functions. With it you can:

❑ Snap to any point along an element

❑ Snap to the endpoints of an element

❑ Snap to the midpoint of an element

❑ Snap to the intersection between two elements

❑ Snap to a location of tangency along an element

❑ Snap to a point perpendicular to or from an element

❑ Force the creation of an element to be parallel, through a point or on a point, to an existing one

❑ Snap to the center of a shape

❑ Snap to the origin of a cell

When it comes to associating one element with another, MicroStation gives you plenty of ways to do it.

The Tentative Point Revisited

So, how do you activate and use the snap functions in MicroStation? Thinking back to the kitchen design exercise in Chapter 2, you may recall the instructions to use the tentative point button on your mouse or graphics tablet puck. Believe it or not, that is how you invoke snaps.

Depending on what type of cursor control device you are using, the tentative point button may be a separate button (a typical example is a graphic tablet puck) or a combination of two buttons (a typical example is a Microsoft 2 button mouse). In the case of a single mouse button (e.g., Apple Macintosh), the tentative point is a combination of a mouse button action and a keyboard keypress, usually the Option key. In all cases, the result is the same: the current snap function is invoked and an action appears on the display.

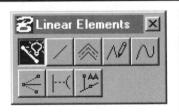 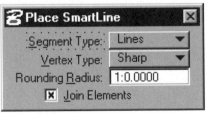

When the tentative point button is selected, the tentative point cursor appears.

In the previous example, the snap mode set was called *keypoint.* In this mode, the tentative point cursor jumped to the nearest keypoint on the closest element. One point to note about keypoints is their temporary nature. The action of generating a tentative point is, as the name implies, not permanent. In other words, as you are placing a line, the act of invoking the snap with the tentative point button does not, in itself, generate a line. Instead, MicroStation requires you to accept the location of the tentative point snap by selecting the datapoint button. As long as you do not hit the datapoint button, you can continue to reselect tentative points or even change the snap mode without any effect on your drawing.

TIMEOUT: *If you are having trouble finding your tentative point button (or for that matter the Reset or datapoint button) or if you have a three-button mouse, don't despair. You can view the current settings for your mouse or tablet puck via the Button Assignments dialog box (****Workspace*** **➡** ***Button Assignments****). Here you will find a list of the standard MicroStation buttons and the actions needed to invoke them. The Tentative button is the second one shown and will normally point to the Left Button–Right Button Chord, which is a fancy way of saying you have to push both buttons down to get a tentative point. To change it, select the tentative entry in the dialog box. Next move the cursor down over the area labeled "Press the button you want…" and hit the middle button or both buttons. This will reassign tentative point to the middle button. Hit OK to accept the change to your button assignments.*

The Common Snaps: Keypoint and Nearest

Prior to version 5 of MicroStation, there were really only two snap modes: Project and Keypoint. Project, now called Nearest, allowed that when you placed a tentative point near an element, the tentative point cursor would jump to the point on the element nearest your cursor. Keypoint, by contrast, forces the tentative point to jump to key locations on the element. In the case of a line, this would be the closest of the two endpoints. A circle keypoint would be the closest quadrant (or its origin point), a line string the nearest vertex, and so on.

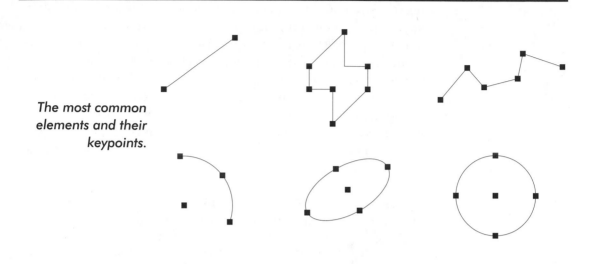

The most common elements and their keypoints.

The keypoints shown in the foregoing illustration are for the default snap divisor of 2. By setting your snap divisor to a higher value (for instance, KY=4 keyed in the Key-in window), you can snap to additional points between those shown.

Even with the additional snap functions added to recent MicroStation versions, Keypoint and Nearest are still used the most. In fact, with the majority of new drawings, the default snap mode is Keypoint.

NOTE: *To identify what snap mode you are currently in, just look at the status bar. In the field just to the right of the message field, you see an icon representing the active snap mode. You should get into the habit of checking this status field as you work.*

Exercise: Using Keypoint and Nearest Snaps to Build a Picture Frame

Are you ready to try out the most basic of snaps? Good! The object of this simple exercise is the creation of a picture frame consisting of two blocks, one inside the other. You will use the snap lock to build the beveled corners. Let's begin.

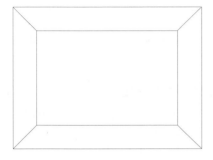

1. Open a new 2D design file. If you've installed the companion disk, open the PIXFRAME.DGN file.

2. Select the *Place Block* tool and draw a large rectangle in view window 1. Inside this box, place another block more or less equidistant from the edge of the first box. The result should look like a picture frame without the corners.

3. Next, we need to connect the corners of the two rectangles to make the miters. Activate the *Place Line* tool with no options turned on.

4. With the *Place Line* tool selected, verify that Tentative Point is set to Keypoint (hint: check the status bar's snap status field). If it is not set to Keypoint, click the snap status field to display the Snaps pop-up menu and select Keypoint with the Shift key pressed on your keyboard. This sets your default snap to Keypoint.

5. With Keypoint your active snap mode, now move your cursor over the upper left corner of your picture frame. Hit your tentative point button. A large cross cursor should snap to this corner and the element should then be highlighted. Accept this location with a datapoint.

6. Now, move your cursor over the upper left corner of the inner box and place a tentative point, followed by a datapoint. The result should be a line that goes from the inner box corner to the outer box corner.

7. Repeat this process for the other three corners.

NOTE: *Simply clicking a snap mode on the Snaps pop-up menu makes it active for only a single snap operation. To make it the default snap mode, you need to press the Shift key while selecting the snap mode.*

Setting Your Snaps Couldn't Be Easier

In the exercise just presented, you were instructed to go to the status bar and set the snap to Keypoint. While there, you should have seen a number of other snap options available for your use. In fact, if you had accidentally selected the wrong option, the results of the exercise may not have been what you expected. Let's explore these various snap options.

Finding and setting your snap is easy. MicroStation provides no fewer than four places at which you can set your active snap. They are:

❑ From the Settings pull-down menu (**Settings ➡ Snaps…**)

❑ Via the Snap Mode button bar (**Settings ➡ Snaps ➡ Button Bar**)

❑ Via the Locks settings box (**Settings ➡ Locks ➡ Full**)

❑ Via the Snaps pop-up menu invoked by either clicking the Snap Mode field on the status bar or by clicking the Tentative button with the Shift key pressed.

The Snaps Pull-down Submenu

Let's look at the Snaps submenu under the Settings menu.

The Snaps submenu is located under the Settings menu.

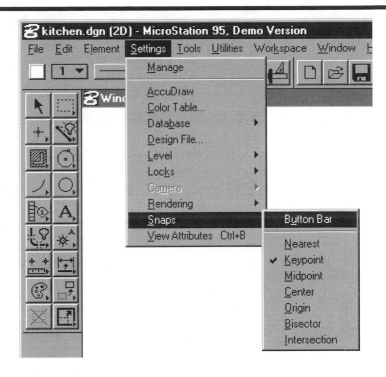

With the *Element Selection* tool selected (that's the arrow icon in the upper left corner of the Main tool palette), the list of snaps available under the Snaps submenu represents what could be considered the generic snaps.

NOTE: *These snap actions always operate on the element closest to the cursor.*

The Generic Snaps	
Snap Name	**Its Action**
Nearest	Jump to the nearest location
Keypoint	Jump to the nearest keypoint (endpoints, center points, and so on)
Midpoint	Jump to the midpoint of the nearest element segment
Center	Jump to the center point or centroid of the element
Origin	Jump to the origin point of a cell
Bisector	Jump to the midpoint of the entire element (not just the closest segment)
Intersection	Jump to the intersection point of two elements

✔ Keypoint

When you pull down the Snaps menu, one thing you should see is a check mark next to one of the snap options. This check mark identifies the active snap. When you select a different snap, this check mark will move to that snap option. Snap modes selected from this menu are active for only a single snap operation.

The Snap Mode Button Bar

Introduced in version 5, the Snap Mode button bar provides an on-screen tool palette, with all of the snaps available at your fingertips. This is most handy when you are constantly changing your snap mode. In addition, it helps stimulate the design process by reminding the user what options are available.

To activate the Snap Mode button bar, choose **Settings ➡ Snaps ➡ Button Bar**. The Snap Mode button bar will appear on your screen ready for you to choose the appropriate snap mode. Instead of names for each of the snap modes, you are presented with icons representing each snap.

The default shape of the Snap Mode button bar. Like any toolbox, you can change its shape by dragging its border.

You will notice that one of the snap mode buttons is depressed. This is the default snap mode. If you click another snap mode, you will see that the default button comes up but still remains shaded. This takes a little explaining.

Default Snap Versus Snap Override

To enhance productivity, MicroStation allows you to temporarily change your default snap to another snap option. Called "snap override," this snap option remains active only for the duration of the present operation.

For example, if you are placing a line with the Nearest snap as your default but decide that *for this one time* you want to use the Center option, you select Center and snap to the arc or circle's center. The dynamic line appears from this center location ready to be completed. With a datapoint you not only accept this new endpoint but cancel the Center snap option. This returns the snap to the Nearest option, your default snap.

In this example, if you looked at your Snap Mode button bar while Center was active, you would have seen the Center button depress and the Nearest button turn gray.

Here, the Nearest option is the default, whereas the Center option is an override for one tentative snap operation.

To actually change your default snap, you must double-click the desired snap button. The reason for this need to double-click has to do with predictability during the design process. Nothing is more frustrating than having a design operation not work the way you expect it to. If you continually changed the snap option, you could never predict what would happen the next time you hit the tentative point button. Instead, you would find yourself constantly checking the Snaps pull-down menu or reading the Command window. This can be very confusing and downright irritating (remember, you'll be doing this day-in and day-out). With the concept of setting your snap to a default selection and temporarily using a different snap, you always know how your tentative point is going to react.

In general, you will use Keypoint snap as your default. When working in a drawing, you find yourself constantly placing elements at the ends of others, thus Keypoint makes the most sense.

Let's recapitulate. To set your default snap you double-click the desired snap icon. The icon you so select will appear depressed. When you select a snap override by clicking once on an icon, the default snap is highlighted in gray.

Your First Visit to the Locks Settings Box

As mentioned earlier, there is more than one way to select a snap option. The Locks settings box provides yet another way to do this. However, it does more than give you access to snaps. It gives you additional control over the snap process.

To access the Locks settings box, choose **Settings** ➡ **Locks** ➡ **Full**. You will be presented with a rather large settings box containing much more than snap options (why do you think they call it the *Full* Locks settings box?).

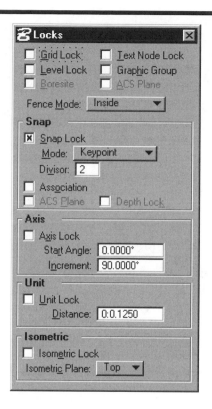

The Full Locks settings box provides access to a great many options. Note the Snap section and its options.

If you look at the Snap section of this menu, you will see a Mode selection field that lists all available snap modes. Unlike the Snaps pull-down submenu, one click will make your selection the default.

More important, though, are the other options found in the Snap section. This is where you can turn the *entire snap operation on or off.* This is done by selecting the Snap Lock checkbox.

Another important option located here is the Divisor field. When used in conjunction with the Keypoint snap, this value tells MicroStation how many additional keypoints to use along an element segment. For instance, if you set the Divisor value to 5 and tentative point along a line, you will have six equidistant tentative points along its length. The reason there are six and not five is that the divisor represents the number of element segments, not the number of tentative points to create. By default, the divisor is set to 2, allowing the Keypoint snap to emulate the Midpoint option (after all, when you divide an element in half you have found its midpoint).

TIP: *If you find yourself working with a lot of small line segments, be sure to set the divisor to 1. This avoids the hazard of accidentally snapping to something other than the vertex or endpoint you really wanted. In addition, the Keypoint snap will work faster in a congested area.*

TIP: *A shortcut for changing the divisor value is the use of the* KY= *key-in. Entered in the Key-in window, this key-in will set the value of the Divisor field without having to call up the Full Locks settings box.*

For now, the other options found under the Snap section will go undefined. These will come into play later, as you learn more about MicroStation's other features.

The Pop-up Snaps Menu

One last method for selecting your snaps is the pop-up menu. There are two ways to invoke it. Hold the Shift key and hit the tentative point button, and the Snaps pop-up menu will appear at your cursor location. Click the Snap Mode field in the status bar, and the Snaps pop-up menu will appear next to it, just above the status bar.

The Snaps pop-up menu is activated at the cursor location by clicking the tentative button in conjunction with the Shift key.

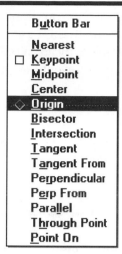

Notice the diamond and the square shapes next to a couple of options on the pop-up snap menu? The square shape designates the default snap, and the diamond designates the snap override. If you select an option with the Shift key pressed, that option becomes the default. Otherwise, it activates for only a single operation.

Precision Input

Or How to Get Those Elements Where You Want Them

Precision input is one of the cornerstones of CAD, and any CAD package worth its salt will have a rich selection of tools for accurately controlling the placement of elements within the drawing. Fortunately, MicroStation is no exception and incorpo-rates a wide variety of controls, tools, and other aids for element placement.

The Precision Key-in

In the sample design session, in which you drew a kitchen plan, you placed the first corner of the kitchen wall with the text

XY=0,0. You didn't know it at the time, but you used a *precision key-in*. In this case, XY= tells MicroStation you want to specify the absolute location of the element on the design plane. The general format for entering key-ins is

XY= Xvalue,Yvalue,Zvalue

where XY= is one of four key-in shortcut prefixes, and X,Y and Z value are the X, Y, and Z coordinate values or distance and angle values (DI= only).

Precision Key-ins and Their Function		
Key-in Name	**Shortcut Prefix**	**Description**
Point Absolute	XY=	Absolute XY location
Point Delta	DL=	Delta distance
Point VDelta	DX=	Delta distance (same as DL=F255 in 2D)
Point Distance	DI=	Distance and angular direction

It should be noted that while you can key in the key-in name as presented, the shortcut key-ins are much quicker to enter (and as we all know, CAD users are infamously bad typists).

The Point Absolute or XY= Precision Key-in

This key-in is used to pass absolute coordinate information to the active tool. The coordinates specify an exact location on the MicroStation design plane. These coordinates are always with respect to the XYZ origin point. For instance, entering XY=0,0 while placing a line will set the line's endpoint at the X and Y axis origin point (commonly referred to as "X0Y0"). Keying in a negative value will place the endpoint somewhere to the lower left of this origin. MicroStation uses Cartesian coordinates as its default coordinate system.

Most MicroStation designs work with an X/Y axis set to the middle of the design plane. This results in an equal number of positive and negative X and Y values. There are commands available to change this configuration.

The Point Delta or DL= Precision Key-in

The next key-in mentioned is Point Delta (DL=). This is often referred to as the *delta distance* key-in. It allows you to specify an X and Y distance from the last datapoint, which, in turn, allows you to draw a line "three units over and four units up from my last datapoint" (DL=3,4). This delta distance is always calculated in reference to the design plane's axes. In most design situations, you will find yourself using the DL= or DX= key-in at least twice as often as the other precision input key-ins.

The Point VDelta or DX= Precision Key-in

Similar to the DL= key-in just described, the VDelta key-in also allows you to specify distances as a change from the present location. In this case, however, the axes from which the distances are derived are always normal to the view. In 2D this does not present a problem, as the view axes and the design plane axes are the same. However, when you begin to work in 3D, the differences between DL= and DX= become clear.

Delta Distances and the Tentative Point

Although precision key-ins provide a method to place any element with exactitude, one of their most powerful capabilities is their association with the tentative point. Earlier it was explained how a tentative point must be accepted with a datapoint. If you enter a precision key-in instead, the tentative point will be used as the point of reference for any delta or change in position.

This means that if you tentative point at the end of a line, and then enter DX=2,3, the result will be a new line extending two units over and three units above the tentative point's previous location.

This illustration shows how the tentative point and key-in DX=2,3 changes the outcome of the element placement operation.

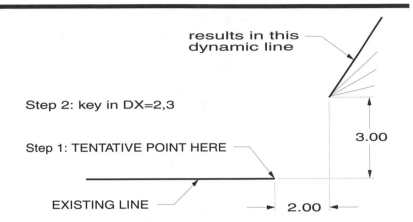

results in this dynamic line

Step 2: key in DX=2,3

Step 1: TENTATIVE POINT HERE

3.00

EXISTING LINE

2.00

The Point Distance, or DI=, Precision Key-in

The Point Distance, or DI=, provides a slightly different function. Instead of using a Cartesian type of geometry, the DI= key-in provides a radial distance and angular direction. Sometimes referred to as "distance and direction," this key-in uses the counterclockwise angular information system similar to the *Place Arc* tool. You enter the key-in prefix, a distance you want to extend out from the last datapoint (or tentative point), and the angle at which to strike out.

Combining the function of the drafting compass and protractor, the DI= key-in provides the easiest method for specifying radial distances.

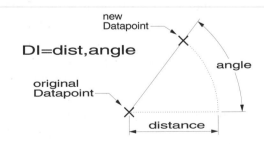

new Datapoint

DI=dist,angle

angle

original Datapoint

distance

Let's try a simple example to illustrate the use of the Point Distance key-in. Starting with a new 2D design file, select the *Place Line* tool. Datapoint once in the lower left corner of view window 1. Be careful not to datapoint a second time. Releasing the mouse or puck, type the following in the Key-in window:

```
DI=1,0↵
DI=1,60↵
DI=1,120↵
DI=1,180↵
DI=1,240↵
DI=1,300↵
```

The result should be a hexagonal shape (see the following diagram). If it didn't fit in the view, or is a tiny dot, don't worry. Just click the Fit View icon on the lower left border of the view.

An example of an object created with precision key-ins.

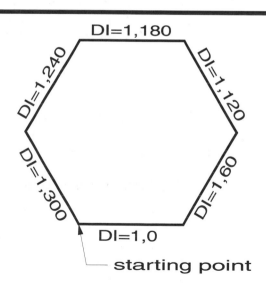

In this brief example you used the DI= key-in to specify the length of each line and its angle of placement. Incrementing this angle repeatedly by 60 degrees results in a hexagon. With each successive key-in, the hexagon was constructed in a counterclock-wise direction.

The final segment's endpoint falls right on top of the first datapoint's location. This simple example points out a critical cornerstone of CAD: the reliable, precise, and consistent place-ment of elements. When you begin using MicroStation for real design problems, you will rely on the computer's ability to maintain this accuracy.

NOTE: The Origin of Key-ins *By now you may be wondering why key-ins feel so foreign. You shouldn't have to type in so much stuff to make MicroStation respond, should you?*

The key-in traces its origins back to Intergraph's early days when MicroStation's predecessor IGDS ran on the DEC PDP11 mini-computer. To simplify IGDS's job of interpreting the CAD user's intentions, Intergraph used the concept of registers to store and pass key information back and forth to the computer. This particular user interface was simple and efficient, although by today's standards a bit archaic. However, it had the advantage of being an extremely fast way to pass very specific information to the computer.

Intergraph has been careful to select a mnemonic pair of letters to represent the key-in's function. This was very nice of them, considering there are over a hundred such key-ins!

Introducing the *ccDra   * Tool

Although you can key in these commands directly, MicroStation does give you another method of entering this important coordi-nate data. On the Primary toolbox you will find the *AccuDraw* tool. Clicking the icon depicting a T-square and triangle activates this new tool designed to both speed up and simplify placement of precision points.

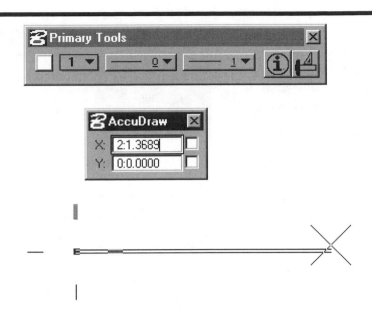

MicroStation's new AccuDraw tool lets you achieve precision with the simplicity of freehand sketching. Note how a line automatically aligns itself to the horizontal or vertical axis with the Place Line tool when AccuDraw is active.

Although the AccuDraw window looks very small and simple, it packs an enormous amount of functionality. As soon as you click the first datapoint for an element placement command, such as Place Line, a rectangular compass attaches there, ready to help simplify your precision key-ins. As your cursor moves along an axis within *AccuDraw's* tolerance specification, a dynamic preview of the axis alignment displays and a datapoint places the element perfectly aligned to the axis without having to separately invoke the axis lock command.

The AccuDraw compass understands both rectangular and polar coordinates. You switch between these modes by pressing the space bar. Additionally, *AccuDraw* understands a host of single- and double-letter key-ins to simplify snapping and controlling its operations. For instance, if you press the letter P while the focus is on the AccuDraw window, the Datapoint Key-in window pops up to let you supply precision key-ins without the need to type in the two-letter shortcut prefix, such as XY=.

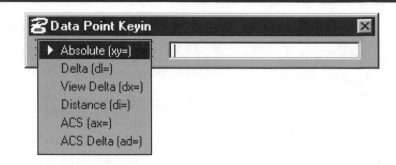

AccuDraw is a powerful tool, with the capability to speed up drawing production. A description of its functional details will have to wait until a later chapter, after you have become familiar with MicroStation's basic operations. In fact, we will discuss *AccuDraw* in its own chapter.

If this brief introduction to *AccuDraw* has piqued your interest, feel free to press the "?" key in the AccuDraw window to display a list of its shortcuts. Of course, if you wish, you may also digress and read the *AccuDraw* chapter at this point and return here later.

Using Grids

Analogous to grid paper, another design aid available in Micro-Station is the *grid lock*. The grid function allows you to control how MicroStation treats your datapoints when entering, modify-ing, or otherwise manipulating elements on the design plane.

If you've spent any time exploring the sample drawings Bentley supplies with MicroStation, you have probably seen this grid system. In its simplest form the grid is nothing more than a regular spacing of dots that can be turned on or off in any active view.

As a visual aid, these "dots" are very helpful in sizing up a design project. But if all the grid system did was display a "pretty picture" of dots, its usefulness would be limited. In fact, it has the ability to force all datapoints to the nearest grid point.

Any application that requires drawing straight lines at regular intervals can benefit from using grid lock. You can place lines more accurately using the grid system than by trying to "eyeball" the linework.

The small dots represent the grid units. The larger tics are the grid reference markers.

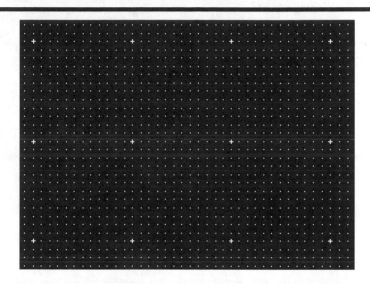

The Grid Controls

Just as you can buy many different types of grid paper, you can adjust MicroStation's grid to suit your needs. The size and type of grid is controlled under the Grid category of the Design File Settings dialog box accessed via the Settings pull-down menu. Here you set the size of your grid (Grid Master option) and the number of grid dots between grid reference points (Grid Reference option).

The Grid category of the Design File Settings dialog box controls the grid settings.

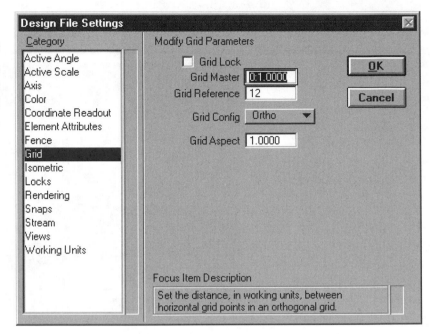

Alternately, you can set these two major values of the grid system via key-ins: the Grid Unit and the Grid Reference. The Active Grid Unit (GU=) key-in sets the distance between each individual grid "dot." The second key-in, the Active Gridref (GR=), sets the number of grid units or dots between each grid reference "tic."

This is sometimes confusing for the first-time MicroStation user. In the previous illustration, if you count the number of dots between each tic, you would find twelve. In this case, the grid unit has been set to :1 (GU=:1) and the reference grid has been set to :12 (GR=:12).

The result, in this case, is one dot per inch, with a reference tic every 12 inches. If you were to set the grid unit to 0.5 master units (same as 6 inches), the result would be an enlargement of the grid six times. However, the reference grid would still be set to 12. Thus, the distance between each GR tic would be :6 times 12.

To use the grid for precision placement, you must first use the Grid Lock command. Usually selected from the Locks dialog box (available via the Settings pull-down menu), you can also key in LOCK GRID ON in the Key-in window. MicroStation lets you know the condition of the grid lock with a "Locks=..." message in the status bar. To unlock the grid, key in LOCK GRID OFF. LOCK GRID TOGGLE reverses the current grid lock condition from on to off and off to on.

You cannot tell if Grid Lock is on by observing what's on a view because grid display is totally separate from grid lock. You can display (or not display) the grid in any active view with the Set Grid command. You can also set the grid display via the View Attributes settings box (**Settings ➡ View Attributes**).

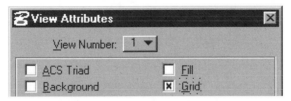

In addition, as you zoom out, Micro-Station will turn off the dots when the density of the grid is such that it obscures the design. This will also occur with the grid reference tics, but at a greater distance out.

Exercise: Understanding Grids

In this exercise you are going to use the grid feature of MicroStation to accurately place some lines.

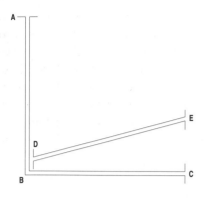

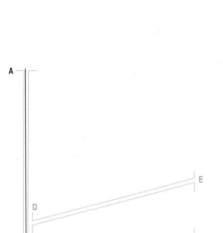

1. If you've installed the companion disk, open the GRID.DGN file. View window 1 should contain the image shown here.

2. Activate the *Place Line* tool. Next, as accurately as you can, place a line between the vertical parallel lines from point A to point B. Try to place it perfectly straight and evenly between these two lines. How did you do? With the grid turned off, you probably didn't do very well. Trying to place a line by eye is not easy. Observe the Locks status message, or click the Lock icon in the status bar, and notice that Grid Lock is off.

Let's start over with your linework. Use the Undo command to remove the line you previously placed (**Edit ➡ Undo Place Line**).

3. Let's review the Grid value. Open the Locks pop-up menu by clicking the Lock icon on the status bar. To activate Grid Lock, select the Grid checkbox.

4. Place the same line between points A and B. This time the line should fall nicely between these points. Next, click the datapoint button at point C. All of your lines should be parallel to the existing ones.

5. Let's display the actual grid points on the screen. Activate the View Attributes settings box (**Settings ➡ View Attributes**). Select the Grid checkbox and hit the All button. What happened?

The large tic marks you see are your reference grid. To see the actual grid points, you need to zoom in a little closer. Click the Zoom In icon on the View Control bar located along the lower left border of your view window and place a datapoint to enclose point B. You should now see dots all over your view. Note how the line you placed is on one of these dots.

6. Now fit the drawing in your view by selecting the Fit View icon on the View Control bar. You should see your entire drawing again. Hit the Reset button once.

 NOTE: *The view manipulation commands are covered in the next chapter.*

7. Next, try placing a line parallel and evenly spaced between points D and E.

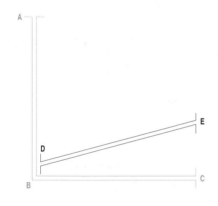

8. What happened? Most likely, no matter how hard you tried, the line just wouldn't stay between the two lines. The reason is simple. MicroStation's grid system is orthogonal in nature, and the two lines you are trying to split with your new line are obviously angular (15 degrees, to be precise). This is an example in which a key-in after the first datapoint is appropriate:

```
DI=7,9,15↵
```

Key this in only after you have datapointed at point D.

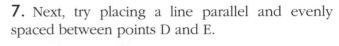

This exercise showed you the basics of turning on your grid lock and displaying your grid. In addition, it showed in an example where not to rely on the grid for element placement.

Exercise: A Simple Drawing Session

Now that you have seen how to place primitive elements, let's draw a common object, an old-style key.

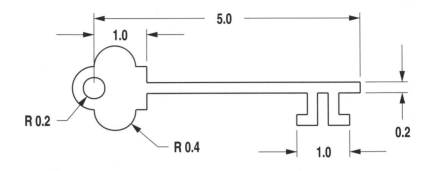

To begin, we need to create the key's handle, consisting of three arcs, a circle, and some lines.

1. Open the KEY.DGN design file. To establish a beginning point, let's put in the hole for the key chain using the *Place Circle* tool. The circle has a 0.2-inch radius, so select the Radius option and key in 0.2.

2. Next, place the circle using an absolute key-in:

XY=0,0

3. This establishes the starting point for your drawing. Now, let's place the three arcs. If you look at the drawing you will see that all three arcs have the same radius: 0.4 inches. Activate the *Place Arc* tool and select the Radius option and key in `0.4`.

Keeping in mind the counterclockwise rule, place the three arcs. It is probably easiest to place the arc around the circle first, as this establishes the endpoints of the two other arcs.

4. Next, draw the shoulder of the key handle with the *Place Line* tool. Turn on the grid display (**Setting ➡ View Attributes ➡ Grid checkbox**) and the Grid Lock (**Settings ➡ Locks ➡ Grid**) and place datapoints for the line endpoints. Don't forget to hit Reset between each pair of lines.

5. To finish off the key, activate the *Place Smart-Line* tool (on the Linear Elements toolbox) and place a datapoint at the top shoulder of the key handle. Next, key in the following:

```
DL=4,0↵
```

This establishes the top edge of the key shaft. Now, using the grid lock, finish off the shape of the key. The thickness of the key shaft and blades is two grid dots. What is that in inches? (Hint: Open the Design File Settings dialog box and select the Grid category.) Don't forget to hit Reset after your last datapoint to accept the SmartLine.

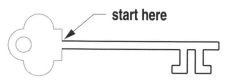

start here

Done!

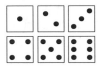

That completes this exercise and this chapter. As a further exercise you may want to try creating the following picture of die faces, consisting of 6 squares and 21 circles. Try your hand at tools such as *Place Block* and *Place Circle* with the *Center* snap tool (and others). The design file DICE.DGN has been provided as a starting point for this exercise. Good luck!

You have been introduced to some of the basic element types used in MicroStation. In addition, you have learned how to place these elements with a certain degree of reliability. By now you may have some idea of the power of MicroStation's tools and how they interact with one another.

In the next chapter we explore this interrelationship and how you can use MicroStation's various tools to construct your designs. In addition, you will learn how to navigate within your design and how to make all of those elements take on characteristics beyond their appearance as plain white lines.

2D Basics:
Part 2

Mastering Screen Control and Element Manipulation

In the previous chapter you were introduced to the primitive elements that constitute the bulk of all CAD drawings. A key feature of any CAD package is its ability to modify objects once they've been placed in a drawing. In this chapter we'll learn how to manipulate elements in a number of ways with MicroStation.

But first, let's learn how to navigate within MicroStation's design file environment.

Screen Control at Your Fingertips

Most of us don't have the luxury of working where we live. Most times we drive, walk, or even fly to work. At the end of the day, we return home, where we have additional duties to perform (taking out the trash, painting the house, cooking…). Of course, we can't perform these "domestic" duties while at work, and vice versa. Working within a design file is very similar.

When working within MicroStation, we perform the various design functions in specific parts of the drawing. We may need to fill out a title block, then go on to modify a preliminary plan layout or create a blown-up detail of a complex part. Unless working on a very small drawing, these functions are performed at locations in your drawing that are at a considerable distance from one another.

Fortunately, MicroStation provides a set of tools and capabilities for navigating—or commuting, as it were—within or about a design file. Collectively, we call these *view control* functions.

Overview of MicroStation's Video Frontier

In previous chapters you were directed to create drawings using many of MicroStation's tools. One common thread of these exercises was *where* you created these drawings. In all cases, you worked within a view window labeled *Window 1*. Now, here's a pop quiz question: Why do you think this view window is labeled Window 1? Because, MicroStation supports more than one view window! In fact, MicroStation supports a total of *eight* independent view windows.

An example of MicroStation's views in use. Note how each view is labeled with its corresponding window number. Also note how all the views are from the same design file (identified by name in the title bar).

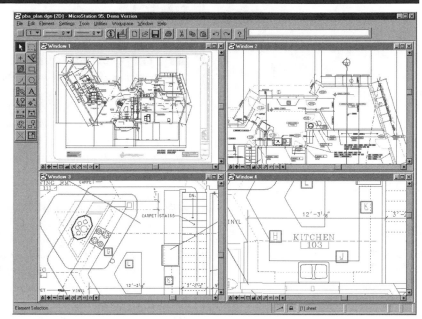

Views: Windows on Your Design

One of the cornerstones of MicroStation has been its excellent view control commands. MicroStation gives you complete visual control over its eight views. Video is one of the major strengths of MicroStation. In fact, as mentioned in Chapter 1, support for dual graphics screens and the display of multiple views have been IGDS/MicroStation hallmarks since the PDP11/VAX days. Giving you the ability to "zoom in" for detailed work while maintaining an overview of the design goes a long way toward eliminating the dreaded CAD "tunnel vision" syndrome.

TIMEOUT:
An Experiment in Tunnel Vision

Step 1: Procuring Supplies

Let's perform a little experiment. Go find a discarded cardboard tube, the type found in the middle of paper towel rolls or (heaven forbid!) toilet paper. Found it? Good. Now find a quiet place where your fellow workers won't see you performing the next part of this experiment (don't worry, no pain is involved—unless you run into a wall).

Step 2: The Experiment

Are you alone? Good. Now, look around the room. Find a picture or other object on a wall that you can identify. Turn your back to the wall containing the picture or object and move to the right, left, or forward (or any combination). Now, place the cardboard tube over one of your eyes, closing the other (assuming you only have two eyes). Now, without prior calculation, turn around and peer through the cardboard tube, trying to locate the upper right corner of the picture frame. Not so easy, is it? This is an example of tunnel vision, the restriction of your visual frame of reference (no pun intended).

When working at a drafting table, you constantly use your eyes' peripheral vision. By remaining aware of your entire drawing, you never have to think about your frame of reference.

In CAD this is not the case. On most systems, when you zoom in to work on a specific area of the design, the rest of the design lies outside your vision, like what you were unable to see through the cardboard tube (you did perform the experiment, didn't you?). The only way to keep track of where you are within the design is by keeping a mental picture of the entire drawing.

Sometimes, probably more often than we want to admit, we get lost inside our design. The only way to get reoriented is to back out. This reorientation can be a real time waster.

Developers of MicroStation recognized this problem and devised the multiple-view concept to overcome it. By allowing several active views within the design file at the same time,

MicroStation provides a way to get up close and personal while maintaining that crucial overview. Up to eight of these views can be activated. Although all of these views can be accommodated on one monitor, in most instances you use four views at a time. If you have dual monitors, you can display all of these views (four on each monitor). This isn't written in stone, but this is usually the case.

A Ship at Sea

Still not clear on views? A good analogy of these views are the views one has from the portholes on a cruise ship. When far from a viewed object, the portholes on the same side of a ship show the same scene: the ocean, or an island, for instance. As the ship approaches land, these portholes would still show the same view, such as the dock and harbor features. At this point you could call someone in another cabin and point out an object that they would be able to see through their own porthole.

When far out at sea, the view out any given porthole is essentially the same.

But once the ship is docked, this changes. Whereas you might have a view of a cleat, for instance, out your porthole, your neighbor may see nothing more than a dock piling (your neighbor must be in the cheap cabins). There is no doubt you are both looking at the same dock, just different parts of it. This is an example of tunnel vision. In fact, if by chance both cabins were adjacent to similar pilings, you would have a difficult time telling them apart.

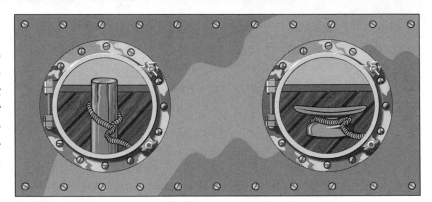

Although you are looking at the same scene, the dock looks very different from each porthole view when you are up close.

This is how the views of MicroStation work, except for one important difference. Unlike the portholes that must maintain the same "zoom factor" because they are bolted securely to the ship, MicroStation's views can simultaneously see the long-distance view of your drawing and the close-up details.

To control what you see through these "porthole" views, MicroStation offers an entire collection of commands. An example of these view control commands are the ones that set the scale of what you see in each view: *Zoom In* and *Zoom Out*. The scale factor applied to the zooming process can be user-selected, although most designers use the default value of 2 (i.e., zoom out 2x, zoom in 1/2).

MicroStation's most common view control commands reside on the horizontal scroll bar of each view window. This group of nine icons is called the View Control bar. Additionally, these commands along with the Copy View command can be found in the View Control toolbox (**Tools ➡ View Control**). Some of the other view control functions are found under the Window option on the menu bar. And then there are some you can access by keying in at the Key-in window, or by using a special mouse operation.

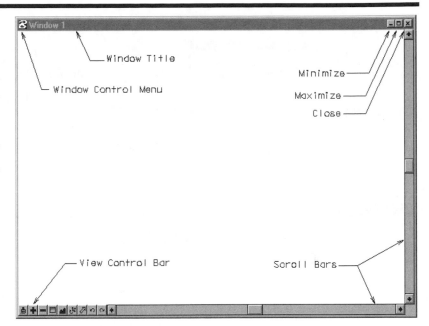

MicroStation's view control commands are located on the View Control bar, the View Control toolbox, and the Window menu.

Before getting into the details of these commands, let's try a couple out. The following exercise shows how to perform some basic view manipulations.

Exercise: Using a View Manipulation Command

1. Open the PORTHOLE.DGN design file. You are presented with what is apparently an empty drawing. But wait, if you look closely you will see two tiny dots in the center of window 1. These two dots are the main elements of this drawing. Let's get in closer to these elements using the Fit View command. Select it either from the View Control bar on the horizontal scroll bar of the view window or from the View Control toolbox (see the adjacent illustration). If you selected it from the View Control bar, the extents of the drawing immediately fit in the view window. If you selected it from the View Control toolbox, and you have more than one view window open, you are prompted to "Select view to fit"; in which case you will need to click a datapoint anywhere in window 1.

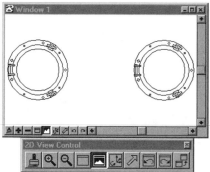

2. Now you see the two portholes in the drawing. Let's zoom in on one of them. To do this, select the Window Area command and click the first datapoint to the left and below the latch on the right porthole as an answer to MicroStation's prompt "Define first corner point." Next, click the second datapoint to the right and above the latch.

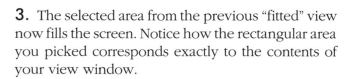

3. The selected area from the previous "fitted" view now fills the screen. Notice how the rectangular area you picked corresponds exactly to the contents of your view window.

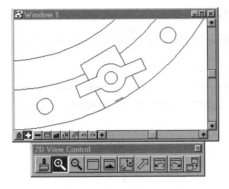

4. Note the small "imperfection" just below the latch. Let's investigate it. Zoom in closer to the imperfection, again using the Window Area command.

   Alternately, you could have used the Zoom In command with an appropriate zoom factor specified in the Tool Settings window (remember, the default is 2X).

5. Still not clear what's there? Try again. Zoom in closer on the imperfection.

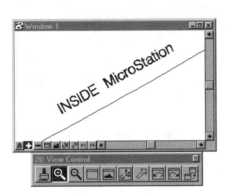

6. There! It's nothing more than the title of this book. Isn't it amazing how much detail you can cram into a drawing?

When You Can Use View Commands

Here's one very important feature about view manipulation commands:

NOTE: *View commands can be used while performing any operation with MicroStation without interrupting the current command's operation. For instance, if you are placing a line and find you need to change a view's perspective to finish the line you can change the view without canceling the line command.*

Anatomy of a View Window

Before proceeding with the individual view commands, let's look at the view windows themselves.

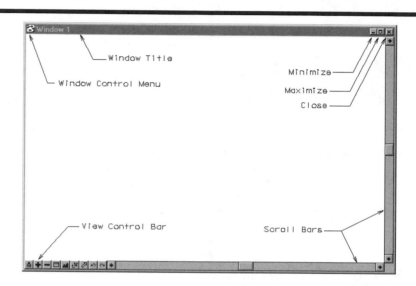

This diagram points out the major features of a view window.

The Border

Surrounding each view window is a rectangular border that limits the size of the view. This border may be used to resize the view by dragging (holding the mouse button down while moving the mouse) the border you wish to move. In addition, the border corners allow you to vary both the horizontal and vertical dimension of the view with one drag operation.

The Title Bar

Located at the top of the view, the primary use of the title bar is to move the entire view. This works the same as with other windows and palettes. To move the entire view, you click and drag the title bar, and the view follows. If a view is obscured by other view windows, clicking on one view's title bar or any part of the view's border brings that view window to the top.

The Minimize and Maximize Buttons

In the upper right corner of each view are two (three under Windows 95 and Windows NT version 4) important view control buttons. Selecting the Minimize button causes the view to shrink to its minimum size. Selecting the Minimize button, called the Restore button when the view is minimized, a second time will restore the view to its previous size and on-screen location.

The Maximize button is located to the right of the Minimize/Restore button. Clicking it expands the view to fill the screen. When the view is maximized, the Maximize button also becomes the Restore button, so that clicking it again restores the view to its previous size and on-screen location.

Under the Windows 95 graphical user interface, also implemented by Windows NT 4.0, and used for screen shots throughout this book, there is yet another icon with an "x", called the Close button, to the right of the Maximize/Restore icon. Clicking the Close button closes the view window. If you accidentally close a view window and wish to reopen it, you will need to use the Open/Close submenu under the Window option on the MicroStation menu bar.

The result of a maximize view operation when the Main toolbox is left floating on the screen…

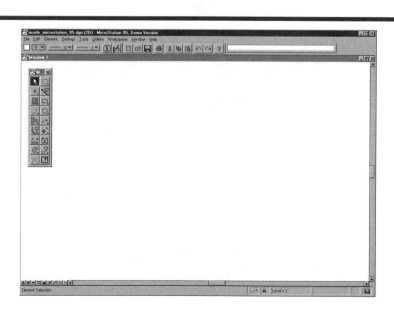

...and the result when the Main toolbox is docked along the left edge.

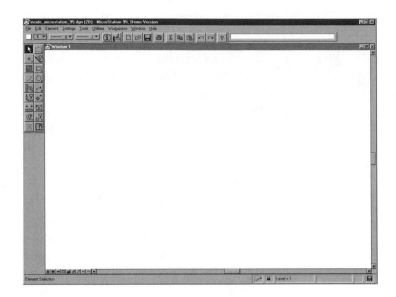

The Window Control Menu

Located in the upper left corner of each view is the Window Control menu. Common to all windows in MicroStation, the commands found here are used to manipulate the entire window.

❑ *Restore:* Restores the view window to its former state after a maximize/minimize operation.

❑ *Move:* Lets you move the view window using the keyboard arrow keys.

❑ *Size:* Lets you size the view window using the keyboard arrow keys.

❑ *Minimize:* Minimizes the view window to its minimum size. This is the same operation as invoked with the Minimize button.

❑ *Maximize:* Maximizes the view window to its largest size. This is the same operation as invoked with the Maximize button.

❑ *Close:* Closes the view window. This is the same operation as invoked by double-clicking the Window Control menu icon, or clicking the Close button on the title bar.

❑ *View Attributes:* Another way of opening the View Attributes settings box. You might remember, it is also found under the Settings menu.

❑ *Level Display:* Opens the View Levels settings box. This settings box can also be invoked using the **Settings ➡ Level ➡ Display menu** sequence.

❑ *View Save/Recall:* Opens the Saved Views settings box. This settings box can be invoked using the **Utilities ➡ Saved Views menu** sequence.

Controlling a View's "Point of View"

There are many view manipulation commands to choose from. The following is a short list, with descriptions.

Window Open/Close	Opens and/or closes a view window.
Update View	Redraws the contents of a view window.
Zoom In/Out	Changes the magnification of a view window.
Window Area	Explicitly defines the viewing area in a view window.
Fit View All/Active/ Reference/Raster	Redefines a view window's magnification by the extents of the design plane and/or reference files.
Rotate View	Redefines a view window's orientation by rotating it based on two specified points.

Pan View	Moves a view window's point of view by a distance and direction specified by two points.
View Previous	Displays the content of a view window as it existed before you changed it with a view control operation.
View Next	The reverse of the View Previous command.
Copy View	Copies a view window's contents and attributes to another view.

Window Open/Close

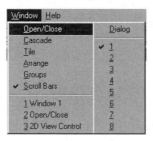

The Window Open/Close command is accessed from the Window pull-down menu. You open or close a view window by selecting the number corresponding to it in the Open/Close submenu.

Alternately, you can activate the Open/Close box, which lets you activate or close multiple view windows without resorting to the pull-down menu.

Activated by selecting the Window Open/Close Dialog command, the Open/Close box provides a convenient method for manipulating your views.

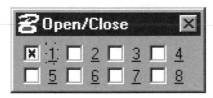

In addition to menus and dialog boxes, you can key in the View On or View Off commands in the Key-in window. The View On command requires the view number (example: View On 3

turns on view 3), whereas the View Off command prompts you to place a datapoint in the view. View Off can also be entered with a view window number. The effect is the immediate closing of the view window without further input from the user. You can also key in VIEW ON/OFF ALL to turn all of your view windows either on or off at one time.

MicroStation provides a default layout for your view windows through the use of the **Window Cascade ➡ Window ➡ Cascade and Window Tile ➡ Window ➡ Tile** commands.

The Window Cascade command stacks all open View Windows like this...

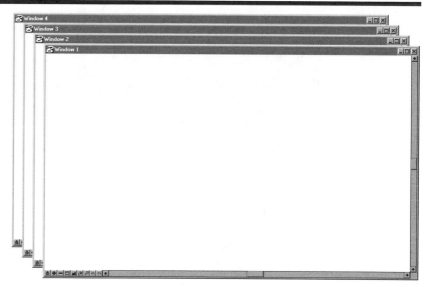

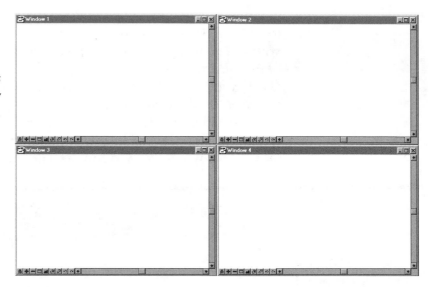

...and Tile positions the open view windows like this.

Note the order of these views. Cascade always positions the lowest view window number first, in sequential order. Tile starts with window 1 in the upper left, window 2 upper right, window 3 lower left, and window 4 lower right. If you have fewer than four view windows active, the positioning will vary.

Update View

During the course of a design session, the various views you have turned on can start to look bad, with tiny line fragments not completely erased during a delete command, or grid dots that were jumbled by moving a line. This is especially true after performing a dynamic pan and an element manipulation command. To clean up the appearance of a view, the Update command is supplied. Selecting it from the View Control bar along the bottom edge of a view window refreshes the contents of that window. When Update is selected from the View Control toolbox you are prompted to select the view window to update. In either case, an Update All Views button appears in the Tool Settings window, which when pressed redraws the contents of all open view windows.

Update Key-ins

In addition to the Update View command previously discussed, MicroStation supports several variations of the command via key-ins. When you key in UPDATE GRID, the grid dots on the selected view window update. When you key in UPDATE LEFT, the view window on the left screen updates. When you key in UPDATE RIGHT, the view window on the right screen updates.

And if you are working on a very congested drawing and wish to update only a partial area bounded by a fence, you have the UPDATE FENCE key-in. Of course, a fence must already be placed in your drawing for this command to work. Additionally, if you wish to update the contents of a view window that are outside a fence, you have the UPDATE FENCE OUTSIDE key-in.

Zoom In and Zoom Out

 Back to the view control commands. Zoom In and Zoom Out affect the magnification scale of the view window. Once invoked, MicroStation prompts you to identify a point about which to zoom. The datapoint you place becomes the center of the new, zoomed view. The default zoom ratio in the Tool Settings window is 2; however, you can change it to whatever value you choose.

If you choose to key in a Zoom command, you can still enter a zoom ratio. Keying in ZOOM OUT 3↵ tells MicroStation to view 3 times more area in the design file.

Conversely, if you ZOOM IN 3, the view would be enlarged by a factor of 3. Keying in the Zoom command without a parameter selects the default ratio of 2.

Once you have selected the Zoom command, it stays active until you hit Reset. This means you can perform multiple zooms in various open view windows. And, of course, once you are done with the view command, hitting Reset returns you to the active construction command.

Window Area

Used to define a view window's exact contents, the Window Area command allows you to identify an area of your design for display in a selected view window. Select two points describing a rectangular area around your area of interest, and the view zooms as necessary. If you wish to display the rectangular area in a view window other than the one it is picked in, choose that view window in the Apply to Window field in the Tool Settings window prior to selecting the area.

MicroStation's ability to let you select a separate target view different from the source means that if you have view windows 1 and 2 active you can define the area you wish to view in view window 1 and have the outcome placed in view window 2. This feature can be very convenient. It lets you display the entire drawing in one view window, on perhaps a secondary screen, while conveniently displaying "window areas" for detail work in another view window, thus minimizing the need for constant zoom and pan operations.

An example of displaying a Window Area from window 1 to window 2.

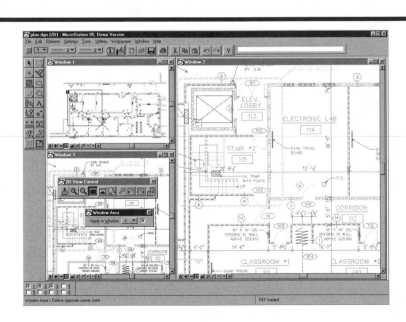

Fit View

 Sometimes after you have zoomed, windowed, and gotten in close to your work, you need to view the overall perspective of your design. To do this requires either a number of Zoom Outs or the Fit View command. When selected from the View Control bar on the horizontal scroll bar of a view window, the contents of your design file, along with its reference files, zoom to fit your view. When selected from the View Control toolbox, MicroStation prompts you to select the view to fit. When you key in FIT, MicroStation prompts you to select the view to fit, but only fits the active design file contents, not the reference files.

When the command is invoked from an icon, the four options on the Tool Settings window are All, Active, Reference, and Raster. These fit the design file, along with reference files, in various combinations.

Rotate View

 The Rotate View command allows you to rotate the contents of a view window for display purposes. The actual elements in your design file are not rotated or moved in any way; only the display axes of the selected view window are rotated. Why would one want to do this? Consider the layout of a highway that runs in a northeasterly direction. Rather than drawing it along a diagonal direction on a standard rectangular border sheet, it is conventional to draw it running left to right parallel to the border sheet edge. Now, for the sake of maintaining its precise north and east coordinates, you do not want to rotate the lines and arcs that constitute the highway; you only want to rotate the view to plot the highway along an orthogonal direction.

When you invoke the command, you are asked to define the first point, followed by another point to identify the X axis of the view. And if you wish to negate the view rotation operation, you can select the Unrotated option on the Tool Settings window.

Pan View

 The Pan View command allows you to relocate the view's point of view within the design file. MicroStation simply moves the view along the vector (length and direction) specified by the two datapoints it requires. A dynamic arrow attaches to your cursor as you click the first datapoint. This arrow indicates the location and direction the initially clicked datapoint will move to.

 NOTE: *Do not forget the scroll bars on each window as a view navigational tool. Clicking an arrowhead on the scroll bar scrolls the view in that direction by a distance that is one-tenth of the view. To pan a screenful at a time, click the scroll bar between the slider box and the arrowhead in the direction desired.*

 NOTE: *Another view navigational command that helps you maneuver through the design is the Move command. This command is only available as key-in and should not be confused with the Move Element command. By keying in* MOVE UP, MOVE DOWN, MOVE LEFT, *or* MOVE RIGHT, *the view you select with a datapoint slides in the direction indicated by a quarter of the screen width.*

Dynamic Panning

Pressing the Shift key down while dragging your mouse (hold down the mouse button) activates MicroStation's *dynamic panning* function. As you move your mouse farther from the initial point you started the drag operation, MicroStation responds by increasing the panning speed. As the image moves across the screen, MicroStation updates the portion of the screen in the direction of your pan. This results in a continuous update process along the edge of your view.

NOTE: *An excellent tool for fine-tuning your view's location, dynamic panning may be a little slow if you are moving from one end of your drawing to the other. In such cases, you might want to use the Window Area command in conjunction with a view in which your entire design is displayed.*

Exercise: Moving About in the Drawing

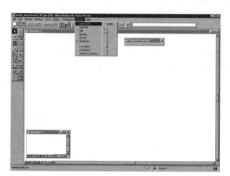

1. Start MicroStation and create a new drawing, giving it any name you like. Pull down the Window menu and in the Open/Close submenu ensure that view windows 1 and 2 are open. Drag the corners of view window 2 such that your screen looks similar to the figure shown at left.

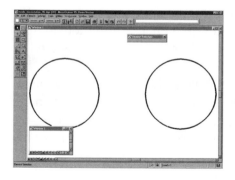

2. Using the *Place Circle* tool, draw two circles side by side in view window 1. The exact dimension of the circles is not important for this exercise; just make sure they fill the view as shown in the figure at left.

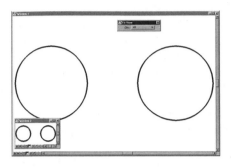

3. Click the Fit View icon on the border of window 2. This will fit the contents of your design file in that view window. Now hit the Reset button to cancel the command. Now the two circles should be displayed in both your view windows.

4. Now, click the right arrowhead two to three times on the horizontal scroll bar of window 1. This will move the contents of the view to the left. It is like moving to the right, so the contents of the view move to the left. As noted earlier, each click pans the view by a distance equal to one-tenth the view dimension.

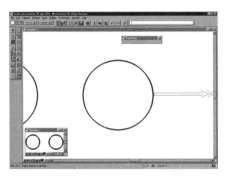

5. Now, click the Pan View icon on the border of window 1. MicroStation prompts you to select the view. Click a datapoint on the circumference of the rightmost circle. Then move the cursor to the right edge of the view and click another datapoint. Both circles should now appear in your view again.

6. Finally, practice the dynamic pan movement by holding the Shift key as you press the left mouse button and drag the mouse in the direction you wish to pan. Once the view starts to move, you can lift your finger from the Shift key. Panning will continue until you release the mouse button. You can change the speed and direction of the dynamic pan by simply dragging the cursor farther from the point initially selected in the direction desired.

View Previous/Next

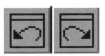

Similar to the Undo and Redo commands for drawing and editing operations found under the Edit menu, this set of commands lets you undo and redo view operations. View Previous negates a view operation. View Next negates a previously negated view operation. Because you can manipulate each view window independently, MicroStation lets you perform this command separately on each. Up to six previous view operations are maintained in its buffer by this command set.

Copy View

MicroStation supports the ability to copy one view's parameters into another view. Choose the Copy View icon from the View Control toolbox. You will be prompted to first select the "source" view, and then the "destination" view. If the View Control toolbox is not on your screen, you can call it up by selecting View Control from the Tools menu. Do not confuse Copy View with the *Copy Element* tool. In essence, all this command does is take what you see in one view, along with its view attributes, and copy it into another view.

This can be helpful when you have certain view-dependent features set up the way you like. Rather than going through the tedious process of setting each of these parameters for each view, just copy the established view to other views.

NOTE: *View Control commands are also available as a pop-up menu at your cursor location. Simply press the Shift key and click the Reset button in a view window. This pop-up menu is a holdover from version 5, as is obvious from the sequence and names of commands displayed.*

Swap View

The hardware-dependent command Swap View only works correctly with very specific hardware configurations. If you have a single-display PC system using a video card that supports an extra video "page," MicroStation will treat this second page as a virtual screen. Key in SWAP to activate this command. You get a message stating "Swap Illegal on this hardware" if your hardware does not support it.

The purpose of this command is to allow you to emulate MicroStation's dual screen capability on a single-screen setup. The

Swap View command allows you to instantly flip between the two video pages.

Basic Element Manipulation Tools

Element manipulation is a major cornerstone of any CAD product. If you couldn't modify or manipulate objects placed in your design file, MicroStation would just be an expensive "electric pencil." Fortunately, MicroStation has an enormous array of manipulation tools. You've already encountered one, the *Delete Element* tool. Fortunately, the results of most of the element manipulation tools are not as drastic as those of *Delete Element*. You will find yourself using these tools more often than actual element placement commands. The basic element manipulation commands available in MicroStation are:

Move	Moves an element
Copy	Copies an element
Delete	Deletes an element (already discussed)
Scale	Changes the size of an element
Rotate	Changes the orientation of an element with respect to the design plane
Mirror	"Flips" an element's orientation around a defined axis (X, Y, or user-defined)

All Elements Are Created Equal

All MicroStation elements can be manipulated with these tools. *There are no exceptions*. This simple statement is an extremely important concept related to CAD. By treating all of the various elements as equals subject to these manipulation commands, MicroStation gives you the opportunity to create your design without worrying about how the pieces are going to be affected by the design process.

The Manipulate Toolbox

So, where do these element manipulation commands reside? Appropriately enough, you can find them on their own toolbox, the Manipulate toolbox. You will find yourself frequently using the various tools found here, activated from the Main tool frame, so you will often find yourself tearing this toolbox off to stay on screen independently.

MicroStation's Manipulate toolbox. Note the options associated with the selected tool in the Tool Settings window.

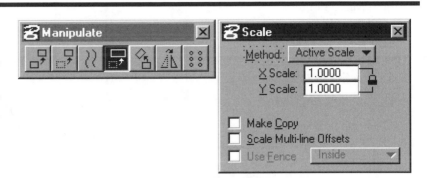

Move Element

The Move Element command is a very rudimentary element manipulation command. You select an element with a datapoint, whereupon it becomes attached to your cursor. A second datapoint establishes the new location for the element.

When you select an element with a datapoint, this location is also the "from" point. The second datapoint selects the "to" location for the element. When using precision input, this be-comes important. By tentative-point snapping to the end of an element and entering an absolute coordinate (the XY= key-in), you can control the precise location of the element move. Another way of explicitly defining the "from" and "to" locations is by first selecting the element using the *Element Selection* tool and then invoking the Move Element command.

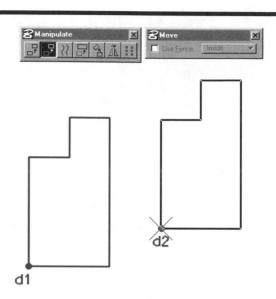

An example of the Move Element tool, demonstrating how the first selection datapoint also defines the point by which MicroStation moves the element. Also note that the Use Fence option is not active in this example.

Copy Element

The Copy Element command is similar to the Move command except that it creates a copy of the original element. The most important part of this command is its ability to make multiple copies of an element. As you datapoint again and again, you create additional copies of the original element. As usual, the Reset button releases the element from the *Copy* tool.

NOTE: *Remember, although you may have no element selected, the copy command can still be active. If you are not careful you may end up with extraneous copies of elements in your design. Always check your status bar for the active command.*

Scale Element

The *Scale Element* tool is the first of the manipulation tools that require additional information in order to operate. In this case, a parameter set collectively called the Active Scale is needed. Consisting of two parts (actually, three parts when working in a 3D design file), these are the X scale (XS= key-in) and the Y scale (YS= key-in).

In most instances you work with both scales set to the same value, so MicroStation provides you with a locking of the two scales via the AS= key-in or a lock icon with the associated key-in data fields. The active scale can be entered in a number of ways. The *Scale Element* tool provides access to the X Scale and Y Scale data fields with the ever-present lock symbol.

The Scale Element tool is found on the Manipulate toolbox. Note the small lock symbol to the right of the X Scale and Y Scale fields. Clicking on this lock will "unlock" the two scale fields, allowing you to enter a different scalar value for each axis.

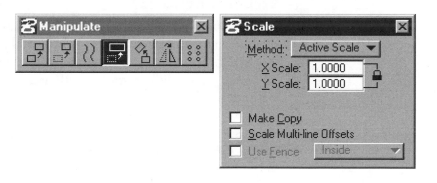

The scale associated with the *Scale Element* tool is also used by other tools within MicroStation. As a result there are other ways of entering this global, active scale. The most direct method is to use the AS= key-in. By keying in AS=.5, you are setting the active scale value to 50%. Conversely, if you key in AS=2, you are establishing a 2:1 ratio, or 200% scale factor.

The Make Copy Option

You may have noticed that there is the Make Copy checkbox on the Tool Settings window for the *Scale Element* tool. Rather than implement two separate commands, one to scale the original element and another to scale a copy of the original element, MicroStation modifies the behavior of the same command with this checkbox. In other words, when you use the Make Copy option, the original element is left in place, and a copy of it is scaled. With the checkbox off, the original element is scaled, essentially replacing the existing one with a new element using the new scales.

MicroStation prompts you to identify an element. It doesn't matter where in the element you datapoint; the second datapoint is what is important. This second datapoint determines the location of the newly scaled element.

Understanding Scale Element's Seemingly Eccentric Behavior

Once you've selected the element to scale, you will see this element move in relation to the cursor on the screen. However, you will notice that it does not necessarily touch the cursor. This is due to a complicated bit of mathematics being applied to this operation.

Many times when you scale an element, you want it to maintain some sort of relationship to the original element being scaled. For instance, a gear train may need to be designed with an inside gear, commonly known as a planetary gear, nested at a convenient tangent point on the original circle.

In order to guarantee that the newly scaled circle will lie on this tangent point, Scale Element also scales the distance from the original object. In this way, if you select a one-third scale and tentative point on a circle, the resulting circle will touch the original circle on its circumference no matter where you move the cursor. Let's try it.

Exercise: Scaling a Circle

1. Open the example design file SCALEXER.DGN. You will see a large circle displayed in window 1.

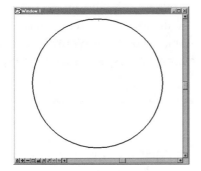

2. With this large circle, let's create scaled replicas. First, activate the *Scale Element* tool from the Manipulate toolbox.

3. Enter `.25` in the X Scale data field. Note how the Y scale changed to match the X scale value. If it did not, the lock to the right of these fields would appear unlocked. Click on the lock to close it, and reenter the `.25` value.

4. Before continuing, we need to set one more option: Make Copy. Click on this option in the Tool Settings window. One item to note is how the tool name changes in the status bar as a result of selecting the Make Copy option.

5. Datapoint once on the circle. A circle 25% the diameter of the master circle should now appear attached to your cursor. Now move the cursor around the circumference of the master circle. Notice anything strange? No matter where you move the cursor along the circle's perimeter, the smaller circle is *tangent* to the larger one. MicroStation always performs the scaling operation with respect to the center of the selected object, no matter where you clicked a datapoint to select it.

6. Tentative point and datapoint anywhere along the source circle. A circle 25% the size of the previous circle appears. Again it remains tangent to its parent circle.

The secret to the *Scale Element* tool is how it applies the active scale to both the object and the distance from the selected object's center point. This applies to all elements, not just circles.

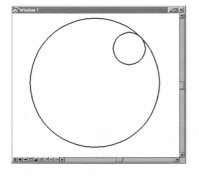

Go ahead and try it with a block shape or a polygon. Try it with other scales as well. Once you see how the distance scaler works, it will no longer be a mystery why the scale command acts as it does. Many long-time MicroStation users don't understand how this distance scaling works, so now you are one up on them.

Active Scale Setting

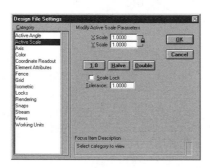

Another method for entering the scale parameters is via the Active Scale category in the Design File Settings dialog box. Accessed from the Settings pull-down menu (**Settings ➡ Design File…**), this dialog box allows you to set both the X and Y scale values. As with the *Scale Element* tool, you can lock the two values together via the lock symbol located to the right of the scale fields. Clicking on the lock symbol toggles its effect.

Also found on the Active Scale category of the dialog box are three buttons to perform some common scale manipulations. The 1.0 scale button resets the active scale to 1 (equivalent to entering an AS=1 key-in). The Halve and Double buttons change the present active scale values. If the active scale was set to 3.0 and you were to hit the Double button, the result would be an active scale of 6.0.

The final feature of the Active Scale settings box is the Scale Lock. By activating this feature and selecting an appropriate tolerance value (normally set to 1.0), you can force the scale value to be a multiple of the tolerance. Leaving the tolerance set to 1 essentially provides you with a method to force the active scale to an integer value.

The active scale can be any number—large or small. For instance, if you wanted to reduce an object by 50%, you would key in AS=.5. A key-in of AS=20 would multiply an element's size twenty times. The default value is 1, meaning no scaling is done to the element.

TIP: *You can also change the active scale using simple arithmetic expressions. For instance, to double the current active scale you can enter* AS=*2. *To change the current active scale to a third of its present value you can enter* AS=3. *Note, however, that any such change is subject to the current scale lock.*

Rotate Element

Now that you've mastered the *Scale Element* tool, let's look at the tool most closely related to it, the *Rotate Element* tool. Instead of applying a scale to a selected element, *Rotate Element* applies an angular rotation. As discussed earlier with arc placement, *Rotate Element* uses a sweep angle to affect the element selected.

In its most basic form, *Rotate Element* gives you the ability to rotate an element by graphically specifying the angle of rotation. To do this with the 2 Points method you must give MicroStation three datapoints: one to select an element, one that specifies a pivot point, and one that defines the angle of rotation.

The actual angle of rotation is calculated by the angle between the X axis passing through the pivot point and the third rotation termination point. This is one of the more visually stimulating commands. Don't resist spinning your element a few times before clicking the datapoint button. Go ahead, have some fun!

Using the Active Angle Method

Although the "spin cycle" of the *Rotate Element* tool is important, most users operate this tool with the Active Angle method. By keying in an angle and selecting the element to be rotated, the user maintains precise control over how MicroStation rotates this element.

The Rotate Element tool in use with the Active Angle method. This is probably the most common use of Rotate Element.

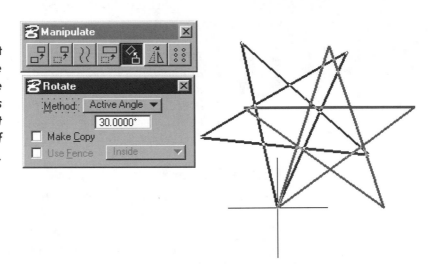

By keying in an angle of 45 degrees, you can select any element and MicroStation will rotate it for you. The first datapoint you supply will select the element; the second datapoint selects the point of rotation. If you tentative point to the actual element, the result will be a rotation about this point. This results in the figure rotating about that point. As is the case with the scale command, there is the Make Copy option.

Exercise: Rotating an Object

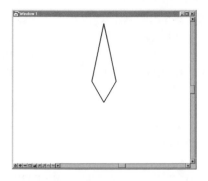

1. Activate the ROTEXER.DGN design file. You should see a diamond shape in view window 1, as pictured. We will be creating rotated copies of this image.

2. Activate the *Rotate Element* tool from the Manipulate toolbox. Select the Active Angle method in the Tool Settings window and enter 30.0. Next, enable the Make Copy option.

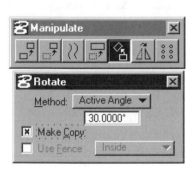

3. Place a datapoint anywhere on the diamond shape. A dynamic and rotated copy of the diamond will appear on your cursor. Notice how it follows your cursor if you move it along the perimeter of the original element.

4. Place a tentative point followed by a datapoint at the bottom vertex of the diamond. Another dynamic shape appears rotated an additional 30 degrees.

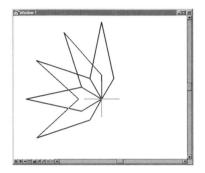

5. Place a tentative point on the second datapoint at the same bottom vertex of the diamond. Again, another copy of the diamond appears rotated a further 30 degrees. You can continue the tentative point/datapoint sequence to create an interesting flower-like pattern. Because each successive data-point was in the same location, the result is a circle of shapes that returns to the original element's initial location. If you did not achieve the same result, one or more of your datapoints was not at the exact point on the diamond.

Try rotations with other shapes or alternating datapoints. In most instances, the result of such successive rotations will be some sort of geometric pattern.

The Active Angle Parameter

As with the Active Scale setting, MicroStation's Active Angle is a global parameter used by a number of commands and tools. As a result, there are a number of ways to enter active angle values. The simplest is the AA= key-in entered in the Key-in window. MicroStation responds by displaying the active angle on the status bar.

This key-in of the active angle automatically updates any active angle data fields presently displayed on your screen. In addition, you can enter the active angle via the Design File Settings dialog box.

The Active Angle Setting

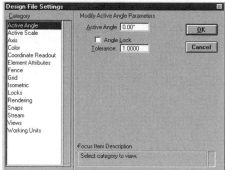

The Active Angle category on the Design File Settings dialog box (**Settings ➡ Design File...**) gives you another way to set the active angle. You simply key in the angle in the data field provided. Note the presence of the Angle Lock checkbox and the Tolerance field. If you enable Angle Lock, you can only set the active angle to a multiple of the tolerance value specified. Thus, if the tolerance is 1.0000 and the Angle Lock checkbox is enabled, any active angle you key in is rounded to the nearest integer.

Further Thoughts on Active Angle

As discussed earlier, MicroStation always measures angles from the horizontal in the counterclockwise direction. However, there are two other angular measurement systems in wide use in design work: azimuth and bearing.

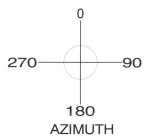

Azimuth refers to angular readout from the vertical as in a north direction and following a positive angular degree *clockwise* through 360 degrees. Bearing angle measurement follows the four points of a compass and is expressed in a primary direction followed by a degree of rotation and a secondary direction. For example, N30E refers to North 30°. toward the East.

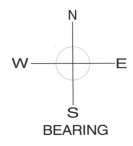

BEARING

Recognizing the need to support these systems, MicroStation is equipped with the ability to accept input and read out angular data in both azimuth and bearing methods, as well as what we term the "conventional" counterclockwise from horizontal shown so far. Additionally, MicroStation can also use and display the *degrees, minutes,* and *seconds* necessary for most surveying and mapping work. Configuration of the angular measurement system used by MicroStation is controlled with the Coordinate Readout category in the Design File Settings dialog box.

The Coordinate Readout Setting

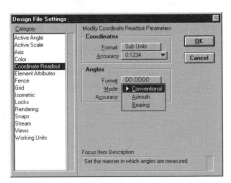

The various methods of angular readout previously discussed are set in the Coordinate Readout category of the Design File Settings dialog box (**Settings ➡ Design File...**). In the Angles section you select the appropriate angular measurement system via the Mode popdown field. Clicking on the Mode field and dragging the mouse over the appropriate measurement system sets this as the default angleentry system. You also set the format of the angular degree readout in a similar fashion. Last, you have control over the accuracy of the readout.

You may have noticed the Coordinates section of this dialog box. This is where you determine how MicroStation displays coordinate information in the various data fields and on the status bar. You can select whether MicroStation displays such information in working units, subunits, or master units.

Mirror Element

 An extremely powerful function of CAD, the *Mirror Element* tool provides you with the ability to take an element and mirror it. Just as looking in a mirror you see a reversed image of yourself, this tool creates a reversed image in your design.

If you take a small pocket mirror and stand it vertically on a drawing, the resulting image shown in the mirror is controlled by how and where you place it on the drawing (see the following diagram). The bottom edge of the mirror is the axis about which the image is mirrored. When using the *Mirror Element* tool in MicroStation you must define this axis. Two such axes are readily available to you in the form of the X and Y axes. In addition, you can define your own. This leads to three mirror options, thus the Mirror About pop-down option field. As with the previous element manipulations, you have the Make Copy option.

The Mirror command uses the bottom "edge" of the mirror to define the axis.

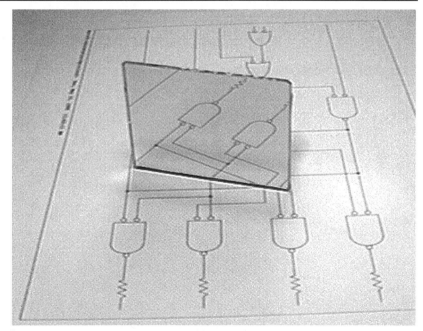

The Mirror About: Horizontal option allows you to mirror an element about the horizontal, or X, axis. First-time users of these commands may be surprised by the results of this option. Because the mirroring occurs about the horizontal axis, the mirrored element flips *vertically,* not horizontally, as the option name suggests.

To flip the element horizontally use the Mirror About: Vertical option. Once you have used these commands a few times you will understand their relationship to the X and Y axes.

The Mirror About: Line option lets you define any line about which to mirror an element. You first select the element to mirror, then specify the first point on the *mirror axis,* and finally, click a data-point to identify the direction of the axis. The adjacent diagram should help you visualize the mirror axis.

Exercise: Mirroring an Object

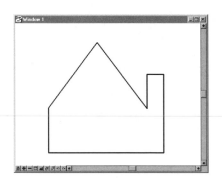

1. Activate the MSHAPE.DGN design file. You should see a shape as shown here, in window 1. Through this exercise you will mirror this element along various axes to demonstrate how the *Mirror Element* tool works.

2. Select the *Mirror Element* tool from the Manipulate toolbox. Set Mirror About to Vertical and enable the Make Copy option.

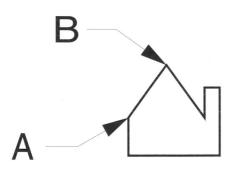

3. Datapoint anywhere on the shape. As you move the cursor away from the original object, note how the distance from the object to the cursor is also mirrored. Datapoint to the right of the original object. The *Mirror* tool will continue to prompt you for a new location of the copy. To release the shape hit Reset. Before proceeding, select the Undo command from the Edit menu to remove the mirrored copy of the shape.

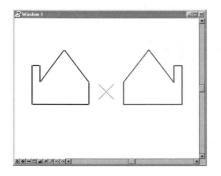

4. Next, let's try the Mirror About: Line option. With the Line option set, datapoint anywhere on the original shape. Next, click a tentative point followed by a datapoint at the location labeled A in the diagram. A dynamic mirrored image of the shape will appear to rotate from this location. Don't be fooled, however; this rotation is actually the mirror process shown as the axis of mirror passes through your last datapoint and the current position of your cursor.

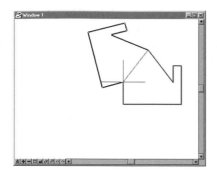

5. Click a tentative point at point B in the previous diagram. The sloping line from point A through point B becomes the axis of mirror and results in the final image shown here.

Remember that all mirror operations occur about the selected axis. *Vertical* and *Horizontal* refer to the axis, not the mirrored results.

Undoing and Redoing Operations

A necessary feature with today's high-performance CAD products is a method by which we can undo an operation we've just performed on our design: an OOPS! fixer. MicroStation is no exception. In fact, MicroStation's implementation of this feature, the Undo command, has some bells and whistles not found in other products.

In a nutshell, Undo reverses your last action. Subsequent undos reverse each previous action in turn. This multiple undo capability is not found in many software products, much less many CAD programs. Theoretically, you could keep undoing your actions until you have a blank screen. There are a couple of limitations, however.

NOTE: *When first installed, MicroStation sets aside a special area in memory called the Undo buffer. By default this buffer is set to 256 kilobytes (1Kb equals 1,024 bytes). You can change this default in the Memory Usage category of the Preferences dialog box (**Workspace ➡ Preferences**).*

The other limiting factor is that Undo will only work on commands performed during the current session. It does not remember changes you made during a previous session.

In other words, if you worked on your drawing just before lunch, exited MicroStation, then came back after lunch to find you made a mistake, you would not be able to undo it. This is not an excuse for leaving your computer on with MicroStation loaded all through lunch, but it points out that you should review your progress whenever you are about to exit MicroStation.

The Undo command can be found under the Edit pull-down menu (**Edit ➡ Undo...**). One nice touch of the Undo command is the way it presents itself on the Edit menu. When you pull down this menu, you will see both the Undo command and the name of the command that would be reversed if you were to go ahead with Undo.

The Undo command. Note the description next to Undo of the command to be undone.

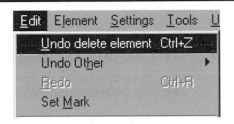

The Redo command does as its name implies: it reverses the last Undo command. As a matter of fact, it will redo as many consecutive undos as your Undo buffer can hold. Like the Undo command, it also lists the name of the last command; in this case, to be "redone."

Undo Other and Setting File Markers

Let's say you are about to take on a particularly nasty design session that will markedly alter the design file. You aren't sure that what you are about to do will create a solution to your design problem; however, you must try. And let's say it may involve so many changes that you aren't sure the Undo buffer will hold them all.

Not to worry! MicroStation provides for such design process considerations with the Set Mark and Undo Other Marked commands.

By "setting" a mark (**Edit ➡ Set Mark**) prior to starting the design process, you can return the design to the premarked condition by using the Undo Marked (**Edit ➡ Undo Other ➡ To Mark**) command. This provides the equivalent of a "What if…" function.

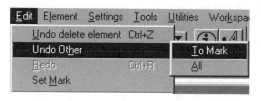

An additional option under the Undo Other pull-down menu is the Undo All command (**Edit ➡ Undo Other ➡ All**). This command essentially reverses all of the work performed on a design file since it was called up in the current MicroStation session. Because of its destructive nature, and the fact that there is no Redo All equivalent, you are presented with an Alert where you have to OK the completion of this operation.

Manipulating Multiple Elements

Fence Manipulations

With all of the element manipulation tools just described you may have noticed an option associated with them called Use Fence. This option refers to MicroStation's ability to act on more than one element at a time. Collectively called the Fence capability, this feature is an important part of how you work with MicroStation.

To have MicroStation operate on the contents of a "fence" with the element manipulation commands discussed earlier, you first need to place a fence around those elements. This fence element you create is not really a true element but rather a temporary construct that allows you to identify a part of the drawing you wish to modify. When the Use Fence checkbox is enabled for a tool, MicroStation acts on the elements enclosed in the fence.

NOTE: *Fence manipulations can operate on a large number of elements. If the Undo command does not restore your manipulations, you need to increase the size of the Undo buffer.*

Place Fence

Although there is only one fence placement tool, *Place Fence,* it implements six different methods of placing a fence. The Place Fence icon can be found in the Main tool frame or in the Fence toolbox. As always, do not overlook the options provided in the Tool Settings window.

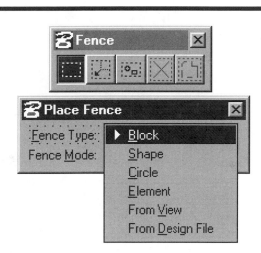

The Place Fence tool implements six ways to invoke it, as seen in the Fence Type pop-down filed in the Tool Settings window.

The various ways to place a fence are summarized in the following table:

Fence Type	
Block	Places a rectangular fence when its diagonal points are specified
Shape	Places an irregular-shaped fence with datapoints supplying its vertices
Circle	Places a circular fence upon specifying its center and a point on its circumference
Element	Uses an existing closed shape in a design file and places a fence around it

Fence Type	
From View	Places a rectangular fence around the perimeter of a view window
From Design File	Places a rectangular fence that surrounds all elements in a design file

The most commonly used type of fence is the Block, a rectangular shape. You place it by clicking two diagonal points. The Shape fence is also commonly used when trying to operate on a specific group of elements in a congested area. The remaining four fence types are new to MicroStation 95. Play with them, as you are sure to find good use for them as you get more acquainted with MicroStation.

Using the Fence with Your Tools

By placing a fence and then selecting the Use Fence option, your chosen tool will act on those elements enclosed by the fence. Once you have surrounded the elements with your fence and have activated the appropriate tool, additional datapoints are needed to direct the tool's operation. Unlike the single-element operation, wherein your datapoint typically identifies the element and the focus point of the tool, fence operations require you to provide this *from/to* coordinate information with two datapoints. In all cases, the fence versions of the element manipulation commands function the same as their single-element cousins.

It is easy to see how a fence manipulation command can modify an element totally enclosed within the fence. What's less obvious is what happens when an element crosses the fence boundary. Associated with all of the element manipulation tools and the *Fence* tools is something called the Fence Mode. Seen as a pop-down field next to the Use Fence option, these modes control what happens when a fence-enhanced operation is executed. The following are the Fence Modes.

Fence Modes	
Inside	Acts on all elements totally enclosed within the fence
Overlap	Acts on all elements within the fence and those that overlap the fence boundary
Clip	Acts on all elements within the fence and only that portion of any element that crosses the fence
Void	Acts on all elements completely outside the fence
Void-Overlap	Acts on elements outside the fence and those that overlap the fence
Void-Clip	Acts on all elements outside the fence and only that portion of any element lying outside the fence

The last three fence modes—Void, Void-Overlap, and Void-Clip— complement the first three modes. Think of the void modes as the "inside out" modes. In most cases, you'll want to *avoid* the default use of these three modes; instead, use them only when needed and return to one of the three normal fence modes. In fact, it is safest to return to the Inside Fence mode at the conclusion of most operations, as the accidental use of the Clip operation could be disastrous.

When you invoke a fence manipulation command you are affecting a large number of elements at one time. If you are indiscriminate with the placement of your fence, this manipula-tion may lead to changes you did not anticipate or desire. For this reason it is a good idea to understand the fence modes thor-oughly.

The Clip Fence Mode

Clip is by far the most dangerous option of all. In this case, *dangerous* is not too strong a word to use. This fence mode chops any elements that cross the fence into separate pieces lying inside and outside the fence.

The ones lying inside the fence are then affected by the fence command chosen. Those lying outside the fence are "left alone," but the act of chopping has, of course, changed those elements as well.

The Clip option also points out an ability of MicroStation: constructing one type of element out of another. If the overlapping element were a circle, the result—after, say, a Move Element operation—would be two arcs. A block would become two line strings.

The indiscriminate use of the Clip option can lead to a disaster. So how do you avoid problems with it? By developing the habit of *always* selecting the Fence Mode/Inside option when you have completed use of a fence clip manipulation. This also applies to the use of the Overlap option. This does not mean that you should avoid using the clip function. It is a very important and powerful function and has its place. Just remember to turn it off when you are finished with it.

Modify Fence

The Modify Fence command allows you to relocate a specific vertex of a previously placed fence, or to move the location of the entire fence. You select the tool, then the option, Vertex or Position, from the Modify Mode pop-down list in the Tool Settings window, and click to identify the vertex or fence. Finally, another datapoint identifies the new location for the vertex or the fence.

The Modify Fence icon implements two commands: Modify Fence Vertex and Modify Fence Position (or Move Fence).

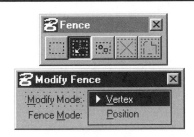

Manipulate Fence Contents

As noted earlier, if you enable the Use Fence checkbox while using tools in the Manipulate toolbox, MicroStation switches to operate on the contents of the fence. However, this is not the only method, or even all the commands available, for manipulating the contents of a fence. There is the *Manipulate Fence Contents* tool in the Fence toolbox. In addition to providing another way to copy, move, rotate, scale, or mirror fence contents, it implements the Fence Stretch command.

The Operation pop-down list for the Manipulate Fence Contents tool includes the Stretch command not found on the Manipulate toolbox.

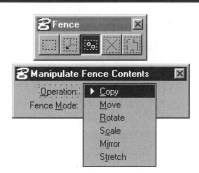

The following table summarizes the function of each fence operation.

Fence Manipulation Operations	
Copy	Copies the contents of a fence after you specify the "from" and "to" points
Move	Moves the contents of a fence after you specify the "from" and "to" points
Rotate	Rotates the contents of a fence, but does not offer the 3-point rotation method otherwise available if the *Rotate Element* tool with the Use Fence option is used
Scale	Scales the contents of a fence

Fence Manipulation Operations	
Mirror	Mirrors the contents of a fence about the vertical or horizontal axis
Stretch	Only available from the Fence toolbox, it allows relocation of the vertices of elements that fall within a fence

As you may have noticed, in general, the tools found on the Manipulate toolbox, with Use Fence enabled, offer greater flexibility than similar tools in the Fence toolbox.

Delete Fence Contents

Remember our old friend the *Delete Element* tool? You may have noticed that this important tool has no options. There are times, however, when you may want to delete entire portions of your design. As a safety precaution, MicroStation provides this *Delete Fence Contents* tool in the Fence toolbox. In this way, you are reminded of the current fence mode so that you won't accidentally delete the wrong portion of your design.

The Delete Fence Contents *tool on the* Fence *toolbox.*

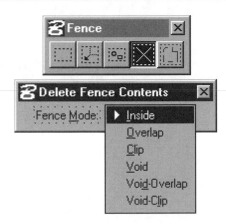

NOTE: *Whenever you select the Use Fence option, the Command Window displays the current fence mode. You should always check this information prior to performing your tool's operation.*

Exercise: Fence Manipulations

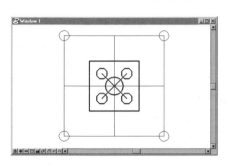

1. Activate the FENCEXER.DGN design file. You should see the elements shown in window 1. Now, place a fence block surrounding the highlighted elements in the center of this design.

2. Next, let's move the elements inside the fence using the *Move Element* tool. Select the Use Fence option and the Fence Mode/Inside. Click a datapoint once at the center of the elements (the big X) inside the fenced area and about a quarter of the way up from the bottom of the screen.

3. The elements enclosed in the fence moved to the new location based on your datapoints. Note how the fence shape travels with your cursor.

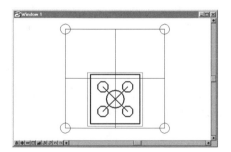

4. Only those elements totally enclosed within the fence block were moved. Those elements crossing over the fence were not affected. This was due to the Fence Mode setting of Inside.

5. Now, set the Fence Mode to Overlap. Click a tentative point, followed by a datapoint on the center point of the objects you just moved, and click a datapoint once at the center of the large square. (Hint: Use the Center snap mode.) Now click a datapoint again. The result should be that elements that overlapped were moved as well.

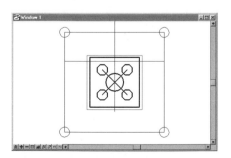

6. What happened? The elements moved back to the center of the square but the intersecting lines have now moved down. Because they crossed the fence boundary, they were moved as well.

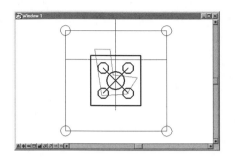

7. Next, let's try the most dangerous of all, the Clip fence mode. Use Place Fence Shape and create an irregular fence that overlaps various elements in the middle of the design. Cut through the circles and the square.

8. Choose the *Move Element* tool once again and select Use Fence with the Clip fence mode. Click a datapoint once inside the fence and a second time just a little to the left of the fence. What happened?

9. Now, instead of circles and blocks you have arcs and line strings. The clip mode radically changes the appearance of your design file. This is why the clip lock is so dangerous. In fact, if you had a large number of elements modified in this way, and your Undo buffer was not large enough, you might not be able to recover from such an inadvertent command.

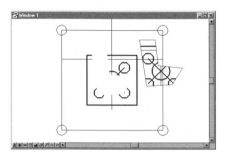

10. Make sure to set your fence lock to Inside before proceeding—an excellent habit to develop, starting *now*.

The Selection Set

An alternative method for working with more than one element is the *Selection* tool. *Selection set* is the name given to the collection of elements you have either identified with the *Element Selection* tool, selected with the Select All command, or established with the Select by Attributes facility (**Edit ➡ Select by Attributes**). This last function is discussed in a later chapter, but the first two are easy to understand.

Select All

This command is very simple. Once activated (**Edit ➡ Select All**), it selects every element in your current design file as your selection set. Any command or tool selected after this will act on all of the elements in your design file. *Be careful!* This command is similar to using one of the more dangerous fence modes, and you may not be able to undo it.

Element Selection Tool

Located on the Main tool frame, this arrow-like tool is the main method for selectively identifying elements for incorporation into the selection set. The element selection tool is simplicity itself. You identify elements by clicking on them one by one while holding down the Ctrl key. You can select more than one element by clicking and holding the datapoint button and dragging the cursor diagonally across the elements desired. In either case, the selected elements will be highlighted with small filled boxes called handles.

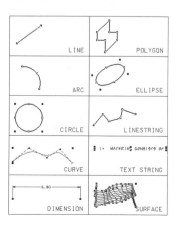

These handles serve two functions. First, they identify elements that are already part of the selection set. Second, by clicking on a highlighted element's handle you can change the location of the endpoints of a line, the diameter of a circle, or the corner of a shape. If you click and drag somewhere along an element's length, the result is similar to the *Move* tool. This is as close as you can get to a modeless operation in MicroStation.

Selection Set and the Element Manipulation Tools

One of the main features of the selection set is its effect on many of the element manipulation tools. When you have a selection set active, all you have to do to act on these elements is select the appropriate tool. The act of selecting the tool actually executes its operation. No "Accept/Reject." No "Datapoint to accept." Even tools such as *Delete Element* offer no prompting when invoked with a selection set active. In fact, with a selection set active, all you have to do to delete these elements is hit the Delete key on the keyboard.

In the case of a tool that may require a datapoint to proceed, the selection set is treated like a fence. For instance, the *Move Element* tool requires two datapoints to perform its task. One minor difference in the operation of *Manipulate Element* tools with selection sets is how they terminate. With the "normal" tool, like *Move Element,* you are prompted to keep moving the element (or fence) until you hit Reset. With a selection set active, the *Move* tool prompts you for the obligatory from-to datapoints, drops the element handles, and then returns active control to the *Element Selection* tool. The elements in the selection set remain high-lighted, waiting for your next command.

Deactivating the Current Selection Set

To discontinue the use of the selection set feature you click in an empty area on your design plane without holding down the Ctrl key. This assumes the *Element Selection* tool is active. You can deselect an individual element of the selection set by selecting it with the Ctrl key held down.

Element Symbology

So far you have been dealing with elements that look, well, rather plain. When performing real drafting, you use a variety of pencils or technical pens to create a number of differing line thicknesses. In addition, you use a series of predefined line styles to describe different parts of a drawing.

In its ongoing battle to duplicate all things traditional, CAD can do the same thing. The term for the appearance characteristics of elements is *element symbology*. MicroStation allows you to alter an element's line thickness (referred to as weight), style, and color.

Setting Line Weights

When you use a technical pen to create a drawing, you expect uniform and predictable line thicknesses. You put up with the mess and maintenance that curse all technical pens for the excellent results such pens provide. When you use a CAD system, you expect the same uniform results.

MicroStation gives you 32 different line weights, which would be comparable to 32 different technical pens. The use of the word *weights* is intentional. MicroStation does not assign a specific line thickness to each weight. Instead, these weights are considered a "logical" characteristic of the element. This refers to the fact that although there are 32 different thicknesses attainable with Micro-Station, as to which weight represents which pen thickness is a decision made at the time of plot generation.

The first 16 line weights are directly accessible from the Primary toolbox.

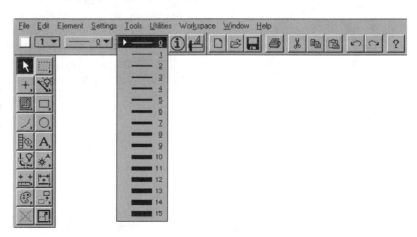

This all sounds very complicated but is simple in practice. Seldom, if ever, will you find a need to use all 32 weight values. In fact, most of the time you will find that the first eight suffice. When we begin to plot the results of our designs you will find that there are some extra benefits to using the various weights.

When you select a line weight from either the Primary toolbox or from pop-down fields in any other tool, it becomes the active line weight. The active line weight means that any new elements you place in your design file from this point on will take on this value.

Because these weights are an abstract, logical characteristic of an element, how they are displayed on the screen can be somewhat disconcerting the first time you see them. The follow-ing exercise demonstrates how MicroStation handles line weights.

Exercise: Working Out with Weights

1. MicroStation uses weights something like line thicknesses. This, however, can be very misleading when trying to associate a weight with a specific line thickness. Let's test this. Activate the LINEWT.DGN design file. Note the two circles. The bottom one is apparently "thicker" than the top one. This is due to its use of a different line weight.

2. To verify this, use the *Element Selection* tool (the arrow icon) to select the top circle. Once selected, choose *Analyze Element* from the Primary toolbox. The weight field displays the number 0. Repeat this step after selecting the lower circle. This time, the circle has a weight of 31, the maximum value allowed. This explains the difference in appear-ances between the two identical circles. You probably also noticed that the line appears to be "broken" every 45 degrees. This is a display anomaly due to the weight "flipping" as it travels around the circle. This appearance hints at the true nature of

MicroStation's weights. Close the Information window.

3. Next, let's zoom out to get a better "view" of these elements. Select the *Zoom Out* tool from the View Control menu (the magnifying glass with the minus sign). Click between the two circles.

4. Surprised by the result? The heavy-weight circle appeared to get thicker. In reality it remained the same as before, the difference being that the circle's diameter shrank in response to the zoom action. Try it again.

5. It almost appears as though the heavier circle is overwhelming its lesser-weight cousin. Now zoom out a few more times.

6. The "fat" circle now looks like a cross. This again is due to the display characteristic of line weights. Even when the circle is too small to really make out, the weight routine will still "paint" it at the weight given.

The key to *weight* is that it is a computer "construct," a logical device to differentiate the apparent thickness of one element from that of another. The actual assignment of a thickness to the weight is performed at the plotting stage through the use of MicroStation's plotting software and the physical pens used in the plotter.

As you can see, the effect of the heavy weights is dependent on the scale of the view. MicroStation paints all weights with the same number of screen pixels no matter what the zoom scale of the view. This leads to what you just saw.

When zooming out, you come to a point where the element's length is less in pixels than that of its width. The result is the drawing distortion. However, rest assured that the final plotted results will not display this same disregard of reality.

Working with Line Styles

The other major feature you are familiar with in traditional drawing is the use of various line styles. Dashed, dotted, and even phantom lines are immediately recognized in a drawing and don't require further description.

As far as MicroStation is concerned, there are two distinct types of line styles. The first type is a set of eight "line codes" that are an integral part of the software. The second type is referred to as *custom line styles*. These were introduced in version 5 and allow you to create your own line styles by way of defining stroke (dash-gap) patterns, point symbols (much like cells embedded in a line definition), and complex styles (a combination of stroke patterns and point symbols).

To see what MicroStation offers for line styles, all you have to do is select the line style pop-down list from the Primary toolbox. What you see is the "traditional eight" line styles as they existed since the beginning of time, or at least the beginning of MicroStation. (In fact, these line styles predate MicroStation. They have been defined in Intergraph's IGDS CAD product since the early 1980s.)

At the bottom of the Line Style hierarchical menu is the word *Custom*. This simple word hides the real power behind MicroStation's user-defined line styles. Selecting Custom brings up the Line Styles settings box. Here you'll find a couple of dozen additional line styles, ranging from { Border } to { Wide Dash }. All of these are available for use in your design file. To see the actual elements of the line style selected, choose the Show Details option. However, before we go totally nuts and start drawing "cute" tree lines and railroads, let's look at the basic line styles that are an integral part of MicroStation.

MicroStation is delivered with dozens of custom line styles. The list you see will depend on a number of factors. The ones seen here are part of MicroStation's default workspace.

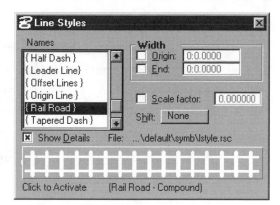

The Basic Line Styles

As mentioned, MicroStation has always supported eight built-in line styles. Instead of descriptive names, as appear in the Line Styles settings box for custom line styles, these are identified with a *line code* number. When you select a line code number from the Primary toolbox, it becomes the active line style. Any new elements you place take on that line style. For the sake of compatibility with prior versions, you can select line codes by also using the LC= key-in. Thus, if you key in LC=6, the line style field in the Primary toolbox also changes to display the number 6, preceded by a graphical representation of the line style; in this case, a large-small dash pattern.

	LC=0
	LC=1
	LC=2
	LC=3
	LC=4
	LC=5
	LC=6
	LC=7

The eight basic line style types supported by MicroStation.

As mentioned, MicroStation treats these eight line styles as other logical characteristics. In most cases, however, you will probably use them as they appear on the screen. Just be aware that should the need arise to modify the appearance of a given line style, it can be adjusted at plotting time by editing the plotter configuration file.

NOTE: *We will be revisiting line styles later in the book. For now, you should stick with the eight default line styles. In fact, your system administrator may restrict the use of the custom line styles until all company procedures can use them. There are few things worse in a project than to see a mix of line styles representing the same types of objects.*

Using Color

Color is a great tool for differentiating the various components of your drawing. You can color the design itself white, the dimensions red, the drawing border green. Another scheme is to use colors to differentiate the types of information found in your drawing. For instance, a roadway plan and profile sheet could use different colors to differentiate between various alignments and other features of the design.

MicroStation includes excellent color support. Depending on your system's color capability, MicroStation is capable of displaying up to 16.7 million colors! However, before you run out and upgrade your system, keep in mind that MicroStation provides direct use of only 256 colors. The key here is *use* versus *display*.

MicroStation provides a very powerful image-rendering capability for generating near-photographic-quality images from your design file. It is in the rendering process where the colors greater than the 256 you can assign come into play.

MicroStation allows you to assign any of the 256 colors in the color palette to any element in your design file. If you click the color picker in the Primary toolbox, the first field in the toolbox, you will see a palette of 256 colors. Selecting one of these colors sets the *active* color. The next element you place will be drawn in this color.

The color palette is most readily accessed from the color picker in the Primary toolbox. A black-and-white image doesn't do justice to this most colorful menu selection.

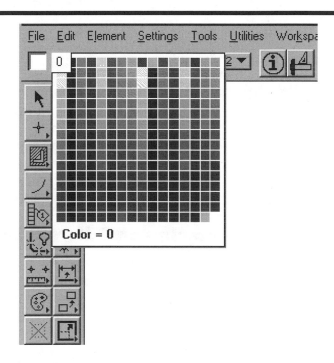

When you choose a color from this palette, MicroStation displays that color's numeric identifier along the bottom of the palette, and in the color box as you move your cursor. For the record, the numbering of the colors in the palette goes 0 to 16 along the top row, 17 to 32 on the second row, and so on.

You can directly enter the color's number using the CO= key-in, followed by a number matching the color desired. In addition, if you are using the default color table (like most users), you can also type in the names of the primary colors desired. This will work only for the first seven colors. The colors and their numbers are:

Size	Standard Colors
0	White
1	Blue
2	Green
3	Red
4	Yellow
5	Violet
6	Orange

When you enter the color's name with the LC key-in, Micro-Station also updates the display of the color in the Primary toolbox. If you are using a plotter capable of plotting in color, either through the use of colored pens or one of the electro-static/ink-jet color plotters, you can set your plotter up to plot using these colors.

Drawing on Different Levels

All of the symbology settings discussed so far have been easy to relate to their manual drafting counterpart. Now, however, comes a new type of symbology that although not unique to CAD is the one most extensively used in CAD systems.

Overlay Drafting

Overlay drafting has been around awhile but has only become very popular in the last twenty years. Overlay refers to the drawing of a design on multiple sheets of drafting media. To create a final print of a specific drawing, the appropriate sheets are merged using the photographic or lithographic process. The concept behind overlay drafting is "don't draw the same line twice."

When you design a house, you show the walls of the building on different sheets in the plans. Using overlay drafting, these walls are drawn only once, usually on their own Mylar sheet. Each major feature of the building is drawn on a separate drawing sheet. By combining the various sheets, you construct the complete design (an electrical plan, for instance).

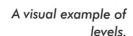

A visual example of levels.

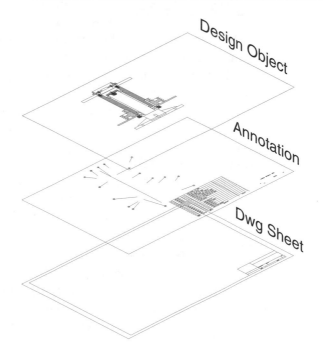

The concept behind MicroStation's levels is the same. By drawing your walls on one level and windows on another, you can control how your final drawing will look. MicroStation supports 63 levels.

There are several commands used to control the levels. Unlike the previous symbology types, levels are most closely associated with the view commands. Using a variety of tools, you select which levels are displayed in which views. Chief among these level control tools is the View Levels settings box (**Settings ➡ Level ➡ Display**). Opening this settings box provides you with full access to all of your active design file's levels.

In the example of the View Levels settings box shown, levels 1 through 44 are currently turned on in view 1, whereas levels 45 through 63 are off. Using your mouse you can select levels to display or not display. Holding down your mouse and dragging across a number of levels will either turn on or turn off those levels, depending on the state of the first level you touched. When you are satisfied with your level selections, hitting the Apply button applies this level selection to the view shown in the View Number selection box. From a pop-down menu you can select any one of MicroStation's eight views. Alternately, you can apply your level selection to all views by hitting the All button.

The Active Level

You may be asking yourself, "What's with the round symbol on level 1?" Good question. This, in fact, designates a very important feature, your *active level.* When you create elements in your design file they are placed on one of the 63 levels. To control which level they are created on, MicroStation provides you with the active level. To change you active level, either double-click the level in the View Levels settings box or select it from the level selection palette on the Primary toolbox. MicroStation does not let you turn off the display of your active level in *any* view, which is why it appears in the same highlighted color as the other displayed levels in the View Levels settings box.

You should be aware that when you select another active level to work on, the previous active level is not removed from the list of levels displayed. To turn off that level, you must use the View Levels settings box or the OF= key-in.

Using the Level Control Key-ins

Using the View Levels settings box is fine, but you may find yourself wishing for a "quick and dirty" way to move from level to level. You may do this by using MicroStation's level key-ins. There are three key-ins to consider.

LV=   Sets the active level

ON=   Turns on the specified levels and prompts for identification of the view(s)

OF=   Turns off the specified levels and prompts for identification the view(s)

 TIP: *Try holding down the Shift key while dragging a datapoint diagonally across levels 1 to 63 in the View Levels settings box.*

Using the ON= key-in, you turn on a level, or levels, for specific views. Level display can also be turned off using the OF= key-in.

If you had to turn on or off each level individually it would be a tedious operation if a drawing consisted of many levels. Fortunately, you can turn on or off individual levels and groups of levels using a combination of commas and dashes. Examples follow.

ON=1,3,5   Turn on levels 1, 3, and 5 only.

ON=1-20   Turn on levels 1-20.

OF=3,6,11,22 to 40 Turn off levels 3, 6, 11, and 22 to 40.

ON=6,1,11 to 42   Turn on levels 6, 1, and 11 to 42.

In the last example, notice how you can specify your levels in any order and even give a range of levels. Once you have keyed in your levels, MicroStation prompts you to select a view. Datapoint on each view you want.

NOTE: *If you are going to be using levels a great deal, it is a good idea to generate a standard-level description. There is no greater time waster than trying to find a specific bit of information in a drawing by turning levels on and off looking for it.*

Most companies that use MicroStation establish such a standard-level list for various drawings. If this does not exist in your case, it would be wise to develop one.

Naming a Level

An alternate level-definition facility introduced with version 4 of MicroStation is the ability to assign an alphanumeric name and description to each level number. The Level Names dialog box **(Settings ➡ Level ➡ Names)** is used to define and review the level names. When selecting an active level or just displaying a level in a particular view window, you can then key in this name. For instance, if you have already set level 10 to represent exterior walls, you could set this as your active level by keying in LV=EXTWALL.

By selecting a level and a name you create a cross-reference that can be used interchangeably in the various level commands.

Saved with the design file itself, these level names are transfer-able by saving them from the File menu of the Level Names dialog box. In this way, as you develop a standard leveling scheme you can include it in your existing designs.

Changing Attributes

This discussion of color, weight, and style would not be complete without giving you some method of making changes. If you select the color red, for instance, and place a line, but realize the color should be green, you can reinsert the line with the correct color. A better way to accomplish the same result would be to modify the existing element's symbology. MicroStation provides a tool for this: *Change Element Attributes.*

Change Element Attributes

Part of the Change Attributes toolbox (**Tools ➡ Main ➡ Change Attributes**), this tool al-lows you to selectively modify an element's various attributes via options boxes and pull-downs that closely match those of the various Element pull-down menu options. Once you've cho-sen the attribute you want to change and set its value, all that remains is for you to select the element of interest and accept the change. You will also note that this tool comes with the Use Fence option.

Changing Attributes with the Element Selection Tool

You can also change the attributes of a selection set by using the Primary toolbox. The act of selecting the weight, line style, or color from this toolbox causes an immediate change in the elements of the selection set.

...And in Conclusion

You have now been exposed to the various element manipulation commands. You now know how to move about in your design with ease.

A couple of parting thoughts before the next chapter. First-time users of MicroStation tend to underuse the views and overuse some of the element manipulation commands. This is natural. The ability to copy, move, and rotate elements gives you a freedom you have never before experienced with drawing.

On the other hand, navigating about the design takes getting used to. Don't worry, as you get comfortable with MicroStation and its viewing ability you will begin to use more and more views. Before long, you will think nothing of having all eight views active and displaying totally different parts of your design. At that point you will be an old hand at MicroStation.

The next chapter is a very important one. There you will learn about additional element types, as well as how to modify your elements. Finally, we'll revisit snaps and how you use them with the tools to construct the objects of your design. See you on the other side!

2D Basics: Part 3

Learning More About MicroStation's Rich Variety of Elements and Tools

It seems the more you learn about MicroStation, the more there is to discover. As we move into the final areas of MicroStation's basic functions, the tools discussed should seem somewhat familiar. This is due to the uniform operation of most MicroStation tools. In other words, once you've mastered a certain number of these tools, the rest will be easier to comprehend, even if you have never used them.

More Elements?

Yes! In the previous chapters we covered MicroStation's basic element types. These included such favorites as Line, Circle, and Block. One very important element type was overlooked until now. Before moving on to other aspects of MicroStation, let's spend a few minutes looking at this fundamental building block: the text string.

Working with Text

"One picture is worth more than a thousand words."

—Chinese proverb

"A picture shows me at a glance what it takes dozens of pages of a book to expound."
—From Fathers and Sons, *Ivan Sergeevich Turgenev, 1818–1883*

The expressiveness of a picture is undeniable. However, it is the written word that rules the world of construction contracts. In addition to depicting your design in graphics, you need to label them with text, and describe the construction sequence in notes on your drawings.

All of the element types discussed so far have been of the geometric variety. However, a typical drawing always has a significant amount of textual information. Whether in the form of dimensions or callouts, general notes, or even the title block text, text conveys very important information. Without such text, your design would not be complete.

Fortunately, text creation within MicroStation is easy. You select the appropriate tool, type in the text, and place it. Sounds easy, doesn't it? Well, before you think it's as simple as placing a line, let's explore text a little more.

You've drawn your dream widget; now you need to label it with its name. You select the Place Text command and key in `widget` and click a datapoint. Of course, it would be nice if the text were drawn in some style other than that atrocious "computer stick figure style." It would also be nice if the text were a little larger (or smaller), and maybe even centered below the design.

You see, there are a number of factors that affect the appearance of your text. The actual text placement is rather simple. However, before you can place it, you need to know more about your text's parameters. These include:

❏ Size

❏ Style or *font*

❏ Angle (not to be confused with *italics*)

❏ Justification

All of these parameters are unique to text, with the exception of angle (this is the same as Active Angle). The standard element attributes or symbology also apply to text (weight, line style, color, and level).

 TIMEOUT: *Text is also the one element that requires you to consider the final plotted size of your drawing. It just wouldn't do to create a fabulous design and have unreadable text.*

MicroStation's text attributes are controlled by various key-ins; however, the most common method for adjusting text attributes is through—you guessed it—the Tool Settings window. However, not all parameters you may want to adjust are available there. You should also get to know the Text settings box. It is invoked from the Element menu (**Element ➡ Text**), and it gives you access to every aspect of the text element. Let's look at each of these settings and what they do to your text.

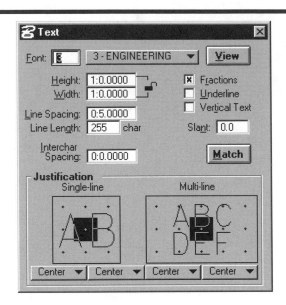

The Text settings box provides access to all text-specific attributes.

Setting Text Attributes

A Commentary About Text Styles

Unless you've been hiding under a rock somewhere, you have probably seen the variety of text styles or fonts associated with most computer systems today. Whether you work on a Macintosh, a PC, or an HP workstation, you've worked with text fonts. As part of the push to make documents more readable, fonts used on computers have been steadily improved. These days you can find thousands of different fonts available for just about every computer system.

In MicroStation you have the ability to select different styles of text as well. However, unlike a word processing program whose standard output device is a laser printer, more often than not, the final drawings generated from MicroStation are created on a plotter. Because a plotter language is geared to the creation of geometric shapes, it cannot easily create the types of fonts associated with today's typesetting equipment.

This is not to say that MicroStation doesn't give you access to such high-quality fonts as found in the rest of your office. In fact, since version 5, you can install practically any font you desire. However, unless your final output device, your plotter, supports such fonts, your final plotted results (and the time it takes to generate them) will be less than optimal.

Text Font

This does not mean you cannot generate great-looking text. On the contrary, MicroStation comes with an assortment of very good text fonts. Font 1 (name: Working), for instance, is a match to the standard Leroy text associated with technical pen lettering. Font 7 (name: Compressed) is a stylized newsprint font. There is even an italicized version of the Leroy font (Font 23). To see examples of the fonts available to you, key in SHOW FONT↵ or select the View button from the Text settings box. This activates MicroStation's Fonts settings box.

The Fonts settings box displays examples of MicroStation's installed fonts. Just scroll through the list of fonts and select one of interest. Doing this displays the font in the lower half of the settings box. To select the currently displayed font, datapoint on the example text.

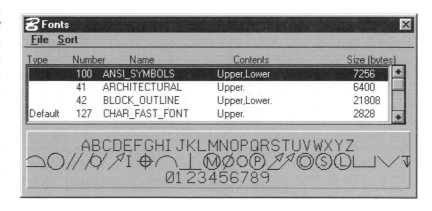

You can also set your *active font* from the Text settings box. This is done either by entering the font number in the Font field or by selecting it from the pop-up option field.

*Selecting the Font
pop-up field
presents you with a
list of all fonts
installed in
MicroStation.*

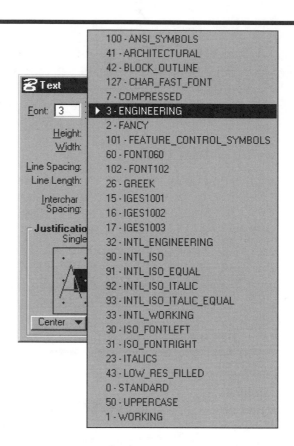

So what's a font number? This is what you can key in at the
Key-in window to tell MicroStation which font to use for your
next text placement, better known as your *active font*. For
instance, FT=1 will give you the Working font.

As mentioned earlier, you can install many third-party fonts
(fonts offered by companies other than Bentley), including Adobe
Type 1, AutoCAD .SHX fonts, and Apple/Microsoft TrueType
fonts. If you've never heard of these, don't worry about it. Font
management is the responsibility of your CAD system administrator. Just keep in mind that he or she may inform you of new and
exciting fonts that have been installed in your system.

Text Size

The foremost decision you must make when selecting your text attributes is your text *size,* which is reckoned in the Height and Width fields. You set your text's size using the Height and Width fields in the Text settings box. As with your Active Scale settings, you have the option to lock the two values to be the same, as noted by the Lock icon to the right of these fields. As with the font setting, there are three key-ins you can use instead of the Text settings box.

Text Size Key-ins	
Text height key-in	**Text attribute affected**
TH=	Height
TW=	Width
TX=	Height and width together

As mentioned earlier, text is one of the element types affected by the final plot scale of your drawing. For instance, if you are constructing a floor plan at a 1/8 scale (1 inch of plotter paper equals 8 feet, or *master units,* of the design), and you want the text height to be an eighth of an inch, your text height/width should be set to 1 master unit (1 foot in this case). The key-in would be TX=1.

Unfortunately, not all scales are that simple. The rule for setting your text height should follow this formula:

drawing text height × (design units ÷ plotter units) = TX= value

To illustrate this, try the 1/8 example:

Target text height: 1/8″, drawing scale: 1/8

1/8″ text height × (8′ design ÷ 1′ plotter) = 1′ design (TX=1)

Another:

Target text height: 3/16″, drawing scale: 1/4

3/16″ text height × (4′ design ÷ 1′ plotter) = 3/4′ design (TX=.75)

A metric example:

Target text height: 2.5mm, drawing scale: 1:50

**2.5mm text height × (50mm design units ÷ 1mm plotter units) =
125mm design (TX=125)**

It is important to note that if you change the scale of the plotted drawing, you will also need to change the size of any text you place accordingly. Text already placed will have to be scaled using the Scale command previously discussed.

Line Spacing

Line spacing refers to the amount of space used between multiple lines of text. When you place notes and other multiple text lines (such as this paragraph), you need to set the amount of space between the bottom of one line of text and the top of the next line of text. This is accomplished with the Line Spacing attribute. As a general rule of thumb, you will want to use line spacing as one half of the text height. The related key-in is LS=<value>.

Justifying Your Text

For now we will skip the other fields found on the top half of the Text settings box and concentrate on the other major text attribute: *justification*. This is the parameter that tells MicroStation where to place your text with respect to the datapoint. MicroStation supports nine different justifications.

The justification most people recognize as "normal" is Left Bottom. This means that the text's origin is at the lower left corner of the text. Left Bottom is most familiar because it matches how you normally print text on a drawing. However, there are times when you will want to use other justifications. They are:

Left Top	Center Top	Right Top
Left Center	Center Center	Right Center
Left Bottom	Center Bottom	Right Bottom

As with the other text attributes, there are key-ins for setting these justifications. The general justification key-in is ACTIVE

TXJ xx. In the preceding table, the letters emphasized are used with this key-in in place of the xx. For instance, to set your justification to Right Center, you would key in ACTIVE TXJ RC↵. For Center-Center, you would key in ACTIVE TXJ CC↵.

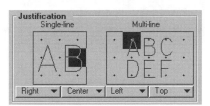

If this seems like a lot of typing, it is. This is probably one of the major uses of the Text settings box. With time you will find yourself using many of the text attribute key-ins as shortcuts; however, few people will want to key in ACTIVE TXJ... every time a justification change is in order. In addition, the visual nature of the Text settings box justification section helps you visualize how your text will appear. It should also be noted that the example text (the AB and ABC DEF) are shown in the active font (FT=). You can also select the justification from the pull-down menus located at the bottom of the justification section.

If you look at the preceding illustration of the justification section, you will see how the multi-line and the single-line justifications are set to different values. This is important to note. Failing to do so is a common first-time user mistake. The reason for this difference has to do with how you place these two different types of text. You normally place text notes from the upper left corner, whereas individual text strings may be placed in a variety of locations with different justifications.

Placing Text

Now that we've gotten through the basic text attributes (others are discussed later), the actual *Place Text* tool will seem rather straightforward in its use. When invoked, MicroStation's *Place Text* tool brings up the Text Editor window. The pop-up Text Editor window is where you enter the text you wish to place in the design file. At this point, all you do is type in your text. As you move your cursor about the view windows, you will see a dynamic version of your text. Clicking a datapoint will set the location of the text. You can continue to place the same text string elsewhere in the design by clicking at each location. When you are ready for another text string, simply revise it in the Text Editor window. To clear all of the text in the Text Editor window, hit Reset.

NOTE: *If you wish to change only some part of the text already in the Text Editor window, do not hit Reset. If you wish to start over with completely new text, hit Reset.*

The Place Text tool in action. Note how even after you've clicked the location of your text, the dynamic cursor and text are still active. This allows you to place more than one copy of the text. Hit Reset to terminate.

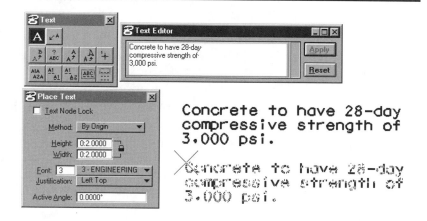

The Text Editor Window

The primary method for entering text in MicroStation is the Text Editor window. Beyond just allowing you to enter text, the Text Editor window is a simple word processor in its own right. By using the mouse and various Control key combinations, you can cut and paste text within this window. The primary functions performed with the Text Editor are:

❑ Entering text for new text placement

❑ Editing previously placed text

❑ Entering text into Enter data fields

When you select any tools associated with these functions, the Text Editor window is automatically activated. To enter your text, just type it in. Note that when you type in more text than can appear on the same line in the Text Editor, the text scrolls horizontally. Hitting the Enter key results in a multi-line text entry with a small dot placed at the end of each line of text.

An example of text being entered in the Text Editor window. Note the use of small dots at the end of some lines to indicate that this is a multi-line text entry.

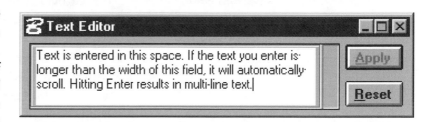

Also note the grayed Apply button in the previous illustration. This button does not "apply" to text you are placing for the first time. Hitting a datapoint applies your entered text to the design file.

Much like most other windows, the Text Editor window can also be resized by dragging its borders. There will be times when you will want to increase the size of this window (as when you are entering general notes), and other times when the window just takes up too much space (as when you are entering callouts or labels).

TIP: *The Text Editor window can be stretched to accommodate more text. This is done by dragging the edges or the corners of the Text Editor window.*

Whether entering text for the first time or editing previously placed text, there are certain functions you may want to perform on text in the Text Editor window. To facilitate these functions, the Text Editor provides limited text manipulation.

Text Editor Functions

Command Name	Description
Insertion Point	The vertical cursor indicating where keyed-in text will be inserted.
Insert/Overwrite Toggle	Normally the Insert key, this toggle controls whether text you enter overwrites the existing text or is inserted at the current text insertion point. The default condition is Insert.
Text Selection	By selecting and dragging the cursor over text in the Text window you select text for further operation. Double-clicking text will highlight the word.
Cut Text	Normally Ctrl-X or Shift-Delete, this command "cuts" the selected text and places it in the cut-and-paste buffer. The selected text is deleted.
Copy Text	Normally Ctrl-C or Ctrl-Insert, this command "copies" the selected text to the cut-and-paste buffer. The selected text is left intact.
Paste Text	Normally Ctrl-V or Shift-Insert, this command "pastes" any text previously cut or copied into the Text window at the current insertion point cursor.

The Text Placement Method

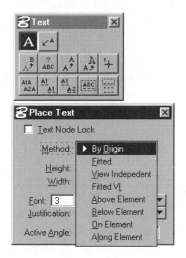

When you select the *Place Text* tool from the Text toolbox, you are presented with a variety of options in the Tool Settings window. The option called Method specifies how the *Place Text* tool will place the text you entered into your design file. The simplest method (and the default), By Origin, will place the text anywhere you click a datapoint, and as often as you click a datapoint. The following is a listing of all the methods and a short description of how they operate.

Text Placement Methods

Method	Description
By Origin	Places text at a datapoint.
Fitted	Places text between two datapoints. Text size and rotation angle are adjusted to fill the distance between the two points.
View Independent	Places text at a datapoint with View Independent attribute turned on. Most effective in 3D design files.
Fitted VI	Same as Fitted but with View Independent attribute.
Above Element	Places text the line spacing (LS=) distance *above* a selected element at the point of selection. Left/Center/Right justification applies to text orientation.

Text Placement Methods	
Method	**Description**
Below Element	Places text the line spacing (LS=) distance *below* a selected element at the point of selection. Left/Center/Right justification applies to text orientation.
On Element*	Places text on the element, cutting an opening in the element and orienting the text along the axis of the element.
Along Element*	Places text above or below (defined by second datapoint) tangent to the element selected. The text "flows" to follow the contour of the element.

* See the text that follows for further information on these methods.

 TIP: *Double-clicking at the beginning of a line highlights the entire line. Dragging a datapoint just inside the left side of the Text Editor window highlights multiple lines of text.*

In the case of the On Element method, the element you select for its insertion will be modified by the *Place Text* tool. The selected element is literally cut in half and the text is placed in the opening. Keep this in mind because from this point on the original element is *two* elements. The text will be placed by the Left/Center/Right current justification.

The Along Element method is one of the more peculiar commands in MicroStation. Each character in your text string is actually a separate string of text. This is necessary to maintain the tangency of the text to the element chosen, especially line curves and arcs. This makes the text much more difficult to change, so use this command only when you are dealing with curving elements, and use the Above or Below method when you are working with lines and linestrings.

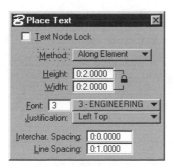

Because Along Element can place text along very convoluted elements, an additional parameter is required: *intercharacter spacing*. As a general rule, if the element along which you are placing text is more than a little curved, use a spacing of 1.5 times the text width.

Setting the Text Angle

In the last chapter you learned about the *Rotate Element* tool and its use of *active angle* (AA=<degrees of rotation>). Text placement is also affected by the active angle. For instance, setting your active angle to 45 degrees (AA=45) will cause all of your subsequent text to be rotated to 45 degrees.

Unfortunately, there is no indicator of the active angle on the Text settings box. You will know right away if the active angle is set to something you don't want because your text will appear rotated prior to actually placing it. Should this happen, just hit the Escape key, which returns temporary control of MicroStation to the Key-in window (i.e., "focus"). Once here, key in AA=0. This will return your active angle to 0 degrees.

More Text Tools

MicroStation provides additional tools for working with text. A short description of some of the commonly used tools follows.

Displaying a Text String's Attributes

The *Display Text Attributes* tool provides you with the selected text string's various attributes. These include height, width, font, and level.

Display Text Attributes > TH=0:2.0000, TW=0:2.0000, LV=1, FT=3

Match Text

Like the preceding tool, the *Match Text Attributes* tool allows you to identify previously placed text. Upon accepting the text, this text element's attributes become the active text attributes. These include the text's height, width, font, line spacing, and justification.

Change Text to Active Attributes

The complement tool to *Match Text Attributes,* the *Change Text to Active Attributes* tool will set any text you select to the current text attributes.

Copy and Increment Text

How often have you drawn an assembly or created drawing notes that use consecutive numbers? "All the time" is probably your answer. MicroStation provides a fast method of copying and incrementing such text. The *Copy and Increment Text* tool is used to select a previously placed text string, and as it creates copies of it, the last number of the string will be incremented by the tag increment value (default: 1). This means that if you have a text string such as "Note 1," the *Copy and Increment Text* tool will create a new copy of the text string: "Note 2," "Note 3," and so on.

1. Place your text string containing the numeric value you wish to increment.

2. Select the *Copy and Increment Text* tool.

3. Select the text placed in step 1.

4. Datapoint at the new text location. The number will increment by the tag increment value.

5. Datapoint again to place another copy of the text. Again, the number will increase by the tag increment value.

Edit Text

 Not to be confused with the Text Editor window, this text element tool allows you to change any text strings you've already placed in your design file. Once you've selected a string of text to be edited, the *Edit Text* tool brings up that text in the Text Editor window. You can edit and change any text in the selected string. When satisfied with the results, you hit the Apply button or Ctrl-Enter or Alt-A to update the text in your design file. If for any reason you decide the changes should not be made, hit the Reset button. The original string will reappear in the Text Editor window.

Working with Multi-lines

While not a true "primitive" element, the multi-line element is so important to many users it deserves special discussion. How many times have you found yourself drawing parallel lines throughout a design to represent some very basic structure? Obvious examples are walls in an architectural plan, pipes in a plant design, air conditioning ductwork, and traces on a printed circuit board, among many others. Suffice it to say, parallel lines are used enough to warrant their own tool. Thus, MicroStation provides the *Place Multi-line* tool.

Place Multi-line

This very powerful tool is related, in a roundabout way, to the *Place SmartLine* tool. You identify the path of your multi-line with datapoints and terminate it with a final Reset to accept it. However, instead of placing just one linestring from datapoint to datapoint, the multi-line tool places a series of parallel linestrings of a predetermined symbology at a predetermined offset from the datapoints. The amount of offset, the symbology, and the number of lines are determined by the multi-line parameters active at the time you selected the *Place Multi-line* tool.

The Place Multi-line *tool in action. Note how the current settings of the multi-line are controlled by what's been set in the Multi-lines settings box.*

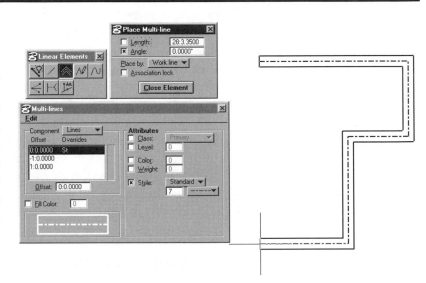

The parameters are controlled by the Multi-lines settings box (**Element ➡ Multi-lines**). From this settings box you define the number of lines (up to 16) that constitute the multi-line, the spacing between the lines, the treatment of the end caps, and the symbology of the individual lines. Let's look at these settings in detail.

The Multi-line Settings Box

When activated, the Multi-lines settings box can appear very intimidating. However, it is relatively easy to use.

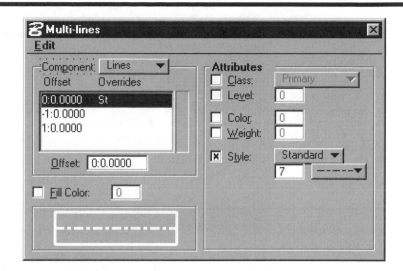

Activated from the Element pull-down menu, this settings box controls the definition of your multi-line.

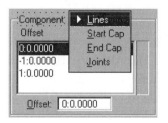

A multi-line really consists of three parts: the *lines, joints,* and two *end caps.* Each of these components has its own settings. The first step when defining your multi-line is to select the component you wish to edit. This is done via the Component pull-down field. When you select the part of the multi-line you wish to define, the appropriate options are displayed in the settings box. In most cases, you begin by defining the lines themselves.

Each time you exit and reenter MicroStation, the multi-line definitions set up in the Multi-lines settings box are lost. Later on, we'll show you how to save your definitions, but for now, assume you lose them each time you exit. This allows us to start from the same place in our discussion of multi-lines.

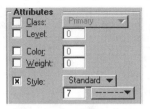

The default multi-line consists of three lines. The first line listed shows a zero offset. This means it is drawn from datapoint to datapoint. However, it is not just a plain line. If you look to the left side of the illustration under Attributes, you will find the Style option selected and at the lower right a line style of 7 (long dash/short dash) entered. The word *Standard* refers to the use of MicroStation's eight standard line codes. You can also use a custom line style.

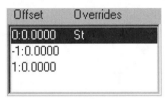

The second line definition is that of the "bottom" edge of the multi-line. In this case, the line does not pass through the datapoints. Instead, it is offset by one negative master unit. By entering a negative number, the line is drawn below the center line. The offset is entered via the Offset field in the Component section.

The third line also shows an offset of one master unit, this time a positive number. This pushes the line above the center line.

To incorporate additional lines in your multi-line definition, all you need to do is *insert* a new definition. This is done via the Edit pull-down menu on the Multi-lines settings box. The new line definition is added in front of the currently selected line definition. You then select this new definition and adjust its values to your needs. In addition to Insert, there are Delete and Duplicate commands on the Edit pull-down menu. The Delete command deletes the selected line segment. Duplicate creates a new line definition based on the one presently highlighted.

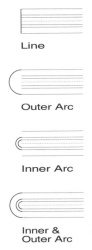

Line

Outer Arc

Inner Arc

Inner &
Outer Arc

The next two components of the multi-line deal with its beginning and ending points. Called *caps,* this multi-line component provides you with many possibilities: a perpendicular line linking all of the line segments, an arc linking the outer-most line segments, an arc linking all inner paired line segments, or any combination of these three. Again, you can override the default element attributes by selecting the appropriate checkbox under the Attributes section. Finally, you can set the angle of each end cap. For instance, if you set the Line option and the Angle to 45, the result is a beveled effect on the endpoint of your multi-line.

The final multi-line component over which you have control is the joints themselves. As you datapoint you create a "kink" in your multi-line. At this kink you can opt to show, or not to show, a perpendicular line that accentuates the joint.

Finally, the entire multi-line can be displayed with a fill. This is a solid color filling the entire area of the multi-line definition. You can set the fill color so that line definitions can be seen through the fill. Why would you want to do this? Remember, you can selectively display or hide the fill attribute. Filling an outside wall of a building will make it stand out while designing; during the plotting process you can turn it off.

Exercise: Placing Multi-lines

In this exercise you will be placing a series of multi-line elements with a variety of multi-line definitions.

> **1.** Open the MULTILIN.DGN design file. Here you will see three boxes labeled *A, B,* and *C.* Using the *Window Area* tool, zoom in on box *A.*

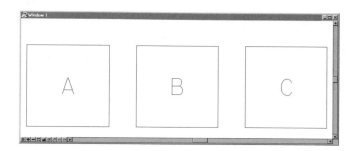

2. Next, activate the Multi-lines settings box (**Element ➡ Multi-lines**). Note the definition for a simple three-line multi-line representing an 8-inch-wide concrete block. Let's change some of its parameters.

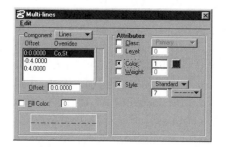

3. Selecting the -0:0.000 definition, change its color attribute to Blue (same as C0=1) by selecting the Color checkbox and either keying in the color or selecting it from the *Color Picker*. Note the change in the Overrides column (changes from St to Co,St). Also note the change in the sample.

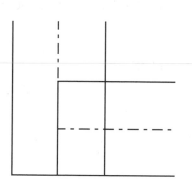

4. Let's place a multi-line. Using the *Multi-line* tool (**Tools ➡ Main ➡ Linear Elements ➡ Place Multi-line**), click a tentative point followed by a datapoint at the lower left corner of box *A*. Continue this tentative point/datapoint sequence at all four corners and hit Reset. Note the "ugly" termination of the multi-line. To avoid this you could have used the Close Element button located on the bottom of the Place Multi-line tool settings window. The result would have been a clean corner.

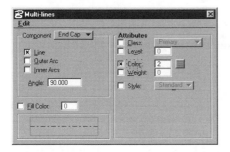

5. Next, let's change the color of the two outer lines in the Multi-lines settings box. Select the -0:4.0000 definition and set its color to Green ($CO=2$). Do the same for the 0:4.0000 definition. Note how the end caps in the sample multi-line still shows White. To change this to the same color as your outer lines, change the Component setting to Start Cap and set Color to Green. Do the same for the End Cap.

6. Zoom in on block B. Select the *Place Multi-line* tool. Before placing your multi-line, set the "Place by" field in the Tool Settings window to Minimum. Now, use the tentative-point/datapoint sequence on the lower left corner of block B to start building your wall and continue clockwise around the block. Note how the multi-line is now created to the inside of the block. In the previous part of the exercise, the multi-line was placed by the center line. Before selecting the lower left corner to conclude this wall, hit the Close Element button. This time your wall is continuous and clean.

7. Back to the Multi-lines settings box. This time, let's add an additional line to our definition. With the Component field set to Lines and the 0:4.0000 line highlighted, select the Insert command (**Edit menu ➡ Insert**). A "0:0.0000" line definition will appear just above the 0:4.0000 definition. With this definition selected, change its offset field to 0:2 and assign it a color of Red (3), and a style of Dotted (1).

8. Using the *Place Multi-line* tool, place another wall, around block C. This time, set "Place by" to Maximum. Tentative point/datapoint on the three corners and hit the Close Element button one more time. Note the new red line on the inside of the wall.

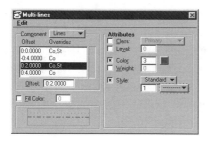

9. Perform a Fit View on view 1. Note how the three walls all appear to have slightly different sizes, although the three starting blocks were exactly the same.

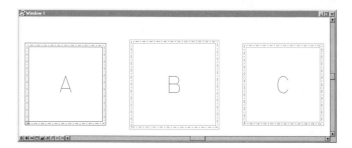

That concludes this exercise. You may want to try changing your multi-line definitions further. Try setting the Joints to On and see what happens when you place your lines. Keep this design file, as we will be using it again.

As you can see from this simple exercise, there is much to the multi-line. You can radically change the appearance of the multi-line by selecting the various options. One other powerful aspect of the multi-line is its ability to be modified for the various intersection requirements found in typical drawings. Before leaving the multi-line element, let's look at one more of its features—its ability to be modified.

Multi-line Joints

When you used the Close Element button in the previous exercise, the *Multi-line* tool did an amazing thing. It cleaned up after itself! The result was an intersection as you would expect it. No nagging leftovers. No extra work to clean it up. Just a nice, clean intersection.

Guess what? MicroStation includes other multi-line maintenance tools that ease the use of multi-lines. Found on their own toolbox (**Tools ➡ Multi-line Joints**), these tools perform some rather extensive modifications to any multi-lines you've already placed.

The secret to the multi-line element is its "modifiability." As witnessed by the number of modification tools, you can alter the appearance of the multi-line to exactly fit your needs. Such control over even complex elements as multi-lines is a particular strength of MicroStation.

You can, for instance, cut openings in a multi-line wall for doors, windows, and other components of a floorplan. Another remarkable capability is what you can do when you have two intersecting multi-lines. You can clean up these intersections in numerous ways.

Element Modification Tools

In the previous discussion, a category of tools specific to the modification of multi-lines was introduced. These tools work exclusively on the multi-line, having no effect on other element types. There are, however, more general-purpose modification tools designed to operate on most types of elements.

In the previous chapter we discussed tools that "manipulated" elements in a global manner. You could change an element's overall size using the *Scale Element* tool, mirror it, and even delete it. What you couldn't do was modify a part of an element.

Another category of tools is collectively known as *element modifiers*. These tools reside on the Main tool frame and have their own toolbox (**Tools ➡ Main ➡ Modify**). The tools located here allow you to adjust the geometry of elements you've already placed in your design file.

Modify Element

A versatile tool you will use often is *Modify Element*. This tool allows you to change most of an element's XY coordinate geometry. This means moving individual vertices on linestrings, changing the diameter of circles, moving the side of a block, and so on. Its operation depends on the type of element you select.

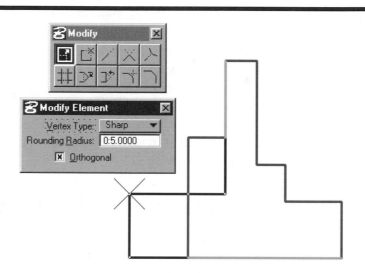

The Modify Element tool in operation.

When you select linear elements such as lines and linestrings, *Modify Element* allows you to "push" and "pull" the individual vertices associated with the element. When you select arcs, it lets you modify the endpoints, or the radius, depending on where you select the element.

Partial Delete

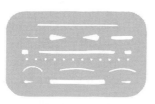

Whereas the *Modify Element* tool concentrates on shortening or stretching your selected elements, the *Partial Delete* tool chops off segments of elements with which it is used. Think of it as the eraser shield of MicroStation. Just like that little metal plate, the *Partial Delete* tool provides a much needed function: it breaks your elements into pieces.

 You have already been exposed to what this tool does. Similar to *Fence Delete* with the Clip Fence mode selected, the *Partial Delete* tool clips out a portion of an element. At least that is what appears to happen when you use this tool. In fact, what the tool really does is delete the element you have chosen and replace it with one or more new elements. These elements share some characteristics of the original element, such as the endpoints, and the radius if it was an arc or circle. Let's try it out to show what we mean.

Exercise: Partially Deleting a Line

1. Open the PARTIAL.DGN design file.

2. Select the *Partial Delete* tool from the Modify toolbox.

3. Place a datapoint about midway down the line. Note how a portion of the line "disappears" as you move your cursor along the line.

4. Datapoint toward but not past one of the endpoints. The result should be two small line segments where the original line was.

As you can see from the exercise, *Partial Delete* is very simple. If you were to investigate the resulting lines from the exercise, you would not find anything odd about them. In a manner of speaking, the original line "begat" the two new lines.

However, this is not always true. Closed elements such as circles and blocks have a problem with the *Partial Delete* tool. By its very nature, this tool creates endpoints in the resulting elements. This is contrary to the nature of the circle, which by definition does not have any endpoints.

So what happens? *Partial Delete* replaces the circle with an arc. A block is replaced by a line string, an ellipse by a partial ellipse, and so on.

Partially deleting a closed element also requires an extra step in its use. Because there are two halves to all such partial deletions—the half you want and the half you don't—you must identify the part you want *deleted*. This is done using the *from-through-to* method.

Exercise: Partially Deleting a Circle

1. With the PARTIAL.DGN still called up and the *Delete Part of Element* tool still active, datapoint anywhere along the circle.

2. The next datapoint will tell MicroStation which portion of the circle you wish removed. Datapoint the "through" location.

3. As you move your cursor, the gap in the circle will extend from the first datapoint through the second and toward your cursor. A final datapoint will complete the deletion. This time, the result is not two lines but one arc.

The result of this exercise will be an arc of the same radius as the circle. The endpoints of this new arc will correspond to the first and third datapoints you entered. The second datapoint is lost with the deleted segment of the circle. This procedure applies equally to the shape and ellipse elements.

Extending Lines

The *Extend Line* tools perform a very simple task. They "push" or "pull" a line's endpoint along the axis of the line in response to your datapoint. The difference between this command and the *Modify Element* tool discussed earlier is the rigid adherence to the *orientation* of the line.

Quite often you place lines in a design more for orientation than for length. "Striking" a line to temporarily define an edge of a design object is a common design practice. Once the planes of the object have been defined, all that remains is to clean up the various intersections and set the element attributes.

That is precisely what the *Extend Line* tools do. They allow you to concentrate on building your object geometry without worrying about whether this line touches that. *Extend Line* does this with *precision*. Later on, you will learn how to use measuring tools to verify this accuracy.

One other useful function of *Extend Line* is in finding obscure intersection points. Using some of the tangent and perpendicular snaps with the *Place Line* tool, you can define key relationships between various elements. The *Extend Line* tools let you finesse these relationships by providing those critical intersection points.

Extend Line

 The *Extend Line* tool does just that. It changes the endpoint of a line in association with your datapoint while maintaining the direction of the selected line. This means that if you select a line for extension and datapoint past its endpoint, *Extend Line* will stretch the line to its closest approach to your second datapoint. Conversely, if your second datapoint is somewhere along the length of the existing line, *Extend Line* will reduce its length to that point.

So how does MicroStation know which end to stretch? By selecting the endpoint closest to the your selection datapoint (the one you used to select the element).

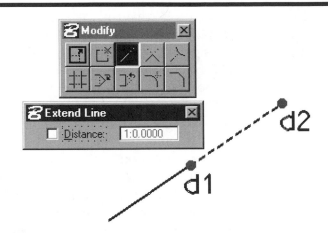

The Extend Line tool in action.

Extend Line by Key-in

When you select the only option under *Extend Line,* the Distance option, you activate a slight variation of the *Extend Line* tool, the *Extend Line by Key-in.* This tool moves the endpoint the distance entered. To extend an element, key in a positive value. A negative value results in a trimming operation.

Bringing Two Elements to an Intersection

The *Extend 2 Elements to Intersection* is one of the most useful forms of the *Extend* tool. By selecting two elements in turn, MicroStation will extend or trim them to their intersection. This applies to lines, linestrings, and arcs.

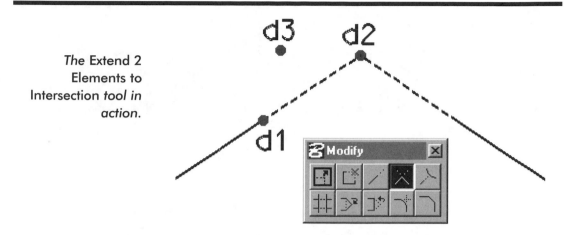

The Extend 2 Elements to Intersection *tool in action.*

As with most of the *Modify Element* tools, where you select each element is important. In the case of overlapping elements, you will want to select the element on the side of the intersection you want MicroStation to *keep*. Selecting the wrong side of the intersection will lead to the element being trimmed opposite to the side you wanted. Just remember, Undo will let you back out of this.

Extending One Element to Intersect Another

Of course, there are times when extending two elements to an intersection is overkill. For that reason, MicroStation also includes *Extend Line to Intersection*.

This tool works like half of the *Extend 2 Elements to Intersection* tool. You select the element to be modified and the element to extend to. Again, it is important to select the portion of the first element that corresponds to that you want to keep.

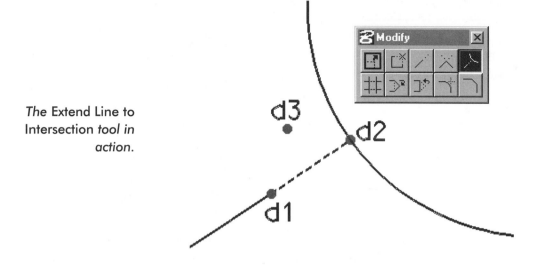

The Extend Line to Intersection *tool in action.*

One note about selecting the intersecting element. In the case of an element that has two or more possible intersection points (e.g., a circle that lies across the path of the line), you must select the element on the side you wish the intersection to be calculated to.

Trim Elements

When you have intersecting elements and wish to trim one back to its intersection with the other, you can use the *Trim Elements* tool. This tool may seem redundant, in that you can perform the same action with the *Extend Element to Intersection* tool, but the former really comes into its own, as it can dramatically cut down the number of clicks needed, when you need to trim multiple elements against a single element.

When you activate the tool, MicroStation prompts you to select the cutting edge. This is the element you wish to use as an edge to cut intersecting elements to. It next asks you to identify the element to trim. The side of the element you identify gets trimmed.

The Trim Elements tool is very efficient in clicks needed when trimming multiple elements against a single element.

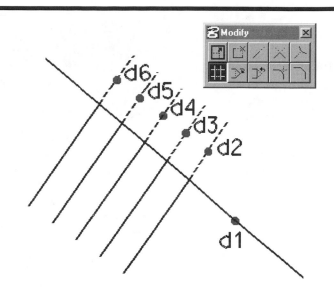

Another use for this tool is to trim a segment from an element that intersects and lies between two other elements. The trick to using the tool this way is to first highlight the cutting edges with the *Element Selection* tool, and then select the *Trim Elements* tool. Remember, you need to hold the Control key when making multiple elements a part of the selection set.

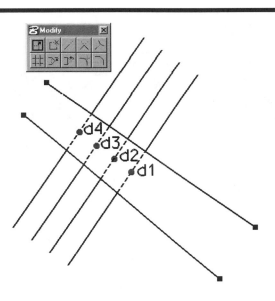

The two cutting edges were first selected with the Element Selection tool prior to invoking the Trim Elements tool.

Modifying Vertices

As we saw earlier, the *Modify Element* tool allows you to change the location of element vertices; however, it does not allow you to add or eliminate them. Fortunately, MicroStation supplies a number of tools to do just this.

Insert Vertex

The most important point to remember about *Insert Vertex* is that the segment where you select the line or linestring is the portion along which your vertex will be inserted. A second datapoint sets the location for the new vertex.

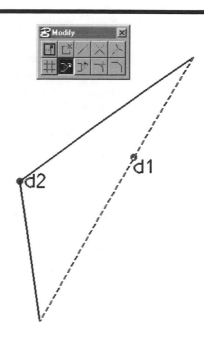

Adding a vertex to a line converts it to a linestring that has two segments.

Another important aspect of this tool is how it modifies a line element. When inserting a new vertex in a line, MicroStation converts the original line into a linestring. This is because, by definition, a line can only have two vertices: its two endpoints.

Delete Vertex

The *Delete Vertex* tool does what its name suggests: it deletes existing vertices. Selecting an element with this command will delete the vertex closest to your selection datapoint. This tool works as you would expect, except when you reach the minimum configuration of a particular element type.

A shape is defined as having at least three points—otherwise it wouldn't be a shape. When you try to delete a vertex on a three-sided shape, MicroStation will respond with the message: "Minimum Element Size." This is also true when you try to delete a vertex on a linestring having just two endpoints.

So, what happens when you delete a vertex on a line? It turns into a point. A point is nothing more than a line with both endpoints at the same location. This is one ability the linestring cannot emulate. If you accidentally reduce a line to a point, just use the *Insert Vertex* tool to "pull" it back out.

Placing Fillets

First-year drafting classes inevitably include exercises in placing fillets. The traditional method for relieving stress points on castings, the fillet is, in reality, nothing more than an arc of a given radius tangent to two lines.

Construct Circular Fillet

One unique aspect of the *Fillet* tool is its ability to modify or *truncate* the elements used to define an arc's location. This results in three possible truncation scenarios.

❑ Truncate both elements.

❑ Don't truncate either element.

❑ Truncate only the first element.

As a result, there is a Truncate pop-down option field associated with this tool. In addition, a radius is needed to set the size of the resulting fillet. Once again, *where* you select the line is critical. The fillet will face in the direction of these datapoints.

In case the command creates a fillet in an unexpected direction, don't worry. There is always the Undo function.

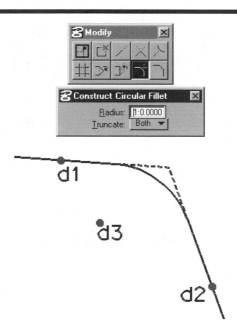

The Construct Circular Fillet tool used with the Truncate Both command is the most often used fillet operation.

One last note. The Fillet command can actually be used to place a fillet between arcs and circles, as well as lines. However, none of the commands can modify either a circle or shape. The fillet will still be placed in either case.

Construct Chamfer

Fillets have a cousin in the construction world, the *chamfer.* Consisting of a straight "face" (actually a line) placed between two intersecting lines, the chamfer is defined by providing a distance along each selected line. If these distances were equal, you would be defining a 45-degree chamfer. By selecting the amount of distance along each line, you can vary this as needed.

The Chamfer command includes two fields in which you enter the distance along each element where the chamfer begins.

Modifying Arcs

Although the *Modify Element* tool can be used to modify arcs, the way it behaves depends on where on the arc you click your datapoint. If there is a specific aspect of the arc you need to modify, you might want to use one of the three arc modification tools found on the Arcs toolbox. Each of these tools specializes in modifying a different aspect of your arc.

Arc Modifiers	
Tool Name	**Description**
Modify Arc Angle	Changes the "sweep" angle of the arc
Modify Arc Radius	Changes the radius value of the arc
Modify Arc Axis	Changes the axis of the arc

Modify Arc Angle

The Modify Arc Angle command is unquestionably the most useful of the three arc modification tools on the Arcs toolbox. By selecting either end of the target arc, you can specify the sweep of the arc. Although the *Delete Part of Element* tool can perform the same duty when it comes to shortening an existing arc, it cannot lengthen an arc's sweep.

Modify Arc Radius

The *Modify Arc Radius* tool "stretches" an arc's radius and at the same time moves the center point of the arc. This is necessary because the endpoints of the arc are maintained. The result is sort of like a soap bubble expanding.

Modify Arc Axis

The *Modify Arc Axis* tool changes an arc's usually equal minimum and maximum radii to create a partial ellipse. Again, the arc's endpoints are maintained.

Manipulate Element Revisited: The Move and Copy Parallel Tools

There are many times in the design process when you want to create an element that is parallel to an existing feature. By *parallel* we mean maintaining a set distance from the selected object at all times. This is quite different from, say, the Copy Element command, where the distance between an element and a copy is set only for the single location you've selected. Instead, the *Parallel* tools actually recalculate the location of each vertex of the parallel element and construct this new element using the selected element as a template.

Move Parallel by Distance

Although not found on the Modify toolbox (actually it is found on the Manipulate toolbox), the *Move Parallel* tool resembles the *Modify* tools more than the *Manipulate* tools.

In its no-options-selected mode, *Move Parallel* does just that. It modifies the vertices of the selected element so that they will be parallel to their original location. Most users find the two options associated with the *Move Parallel* tool more useful: the Distance and Make Copy options.

Copy Parallel by Distance

Selecting the Make Copy option in the Tool Settings window invokes the *Copy Parallel by Distance* tool. In this case, the selected element is left intact and a parallel copy is made at the distance specified by a second datapoint.

Copy Parallel maintains the parallelness of an object by adjusting the length of each element segment.

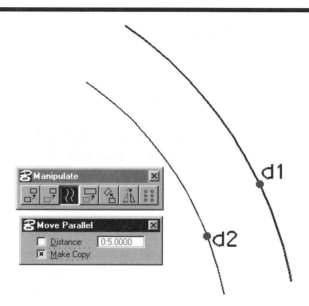

As you can see in the figure, Copy Parallel would be very useful in a great many objects. However, without the ability to specify the spacing between the copies, this command would be of limited use. Thus we have the other derivative of the Copy Parallel command, *Copy Parallel by Key-in*.

Copy Parallel by Key-in

By selecting the distance option, you can specify the exact distance between the original element and the new copy. There is one item of interest about the *Copy/Move Parallel* tools. If you copy parallel a linestring that has a relatively short segment, you will find that in the resulting copy you may not have this line segment at all. This is due to the parallel distance exceeding the length of the linestring segment.

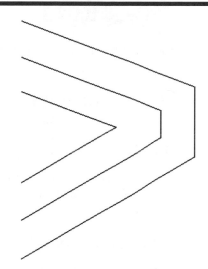

If you try to copy parallel this linestring, you will find that more and more of the middle segment will disappear the farther to the left you go.

Does Your Drawing "Measure" Up?

All of this talk about accurately placing elements would be more reassuring if you could somehow check their placement with some sort of measuring stick. Indeed, MicroStation comes equipped with a number of measurement tools for analyzing your design.

Your Measuring Tools

MicroStation's measurement tools can be found on the Main tool frame's Measure toolbox (**Tools ➡ Main ➡ Measure**). With the options associated with each measurement tool, you have many more measuring techniques than the six icons shown in the illustration.

Measure Distance

The simplest of the measurement tools, *Measure Distance,* relies on your setting the distance measuring method through the Distance pop-down field in the Tool Settings window. Each of the four Distance options provides a method for measuring your design file elements. Let's look at each one.

...Between Points

The simplest of the *Measure Distance* options, Measure Distance Between Points, prompts you for two datapoints. Upon entry of the second datapoint, the *Measure Distance Between Points* tool will return the minimum distance between them as a number in the status bar. The distance is measured as a straight line from the first datapoint to each subsequent datapoint.

The results of the Measure Distance Between Points command is displayed in the status bar.

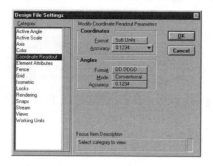

In the foregoing illustration, the units displayed are in *master units* (the 9mu) and *subunits* (the 8.6125su). This coordinate readout is set in the Coordinate Readout category of the Design File Settings dialog box (**Settings ➥ Design File**). You will get either the master units, subunits, or working units, with various levels of accuracy, depending on how you set these options.

...Along an Element

There are times when a straight line distance is not enough. You may need to know the distance along a nonlinear element—an arc, for instance. The Along Element option comes in handy here. By datapointing on an element at the point from which you wish to know the length, all subsequent datapoints on the element will result in a measured distance. This applies to arcs and circles, as well as to lines, linestrings, and chained elements.

...Perpendicular from an Element

Sort of a right-angle version of the Along an Element, the Perpendicular option prompts you for an element. Upon selecting one, a perpendicular dynamic line appears. When you datapoint, the distance from the chosen element to that point is measured along this perpendicular line.

When the Measure Perpendicular Distance from Element tool is invoked, a perpendicular dynamic line is displayed until you place your second datapoint.

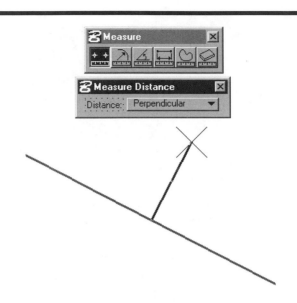

...Minimum Between

In many instances you need to know how close one object is to another. That is the purpose for this last option of the *Measure Distance* tool. When two objects are selected and accepted, the distance is given and a dynamic line is displayed, representing the closest approach between the chosen elements.

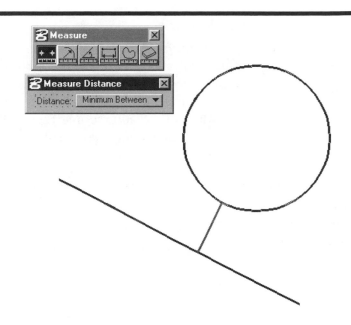

Selecting two elements results in a dynamic line displaying the minimum distance between the elements. This is helpful for knowing both the distance and where it occurs.

Measure Radius

The *Measure Radius* tool is used to find out the radius of either a circle or an arc. Selecting and accepting such an element results in the display of its radius value.

Measure Angle

The *Measure Angle* tool prompts you to select two lines (or linestring segments). It then returns the positive angle between the chosen elements. The format of the angular data is also set via the Coordinate Readout category in the Design File Settings dialog box.

Measure Area...

The *Measure Area* tool provides a number of advanced measurement options. For now, we will discuss only two of the most common area-measuring methods: *Element* and *Points.*

...Element

The *Measure Area* tool calculates the area occupied by *closed* elements. Blocks, circles, and closed complex elements are examples of closed elements. By their very definition, all of these element types enclose a finite portion of the design plane, thus allowing MicroStation to interrogate them for this data. Selecting and accepting an element results in its area and perimeter being reported in the status bar.

The Measure Area tool displays its results on the status bar.

...Points

Measure Area Points allows you to datapoint a fence-like area, and upon closure of the this fence, reports the area enclosed.

Compressing Your Design

As you add, delete, and modify elements on your video screen, MicroStation is continually updating and changing your design file. Referring back to the shopping list analogy from previous chapters, these changes consist of two distinct operations: those that modify an element *in position* within the design file, and those that add elements to the design file. The *Move* tool and all of the *Change Element Attributes* tools are examples of in-position modification tools. Copy Element and Delete Partial are both examples of commands that add elements.

Notice that nothing was said about the Delete command. With good reason: Delete is a special type of manipulation command. Whenever you delete an element from the design, you are telling MicroStation to ignore that element. It still resides in your design file, and theoretically can be resurrected through the use of the EDG utility (which is beyond the scope of this book).

Compress Design

The actual elimination of these elements occurs when you invoke a special file maintenance command: the Compress Design command (**File ➡ Compress Design**). When you invoke Compress Design, MicroStation suspends interactive operation (it won't let you work on the design file) while it goes out and physically deletes the elements marked for deletion.

Of course, as these elements are eliminated, the result is a design file with empty records. MicroStation takes care of this by moving all of the "good" elements up in the design file to *compress* these empty records out. The result is a clean design file ready for further work. An overview of this operation is shown in the following illustration.

The effect of the Compress Design command on a design file.

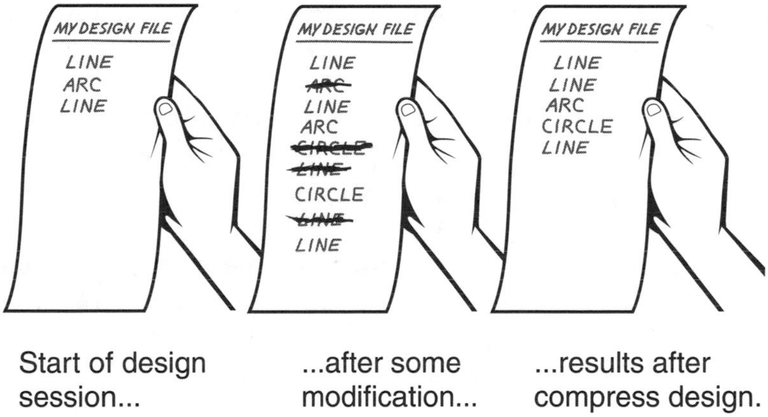

MY DESIGN FILE
LINE
ARC
LINE

MY DESIGN FILE
LINE
~~ARC~~
LINE
ARC
~~CIRCLE~~
~~LINE~~
CIRCLE
~~LINE~~
LINE

MY DESIGN FILE
LINE
LINE
ARC
CIRCLE
LINE

Start of design session...   ...after some modification...   ...results after compress design.

Compressing your simple designs won't produce a great deal of improvement in performance. However, in monster design files or after large fence deletes, the improvement is substantial. So, how often should you compress? There is no set rule for when it's best to compress, but the following note and tip offer some guidelines.

NOTE: *Once you compress, you cannot undo any operations performed prior to the compression.*

TIP: *A good habit to develop is compressing your design file just prior to exiting the design.*

Line Construction Tools

Earlier in the book you learned how to use MicroStation to create lines by datapointing and tentative pointing to other elements. There are times when the Place Line command needs a little extra help. For instance, you may need to create a line bisecting the angle between two elements. Unfortunately, there is no snap mode designed to give you this. However, there is a separate tool for performing this very task. In addition, there are other *Construction* tools for performing a variety of specialized design tasks. Many of these tasks are critical to the design process.

Construct Angle Bisector

A construction line commonly required in design work is one that divides an angle. This is accomplished using the *Construct Angle Bisector* tool (**Tools ➡ Main ➡ Linear Elements ➡ Construct Angle Bisector**). Although it does not require any type of element to provide the angle, it is commonly used with lines or arcs.

By tentative-point snapping to the endpoints or center points of elements, you provide the angle that this command then divides in half. A line is placed at this angle. The length of the line is set by an imaginary line drawn between the "horns" (i.e., the first and third datapoints) of the angle. This line defines the maximum length of the line.

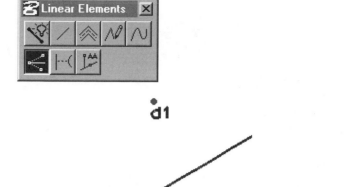

The Construct Angle Bisector *tool in action.*

Construct Minimum Distance Line

The *Construct Minimum Distance Line* tool is very useful when you are trying to establish a line perpendicular to an arc and a line. To do this manually would be a tedious job. With MicroStation you need only select the two elements in turn, and the result will be the perpendicular line.

Why is it called *construct minimum distance line* instead of, say, *construct perpendicular to two elements?* Because perpendicularity only results in the use of arcs or circles.

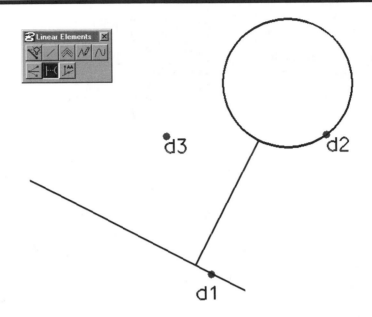

Construct Minimum Distance Line is a handy way to construct a line perpendicular to a line and an arc.

Other times, the resulting line will not be perpendicular. Thinking back to the line perpendicular to an arc, you will recall what happens when the line comes to the end of the arc. A similar thing happens here. The minimum distance between two skewed elements will not have any resemblance to the perpendicular lines seen so far, as is shown in the next illustration.

Note how the resulting line forms nothing that is tangent or perpendicular.

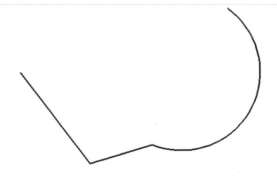

Lines with an Angle on Things

Another important drafting function performed with lines is setting various angles. Quite often you need to strike a given angle off an existing line in order to develop your object.

Using the *Place Line* tool, you could use a combination of tentative points and the DI= key-in to perform this function. This, of course, assumes you know the angle of the baseline from which you are drawing your elements. More often this angle is unknown.

Construct Line at Active Angle

When constructing a line at an angle from another element, you have two distinct methods for calculating the position and length of the constructed line. You can choose a point on the target element and have the tool create the line from this point (the From Point method). Alternately, you can choose a point in space from which the *Construct Line* tool will project the line back to the target element (the To Point method). The *Construct Line at Active Angle* tool provides a Method pull-down field for selecting one of these two methods.

...From Point

The From Point method creates the line from the point at which you selected the original element. If your active angle is set to zero, this command will give you an error message:

        Unable to construct line at 0 or 180 degrees

It will not let you proceed with the command. Entering a value in the Active Angle field will take care of this.

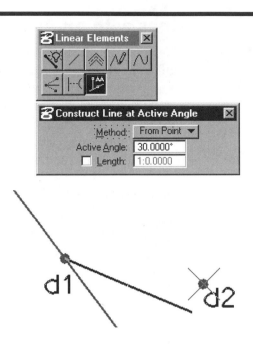

The Construct Line at Active Angle *tool used with the From Point option requires the entry of the angular information prior to selecting the target element.*

In the previous figure, the datapoint d2 is perpendicular to the line being constructed. This is how MicroStation calculates the length of the line for this command.

...To Point

The To Point method allows you to select the element from which the new angled line will appear dynamically attached to the cursor. Once satisfied with its location, you datapoint to set it. One note about both methods. If you select an active angle greater than 180 degrees, the result may not be what you expect.

Because you set which side of the line the angled line should emanate from, angles greater than 180 degrees can produce strange results. In the case of an active angle greater than 180 degrees, MicroStation subtracts 180 from the active angle and uses this in subsequent line placements.

This, combined with the fact that you can place such a line in your design file that doesn't even touch your original line, can lead to some confused results. Try placing a line with an active angle of 185 degrees. The result will usually be an enormously long line set at an angle of 5 degrees.

The Length Option

As with other tools, *Construct Line at Active Angle* can create a construction line with a fixed length. By selecting the Length option and entering a value, you force the tool to do just this.

On to the Exercises!

This concludes the basic discussion of MicroStation's construction and modification tools. You've now learned enough about Micro-Station to attempt to use these tools in a real project. In the next chapter you will learn how to use many of these tools and various snaps to construct some real-life designs.

Construction Techniques and Tools

Using MicroStation to Solve Real Design Problems

Up to now you've used MicroStation as you would a drafting table, with maybe a few bells and whistles. The strength of MicroStation, however, lies in its formidable construction tools and object manipulation techniques. In this chapter we will explore these techniques and tools in greater detail. In addition, you will have an opportunity to work through some real designs using Micro-Station's various tools.

Revisiting the Snaps Option

In a previous chapter we introduced MicroStation's Snaps feature. In describing the Snaps facility, we pointed out how powerful snaps are in helping you to place your elements accurately. This is true but incomplete. Not only are they powerful, they are invaluable. To show you how this is so, let's look at snaps once again.

Nothing Substitutes for Good Geometric Construction Technique

When you are creating your masterpiece design, you often run into situations in which "you just can't get there from here." For instance, you may have a design in which some of the dimensions are fixed but others are subject to the design process.

In the following example of a flower vase, you have two arcs obviously tangent to each other. The problem is that the only known dimensions for this object are its height, width, and the radii of its curves. The center points of both arcs are not available and must be indirectly determined.

With a few known dimensions, this vase can be created using simple geometric construction techniques.

No amount of "banging on the tools" will give you a one-stop command to magically locate these elements. Instead, you are going to have to work it out using geometric construction. Let's look at this problem in detail.

Exercise: Creating a Flower Vase

The key to creating this vase is to start from what you know and calculate the locations of those elements about which you have incomplete information. In this case, you know the heights and widths of the base and mouth, and the radii of the arcs. In addition, the vase is symmetrical, so we can work with one half of it and mirror-copy the other half. Let's do it.

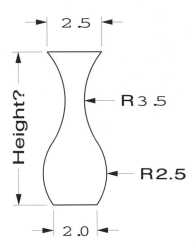

In this exercise, the flower vase presents a designer with the challenge of locating the two tangent curves.

1. Open the design file VASE.DGN. This is essentially an empty design file, so you will need to establish a starting point for this project. We suggest using the bottom center point of the vase as the origin point (X0Y0).

2. Let's draw some lines establishing the two known entities, the base and the mouth of the vase. Select the *Place Line* tool and place these two lines as shown. By now you should be able to locate these two lines with accuracy. (Hint: Use the XY= and DL= key-ins.) The results are shown in the figure at the left.

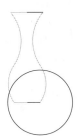

3. With these two lines established, we need to locate the center point of the bottom arc. This cannot be done directly without a lot of math. However, using a simple geometric trick, we can easily locate it. Start by selecting the *Place Circle by Center* tool. Select the Radius option and set the value to 2.5′ (the radius of the curve that forms the bottom part of the vase). Making sure the tentative point snap is set to endpoint, tentative point/datapoint on the right end of the line. The results are shown in the figure.

You have taken advantage of the fact that a circle's radius is symmetrical, meaning that any point through which the circle passes can inversely be used to locate its center point. One of the points on the circle that we have drawn is the center point for the bottom arc. What remains is to find the distance of the center point from the vase's opening. How do you do that?

Because we know that the two arcs that constitute the graceful curve of the vase are tangent, we also know that the center point of the bottom arc must lie the combined distance of the upper arc's radius and the bottom arc's radius from the vase's mouth. If you strike an arc (or circle, in this case) of this combined value from the upper right line endpoint through the previously placed arc of step 2, the intersection between these two arcs must be the center point of the bottom arc.

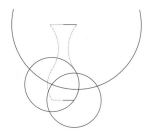

4. Set the Circle by Center Radius option value to 6.0′ (that's 2.5 + 3.5). Again, using the endpoint tentative snap, tentative point to the right end of the vase's mouth. The result should be two circles that intersect, as shown in the figure at the left.

You've now overcome the hardest part of this exercise, that of locating the base arc's center point location. Let's place the circle.

5. With the *Place Circle by Center Radius* tool active, set the Radius value to 2.5 (remember to select the Radius option). Next, we need to override the default snap (Keypoint) with the Intersection snap. Choose **Settings ➡ Snaps ➡ Intersection** and tentative point/datapoint at the leftmost inter-section of the two arcs. A circle of the desired radius should now touch the endpoint of the bottom line. This will later be trimmed into the correct arc using the *Delete Partial* tool.

If you want, you can delete the two circles you placed in step 3; they have done their job. Next, we need to locate the upper curve of the vase. Geomet-rically speaking, the upper arc is tangent to the circle placed in the previous step and passes through the line representing the mouth of the vase. If you were drawing this by hand with a compass, you would strike two arcs or circles, as we did in step 5, to locate the center point for this arc. However, with MicroStation we can simplify this with the creative use of the Tangency Snap option.

6. A *Circle* tool is used, but this time the *Place Circle by Edge* tool is needed. Select the Radius option and set its value to 3.5 (the radius of the upper arc). To tie down one end of the circle, tentative point/datapoint once on the right end of the top line (the "mouth" of the vase). A dynamic circle appears attached to this point.

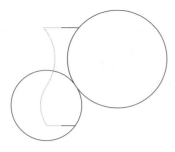

7. Before placing the circle, you will need to temporarily override the tentative point snap (the default is currently Keypoint) with the Tangent option. Select this from the Snaps submenu (**Settings ➡ Snaps ➡ Tangent**). With this selected, tentative point/datapoint to the circle we placed in step 5 on its right-hand side. See the figure to the left.

You may experience some confusion with the dynamics of the circle you are placing. This is due to the fact there are two possible solutions for a circle passing through a point and tangent to another circle. The way to control the circle is to "circle" counterclockwise closely around the line you just clicked. This will result in the circle being oriented the proper way for you to place a tentative point on it. If you aren't successful the first time, don't worry. Select Undo and try again. This may take some getting used to, but you will master it. All that remains is to trim the circles into the desired arcs and mirror-copy the entire image.

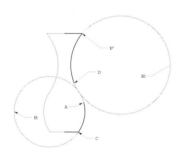

8. Select the *Partial Delete* tool (**Tools ➡ Main ➡ Modify ➡ Partial Delete**) and select the lower circle at the point labeled A (see figure). Next, datapoint on the leftmost edge of the circle at the point labeled B. The dynamics will show you a hole in the circle that follows your cursor. Finally, tentative point/datapoint to the left end of the bottom line (point C). The result will be an arc that follows the contours of your vase. Do the same to the top circle this time; however, start just to the left of the circle/circle intersection (point D) and select your second point on the right edge of the circle (point E). Finally, tentative point/datapoint on the right end of the mouth of the vase (point F).

9. Select the *Extend Elements to Intersection* tool (**Tools ➡ Main ➡ Modify ➡ Extend Elements to Intersection**), and select the two arcs near their intersection point and accept your selection.

10. Finally, select all of the elements in your half vase with the *Element Selection* tool and activate the *Mirror Element* tool (**Tools ➡ Main ➡ Manipulate ➡ Mirror**). Set the Mirror About field to Vertical and select the Make Copy option. Tentative point/data-point on the left end of the line at the top of the vase.

That's it! You have created your vase from minimal dimension information. This closely simulates what goes on in the real world. You rarely have all of the information you want to create your project. After all, isn't that why you are using the computer in the first place?

The main purpose of the previous exercise was to get you thinking about how snaps work and how to use geometric construction to find the missing pieces in your design. In addition, you indirectly created your final elements by converting construction objects (the circles) into finished elements (the arcs).

Experienced users of MicroStation use techniques such as these just demonstrated when working on their projects. Quite often, the difference between a new user and an experienced one lies not in the knowledge of more commands but in knowing how they should be applied to a design problem. With time, you will see the solution to difficult design problems as a series of such construction steps.

In the next example you will create a finished mechanical part using a variety of tools, snaps, and construction techniques.

Creating a Mechanical Part

Until now you have only seen the individual construction commands at arm's length. Now it's time to take what you have
learned and create a real design.

The following exercise creates a bracket similar to the one
shown in the next diagram. This rather simple mechanical bracket
contains an assortment of geometric problems.

The dimensions given are the only ones needed to create this
design. The rest of the dimensional data will be calculated by the
various tools, using construction techniques similar to those
introduced with the vase exercise. Due to the complexity of the
overall design, this problem is broken down into a series of
exercises. Each one concentrates on a single aspect of the design
and highlights a particular set of tools and techniques.

*Starting out.
Familiarize yourself
with the parts of the
bracket.*

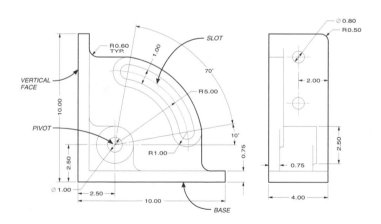

It should be noted that although you will be presented with a
specific set of tools and steps to create this object, this is not the
only method by which you can create the bracket. The purpose
of this exercise is to show you a variety of construction tech-

niques, using as many tools as possible. For this reason, repetitive use of a single technique is avoided as much as possible.

Exercise: Establishing the Drawing Origin and Placing the First Elements

1. To start, open the design file BRACKET.DGN found on the companion disk. This is an empty file, with the working units and coordinate readout set appropriate for a mechanical project. For the record, the settings are shown in the figure at the left.

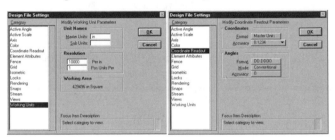

A starting point must be established. For this project, the pivot point has been chosen. This will become our X0Y0 point.

2. Activate the *Place Circle by Center* tool (**Tools ➡ Main ➡ Ellipses ➡ Place Circle by Center**), and select the Radius option and set it to .5 (half the diameter of the pivot hole). Key in XY=0,0↵ to place this circle. Don't forget to hit the Escape key to set the focus on the Key-in window before typing in the XY key-in. While we're at it, let's place the larger concentric circle at the same location. Set the radius to 1.25 and place it at the same location. (*Hint:* Use the up arrow to retrieve your previous key-in, and hit the Enter key.) You can also use the tentative point/datapoint sequence to snap to the center of the first circle.

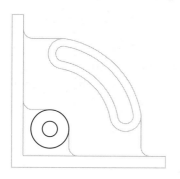

The results should be the two concentric circles shown in the figure at the left. Next, we'll create the base of the part using the *Place Line* tool. You could key in each location of the line, but where's the fun in that? Instead, we'll be using the Place Line options to establish the base.

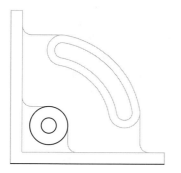

3. Activate the *Place Line* tool (**Tools ➡ Main ➡ Linear Elements ➡ Place Line**). Select the Length option and set it to 0 (the length of the base). While you're at it, select the Angle option and set it to 0. To place the line, use the key-in XY=-2.5,-2.5↵. The results are shown in the figure.

You have just placed the starting elements for your design. Continuing with the construction of the base and vertical face of the bracket, we will place elements using the *Active Angle* parameter.

Exercise: Constructing Elements by Active Angle

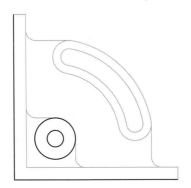

Looking at the bracket drawing, you can see that the vertical face of the bracket is the same length as the base. Let's use the *Rotate* tool to create this face.

1. Activate the *Rotate* tool (**Tools ➡ Main ➡ Manipulate ➡ Rotate**). Select the By Active Angle option and set it to 90 degrees. Also, select the Make Copy option. Datapoint on the baseline created in the previous exercise. A dynamic element will appear. To tie it down at the correct location, tentative point/datapoint at the left end of the base line. This will result in the vertical face of the bracket (see figure). Hit Reset before continuing the exercise. Next, we'll begin on the slot construction by defining the extents of the slots with two construction lines.

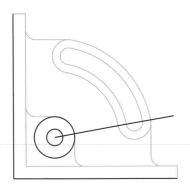

2. Activate the *Place Line* tool again. Make sure the Length option is OFF. Select the Angle option (it should still be on) and enter 10 degrees. This is the angle of the bottom of the slot (see the master diagram). The length of the line is not critical; however, its origin point is. Tentative point/datapoint to the center of the circles (as shown in the figure). Next, datapoint out far enough to define the arc distance. A point around the right end of the base is fine. We need to define the other end of the slot. We could set our angle to 80 degrees (the sum of two angles to arrive at the absolute angular data). Instead, however, let's try another tool: *Construct Line at Active Angle.*

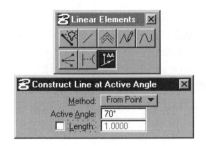

3. Activate the *Construct Line at Active Angle* tool (**Tools ➡ Main ➡ Linear Elements ➡ Construct Line at Active Angle**). Set the Method to From Point. Next, set the Active Angle option to 70, the angular length of the slot.

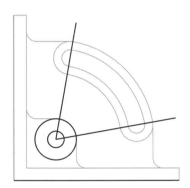

4. Next, tentative point/datapoint at the left end of the 10-degree line previously placed. A dynamic line, offset 70 degrees from this point, should appear. To complete the line, datapoint once toward the top of the bracket (the length is not critical, it is only a construction line).

You have successfully completed the first part of the bracket's design. Next, you'll define the centerline of the slot, which you will use, in turn, to define the slot itself. You will actually only place one arc, but will end up with a total of five through the use of the *Copy Parallel* tool. Let's place that first arc.

Exercise: Creating the Slot

To locate this first arc you will be using a bit of trickery. Due to the sequence of datapoints required by the *Place Arc by Radius* tool, a "workaround" will be used to establish the first arc.

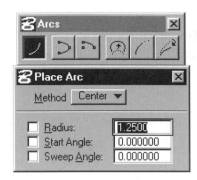

1. Activate the *Place Arc By Center* tool (**Tools ➡ Main ➡ Arcs ➡ Place Arc**) with the Center method selected in the Tool Settings window. Make sure all of the options are turned OFF. Remembering the counterclockwise rule, tentative point/datapoint on the right end of the 10-degree line. Next, tentative point/datapoint at the common vertex of the two angled lines (this is also the center point of the circles).

Before proceeding, note that the Radius option has magically turned itself ON. The radius length was derived from the first two datapoints. This length is not correct for this arc, so you'll need to change it.

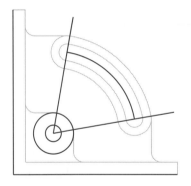

2. Before placing the third datapoint for the arc, select the Radius data field, key in 5.0, and hit Enter. The dynamic arc is now set to 5 master units. To tie down the end of the arc, tentative point/data-point on the end of the second angled construction line (the one set 70 degrees from the first). The result should be an arc of 5 units centered on the circles and terminating at the two angled lines (see figure).

The next step is to create the edges of the slot itself. This is done with the *Copy Parallel* tool.

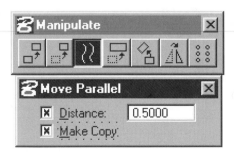

3. Activate the *Move Parallel* tool (**Tools ➡ Main ➡ Manipulate ➡ Move Parallel**). Select the Distance option and set it to 0.5. Also select the Make Copy option. Note how selecting these options changes the tool name shown in the status bar from *Move Parallel* to *Copy Parallel by Key-in*, the tool you want for the next step.

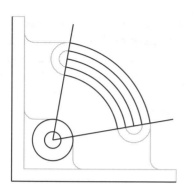

4. Datapoint on the slot's centerline arc. As you move your cursor to either side of this arc, a dynamic arc appears parallel to this arc exactly a half unit over. Datapoint twice on each side of the centerline arc to define both the inner and outer edges of the slot. This results in five arcs equally spaced (see figure). Hit Reset to release the arc.

Before finishing the slot, let's take a break and work on the base and vertical face. To do this we'll use the *Copy Parallel* tool one more time; but first, the results of this operation need a little cleaning up to be useful. This will be accomplished with the *Extend Element* tool.

Exercise: Closing the Bracket's Base

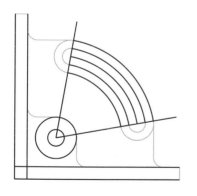

1. With the *Copy Parallel by Key-in* tool still selected, enter a new distance value of 3/4 (or 0.75). Datapoint once on the baseline and once just above it. This results in the top edge of the base. Hit Reset to release the line. Next, datapoint once on the vertical face line and once just to the right of it.

Note that the intersection of the two lines is not as it should be (see figure). This is where the *Extend* tool comes into play.

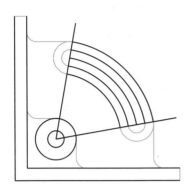

2. Activate the *Extend 2 Elements to Intersection* tool (**Tools ➡ Main ➡ Modify ➡ Extend Elements to Intersection**). There are no options to set with this tool, so datapoint once on each line to clean up their intersection and a third time to accept. You *must* datapoint on the portion of the line you wish to keep; otherwise, the results will not be what you expect.

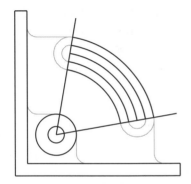

3. Before leaving the base and face, let's close up the two ends of the bracket. Use the *Place Line* tool and the Keypoint snap to place two lines on each end. Be sure to deselect the Angle Lock.

The next part of the bracket's construction is fun. You are going to construct a couple of arcs using the endpoints of the arcs you created in Exercise 4. This ensures that the rounded end of the slot is of the same uniform thickness as the rest of the slot.

Exercise: Capping Off the Slot and Creating the Shoulder of the Bracket

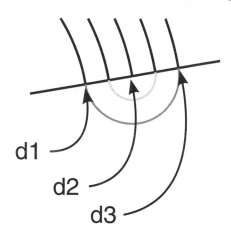

d1

d2

d3

1. Activate the *Place Arc by Center* tool again. This time, turn off all of the options. You won't need them to construct the slot's end cap arcs. The key here is the order in which you tentative point/data-point on each arc's endpoints. Repeat the sequence for the inner edge of the slot.

You could just go ahead and cap the other end of the slot using the same operation just discussed. Don't! Later we will use the *Mirror Copy* tool to do this and more. For now, let's finish the bottom half of the bracket, which leads us to the shoulders. The two lines that attach the slot and pivot to the base are collectively referred to here as the *shoulders* of the design.

At first glance, it looks as if you could place a line at AA=90 and somehow get it to be tangent with the slot's outer arc. In reality, what you are looking for is a tool that gives you a line tangent to the arc while perpendicular to the base. Although it may appear there is no such tool in MicroStation, there is a way to get the *Place Line* tool to perform this task for you. It involves the use of the snaps.

2. Activate the *Place Line* tool. Deselect all of its options. Next, select the Tangent snap (**Settings** ➡ **Snaps** ➡ **Tangent**). You may want to set this as your "permanent" snap by holding down the Control key while selecting it from the menu. Alternately, you can choose the Tangent snap from the Snap Mode button bar if you have it active (see figure), or from the snap field on the status bar.

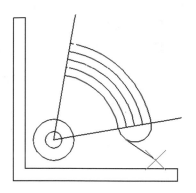

3. With the Tangent snap selected, tentative point/datapoint on the small outer arc of the slot. A dynamic line will appear, and depending on where you clicked the tentative point on the arc, it may or may not be facing the right direction. In this example, the line is definitely *not* facing the way you want. This is easy to fix: just do a "loop-de-loop" counterclockwise around the right edge of the arc.

"A LOOP-DE-LOOP?" This isn't exactly the most technical term used; however, it is the action performed to change the orientation of a tangent dynamic line. By crossing over the line's source element (the arc) and back out in the direction you want the tangent line to face, you direct MicroStation to change the orientation of the tangency.

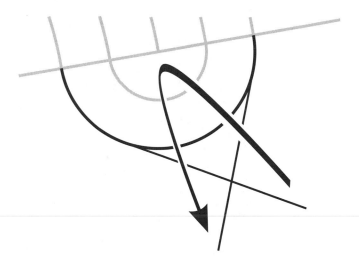

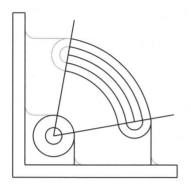

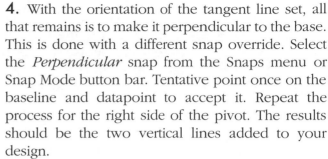

4. With the orientation of the tangent line set, all that remains is to make it perpendicular to the base. This is done with a different snap override. Select the *Perpendicular* snap from the Snaps menu or Snap Mode button bar. Tentative point once on the baseline and datapoint to accept it. Repeat the process for the right side of the pivot. The results should be the two vertical lines added to your design.

With the shoulders on half your bracket, all that remains is the creation of the fillets and the much-anticipated mirroring operation. First, the fillets.

5. Activate the *Circular Fillet* tool (**Tools ➡ Main ➡ Modify ➡ Construct Circular Fillet**). Next, set the Radius to 0.6. Finally, because the fillet to be applied modifies only one element (check the main drawing, it's true!), select the Truncate: First option.

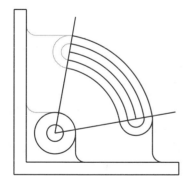

6. Because the First option has been specified, the order in which you select the elements for the fillet operation is important. Datapoint on the first shoulder line placed in step 4, followed by the baseline. Where you select the baseline will establish the direction of the resulting fillet. Datapoint on the side you wish the fillet to face (in this case, to the right of the shoulder line). Repeat for the Pivot shoulder. The result of this step is shown in the figure.

Finally, we get ready to perform the Mirror Copy operation. However, before this can be done, the axis for the mirror operation must be established. For visualization purposes, a line will be constructed to follow this axis. To do this requires the use of yet another construction tool: *Construct Angle Bisector*.

Exercise: Using Construct Bisector

Activate the *Construct Angle Bisector* tool (**Tools ➡ Main ➡ Linear Elements ➡ Construct Angle Bisector**). Set your Snap mode to Keypoint.

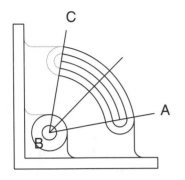

1. Tentative point/datapoint at the point labeled A in the figure. This defines one leg of the angle. Next, tentative point/datapoint at point B, the center point of the pivot. Finally, tentative point/datapoint on the end of the second line (point C). A line bisecting the angle you just described with your datapoints will appear.

With the mirror axis in place, it is time to perform the Mirror Copy operation and thus complete the design. Prior to actually mirroring the elements, you must select them.

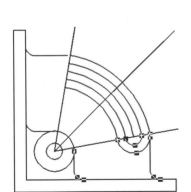

2. Activate the *Element Selection* tool (the Arrow icon). Drag a selection rectangle around the elements to be mirrored. This includes the two small arcs of the slot, the shoulders, and their fillets. If you missed one or two elements, select them now while holding down the Control key. This adds the wayward elements to the present selection set.

3. Activate the *Mirror Element* tool (**Tools ➡ Main ➡ Manipulate ➡ Mirror Element**). Select the Mirror About: Line and Make Copy option. The status bar should report the tool in use as *Mirror Element About Line (Copy)*.

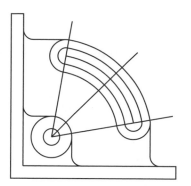

4. Tentative point/datapoint at the origin point of the bisector line created in step 2. Next, tentative point/datapoint at the opposite end of the same bisector. The result should be a copy of the selected elements in their correct location. In fact, you should see the completed design right before your eyes!

Complete!

This little exercise shows you how the various tools interact to create your finished design. With a little bit of practice, you will begin to see that there are many different combinations of tools you can use to get the same end results.

Every person will develop his or her own style of construction. Some will choose to use a lot of construction-type elements to sketch out the design, whereas others will place the elements using precision key-ins and tool options. No one way is better than another. Some tools will become your favorites, and you will avoid others. Remember to try some of those other (little-used) commands from time to time. Just think of what you might be missing!

Complex Elements

Working with Cells, Complex Shapes, Chains, and Other Sophisticated Elements

It is not unusual that while creating a drawing you will want to use a common symbol over and over. Examples of such symbols include street signs on a signing and marking plan, a NAND gate on an electrical schematic, or a North arrow on a site plan.

If you were limited to the commands you have learned so far, you would use something like a Fence Contents Copy command, or else you would copy each element of the desired symbol one at a time. This goes against the CAD mission of making your job easier and more efficient, which means, of course, that there is a facility in MicroStation for duplicating symbols.

What Is a Complex Element?

Up to this point you've been dealing with what are commonly referred to as "simple" or "primitive" element types. Another type of object used in MicroStation is the *complex element*. Consisting of a varying quantity of primitive elements, a complex element is a method by which MicroStation can describe complex geometric shapes while manipulating them as single elements. Chief among this class of elements are the *cell,* the *text node,* the *chain,* and the *shape.* In this chapter, each of these element types is discussed in detail. Let's start with the cell.

What Is a Cell?

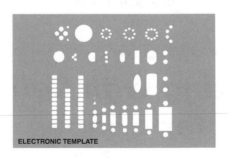

ELECTRONIC TEMPLATE

When you copy a line, you select that line and datapoint where you want the new copy to appear. If you have several lines, you use a fence to identify them, and then invoke the *Copy* tool with the Fence option selected. In either case, at the conclusion of the operation, what you have is simply more elements. There is no association of one element with another. There are times, however, when you want a group of elements to be treated as one element. What is needed is a way to associate, or fuse, fenced elements together as a single entity.

That is what MicroStation calls a "cell." A collection of simpler elements, a cell is an example of a complex element. Put simply, a cell is a name associated with a set of lines, arcs, circles, and other primitive elements that act as one object.

You manipulate a cell the same way you would any other element. However, you cannot modify individual elements of a cell. Liken it to a preprinted, adhesive-backed decal—a North arrow, for example. Working with this decal, you can move it, rotate it, copy it (using a sheet of adhesive-backed film on a photocopier), or delete it (peel it up and throw it away). Cells work in much the same way.

Cells work in much the same way as preprinted adhesive-backed symbols.

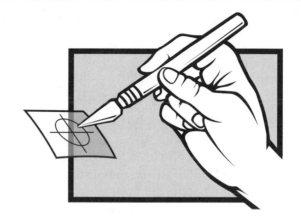

Another analogy to the cell is the drafting template. Repetitive symbols found on such templates are definite candidates for conversion to cells. If you use a symbol more than a few times in a design, you should consider making it a cell.

Some typical cells.

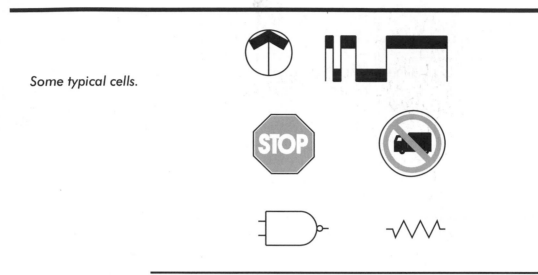

Anatomy of a Cell

A typical cell consists of more than the grouped elements. For one thing, there is the cell origin, the location within the cell definition around which the cell is drawn. A cell also has a name. Limited to six characters, this name is generally used to describe what the cell represents. For instance, a name such as VALVE will likely be used with a valve symbol. Because MicroStation limits the length of the cell name to six characters, it is difficult to get much more descriptive than DOOR or VALVE! Fortunately, when the cell is created and placed in its cell library, there is a description field of 27 characters in which you can provide a proper description of the symbol.

The Relationship of Cells and Their Libraries

Before you can use a cell, you need to create one and store its definition somewhere. MicroStation uses a special file called a *cell library* to hold these definitions. You create this library once and place your cell definitions in it one at a time. A cell library is nothing more than a special type of design file that contains one or more cell definitions. It is not unusual to find cell libraries containing literally thousands of cell definitions.

Because you use a symbol more than once, you will find yourself extracting cell definitions from a cell library and using them in your drawing more often than actually creating new cells. In many companies, the cell library is considered a corporate resource and is protected from unauthorized modification. You are generally given access to cells in a library but are not allowed to create new cells. This makes sense as a way to maintain drawing uniformity within a company or a project. Using a cell from a cell library is a straightforward process.

❏ Attach the appropriate cell library to your active design file.

❏ Identify the cell you wish to use.

❏ Place that cell.

To show you how simple it is, let's work through a brief exercise. We will be attaching a cell library to our active design file, and placing a North arrow symbol from this library.

Exercise: Placing a Cell

1. Open the CELEX01.DGN file. Prior to using any cells, you need to attach an existing cell library. One has been provided for this exercise.

2. Attach the cell library MYCELLS.CEL. For this, you need to invoke the Cells settings box (**Element ➡ Cells**). This settings box offers a File pull-down menu. Select Attach from this menu (**Cell Library ➡ File ➡ Attach…**). You are presented with the Attach Cell Library dialog box. Be sure to navigate to the directory you installed the files on, from the diskette accompanying this book, to find the cell library. As an alternative, you can directly attach the library using the key-in RC=MYCELLS.CEL

3. Next, you must identify the cell you wish to place. Again, for this you will use the Cells settings box opened in the previous step.

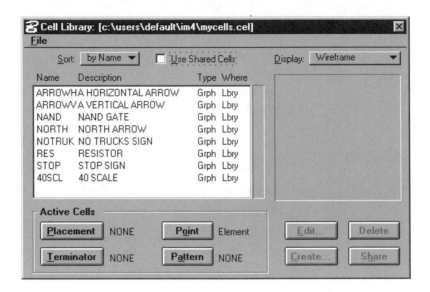

4. You should now have the Cells settings box open on your screen. Note the list of cells on the left side of this window. Select the cell named NORTH. See how MicroStation previews the cell in the Preview window. To make this your active cell, hit the Placement button. Close the settings box by double-clicking its control menu box (upper left corner), or if you are using Windows 95 or Windows NT 4.0, by clicking the "x" button (upper right corner).

5. From the Main Tool Frame, select the *Place Cell* tool. You may also invoke this command from the Cells toolbox (**Tools ➡ Main ➡ Cells**). The North arrow should appear as seen in the preview box of the Cells Settings box. Note how the origin of this cell is the end of the vertical line on the perimeter of the circle. This is defined at the time of the cell's creation.

6. Let's reorient the North symbol more toward the North-Northwest. In the Active Angle data field of the *Tool Settings* window, key in 15 degrees. Note how the North arrow changes direction in the counterclockwise direction. Datapoint once to place the North arrow.

That's all there is to placing a cell. As you can see there are other parameters that affect the appearance of the cell, in this case the active angle. You would be correct if you guessed the active scale (AS=) will also affect the placement of the active cell. This is noted by the existence of the X Scale and Y Scale fields on the Tool Settings window. In addition to selecting the active cell from the Cells setting box, you can directly enter the name of the cell via the Active Cell data field found on the Tool Settings window.

Working with the Cell Library

In the previous exercise, you told MicroStation to attach the cell library MYCELLS.CEL to your active design file. Unlike your regular design file, which you call up and work directly on, modifying the elements in it, the cell library file is only accessed by indirect means. Cells are drawn in a regular design file; then, using the *Create Cell* tool or key-in command (CC=), the cell is created in the cell library.

Cell libraries are blind affairs where you put symbols, and later call them up for use in your design. Because the cell library must exist prior to placing cells in it, you need to first create the cell library.

Creating the Cell Library

Cell library creation is accomplished from within MicroStation. Select the option New from the File menu on the Cells settings box (**Cell Library window ➡ File ➡ New**...). This brings up the Create Cell Library dialog box.

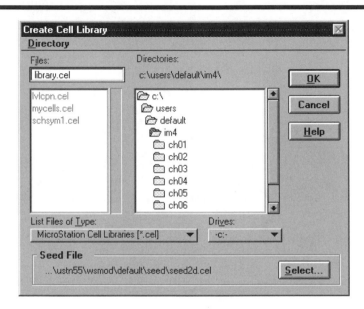

The Create Cell Library dialog box. Type in the name of your cell file. In this example, LIBRARY.CEL is used.

You do not *have* to use the .CEL extension. However, it is a good idea to conform to this standard. By using this extension, and others such as .DGN and .000, you will know at a glance what type of information is stored in the file.

With the name of the cell library entered, all that remains is for you to hit the OK button. If you were to perform a file-listing command (i.e., DIR or ls) of your folder or subdirectory, you would see the LIBRARY.CEL file. In this example, the file name LIBRARY was chosen. In reality, you would use a name that helps identify the contents of the cell file.

So, what does this library file contain? At the moment, nothing. However, as you create cells, this file will contain cell definitions, each of which may consist of hundreds of elements. Because your cell library may contain hundreds of cells, you should give some consideration to the organization of your cell library.

The Cell Library as a Post Office

A good analogy of how a cell library works is P.O. boxes found at your local post office. When you visit a post office, you can see hundreds of post office boxes lining numerous walls. What makes one unique from another is the name each box is given (usually a number). If you've visited several post offices, you know they all have the same basic numbering system for their P.O. boxes (some just have more than others). You know each box contains mail but, beyond that, you don't really know its contents. Unless you look in a specific box, assuming you have the combination code or key, you may never know what a P.O. box has in it.

Each cell library is like a post office. A cell is equivalent to an individual P.O. box. Each cell has a unique cell name; however, this uniqueness applies only within this cell library. Other cell libraries may have the same cell names, but may have totally different contents.

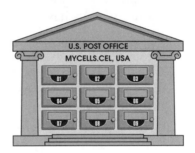

LIBRARY.CEL and MYCELLS.CEL both contain cells with the same name. The contents of each cell can be, and probably are, different.

As mentioned before, a cell name can be no longer than six characters. True, you aren't restricted to numbers only (letters work, but no spaces). To help alleviate this limitation, MicroStation provides a description field with each cell. Here you can write a longer description of the cell. In the previous example, the description field described the cell NORTH as NORTH ARROW. With an obvious symbol like this, the description doesn't seem that important. But what about with a cell named P1THL-? Be wary of this mistake commonly made by first-time MicroStation users: avoid cell libraries riddled with bizarre cell names and no descriptions. This, at best, makes their use difficult.

NOTE: *Another common mistake made by first-time users is the tendency to place all cells in one master library. At first this is not a problem. However, as you add more and more cells to it, you will find that you lose track of what the different cells represent. So, now is a good time to organize your cell library files by their function or contents. It is much better to have multiple cell libraries you attach and reattach to your designs than to have one huge central cell library. MicroStation even provides support for multiple-cell libraries via a cell library search path.*

Creating a Cell

Creating a cell is easy. While in an active design file, all you do is draw your soon-to-be cell, and, using the appropriate tools, create your new cell. The name of the design file in which you draw your cell is not critical; however, it should use the same working units as those design files with which you will be using the cell. In this way, you won't have to deal with scaling the cell later to fit it in your design. Many users build their cells in the margins of their active design and insert them directly into the attached cell library. You can do this as well; however, there are good arguments for using a separate "scratch" file for creating your cell library definitions. The steps involved in creating your cell are as follows:

❑ Draw the contents of the new cell in an active design file.

❑ Attach the appropriate cell library. (This step can occur any time up to the last step.)

❑ Identify the contents of the cell using the *Place Fence* tool or *Element Selection* tool.

❑ Define the origin point of the new cell using the *Define Origin* tool.

❑ Create the cell by defining its name, description, and type of cell.

In reality the cell creation process is not all that difficult to follow. Think of it as a Copy Element command, but instead of making the copy within your design file, you place it in the cell library.

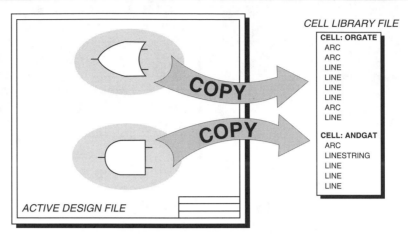

Cell creation in its most basic form is a Copy Element operation between your active design file and the cell library.

As mentioned, cells can consist of any elements supported by MicroStation. This includes all lines, arcs, circles, text, shapes, and so on. All of the weights, line styles, colors, and so on are also allowed. Because the level information about each element is also stored, it is important to make sure your elements are on their correct level before creating the cell. There is nothing more frustrating than having an errant element of a common cell appearing on the wrong level. Of course, this usually happens just as you are ready to go to final plots.

Adding Your Cell to the Cell Library

With the cell library successfully attached, you need to identify the elements of your fledgling cell. This is done with the *Place Fence* tool or the *Element Selection* tool. In either case, the purpose here is to identify only those elements you want to appear in your cell. One final item remains: setting the cell origin.

Every cell has an origin associated with it. When you placed the cell in the earlier exercise, it was pointed out how the elements of the cell fell around your cursor. That was intentional and was the result of placing the cell origin at a specific point in the elements that make up the North arrow.

Define Cell Origin

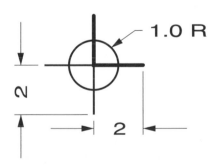 The tool for setting your cell's origin is *Define Cell Origin,* found on the Cells toolbox. This origin point is crucial. Because it is the "handle" by which you place the cell, you need to make sure the point you select for the origin is appropriate to the cell's usage.

In the next exercise you will build your first cell, a simple target symbol. This will be done by placing a circle and a couple of linestrings. By now you know how to place such elements, so we will dispense with the step-by-step approach to element placement. Instead, we will concentrate on the cell creation steps.

Exercise: Building a Cell

1. Open the CELEX01.DGN file. This file was used in the previous exercise. Attach the MYCELL.CEL library if it isn't already attached. To verify if this cell library is attached, key in RC=$. This will give you the name of the currently attached cell library.

2. Let's build the target itself. Using the dimensions shown, build the target with the *Place Circle* and *Place SmartLine* tools. The length of the linestring's legs is not critical. However, be sure to place the middle datapoint of each linestring at the centerpoint of the circle.

3. Next, place a fence around the elements just placed using the *Place Fence Block* tool. With the fence in place, you need to define the cell origin point at the center of the circle.

4. Select the *Define Cell Origin* tool from the Cells toolbox. Tentative point to the center of the circle.

5. An "O" will appear at the origin's location, notifying you that MicroStation is ready for you to store the cell. Open the Cells settings box and select the Create button. This will bring up the Create New Cell dialog box. If this button is dimmed, or inactive, you have either not placed a fence around the cell's elements or you haven't defined the cell's origin. Enter the information in the fields as shown below, and hit the Create button.

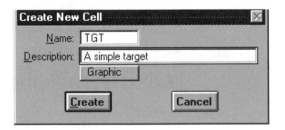

NOTE: *Alternative cell creation method: You can use the following key-in to perform the same operation.*

```
CC=TGT,A SIMPLE TARGET↵
```

6. MicroStation confirms creation of the cell by displaying a message on the status bar. You may want to use the Cells settings box (**Element ➡ Cells**) to browse through the cell library to confirm your cell's creation.

You have now created your first cell. Let's go ahead and use it in our next exercise.

Exercise: Placing the TGT Cell

1. While the Cells settings box is still displayed on your screen and the TGT cell selected, hit the Placement button. This makes your new cell the active cell. If you've already closed the Cells settings box, you can make your cell active by using the key-in AC=TGT.

2. To place your cell, select the *Place Cell* tool from the Cells toolbox. Your TGT cell should now appear on your cursor. Click a datapoint once anywhere in view window 1.

When you keyed in CC=TGT,A SIMPLE TARGET a moment ago, you actually invoked the Create Cell command. The actual name of the cell was TGT. A SIMPLE TARGET is a descriptive text label stored with the cell for listing purposes.

First-time users of MicroStation quite often make two mistakes with cell creation. First, their choice of cell names almost always include MINE or XXX or A, all of which say nothing about what the cell represents.

The second mistake is, of course, not using the description field. When you can have literally hundreds, maybe even thousands, of cells in a library, this description field is important. That is why the description field can handle up to 27 characters. So, a good habit to get into, starting now, is using intelligent cell names. Use the descriptions even if the cell's name makes its contents obvious.

When Element Keypoints Get in the Way

So far, the discussion about cells has covered only a normal cell. This type of cell remembers all aspects of your original graphic elements used to create it, including its color, line style, weight, level, and so on. In addition, all elements that constitute your cell retain their keypoint locations. This means you can snap to any part of the cell as if it were an individual element.

Sometimes the ability to snap to any element of a cell can be a real problem. For instance, when creating site plans, there is a real danger with using a cell that has more than one point to snap to. Depending on your cell, you could have serious problems with accuracy by inadvertently snapping to the wrong end of a cell.

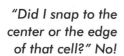

"Did I snap to the center or the edge of that cell?" No!

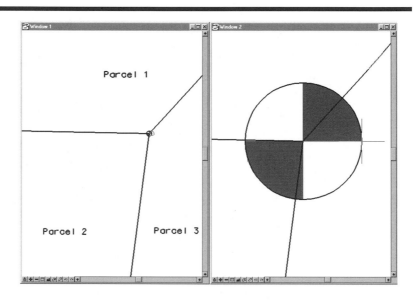

The Point Cell to the Rescue

MicroStation anticipates this possibility and provides a special type of cell called the *point cell*. It differs in two ways from a normal cell. First, a point cell takes on whatever element attributes you have active at the time you use the *Place Cell* tool. If you have CO=RED, WT=5, LV=11, your point cell will take on these attributes at the time of placement. It makes no difference what the source elements were set to when you made the cell.

The other, "minor" difference is that a point cell has only one point to snap to: the origin point of the cell (thus its name). In the previous example, if the target or monument had been a point cell, that error condition could not have occurred.

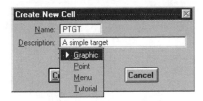

You create a point cell in almost the same way as a normal cell. You set the fence and the origin in the same way. The difference comes when you choose the *type* of cell. By setting the Type field on the Create New Cell dialog box to Point, you tell MicroStation to create a point cell. Using the CC= key-in, you append a comma and the letter P to designate the new cell as a point cell. For instance, to create the target cell as a point cell you would enter:

```
CC=TGT,A POINT CELL TARGET,P
```

The ,P informs MicroStation of your intention to make the cell a point cell. Outside this difference, the point cell acts the same as all cells being affected by the active angle, active scale, and so forth.

The Cells Settings Box in Detail

Over the past several pages we've had you bounce in and out of the Cells settings box a number of times. By now you are probably curious about this settings box and all of the things you can do with it.

One of the first features you see with this settings box is its creative use of the title bar. Instead of identifying the settings box name, you are instead presented with the name of the currently attached cell library.

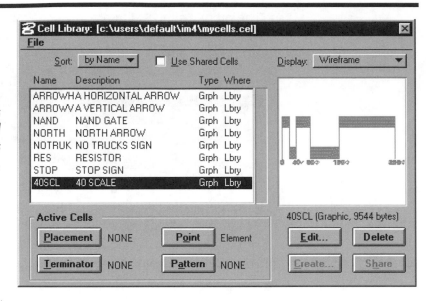

Most cell functions can be performed from the Cells settings box.

You can sort the list of cells in your cell library via the Sort field. Along with setting your current Placement cell, you can set the Point cell, the Terminator cell, and the Pattern cell via buttons in the lower left section of the settings box.

You can also perform maintenance on individual cells. Selecting the Edit button with a cell selected brings up the Edit Cell Information dialog box. Here you can change the name and the description of your cell.

Of course, there is also a Delete button for deleting a cell from your library. An Alert box pops up when you select this command, confirming whether or not you really do want to delete the chosen cell.

The Shared Cell Option

Normally, when you place a cell, you are copying all elements constituting the cell into your design file every time you place a cell. In many cases, this means there is a lot of redundant data in your design file. Recognizing this, MicroStation gives you the option to share one occurrence of a cell's elements among many occurrences. By enabling the Use Shared Cells option on the Cells settings box, you can reduce the size of your design file. In addition, when you replace a cell (use the *Replace Cell* tool) that was placed with the Shared Cell option on, all occurrences of that cell are updated.

NOTE: *There are times when you may want to turn the Shared Cell option off. When using features such as enter_data fields, text nodes, and dimension-driven cells, you must turn this option off.*

Working with Cells

Place Active Cell

You have already been exposed to this tool. Now, however, it is time to look at the options unique to the placement of cells.

The Relative Option

There are times when you want to place a cell's contents on a level other than the one on which it was originally created. This is important when using a level-assignment scheme in which each level represents some specific part of your drawing. A target cell you created earlier would be a good candidate for placing on different levels. Accomplishing this requires the use of the Relative option.

This command uses your active level (LV=) as the base for the levels of the cell's elements. The active level, in fact, becomes level 1 to the cell. This means that any elements in the cell that were on level 1 when it was created will now appear on the active level. Level 2 elements of the cell will appear on the next level higher than the active level (LV = n + 1). Level 3 elements appear on the next level (LV = n + 2), and so on.

Cells placed as Relative start with elements on level 1 of the cell being placed on the active level in the design file.

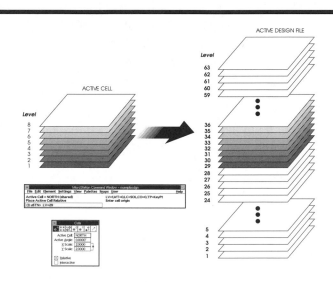

The Interactive Option

Instead of using the current active angle and active scale, this command allows you to specify the scale and angle interactively. In keeping with the abilities of the previous Place Cell commands, the Interactive command can place cells both absolutely and relative to the active level.

Cell Matrix

MicroStation includes a facility to place a rectangular matrix of cells in your design file. This can be used to establish a structure for mapping projects, or a regular spacing of components for printed circuit board design.

Similar in operation to the *Construct Array* tool described earlier in the book, this tool requires you to set the parameters for the number of rows, the number of columns, and the spacing between each. Once set, you datapoint at the lower left corner of where you want the matrix to appear.

There are a number of options you must set in order to use the Cell Matrix tool.

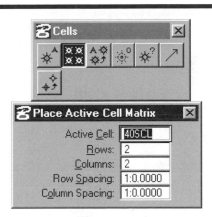

Parameters That Affect Cell Placement

In the cell exercises, you were directed to change your active scale and active angle to show how these affect your cell placement. When laying out your cell, you should keep in mind that in all likelihood the cell will be inserted at various rotations and scales. Remembering the counterclockwise rule of angles, it is a good idea to build your cells in a predominantly horizontal direction. If you do this, the active angle will affect the cell in a predictable manner.

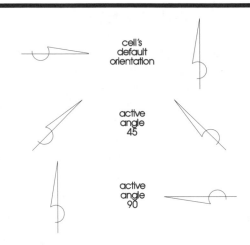

The cell on the left corresponds to the normal active angle rotation. The cell on the right could lead to some confusion.

Select Cell

More often than not, when you are editing an existing drawing, you come across a cell already placed that you would like to use elsewhere. You could use the Copy command, but if scale or angle has been used on the cell, you would have to undo these effects on the copied cell. Instead, use the *Select and Place Cell* tool.

This tool allows you to click a datapoint on an existing cell, which then becomes your active cell. *Select and Place Cell* ignores the rotation and scaling of the identified cell. Thus, only the active scale and angle affect the placement of the new cell. As with the *Place Cell* tool, there is a Relative option.

Identify Cell

So, how do you know what the name of a cell is once it has been placed in the design file a number of times? By using the *Identify Cell* tool, of course. Clicking on any cell returns its name in the status bar.

Replace Cell

One of the disadvantages of the cell library approach adopted by MicroStation is the problem of performing revisions to cells. It is easy enough to update the cell in the cell library, but what about all those cells you have already inserted into your design file?

A partial solution to this problem exists in the Replace Cell command. After selecting a cell in your design, MicroStation will replace it with the current version of that cell from your active cell library.

Reversing the Cell Creation Process

There are times when you may want to return a cell to its constituent components. For instance, you may want to create a new cell roughly based on an existing cell. Instead of recreating it from scratch, it would be easier if you could take a cell, undo its "cellness," and create your new cell from its parts. Well, you can. MicroStation supports just such a command: the *Drop Element* tool. It can be found in the Groups toolbox (**Tools ➡ Main ➡ Groups**).

Drop Complex Element: Dropping a Cell's Status

If you should accidentally delete a cell you absolutely need, there may be a way to recreate it. Earlier in this chapter it was mentioned how MicroStation copies the contents of the cell into the design file from the cell library. This means that each occurrence of a cell is complete and self-contained. If you should need to recreate a particular cell, all you need to do is reverse or drop the cell status on a previously placed cell, fence it, define the cell origin, and perform the Create Cell operation.

So what is this "drop status" operation? The full name of the tool is *Drop Complex Status*. It "explodes" a cell already placed in a design file back into its individual elements. Remember, a cell is one type of complex element among many. You can use the *Drop Element* tool, with the Complex option enabled, on any complex element, including text nodes, chains, and shapes, as well as cells.

When you drop a cell's "status," the result is similar to using the **Delete** *tool, except that the elements associated with the cell are left intact. The* Compress Design *command eliminates the deleted cell headers.*

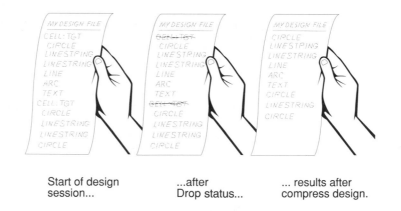

Start of design
session...

...after
Drop status...

... results after
compress design.

WARNING: *You should make sure you have dropped the cell's elements before recreating it. If you don't, it can lead to a self-nested cell, a very nasty error. The result can be a cell that, although shown in the library, may not be accessible and can lead to corrupt elements in the cell library.*

Convert Shared Cell to Unshared Cell

There are times when you want to release one instance of a cell you placed with the Use Shared option on. Maybe you are going to be replacing all but one occurrence of this cell with a new cell. To allow you to "unshare" a cell you have already placed, use the Drop Share command from the Key-in window.

By entering this command and identifying/accepting a cell you have placed, a stand-alone instance of this cell is created. Any subsequent replacing of the cell via the *Replace Cell* tool will not affect this occurrence...unless, of course, you specifically identify it with a datapoint.

Text Revisited

As mentioned earlier, there are other types of complex elements. One you may have already encountered is the *text node*. There are a number of interesting capabilities unique to working with text. Let's look at some of them, starting with the text node.

The Text Node

When we last discussed text, it was pointed out how text involves the largest number of parameters associated with any single element type. It is necessary to set the text's height, width, font, angle, line length, line spacing, and justification, in addition to all of the standard element symbologies.

A common problem found when placing text in a design file is that the text does not fit into the space provided. One solution to this is obvious: use more than one line of text. To support this simple solution, MicroStation uses the text node. Similar in concept to the cell, the text node holds together multiple lines of text as one element.

Placing Multiple Lines of Text

Although there is a separate *Place Text Node* tool, you've probably already created a few text nodes. When placing text, you hit the Enter key; MicroStation interprets this action as "Create a text node and place these multiple lines of text on it."

Sounds complicated, doesn't it? In actuality, MicroStation takes care of the entire process. The only indication that it has happened at all will be shown when you have the Display of Text Nodes turned on. Go ahead, place some multiple lines of text in a design file.

Now, go to the View Attributes settings box (**Settings ➡ View Attributes**), and select the Text Nodes option and your view. You can also key in SET NODES ON and place a datapoint in the view you want this view attribute applied to. When you update this view, you will see small cross lines and numbers at each location where you placed your multiple lines of text. These are the text nodes. Where they appear in relation to your text depends on how your text node justification has been set.

NOTE: *Although you may have inferred this from the fact that a view needs to be identified to apply the attribute to; it is worth noting that you can set the view attributes independently for each View Window.*

With Display of Text Nodes turned on, view windows show a text node symbol for multi-line text elements.

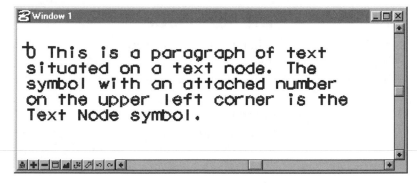

If you tried placing multiple lines of text and they appeared scrunched together, you need to set your line spacing appropriately. Remembering its use with text placement options such as Above and Below, the text node uses the line spacing to place each line of text with respect to the previous line.

The Line Spacing value (LS=) found on the Text settings box (**Element ➡ Text**) specifies the distance in working units between each line of text on a text node. If you are working with 1/8-high text (TX=1/8), and you set your line spacing to 1/8 (LS=1/8), the result will be lines of text an eighth of an inch high, spaced an eighth of an inch apart.

Graphic definition of the Line Space parameter.

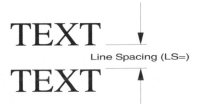

The other critical aspect of text node usage is its *justification.* This doesn't refer to whether you should use text nodes, but rather to the position the text takes up with respect to your datapoint. Text justification was covered in the earlier discussion about regular text. Text nodes have their own set of justification values. They include the nine associated with regular text and six more.

Justification for text nodes is a lot more critical than it is for regular text. The reason is simple. You have a larger set of text to deal with, and selecting the wrong justification can push this text in all the wrong directions.

The standard text node justification positions. Note the location of the text node "plus" sign in relation to its associated text.

This text is left top justified	This text is center top justified	This text is right top justified
This text is left center justified	This text is center center justified	This text is right center justified
This text is left bottom justified	This text is center bottom justified	This text is right bottom justified

Place Text Node

You can also place text nodes that contain no text. The main use of such a text node is in the creation of annotation cells.

For instance, if you are creating a callout balloon for use on your detail drawing, it would be nice to construct it in a way that allows you to set the number or letter of the callout once the drawing is nearing completion.

A text node placed in your callout balloon would allow you to do this. By selecting all of the various text parameters prior to placing the empty text node, all that remains is to place this node within your balloon graphics and create your balloon cell.

The *Place Text Node* tool does have one wrinkle. When you have identified your text node's location, you are prompted to define its angle using a second datapoint. This allows you to align the text node along an imaginary line from the text node datapoint and a second datapoint. If you wish not to do this, you can hit Reset, which instructs MicroStation to use the active angle parameter instead.

The Text Node Sequence Number

One last note on the text node. As you place each text node, you probably noticed a number associated with it. This is the text node sequence number, which is unique to each text node. The text node is a complex element similar to the cell. This number is the text node's name and is used by some advanced applications to process text both onto and off the nodes. MicroStation is delivered with one such application, the Bulk Text application. Database management applications also make extensive use of this feature.

There is a key-in parameter associated with the text node sequence number. Because the node number of the text node is automatically incremented each time you place a text node, there is an occasion when you may want to reset the value of the next node number.

For instance, you just deleted an entire series of text nodes via the *Delete Fence Contents* tool, and you want to start fresh with node number one. You can do this by keying in NN=1.

Conversely, if you want to know what the next node number will be, you can key in: NN=$. MicroStation responds with Node Num = x.

Because a text node is a complex element, you can drop it using the *Drop Complex Status* tool, just as you would a cell. The result is that each line of text becomes a separate element.

Placing Text on a Text Node

So, once you've placed a few text nodes, how do you get your text onto them? If you look at the *Place Text* tool, you will find an option called Text Node Lock. Selecting this option forces all entered text to be placed on preexisting blank text nodes. Clicking anywhere but a previously placed text node results in no action.

The Fill-in-the-Blanks Text Feature

In addition to text nodes, MicroStation provides another form of reserved text. Called *Eenter_Data Fields,* this useful feature of the text tool allows you to set aside individual characters for future updating. In addition, MicroStation includes tools specifically designed for maintaining your enter data fields.

When would you use enter_data fields? How about part numbers on drawings? How about section callouts? How about specification numbers? Any time you have an important string of text of a fixed format (for example, Part Number 360XXXX-001), an enter_data field may be just the ticket.

Enter data fields can be included in cells and updated once they've been placed in a drawing. As with the text node, the Shared Cells option must be turned off prior to placing these cells.

Creating Enter_Data Fields

Creating an Enter_data field is easy. Using the normal *Place Text* tool, all you have to do is enter an underscore (_) character at each location at which you want to reserve a character. When you type in a string of underscores, you create a single, fixed-length enter_data field. A string of text can have any number of enter_data fields in it. For instance, all of the following are legitimate enter_data fields:

❑ Pursuant to Section __ of the Environmental Impact Law, no toxic gases greater than ___ PPB will be allowed.

❑ Refer to design guideline 123__-__ for more information.

❑ Date: __/__/__

❑ Part Number: 471____-__-00__

In each case, the text string contains more than one enter_data field. Each of these enter_data fields is treated as an individual by the following enter_data field tools. Keep this in mind, as it can sometimes be more tedious to fill out multiple enter_data fields than to key in repetitive data. However, the use of prefixes and suffixes with enter_data fields ensures conformance to a part numbering standard, one of the more error-prone aspects of the design process.

So, after placing these strings, how do you fill them in? By using one of two tools: *Fill in Single Enter_Data Field* or *Auto Fill in Enter_Data Fields*.

Fill in Single Enter_Data Field

The *Fill in Single Enter_Data Field* tool allows you to select each enter_data field in turn and fill in the missing text. This tool works a little differently than other text placement tools in that you first select the enter_data field, *then* enter the text. If you enter text that is longer than will fit in the enter data field, the text will be truncated.

This truncation is an important characteristic of the enter data field. Unlike the text node, which allows you to place a text string of any length on it, the enter_data field is fixed in length. This difference may affect your decision as to which of these two element types to use.

Enter_Data Field Justifications

We've discussed what happens when you type in more text than will fit in the chosen enter_data fields. But what happens if you enter text that is shorter than the enter_data field? With the default enter_data field, your text will be left-justified in the field, and spaces will be added to the end of it. There are times, however, when you want to set the justification of the enter_data field to something other than left-justified. To do this requires the use of the JUSTIFY key-in:

❑ JUSTIFY LEFT
❑ JUSTIFY RIGHT
❑ JUSTIFY CENTER

One word about center justification: Because the enter_data field is fixed in length and size, center justification may not always give you the results you want. If you try to put a text string with an even number of characters into an odd-numbered enter_data field with center justification, MicroStation will offset the text by one character. The same is true with odd-numbered text strings in even-numbered enter_data fields.

Auto Fill in Enter_Data Fields

A neat labor-saving command is the *Auto Fill in Enter_Data Fields*. By selecting a specific view, MicroStation will highlight each empty enter_data field in turn, at which time you key in the text.

The order of highlight is the order in which the enter_data fields were placed in the design file. This tool skips any enter_data field that already contains characters.

Copy Enter_Data Field

If you have an enter_data field already filled out and want to transfer this data to another enter_data field, MicroStation provides the *Copy Enter_Data Field* tool. By selecting the first enter_data field that contains the text you wish to copy, you can select any number of other fields. MicroStation will copy this text into the selected enter_data fields one by one.

NOTE: *If you use the* Fill in Single Enter_Data Field *or* Copy Enter_Data Field *tool and select a previously filled-in field, the text you key in will replace the text already there. Only one string can reside in an enter data field at a time.*

Copy and Increment Enter_Data Field

This tool is related to the *Copy and Increment Text* tool previously introduced. In this case, you select the source data field with a datapoint and identify subsequent fields into which you want the source data field's text to be incremented and inserted. As with the other data field tools, any data in the target data field will be overwritten by the incremented data.

Viewing Enter_Data Fields

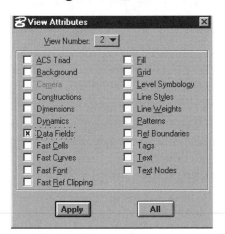

You can make the underscore character associated with the enter_data field invisible. This is done by using the key-in SET ED ON/OFF, or by setting the Data Fields option to off in the View Attributes settings window.

This is an important consideration, because enter_data fields *may* plot on your pen plotter. Depending on your plotter's configuration, you may be able to override the plotting of these fields; however, it's a good habit to be aware of their disposition prior to plotting.

An Exercise in Cells and Text

To show how cells and text work hand-in-hand, a demonstration is in order. When an electrical engineer creates a schematic diagram of a circuit, he or she often uses the same symbol over and over. Owing to the repetitive nature of these symbols, a cell library is an ideal way to manipulate and update them. Additionally, in most instances the gates that constitute the circuit have fixed text values associated with each occurrence. For this reason, the use of enter_data fields is ideal. So, without further ado…

Exercise: Cells and Text

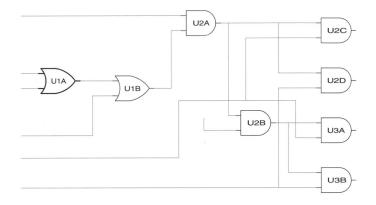

1. Open the SCHEM.DGN design file. Once you have this file active, you will need to create a cell library for your electronic symbols. Use the Create Cell Library (**Command Window ➡ File ➡ Cell ➡ New**) to create the cell library ELESYM.CEL.

2. Setting your grid to .05 (GU=.05) and your grid reference to 2 (GR=2), turn on your grid lock. Using the *Place Arc* and *Place Linestring* tools, create the ORGATE symbol as shown. Make sure to keep the input lines (left side of the symbol) on the reference grid (the large tics).

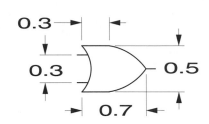

3. Most gate symbols include a text designator unique to each symbol occurrence. To provide for this, we'll use a blank enter_data field. Select the *Place Text* tool and enter four underscore characters. Place the text in the center of the symbol.

4. Place a fence around the symbol using the *Place Fence* tool. Next, select the *Define Cell Origin* tool to set the cell's origin.

5. Next, store the cell in the cell library using the CC= key-in:

CC=ORGATE,A TWO INPUT OR GATE↵

6. Next, repeat the construction process for the ANDGAT symbol shown next to step 7. Use the same lower-left input pin as the new cell's origin. Make sure to place an enter_data field in the center as with the previous cell. Use the key-in:

CC=ANDGAT, A TWO INPUT AND GATE↵

to create the cell. (Don't forget to use the *Fence* and *Define Origin* tools.) Once you've created your two cells, delete the elements you used to create them (*Place Fence/Delete Fence*).

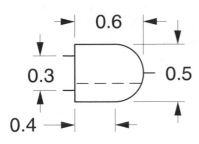

7. Activate the Cells settings box (**Element ➡ Cells**). Select the ORGATE cell and hit the Placement button. The name next to the Placement button should now read ORGATE.

8. Using the figure at the start of this exercise as a guide, place two copies of the ORGATE using the *Place Cell* tool. Then select the ANDGAT cell, and again using the same figure as a guide, place six copies of the cell. Interconnect the cells using the *Place SmartLine* tool. Make sure your grid lock is on during this phase of the work.

9. Next, let's fill in the enter_data fields. Activate the *Fill in Single Enter_Data Field* tool from the Text toolbox. The selected enter_data field should be highlighted with a rectangle. Enter the text associated with the gate in the Text Editor window.

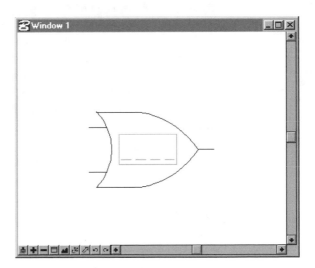

10. With the schematic fitted to your view (the *Fit View* icon on the view's border), select the *Auto Fill in Enter_Data Fields* tool and select your view. Each empty enter_data field should be highlighted in turn as you enter the appropriate text associated with its symbol.

If, when placing your cells in the design file, you did not see the enter_data fields displayed, chances are you had the Use Shared Cells option turned on. Unfortunately, MicroStation cannot give you enter_data fields (or text nodes) within cells with this option turned on. Just set the Shared Cells option to Off and repeat the cell placement, or use the Drop Share command.

More Complex Elements

So far, you have been introduced to two complex element types. In the case of the *cell* you had to complete a certain number of commands in order to create and use your final cell. When you place a cell in your design file, there is little you can do to its individual elements. You can, of course, change the overall size and attributes of the cell, but you cannot change a single vertex of any of its elements.

There are times, however, when you may want to modify vertices of a complex element. Take a road centerline, for instance. On a traditional hand-drawn plan, this centerline is treated as one object. However, in CAD the centerline consists of discrete lines and arcs. There must be a way to relate these individual elements as one while still allowing the design process to be carried out. After all, isn't the purpose of CAD to assist the user in the design process?

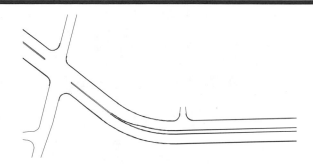

A road centerline is an excellent example of where you would use a complex chain.

Fortunately, MicroStation provides just such an element type. Called the *complex chain* and its close cousin, the *complex shape,* these elements allow the user to take a series of connected elements and link them together. Vertices of the individual elements are modifiable. Even additional vertices are allowed. In fact, all of the element modification tools work on these complex element types as if they were simple lines and arcs.

"Why would I want to do that?" you ask. Imagine drawing a centerline of a road and, with one command, creating the two edges of pavement complete with tangencies along the arcs. If you've created that centerline as a complex chain, you would be able to use the *Copy Parallel* tool in just that way. *That* is what the complex chain does for you. Long-time users of MicroStation rely on this feature and use it to their advantage.

The Complex Chain Versus the Complex Shape

The main difference between the complex chain and complex shape is *closure.* With a chain you naturally have two endpoints to the element. A chain is considered an *open* element. On the other hand, the complex shape is *closed,* meaning it starts and ends at the same XY location. As a result, a shape encompasses a fixed area of the design plane that in turn can be measured using the *Measure Area* tool. Quite often, a complex shape is created in a design for no other reason than to compute an enclosed area.

Chains and shapes really come into their own later when you begin working with 3D designs. The concept of area is very important when dealing with 3D design.

The Groups Toolbox

The tools for creating complex chains and shapes come packaged together on their own toolbox named Groups. Available from the Main tool frame, this toolbox contains three important tools for the creation of these elements.

Create Complex Chain

Used to link previously created elements into a single complex chain, this tool has two distinctly different operating modes. With the manual method, you identify each element you want in your new chain with datapoints. A final datapoint in space (meaning not on any element) accepts the creation of the chain, at which point MicroStation creates the chain.

TIP: *It is always a good idea to hit Reset after the acceptance datapoint.*

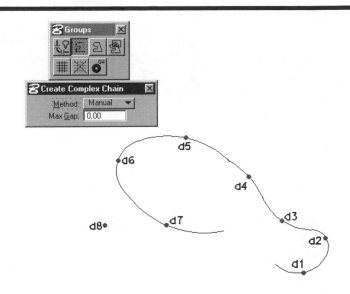

Creating a chain is simply a case of selecting the elements to make up the target shape with a series of datapoints. In this example, the manual method is being demonstrated.

The automatic method, on the other hand, uses your first element selection as the starting point for a search for additional elements that touch. In other words, you identify an element in your proposed chain, and MicroStation will, it is hoped, find all of the associated elements for the chain.

Fortunately, this process does require your approval for each element added. MicroStation highlights each element it finds and, if it is the right one, you datapoint to accept it. In case you meet a "fork in the road," you can hit Reset to deselect an element, and MicroStation will look for the next element sharing the same location.

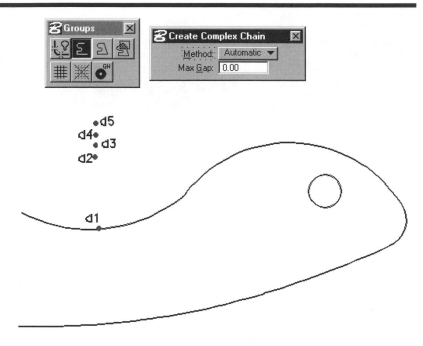

In this example, the Automatic option for creating a complex chain has been selected. Once the starting segment of a series of arcs is selected with a datapoint, the Create Complex Chain tool highlights the next segment and waits for a datapoint to move to the next one.

Of course, for the automatic process to work, the elements must share common endpoints, right? Not necessarily. As an option to the automatic method, you can select the air gap between the end of one element and how far MicroStation will search for the next element. By default, this value is small enough to be treated as zero. However, you can change this value and span short distances.

Create Complex Shape

The procedure for creating a shape is almost the same as that for creating a chain, with one major exception. When you want to close the shape, you can place your final datapoint on the element with which you started your shape, or just datapoint once in space. MicroStation will then provide closure for this shape.

As with Chain, you can set the method to Automatic and have MicroStation make the selection of elements. This tool is smart enough to know when it has closed upon itself, so no further action needs to be taken by you to close the shape.

You may have noticed how the *Complex Shape* tool provides options for setting the area attributes of the new shape. This is consistent with Complex Shape's newly acquired area characteristic. As with polygons and circles, you can set the fill color and type by selecting the appropriate settings.

Create Region...

One of the more powerful tools for creating a complex shape, Create Region *actually performs Boolean operations with existing elements to generate a new shape.*

The *Create Region* tool enhances the search-and-create function of *Create Shape Automatic*. Instead of limiting the creation of a complex shape to using existing linear elements, *Create Region* computes a new shape from the relationship of two or more elements. In other words, you can take two overlapping polygons and create a shape consisting of that area where the two shapes overlap. Or you can create a shape by subtracting one polygon from another. In fact, there are four possible methods for creating a region (i.e., a complex shape) from two or more closed shapes.

... From Element Intersection

Selecting the Intersection method allows you to select two or more closed shapes from which the *Create Region* tool will compute the exact area these elements co-occupy (thus the term *intersect*) and create an appropriate complex shape of this region. Selecting the first two elements will display the computed intersection. A third datapoint accepts this shape. If this third datapoint falls on yet another element, the computed shape will incorporate this element as well.

... From Element Union

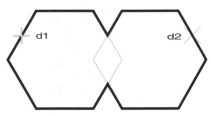

The complement of the intersection, the Union method computes a complex shape by computing the perimeter around both elements. If the two elements you select do not touch, no action is taken. As with the Intersection method, you can continue to add elements to the new complex shape.

... From Element Difference

If Intersection computes the overlapping area and Union computes the combined area, the Difference method should subtract one area from the other. That is precisely what Difference does. The first datapoint selects the source element, the second datapoint the element whose area is to be subtracted.

... From Area Enclosing Point (Flood)

The only method that does not require closed shapes, the Flood option is also one of the more interesting operations performed by MicroStation. By striking lines, arcs, or any element supported by MicroStation that encloses an area of the design file, the *Create Region from Area Enclosing Point* tool will calculate the complex shape that matches this enclosed area. This has real design potential. Now you don't have to be concerned with cleaning up the intersections of your linework. Instead, the judicious use of this tool can speed things up.

Using the Flood option, a single datapoint within a closed region can clean up the construction linework, as shown.

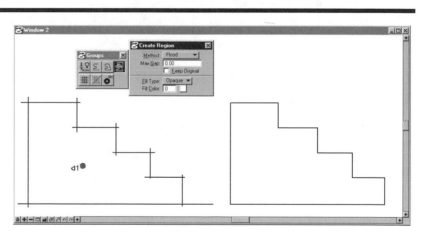

Keep Original Option

One important option associated with the *Create Region* tool is Keep Original. When this option is not set (the default), Micro-Station deletes the elements used to create the new complex element. This may or may not be your intention. Selecting this option ensures the continued existence of your original design elements.

You may wish to turn the Keep Original option off when using the Flood method. In this way you create your objects and clean up at the same time. If you inadvertently "flood" an area, just use the Undo command (**Edit ➡ Undo**) to return your elements.

The Create Region Tool

You use the *Create Region* tool to create a series of complex shapes based on the relationship of various elements. The various elements you will use in the following exercise are provided in the REGION.DGN design file. From these you will create the shapes shown.

Exercise: Using the Create Region Tool

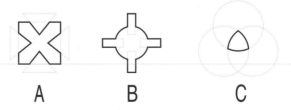

In this exercise, you will be placing a series of multi-line elements with a variety of multi-line definitions.

1. Open the REGION.DGN design file. Here you will see three sets of elements labeled *A, B,* and *C*. Using the *Window Area* tool, zoom in on element set *A*.

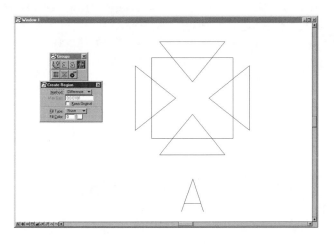

2. Activate the *Create Region* tool (**Tools ➡ Main ➡ Groups**) and set Method to Difference. Make sure the Keep Original option is OFF.

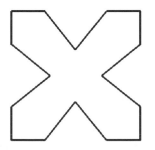

3. Select the square shape in the middle with your first datapoint. Next, select each of the four triangles that intrude on the square. Place a final datapoint and Reset in space to accept the shape. Note how the "square" now has four triangular indentations.

4. Scroll your view to element set *B*. (You can use the scroll bars, or the **VI=B** key-in with a datapoint on your view as a shortcut.) In this example, we'll be combining these shapes to generate the desired symbol.

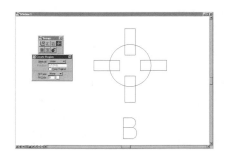

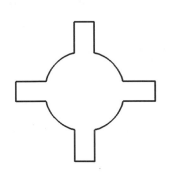

5. With the *Create Region* tool active, set Method to Union. Next, select each shape, starting with the circle. A final datapoint in space will accept the action. Note how the overall shape is the combination of all of the elements you selected.

6. Scroll your view to element set *C* (you can use the ∨I=C key-in with a datapoint on your view as a shortcut). In this example, you'll be creating a shape of the intersection of these three circles.

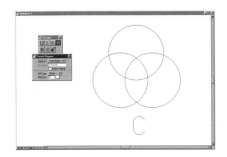

7. Set the *Create Region* method to Intersection. Next, click on each circle in turn and place a final datapoint away from any elements and Reset. You should be left with a small region in which all three circles intersect. Another, more efficient, way to create the same result is to use the Flood method. To try it, select Undo from the Edit menu and with the Flood method selected, click a datapoint within the small region where all three circles intersect. The *Create Region* tool will trace this space and wait for a final datapoint to accept the change. Go ahead and click a datapoint. By setting the appropriate option and selecting the elements in the right order, you can create some rather complex shapes without much effort.

The Composite Curve

Before leaving the world of complex chains and shapes, we need to look at one more tool: *Place Composite Curve*. Not found on the Groups toolbox, but every bit a complex chain/shape tool, *Place Composite Curve* does not require existing elements in order to generate a chain or shape. Instead, it provides options to create such an element on the fly via a number of options. Found on the Curves toolbox, this is a powerful tool you will find many uses for.

Place Composite Curve

By definition, a complex chain can consist of a variety of element types. A tool designed to create such a chain should, in turn, support the creation of such elements, and *Place Composite Curve* does just that. Providing an array of options, this tool allows you to adjust the type and parameters of each element created as part of the Composite Curve construction. Selecting the tool from the Curves toolbox (**Tools ➡ Curves**) presents these options to you.

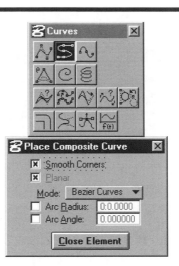

The Composite Curve *tool can be found on the Curves toolbox. The Mode field controls the type of element currently under construction.*

The most important option found here is the Mode field. By selecting the appropriate element type from this field, the *Place Composite Curve* tool presents you with this element as you click your way across the design plane.

...Mode: Line Segments

The simplest of the modes, Line Segments results in a linestring being generated as you datapoint.

...Mode: Arcs by Edge

If, during your placement of line segments, you wish to transition into an arc, this is one of two options that allows you to do just that. With the Smooth Corners selected (the default), this transition will also remain tangent to the last line segment. This is extremely useful, especially in design situations for which such transitions are critical. (Pipes and road alignments immediately come to mind.) You can also control the resulting arc's radius and even its sweep (arc angle) by selecting the appropriate options. This, again, is an important consideration when working with known pipe sizes and minimum bends.

...Mode: Arcs by Center

Similar to the previous option, the Arcs by Center option gives you the ability to set the centerpoint of the arc while maintaining tangency with your previously created linework. Being able to set the radius and angle is especially helpful with known construction details such as cul-de-sacs and the like.

...Mode: Bezier Curves

An element type not yet discussed, the Bezier curve (i.e., B-spline) is a sophisticated, mathematically generated, freeform curve used extensively in design situations for which absolute curve definition is needed (e.g., aerodynamics, mold design, and boat design). This element type is discussed in greater detail in the 3D chapter.

The Smooth Corners Option

As just mentioned, this option controls whether arcs created with this tool will maintain tangency with the previous element segment. Turning it off results in a sharp corner at the point of transition from one element to another. There are times when you may want such a transition, thus this option.

Close Element

The *Composite Curve* tool can create either a chain or a shape. This button selects which of the two element types you want. By hitting the Close Element button, you create a shape. The element under construction is immediately created, with a final segment placed between your last datapoint and the beginning point. Regardless of which mode you've selected, the final segment will be a line.

 NOTE: *The* Place SmartLine *tool discussed in Chapter 4 also creates chains and shapes. However, it is more geared to creating linestrings and lines combined with circular arcs with the ability to automatically generate fillets and chamfers than to composite curves that maintain tangency.*

Grouping Elements

Element "Groups"

A complex chain or shape, though consisting of a variety of primitive elements types, requires that all elements share a continuous set of endpoints. There are times, however, when you may want to group a set of design elements that do not share common endpoints. True, you could create a cell and manipulate your elements as a single group; however, this precludes modification of individual elements.

Recognizing this, MicroStation comes equipped with yet another group facility called *graphic groups*. Whereas cells or complex chains and shapes always behave as a group (unless you *drop* them), graphic groups can act as a group or as individual elements, depending on whether or not you have the graphic group lock enabled. In other words, with graphic groups, you control whether these elements are treated as one element or as individuals.

The Graphic Group

A sort of tag system, the graphic group is an informal collection of elements for common operations. For instance, the steel plate with its holes and text may need to be copied a number of times and then modified. By first creating a graphic group of the elements that constitute the plate, you can quickly and easily copy this group using the *Copy Element* tool, provided you have turned on the Graphic Group Lock.

The graphic group allows you to modify any member of the group using the appropriate modify command. In fact, you can drop individual elements from the graphic group if they are no longer needed. You can also add elements to the individual graphic group as necessary. The key concept of the graphic group is *flexibility*.

Creating a Graphic Group

Because you can turn on or off the graphic group effect at will, the individual elements of each group will act as separate elements until you need them to work as a whole. The tools for creating and dropping graphic groups can be found on the Groups toolbox.

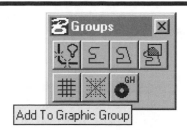

Add to Graphic Group

 So, how do you activate this feature? By selecting the *Add to Graphic Group* tool and selecting your first element.

The *Add to Graphic Group* tool will first check to see if the element you have selected belongs to a graphic group. If it does, you will be prompted to select the next element to add to the existing group. If the element is not a member of a group, a new group will be created. There can be up to 65,536 graphic groups in a design file.

Once your graphic group is started, you select each element in turn to add to the group. Selecting each new element also accepts the last element in the group. This is important. Many first-time users of the Graphic Group command will find that the last element they chose did not end up in the group. This is because the last element was highlighted but not accepted. Remember to datapoint one last time to accept this element.

The Graphic Group Lock

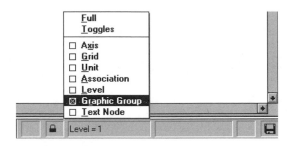

Once you have a graphic group, you control it using the Graphic Group Lock. There are three different ways to toggle this lock. One method is to activate the Locks settings box (**Settings ➡ Locks ➡ Full** or **Toggles**) and select the Graphic Group option. Another way is to key in LOCK GGROUP at the Key-in window. Yet another way is to click the Lock icon on the status bar for the locks pop-up menu.

With the Graphic Group Lock on, all standard element manipulation commands act on the *entire graphic group.* When you select an element for, say, copying, and it is a member of a graphic group, instead of telling you it is a line or arc, MicroStation will inform you that you have selected a graphic group on the status bar.

It is important to read your status bar when working with graphic groups. You can unintentionally alter your design if Graphic Group Lock is on and you meant to manipulate only a single element.

 WARNING: *Always read your prompts when dealing with graphic groups. You can destroy your design without knowing it when elements in a graphic group are out of view. When you select an element for manipulation, the only indication that something might be amiss is the* (GG) *following a description of the highlighted element type on the status bar.*

Graphic Group is a powerful command. In fact, MicroStation uses it in many areas when dealing with complicated construction commands. Examples include dimensions, patterning, and the already-mentioned Text Along elements.

Drop from Graphic Group

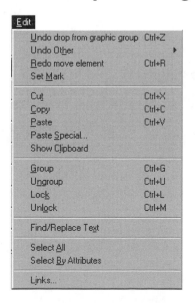 Part of the flexibility of the graphic group is the ease with which you can drop an element from it. You can also drop the entire group, thus releasing all elements from it. This is done with the *Drop from Graphic Group* tool.

The effect of this tool depends on the condition of the Graphic Group Lock. If it is on, and you select an element in a graphic group, you will be prompted to drop the *entire* group. If the Graphic Group Lock is off, the single element is released.

The Select Element Tool Revisited

By now you have probably seen the Group and Ungroup commands found under the Edit pull-down menu. Not to be confused with the graphic group tools just discussed, these two commands work in conjunction with the *Select Element* tool to create yet another type of element association, the *orphan cell*.

The Group and Ungroup Commands

With the introduction of the *Element Selection* tool, a new type of element association is possible. By selecting a number of elements using the element selection arrow and selecting the Group command from the Edit pull-down menu, you in essence create a cell. However, unlike the normal cell, the actual elements you select become the cell. *Orphan* refers to the fact that you created this cell without the benefit of a cell library. Macintosh owners will be familiar with this function, as it is found in many Macintosh programs.

As the Group command's complement, Ungroup does just as you would expect. It breaks apart a previously grouped set of elements.

Locking Elements

While on the subject of working with the *Element Selection* tool, there are two interesting commands to be mentioned: Lock and Unlock. These are located under the Group and Ungroup options on the Edit menu. There are times when working with complex drawings that you wish you could lock a set of elements in place where they are "out of harm's way." When you select an element and lock it, no element modification or manipulation command will work on it.

For instance, let's say you have a complex drawing and wish to globally delete a large area. However, in the middle of the "destruction" area there is a set of elements you wish to save. By first selecting the elements with the *Element Selection* tool, followed by the Lock command (**Edit ➡ Lock**), you can proceed with the mass destruction with no worries. The Unlock command (**Edit ➡ Unlock**) reverses the effect of the Lock command and releases the elements for general manipulation and, yes, destruction.

Conclusion

By now you have realized that MicroStation really does provide you with more than one way to perform your tasks. Using the tools and techniques just described, there is very little that you cannot draw and manipulate quickly, and in the exact manner you want. Many of these features may seem redundant in operation; however, when you start using them on a daily basis, you will find there are times when cells are appropriate, other times when creating a complex shape is the right thing to do, and yet other times when a combination does what you want. Experimenting with these various options and experience will help you work out their place in your design.

PART TWO

2

CREATING A FINISHED DESIGN

Reference Files

Bringing the Work Group Together

In this day and age it is rare to see one person create a design from start to finish, totally unassisted by other individuals. Instead, most designs, whether a new hospital or a microelectronic gadget, involve teams of skilled people, each responsible for a specific portion of the overall design.

For instance, you may very well have architectural, structural, mechanical, and process designers working simultaneously on a project. In such an environment, the need to share information and communicate it as soon as something changes, especially as it might affect others, is crucial to keeping the project on track.

Using Reference Files

To support this teamwork approach to design, MicroStation provides specific tools to assist communication and improve the dissemination of important design data. This is done with the Reference File facility built into MicroStation.

Simply put, MicroStation can "look in on" another designer's drawing file, even while that designer may be currently working on that file. If you are a member of a design team linked by a network, this ability to "look over the shoulder" of the other person provides an entirely new level of communication. Let's look at an example of what this means.

Sharing Files in a Workgroup

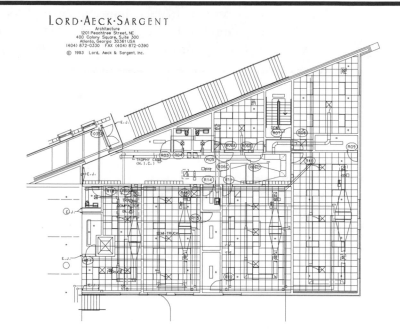

An example of an architect and engineer sharing information. (Courtesy of Lord Aeck Sargent.)

Suppose you are a structural engineer charged with creating a rebar plan. Using the reference file capability of MicroStation, you call up your design and attach the architectural plan to it. By using this architectural reference file as a background to your design, you can quickly pull off the information needed to get started with your design process.

Aha!, you say. You can do the same thing by starting with a copy of the original design file and putting all of your rebar information on one level.

Not so fast! Suppose the architect in the next cubicle/office/building/state/country (pick one; all are possible), the one who is responsible for the architectural plan, has a last-minute change to wall locations in the design. If you had copied the architectural plan into your design, you would be required to edit your drawing to reflect this change. On the other hand, if you were using the reference file capability of MicroStation, a simple reference file update would immediately show the change on your screen. In fact, in some cases (depending on the system configuration), these changes may be immediately apparent *without any direct intervention by either you or the architect.*

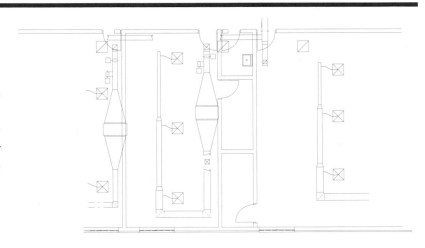

Note the change in the reference file (the floor plan layout) is immediately apparent in the active design file.

This immediate feedback has many benefits. First, it cuts down on the number of reworks of duplicate information required because of design changes, and obviates the inherent ripple effect through all parts of the design process. Second, it cuts down on the duplication of effort required with traditional drafting and CAD. If the wall is in the right place in the original architectural plan, why duplicate it in your plan? Just use it as is.

MicroStation even provides a method for modifying the appearance of the other files when it comes time to plot your design.

Sheet File from a Model File

From the beginning, this book has stressed the importance of creating your designs at full scale. However, when it comes time to annotate the final design, the plot scale you will use to create paper plots determines the size of text and symbols you place in the design file. Thus, if you were to decide to change the plot scale after all text and annotation symbols were in place, you would have to change their size throughout the design file.

If, on the other hand, you were to create your model in one design file and your individual drawing sheets containing all annotation in another, you could then attach the design model to your sheets at the appropriate scale and place your callouts, notes, and other detailing information in the drawing sheet file with consistent parameters (e.g., text size, patterning, spacing, and scale). Let's look at another scenario in which you would use the reference file system in the design process.

Multiple Models from a Main Model

When you design a road, you may produce literally hundreds of drawings with multiple drawing scales. Because a road design can be a large and time-consuming project, it is most often supported by a staff of engineers, designers, and detailers. As the engineers create the road design, the designers and detailers are given the task of drawing up the individual drawing sheets to meet specific standards.

All of the drawings have one thing in common—the stretch of road being designed. Using the reference file approach, drawing sheets would reference the main road model in sections appropriate to the final drawing scale (1:20, 1:50, 1:200, and so on).

By aligning the sheets along the road's main axis, you can generate uniform, detailed drawings and still maintain the modeling approach no matter which way the road curves. Sometimes design changes make subtle shifts in the overall alignment of the road. With traditional hand drawings, such a subtle change is difficult to incorporate across every sheet without tight quality control. Conversely, by changing the road in the CAD model, you can find out immediately what the effect will be on the individual drawing sheets and their numerous details.

An example of how a reference file can "travel" along a road.

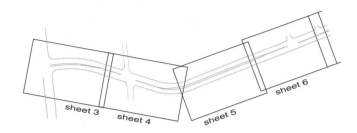

Extending the Design Plane for Large Areas

No matter how capable a CAD package is, there comes a time when you must break up a drawing into more manageable parts. When you do this, you must deal with those features that cross from one drawing into another. In most cases, this is not a critical junction. In an architectural design, for instance, you can plan logical breaking points that minimize such crossovers.

Mapping, on the other hand, deals with many features crossing from drawing to drawing. Physical land features cannot be controlled in the sense of designed layout. In such cases, the mapping professional must deal with matchlines and closely scrutinize those elements that cross between adjacent drawings. In addition, some sort of spatial check must be possible to guarantee that the maps match the real world.

This is where MicroStation comes into its own. By allowing you to connect several separate design files to your active design file, adjacent linework is available for immediate reference and identification. In addition, a master gridwork of monuments, carefully laid out, can provide a useful framework upon which to calibrate the individual map sheets.

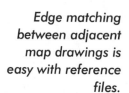

Edge matching between adjacent map drawings is easy with reference files.

No matter how large your design plane is, there will come a time when you exceed it. Because mapping involves large areas and tight dimensional control, you are always running the risk of falling off the edge, so to speak.

However, with proper project planning, you can use the reference file capability of MicroStation to extend this design plane. Because MicroStation allows you to move a reference file's point of origin with respect to the active design file, you can maintain a "traveling canvas" of design files.

The Capabilities of Reference Files

The previous discussion about the various scenarios may have stimulated some thoughts about how reference files can be used in your operation. With this in mind, let's take a detailed look at how MicroStation's reference file system works.

In its most basic form, a reference file facility is nothing more than a way to display the contents of another design file on top of (or under) your active design file. You can have numerous reference files attached (up to 255). Each reference file can be rotated, scaled, clipped, and moved with respect to your active design file. You can do all of this without affecting the actual contents of the reference file itself.

Once you have attached a reference file to your active design, you can use any of the *Copy* tools to copy selected elements of the reference file into your design file. Of course, this defeats one of the advantages of the reference file concept. However, there are many times when you will need to do this. You can also restrict the ability to copy on a reference file-by-reference file basis.

Another important aspect of the reference file is its "snapability." When enabled, the snap feature of the reference file facility allows you to use the tentative point snap functions with elements in the reference file. In this way, you can use the reference file as a starting point for your active design.

Even more important, you can set the reference file to be viewable only—no interaction allowed. This keeps you from accidentally copying elements from the reference file into your active design file. Even the fence copy tool will not work on a reference file whose elements are not "located." This restriction is not available with normal elements in a design file, unless, of course, you've locked them using the Lock command (**Edit ➡ Lock**) on elements in a selection set.

Also of special note: there is nothing to stop you from attaching a design file to itself. Why would you do this? By scaling and clipping the self-referenced file, you can highlight an area of the main design and add text, arrows, dimensions, and so on to better illustrate the object of interest. As you make changes to the main design, this "live" detail is also updated.

A design file referenced to itself is an excellent way to detail a small section of a design without duplicating linework.

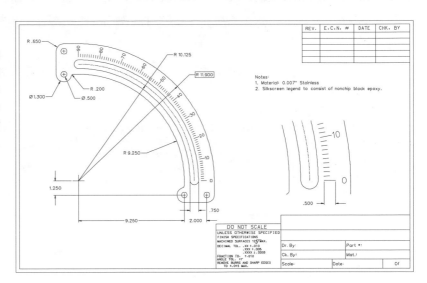

The Reference File Tools

Before we go into detail about attaching a reference file, let's look at these reference file facilities.

A Quick Tour of the Reference File Settings Box

As the starting point for many of the reference file functions, the settings box is the primary tool for working with reference files. From here you can perform every reference file command on any of the attached reference files. The settings box is also where you get the current status of each reference file. Organized by reference file, each operation you perform from here requires you to select first a reference file and then the command. This is different from most MicroStation tools and commands, which prompt you to select the element or object to be worked on.

The Reference File settings box is the primary point of contact with your reference files. Here you set the various parameters associated with each reference file attachment.

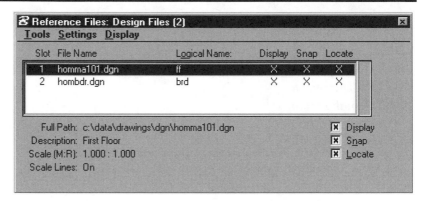

As you select a reference file entry in the settings box, specific details about the entry are revealed. Information on where the reference file is located, its current settings, and its description are provided. To change any of these aspects of your reference file requires the use of a *Reference File* tool or command.

These commands are available from the Reference File settings box under the Tools, Settings, and Display pull-down menus. The Tools pull-down includes these commands:

Reference File Tools Pull-down Menu	
Command name	**Description**
Attach	Attach a new reference file
Detach	Deactivate a previously attached reference file
Detach All	Deactivate all previously attached reference files
Reload	Update the reference file image stored in the computer's memory

Move	Reposition the reference file with respect to your active design file
Scale	Change the working unit to working unit ratio between the reference file and active design file
Rotate	Change the angle at which the reference file is displayed
Mirror Horizontal	Mirror the display of the reference file about the horizontal axis
Mirror Vertical	Mirror the display of the reference file about the vertical axis
Clip Boundary	Clip the area within a fence to display from a reference file
Clip Mask	Clip the area within a fence to hide from a reference file
Clip Mask Delete	Delete the clipping mask for a reference file
Clip Front	Clip the reference file's display on the front of the Z axis (3D only)
Clip Back	Clip the reference file's display on the back of the Z axis (3D only)

As you can see, there are quite a few commands associated with reference files. There are also a number of settings associated with each reference file attachment. These are controlled by the commands found under the Settings pull-down menu.

Reference File Settings Pull-down Menu

Command name	Description
Attachment	Modifies settings of previously attached reference files (includes Display).
Levels	Controls the display of reference file levels in each view.
Level Symbology	Controls the level symbology settings associated with each reference file.

Update Sequence   Invokes the Update Sequence dialog box that allows you to change the sequence in which MicroStation displays attached raster and design files.

Finally, the Display pull-down menu in the Reference Files settings box lets you control the type of reference file you wish to manipulate.

Reference File Display Pull-down Menu	
Command name	**Description**
Design	Enables controls in the settings box for manipulating reference design files.
Raster	Enables controls in the settings box for manipulating raster reference files.

The list of commands on the Reference Files settings box menu (see previous tables) is for controlling design files attached as references to a design file you may be working on. When you select the Raster option under the Display menu, the menu options slightly change to reflect the manipulation of raster reference files, a feature new to MicroStation 95.

Feel free to select the Raster menu option under Display and wade through the menus to see how they change. As you will notice, the terminology used is very similar to that for reference design files. You should have little trouble understanding what the menu options mean.

The Reference File Tool Palette

 All of the commands found under the Tools pull-down menu are also available from the Reference File toolbox (**Tools** ➡ **Reference Files**). However, most first-time users will find the settings box version of these tools a little easier to follow. As you become proficient in their use, don't hesitate to use the toolbox version of each command.

The Reference File Tools

Let's look at the tools used to manipulate and control the operation of your reference design files. The following discussion specifically deals with design files attached as a reference.

Attach Reference File

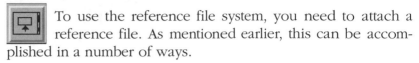 To use the reference file system, you need to attach a reference file. As mentioned earlier, this can be accomplished in a number of ways.

❑ From the Reference File settings box invoked from the Micro-Station main menu (**File ➡ Reference**).

❑ From the Reference Files toolbox (**Tools ➡ Reference Files**).

❑ Key-in the REFERENCE ATTACH command (RF=) via the Key-in Window.

All three of these methods for attaching a reference file perform the exact same functions. When you select the *Attach Reference File* tool, you are presented with the Attach Reference File dialog box (which resembles the Open Design File dialog box). Here you must identify the file you wish to attach as your reference file. Once selected, a second dialog box is presented in which you specify key information about the soon-to-be-attached reference file.

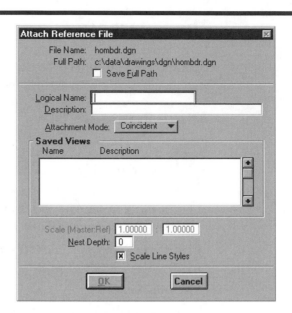

The Attach Reference File dialog box associated with the Attach Reference tool. Here you define key information about the new reference file.

Although you need not enter any information in this dialog box to create an attachment, unless the selected file is already attached as a reference, it is a good idea to fill in the fields provided.

Reference File Dialog Box Fields

Field label	Description
Save Full Path	This checkbox, when enabled, saves the directory path prefix with the reference file name in the design file.
Logical name	The shorthand name by which you can identify the reference file.
Description	A short description of the attached reference file.
Attachment Mode	Coincident (matching the design plane of active design file) or Saved View (attach using parameters defined in view).
Saved Views	Used to select a specific saved view (SV=).

Scale (Master:Ref)	The ratio of MU to MU between the active design file and the reference file.
Nest Depth	The depth of reference file nesting.
Scale Line Styles	This checkbox, when enabled, scales for display the custom line styles in the reference file using the Scale (Master:Ref) value.

Logical names are usually short, consisting of one or two characters by which you can quickly identify the reference file. Many users standardize these names by function: R1 for reference file 1, D1 for DTM file 1, and so on. In this way they know which reference files are used for which elements in the drawing.

This standardization can be extended to other disciplines; for example, adjacent map sheets can be referred to by their relationship to the active design file (i.e., N, NE, E, SE, and so on).

Use Those Descriptions!

The description part of the Attach Reference command is an informational field displayed when performing a directory of the design files attached. This field is often overlooked by even long-time users of MicroStation. This is unfortunate because it is an important way to communicate your intention with the reference file, and other details that are not obvious. At the very least, it should be used to define the relationship of the logical name to the design file (e.g., B = BASELINE).

The Coincident attachment mode means the design plane of the reference file matches your design file exactly. The absolute X and Y coordinates of the two files are precisely the same unless the two files are using different working units. MicroStation does not pay attention to the working units. Instead, it uses the positional units—the 2^{32} number, or 4.2 billion points—for alignment. In other words, the two files' design planes are precisely aligned with no offset.

If, on the other hand, you want to attach the reference file at a scale or with part of it clipped, you can key in a named view you previously created in the reference file using the $SV=$ (save view) key-in. This view defines how much of the reference file you wish to see in your active design file. If you have such a view, and MicroStation finds it, the next question is, at what *scale* do you want it attached?

Unlike the scales you have used so far, the scale factor this time consists of setting a ratio between the master units of the active design file and the master units of the reference file. This relationship is always master unit to master unit, regardless of the subunits or the positional unit values.

This is one of the most important aspects of the reference file system. As mentioned earlier, text and symbols must be defined based on the scale of the final plotted drawing. To make matters worse, the traditional scales, such as 1/8, compare different working units to plotter units (1 inch versus 8 feet of design file, or 1/96 scale). Using the reference file scale system, you can relate a drawing sheet done in inches in your active design file with a design model done in feet without having to deal with the feet-to-inches conversion.

Detach Reference File

 This command is self-explanatory. Selecting this command from the Tools pull-down menu brings up an alert box for confirmation of the operation. The *Toolbox* version requires you to identify the unwanted reference file by clicking on an element within that file or by keying in its logical name.

> **WARNING:** *This is an irreversible command. Once you have identified the reference file, you lose all of the clipping, movement, and scalar information you have painstakingly generated, and there is no undo. If you aren't sure of the effect of detachment, you should first turn the reference file display off and look over (and even plot) your design.*

Reload Reference File

As mentioned earlier, one of the strengths of the reference file is its ability to let you "look over the shoulder" of another person in a design session. For performance reasons, this "spying" feature of MicroStation is limited to the first time you open your design file or first attach the reference file to your design file. After that, the image of the reference file is stored in your computer's memory. In the meantime, if the reference file source is modified, your on-screen version of the reference file will not reflect these changes.

However, all is not lost. The Reload Reference File command forces MicroStation to refresh the reference file contents it holds in memory from the original file on the disk or from the network. With large reference files, you will not want to do this every few minutes; however, if a critical change has been made to the original file, and you are aware of it, you would invoke this command to see the changes.

Moving, Scaling, and Rotating Your Reference Files

The next three tools are used to reposition your reference file with respect to your active file's design plane.

Move Reference File

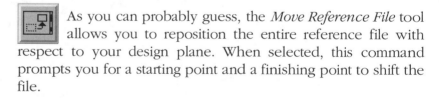

As you can probably guess, the *Move Reference File* tool allows you to reposition the entire reference file with respect to your design plane. When selected, this command prompts you for a starting point and a finishing point to shift the file.

Scale Reference File

This tool allows you to change the ratio of active design file master units to reference file master units. This tool performs the same function as the Scale option in the Attach Reference File dialog box.

NOTE: *The ratio scale between the reference file and the active design file is not cumulative. If you specify a scale of 1:5 followed by a 1:2, the final result will be 1:2.*

Rotate Reference File

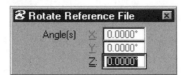

When selected, the tool settings window prompts you for the angular rotation about each of the axes (one for 2D, three for 3D) you want the reference file rotated. You are also prompted in the status bar for the point of rotation.

Mirror Horizontal and Mirror Vertical

These two tools are provided for mirroring the entire contents of the reference file. Once you've identified the reference file in question, you are prompted for the mirror axis. As with other mirror tools, this datapoint defines the axis, *not* the direction of the mirror operation.

Setting the Bounds of Your Reference File

In many instances, you may want to display only a portion of a reference file. This ability is controlled by the various *Clip* tools.

Clip Boundary

The first of these tools, and probably the most used, is *Clip Boundary*. This tool defines the outer boundary of your reference file. Any elements that fall outside this boundary or any portion of elements that cross the boundary and lie outside it will not be displayed.

To define the boundary, you must first place a fence. You can use either Place Fence Block or Place Fence Shape to define the clip boundary. In either case, when the tool boundary has been defined, and the *Clip Boundary* tool is invoked; the result is the disappearance of the elements outside the fence.

A "before" picture of a clip boundary candidate.

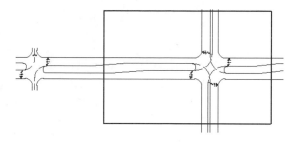

An "after" picture of the same clip-bounded reference file.

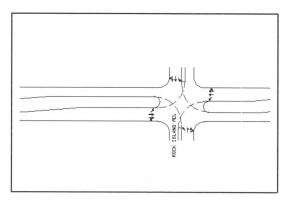

Any type of fence shape is allowed. You can place complex fence shapes and display specific portions of the reference file. However, it should be noted that complex shapes affect the various window commands. To maximize the performance of MicroStation, you have the option of setting the reference file display as fast or slow.

View Fast Reference Clipping

☒ Fast Ref Clipping Either using the key-in SET REFCLIP FAST/SLOW, or selecting the Fast Ref Clipping option under View Attributes (**Settings ➡ View Attributes**), you control how MicroStation displays the reference file clip boundary. With the Slow option (Fast Ref Clipping not selected), the clip bounds are accurately displayed as they were cut. The Fast option causes MicroStation to display the reference file as a rectangular area encompassing the area of the true reference clip boundary.

*A reference file with
Fast Ref Clipping
disabled…*

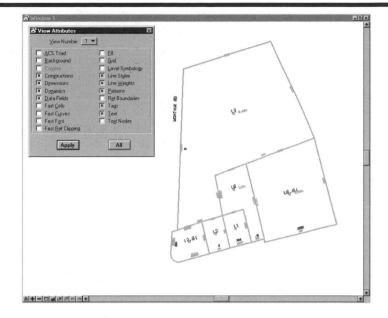

*… and the same
display with Fast Ref
Clipping enabled.*

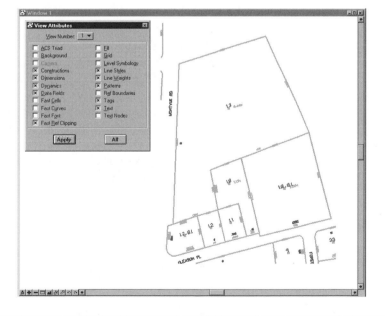

View Reference Boundaries

 One additional display attribute related to the reference file clip boundary is Ref Boundaries (**Settings** ➡ **View Attributes** ➡ **Ref Boundaries**). You have the option to display the boundary on the screen and plot it as well. This is useful when determining where a reference file stops and your active design file begins.

Set Reference Clipping Mask

 Sort of an inside-out boundary, the Reference File Clipping Mask allows you to specify areas within a reference file you do not wish to display. Following the same rules as the normal clip bounds, this command is extremely useful for exploring options with respect to an existing design. For instance, a rehab job on a building would use an as-built plan as a reference file, using this masking to "white out" those parts of the design replaced by the new design shown in the active file.

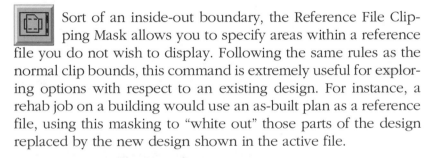

NOTE: *The total number of masks allowed depends on the total number of vertices those masks contain. The total number of vertices cannot exceed 101. In addition, each mask takes up one "point." This means you can have a maximum of 25 three-vertice masks (25 x 3 vertices + 25 masks = 100).*

The Reference File Settings Pull-down Menu Functions

When working with reference files during the design process, there are times you may want to do one or several of the following:

❑ Display or not display entire reference files

❑ Enable or disable the ability to snap to reference elements

❑ Enable or disable the ability to locate elements in a reference file for use with various copy tools

❏ Turn specific levels on and off for display

❏ Set a reference file's level symbology

MicroStation supplies you with commands to perform all of these functions. They can be found on the Settings pull-down menu of the Reference Files settings box.

Attachment Settings

Once you have attached a file as a reference file, there are a number of settings associated with its operation. The three most important of these—the Display, Snap, and Locate options—are defined via the Reference Files (**File ➡ Reference**) settings box.

Selecting Reference from the File menu brings up this settings box. The three checkboxes are its most important functions.

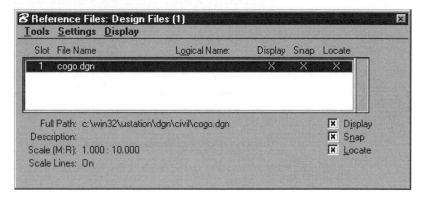

The three checkboxes (Display, Snap, and Locate) control the fundamental relationship between the selected reference file and your active design file.

Attachment Settings Options

Option	Description
Display	Controls the display of the entire reference file on all views.
Snap	Enables/disables the tentative point snap capability to the selected reference file.

Locate   Enables MicroStation to copy one or more elements from a reference file into the active design file.

Selectively Displaying (or Not Displaying) a Reference File

Sometimes you may want to temporarily suspend the display of a reference file. Maybe you have a complicated active file and an equally complicated reference file, and you can't tell what's in which file. The Display option lets you toggle the display of a reference file without actually detaching it permanently.

Locating Reference File Elements

MicroStation's rich set of fence manipulation commands can also be selectively used to copy elements from a reference file via the Locate option (key in REF LOCATE ON/OFF/T). When you select a reference file's Locate Off, the elements shown on the screen are out of harm's way. The fence manipulation commands ignore these elements completely. (T stands for toggle.)

Snapping to Reference Elements

Just as you can locate an element, you can snap to it using the tentative point snap. Enabling the Snap option of a reference file (key in REFERENCE SNAP ON/OFF/T) allows you to tentative point snap to any visible element.

Reference Levels

Similar to View Levels, the Reference Levels settings box (**Reference Files ➡ Settings ➡ Levels**) allows you to select which levels you want displayed (or not) for each of your views. However, unlike View Levels, you can only indicate your levels by number, not by name.

Working with Reference Files: A Site Plan

Now that you have been shown some scenarios in which reference files are especially helpful, and have been shown the basic set of commands to manipulate them, let's try using them. If you have the companion disk, there is a set of design files specifically for this exercise.

Reference File Exercise Design Files	
File name	**Description**
myhouse.dgn	A small house floor plan
mysite.dgn	The site plan to which the other files will be attached
asize.dgn	An A-size drawing sheet

These files will be used in the following interactive sessions designed to help you understand the reference file capabilities of MicroStation. In this series of exercises we will locate the house plan on the site plan and, accomplishing that, we'll place an A-size border around the entire works.

Exercise: Reviewing the Floor Plan

Before actually working with reference files, you should be familiar with the files you will be referencing.

1. Activate the design file MYHOUSE.DGN.

The MYHOUSE.DGN design file on screen.

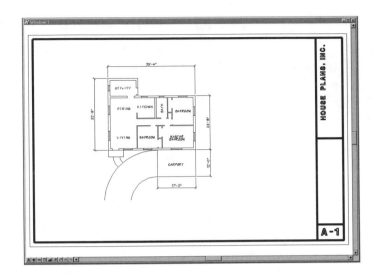

2. Open the Working Units dialog box (**Settings ➡ Design File**... ➡ **Working Units**) and note the values.

3. Note the use of dimensions and the resolution of this file.

Exercise: Attaching the House Plan

On to the real work. In this exercise you will activate the site plan drawing. To this you will attach the floor plan just reviewed.

1. Open the design file MYSITE.DGN. This file consists of a surveyed lot outline and dimensions. To this file we will attach and manipulate the floor plan file you reviewed in the previous exercise.

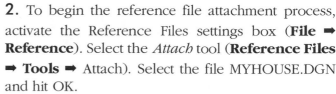

2. To begin the reference file attachment process, activate the Reference Files settings box (**File ➡ Reference**). Select the *Attach* tool (**Reference Files ➡ Tools ➡** Attach). Select the file MYHOUSE.DGN and hit OK.

This brings up the reference file attachment dialog box labeled Attach Reference File. Here you will enter specific information about how you want this reference file to be attached and described.

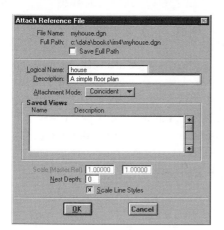

3. Enter the Logical Name and Description. Hit the OK button.

An indication that something happened is a confirmation message in the status bar and the appearance of the reference file name in the Reference Files settings box. Although the house plan may not be visible within the extents of your view window, the house plan is indeed attached to your site plan. To verify this, you need to use the Fit View command, which gives you the complete picture.

4. Choose the Fit View command from the view window border and make sure the All option is selected in the Tool Settings window. This command performs the Fit command on all elements: those active and in all of the attached reference files.

The result was not what you expected, was it? Instead of seeing the site plan, you now see the floor plan. However, if you look in the lower right corner of the view, you will see the site plan smaller than life. The reason for this size discrepancy is in the different working units with which these two designs were made (feet/inches/8,000 pus versus feet/hundredths of a foot/10 pus). However, all you have to do is reset the scale of the reference file.

5. In the Reference Files settings box, highlight the HOUSE reference file entry and choose the *Scale* tool (**Reference Files ➡ Tools ➡ Scale...**). Enter a 1:1 ratio (Master:Ref) in the Tool Settings window.

6. MicroStation prompts you in the status bar for the point to scale the reference file about. Click a datapoint once at the lower right corner of the house drawing border (under the A-1 label).

The house should now appear to be the same scale as the site plan. Although the working units between the two files are dissimilar (FT:IN versus FT:tenths), MicroStation successfully reconciles the working units between the two design files.

At this point you may wish to zoom in on the house plan and look it over. You may even want to try to delete some of the elements. Good luck, though; you cannot delete elements from a reference file. You can, however, copy elements from a reference file, so be careful.

The next step in this process is to clip the floor plan down to size. This means eliminating the surrounding material, such as the format shown to the right of the actual floor plan. This will be performed using the Reference Clip command.

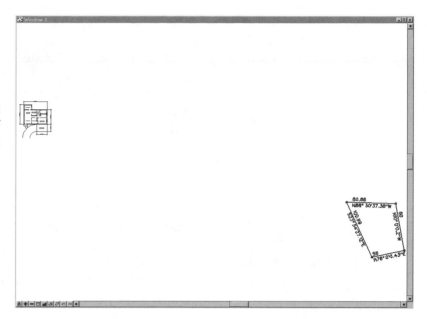

Eliminating the unwanted portion of the floor plan for the site plan preparation.

Exercise: Clipping the Floor Plan to Size

1. Place a fence shape around the house as close as possible without touching the actual walls. Do this with the *Place Fence Shape* tool on the Main toolbox.

2. With the house reference file selected in the Reference Files settings box, choose the *Clip Boundary* tool (**Reference Files ➡ Tools ➡ Clip Boundary**).

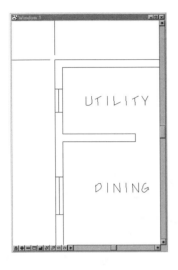

This results in the floor plan drawing being clipped to your fence shape. However, if you look closely at the house plan, you will see part of the witness lines of the dimensions around the house. This will not do for a site plan. To get rid of those unsightly lines, you need to turn off the dimensions level.

3. From the Reference Files settings box, select the Levels command (**Reference Files ➡ Settings ➡ Levels**). Click on level 50, the dimensions level for the floor plan reference file, to turn it off and hit the All button to apply the change to all view windows. The witness lines should disappear, leaving only the house itself.

The house is now ready to be placed on the property. If you want, you can use the Levels settings box from the previous step to turn off other levels of the reference file. (Level 11 is room names, and level 10 is interior walls.)

Positioning the House on the Lot

The shape of the site plan chosen for this exercise is irregular and requires you to turn the house at least 20 degrees to get it situated appropriately on the property. To do this you will use the Move Reference File and Rotate Reference File commands.

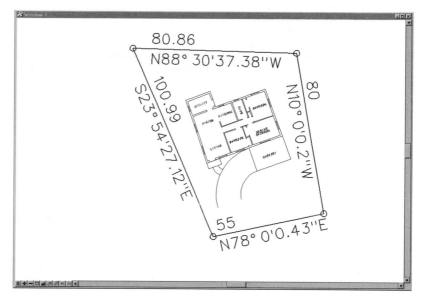

A design of the house sitting on the site plan. You can adjust it to fit as needed.

Exercise: Moving and Rotating the Reference File

1. First, you need to move the reference file closer to the action; in this case, onto the property itself. Choose the *Move Reference File* tool (**Reference Files ➡ Tools ➡ Move**). Select a point within the house for the *from* point (d1), and a point in the middle of the site layout for the *to* (d2) point.

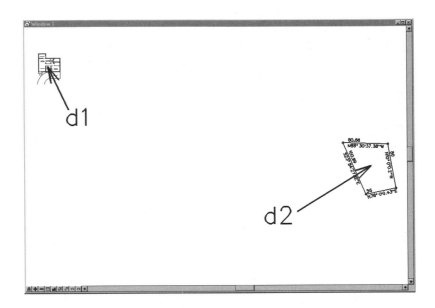

2. Next, we need to rotate the reference file to better position the house on the property. Choose the *Rotate Reference File* tool (**Reference Files ➡ Tools ➡ Rotate**). Now, enter the rotation angle you need to reorient the house. Try using an angle of 20 degrees for input in the Tool Settings window. Of course, you may adjust this value if desired.

3. The reference file's boundary polygon is dynamically active at this point. Position it where you want the house to be located on the property and click a datapoint once.

At this point you can use the *Move Reference File* tool to move the rotated house around on the property to get the best fit. If you want, you can add line work to extend the driveway to the property line. Just remember to turn Snap on so that you can use the tentative point snap with the *Place Arc by Edge* tool.

Placing the Drawing Sheet Format

Before continuing with the exercise, let's take a moment to discuss the use of the border as a reference file. Quite often, first-time users of MicroStation start their project by drawing in the drawing sheet format border. This is probably done from habit; however, there are a number of reasons not to do this.

First, a company's drawing sheet format goes through a number of revisions in its lifetime. Second, by their very nature, such drawing formats are uniform in appearance. When you start your design with a drawing format, its elements will be the first highlighted should you stray too close to them while using, say, the Delete command. This leads to lost elements, nonuniform appearance, and a host of generally irritating problems.

So, what is the solution? Well, you could use a cell for the drawing border, or you could use (dare I say it?) a reference file.

What's the advantage of using a reference file over a cell, you ask? The biggest difference is the global changeability of the reference file over the cell concept. If, for some reason, there are changes to the drawing format, you can implement those changes in the master-referenced design file. MicroStation will make sure the change will be reflected in all drawings that use that drawing format as a reference file. It is sort of like the "other" way of dealing with library parts previously discussed.

*The final drawing of
the house with the
border positioned.*

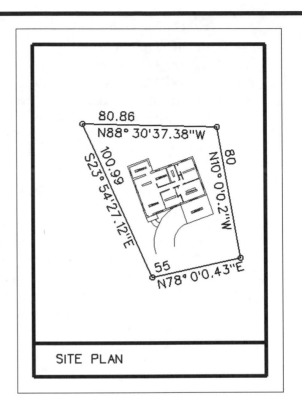

Exercise: Attaching the Drawing Format

In order to perform this next exercise, you must understand the relationship of the master unit (active file) to master unit (reference file). This ratio ignores the subunits and positional units. (Actually, MicroStation calculates the UOR:UOR ratio for you.) So, to establish a 1 inch = 20 feet scale (or 1/240 scale), all that is needed is to attach the design file ASIZE.DGN to the site plan at a 20:1 ratio.

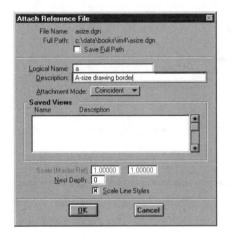

1. Attach the design file ASIZE.DGN to the site plan using the *Attach* tool (**Reference Files ➡ Tools ➡ Attach...**). Give it the logical name A and a short description.

The drawing border appears to the right of your site plan. As you can see, the size of this drawing sheet is not correct. You need to use Scale Reference File to adjust it.

2. Use the Fit All command (hint: the Fit View command on the view window bottom border with the All option selected on the Tool Settings window) to view both the drawing border and your site plan. You may want to use the *Zoom Out* tool to further shrink the image in view window. This will give you some elbow room when it comes time to move the drawing border reference file.

3. With the ASIZE reference file highlighted on the Reference Files settings box, choose the *Scale* tool (**Reference Files ➡ Tools ➡ Scale**). Enter a 20:1 ratio between your master file and this reference file. This defines 20 *feet* equal to 1 *inch* of drawing paper. Click near the lower right corner of the ASIZE reference file. The result should be an overlap of the drawing on your site plan.

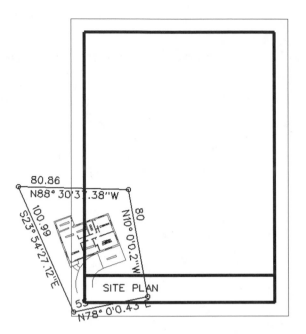

4. Using the *Move Reference File* tool (**Reference Files ➡ Tools ➡ Move**), reposition the drawing sheet over the site plan. Make sure the ASIZE reference file is highlighted in the Reference File settings box before invoking this command or you may be moving the house instead!

In this series of exercises you used the Reference File facility of MicroStation to compose a finished drawing. All you need to finish this drawing is to add in the various notes and descriptions and plot it.

The subject of the next two chapters is getting to the finished product. In the next chapter you will learn how to take your design model and turn it into a finished set of drawings by providing all of the traditional drawing constructs of patterns and dimensions. Combined with the various text commands and the reference file capabilities just discussed, there is no question that you are now well on your way to using MicroStation productively for your design needs, whatever they might be.

Detailing Tools

Finishing a Design with Meaningful Details

Creating the computer model is only half of any project. True, there are methods available to go directly from a computer model to final product (for instance, numerical, controlled machining), but in most cases you must generate detailed drawings in order to ensure that the final product matches your original design.

The process of converting your model into usable drawings is better known by its drafting function: *detailing*. Starting with your computer model, you add drawing details such as hatching, sectional details, dimensions, callouts, notes, and the like. The result of the detailing process will be drawings with enough information for the manufacture of your design to your specifications.

In most cases, such detailing must conform to drafting standards originally designed for manual drafting. This sometimes can lead to compromises between what is efficient for the computer design process and what is acceptable as a final drawing. For this reason, most detailing work is performed near the end of the design process. In this way, if there are major changes in the design, the effect to the drawings will be minimized.

Dimensioning Your Drawings

Paramount in any design project is the need to convey the accurate dimensions of the model. One of the first subjects you learn in any first-year drafting class is the importance and method of dimensioning a drawing. Keeping true to its purpose, MicroStation supports most dimensioning standards. Its dimensioning capabilities are flexible enough to handle both AEC and mechanical design disciplines.

MicroStation provides a bewildering set of dimensioning tools and options. If you thought dealing with text was complicated, wait until you see the dimensioning parameters and setups.

The Anatomy of a Dimension

Before continuing with the initial setup and use of the dimensioning tools, let's look at what makes up a dimension. A dimension is a text label providing spatial information about the design object in your drawing. In other words, a dimension tells you how long something is and whether it is in units of measure or degrees of arc. Additional information may also be included in a dimension, such as tolerance and alternate measurement systems (e.g., metric/English).

Obviously, there is some structure to a dimension. In fact, let's take a closer look at the components of the dimension element.

The components of the dimension element.

Extension line · Dimension line · Dimension text · Tolerance · Terminator

$$3.600 \, {}^{+0.005}_{-0.003}$$

Prefix · Suffix

$$// 2.00 \, \mathbb{C}$$

As can be seen in this diagram, each component of the dimension has a name associated with it. MicroStation allows you to customize practically everything about these components, even eliminate them altogether. For this reason it is a good idea to take a moment to familiarize yourself with their names.

Dimension Line

The most obvious part of the dimension is the dimension line. Defining the measured distance, this line may be a single line with the dimension text resting above it, or a broken line with the dimension text sandwiched in between its two segments.

Dimension Text

This is probably the most important part of the dimension. Used to document a measurement of the design object, this text has all of the standard text attributes, as well as additional dimension-specific parameters (accuracy, format, and measurement system, to name a few).

Extension Lines

Extension lines (that is, witness lines) are used to indicate the point in the design where the dimension originates and ends. This way there is no question as to what is being measured. Again, there are options associated with this dimension component, most important, selectively turning it on and off.

Terminators

Finally, there are the terminators (that is, arrowheads). Always shown at the ends of the dimension line, they serve the purpose of identifying the text and linework of a dimension as a dimension. Without arrowheads, dimensions would get lost in the maze of elements making up the drawing. Arrowheads come in a variety of styles and types to support the various dimensioning standards.

Prefixes, Suffixes, and Tolerances

Additional information critical to interpreting the dimension, these components can be activated and adjusted as needed. These, too, warrant their own settings boxes and provide MicroStation the ability to adhere to some of the more rigorous dimensioning standards (e.g., ANSI Y14.2).

All told, there are eleven separate dimension setting categories dedicated to your dimensions (far more than any other element class within MicroStation). This fact serves to point out the importance of dimensioning within the design community.

Setting Up the Dimensions

Because MicroStation tries to be all things to all people, when it comes to dimensions, it can require a fair amount of setup prior to actually placing your first dimension. The dimensioning options are set via the Dimension Settings box.

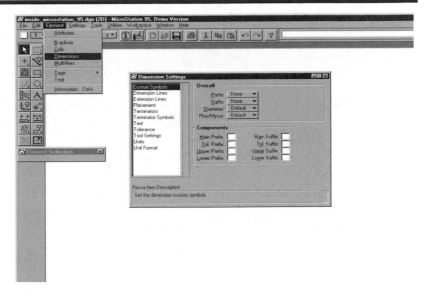

The Dimension Settings box is used to control every aspect of the dimensioning process.

Accessed via the Element pull-down menu (**Element ➡ Dimensions**), the Dimension Settings box offers a list of categories on the left, each of which controls different dimension attributes.

Dimension Setting Categories

Command Name	Description
Custom Symbols	Controls the creation of suffix/prefix annotation
Dimension Lines	Controls the level and symbology settings for dimension lines
Extension Lines	Controls the level and symbology settings for extension lines
Placement	Controls the alignment of linear dimensions relative to the element, and location of text and other placement parameters
Terminators	Controls the geometry, symbology, and orientation of arrowheads

Terminator Symbols	Allows you to select a symbol or a cell for any of the four terminator types: Arrow, Stroke, Origin, or Dot
Text	Used to select text placement and symbology parameters
Tolerance	Controls the geometry and attributes for dimension tolerance text
Tool Settings	Allows adjustment of settings for individual dimension tools
Units	Controls the dimension format (mechanical or AEC), and whether or not to place the dimension in two units, primary and secondary
Unit Format	Sets the format for the units

Let's look at each of these dimension-setting categories in detail.

Custom Symbols

MicroStation provides the option for adding a prefix and suffix character symbol to each dimension you place. This category gives you control over what MicroStation places. By default, no suffix or prefix is placed; however, you can opt to display either a symbol from a text font or a cell from your active design file (shared cells only).

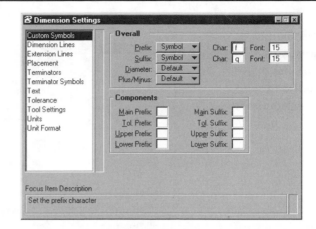

Custom Symbols gives you options for setting dimension prefixes and suffixes. More importantly, this is where you change the default diameter and plus/minus symbols.

In addition, you can change the default diameter symbol and/or the plus/minus symbol used with all dimension tools. In this case, however, you can only specify an alternative font and character (no cells).

In addition to suffixes and prefixes for the entire dimension text string, you can set single-character text for the individual text parts associated with toleranced dimensions. As you can see, this can get very complicated, so the recommendation here is to tread lightly through this settings box, and use only those settings you absolutely need.

Dimension Lines

At first glance, a dimension can be thought of as a series of lines and text. In fact, prior to MicroStation version 4, this was precisely how MicroStation treated the entire dimensioning routine. Now, however, dimensions are seen as elements in and of themselves, subject to the same element attributes as all other elements. However, the individual parts of the dimension can have their own attributes subject to the settings you select.

The Dimension Lines category is used to override the active element attributes for dimension lines placed.

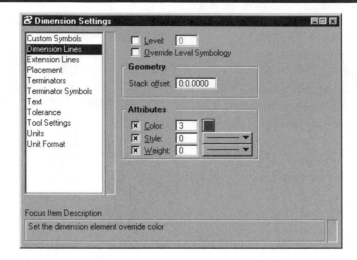

By clicking on the checkboxes of the attributes you wish to override, you ensure uniform dimensional appearances. This is an important aspect of the dimensioning system. Standardizing the color, weight, and especially the level of dimensions will lead to a better- looking final product.

TIP: *The Dimension Level override associated with the Dimension Attributes settings box also has a shortcut key-in. Use* LD=50 *in the Command Window to set the level to which all of your dimensions will go. This is much easier than calling up this rather large settings box.*

Extension Lines

This category is similar to Dimension Lines as far as being able to independently select color, style, and weight for them. Whereas dimension lines are always placed when using a dimensioning tool, the Extension Lines checkbox allows you to control whether or not extension lines are actually placed.

Normally, when dimension text is longer than the gap between extension lines, the text is placed outside, with a gap between the extension lines. When you enable the checkbox labeled Join When Text Outside, the gap between the extension lines is closed with a line.

The Extension Lines category is used to specify extension line parameters.

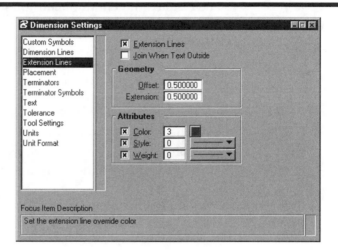

The Offset parameter under Geometry specifies the distance, in text height units (TH=), between the start of the extension line and the element being dimensioned. This measure is a percentage of the active text height associated with the dimension. The default is 0.5000 (or 50%), which means that the space between the witness line and the object is half that of the current dimension text height. The Extension parameter specifies the distance, again in text height units, the extension line should extend beyond the dimension line.

Placement

The Placement category on the Dimension Settings box sets some of the major features of the dimension system. From here you can select such dimensioning aspects as orientation of the dimension text to the dimension line, the text's justification, whether Micro-Station builds the entire dimension itself, and other options.

Alignment

Normally you dimension objects using the X and Y axes of your view as your reference. This is known as the *View* alignment. You may have cause to change this, so there are a number of additional alignments supported by MicroStation. Alignment along the *Drawing* axes uses the drawing's absolute XYZ axes for calculating a distance to be dimensioned, regardless of View's orientation. When you want to dimension an oblique face of an object, use the *True* alignment.

Aribitrary alignment allows you to measure a length without keeping the extension lines perpendicular to the object being measured. This is especially helpful when dimensioning 2D, isometric drawings.

The Alignment control gives you control over how MicroStation calculates distances for the active dimension tool.

view   true   drawing   arbitrary
                          (view rotated 30°)   (using font 30 - Iso_fontright)

Location

The Location option selects what sets the location of the text with respect to the dimension line. In automatic mode, the text is automatically placed by MicroStation using the justification option just described. The manual mode prompts you to click a datapoint at the location of the text along the dimension line.

Semi-auto mode is a little trickier. When a dimension fits between the witness lines, MicroStation automatically places the dimension. If the dimension text is too large, you are prompted to manually place the text. This last option is probably one of the better compromises between human- and machine-generated dimensions. Many times the aesthetics of a drawing are a matter of placing these dimensions with an eye toward clarity of the overall drawing.

Manual dimensioning is most often chosen when working with small distances that require you to crowd the dimensions. MicroStation's automatic dimensioning feature is good, but it does have a tendency to place the dimension string in an arrows-out configuration before the distance being dimensioned really requires it.

The next diagram points this out. The automatic placement results in the dimension at the top of the object. By selecting the manual placement option, the additional step of placing the dimension text allows you to place the text between the arrowheads. This is shown on the bottom of the object.

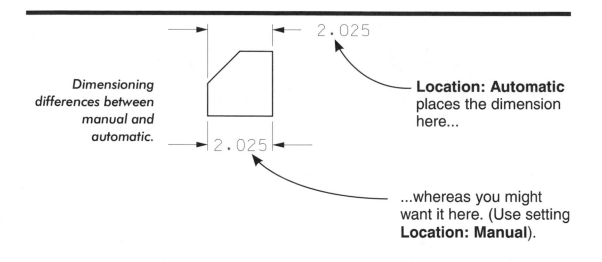

Dimensioning differences between manual and automatic.

Location: Automatic places the dimension here...

...whereas you might want it here. (Use setting **Location: Manual**).

Adjust Dimension Line

This option gives the *Place Dimension* tools some latitude when placing adjacent dimensions. With the Adjust Dimension Line option selected, a second dimension's text, terminators, and arrowheads will be shifted up to clear the first dimension's text.

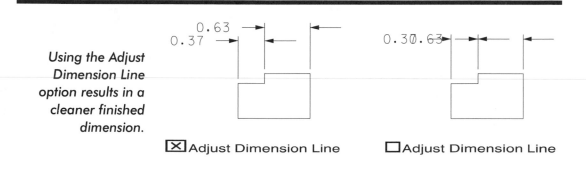

Using the Adjust Dimension Line option results in a cleaner finished dimension.

☒Adjust Dimension Line   ☐Adjust Dimension Line

Reference File Units

Remembering that one of the strengths of MicroStation is its reference file facility, this checkbox option allows you to look inside an attached reference file for dimension measurements. When you identify an element of a reference file with the dimension tool, the working units of the reference file are used to compute the value of the dimension. By attaching your design to a border sheet, you can set up your text and other drawing-related functions based on the final drawing size, while still being able to accurately dimension your design.

Relative Dimension Line

This option affects the operation of the *Modify Element* tool on placed dimensions. Now, the following is a little difficult to follow, so let's look at the following diagram.

The Relative Dimension checkbox option affects the action of the Modify Element tool on dimension elements.

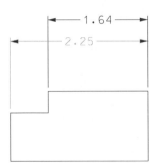

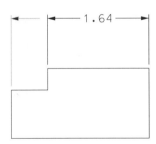

☒ Relative Dimension Line   ☐ Relative Dimension Line

As you can see, when a dimension is placed with the Relative Dimension Line option selected, any changes to the dimension's extension line keeps the dimension line at the same relative distance from the extension line's endpoint. With the Relative

Dimension Line option turned off, the dimension line keeps its original location and only changes its length in response to changes to the extension line location.

NOTE: *The Relative Dimension Line option is effective only at the time you place the original dimension. Changing the setting after the fact will have no effect on existing dimension elements. You can, however, use the* Change Dimension to Active Settings *tool to update an existing dimension to this parameter. Keep in mind, though, that this tool changes all parameters of the chosen dimension to the current settings.*

Center Size

This text field sets the size of the center mark used when placing radial dimensions. The center mark size is specified in the design file's working units.

Terminators

This category controls the orientation of the terminators (read arrowheads) with respect to the dimension line. The Terminators option button under Orientation is normally set to automatic, and MicroStation orients the arrowheads inside and along the dimension line unless there is not enough room for them and the dimension text. In those instances, it will orient the terminators to the outside of the dimensioned distance.

Inside forces MicroStation to always orient the terminators on the inside of the dimension, along the dimension line. Outside forces the terminators away to the outside of the extension lines. *Reversed* flips the terminators from where MicroStation would normally place them.

The Terminators category on the Dimension Settings box.

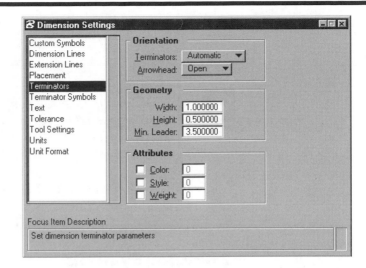

The three terminator options.

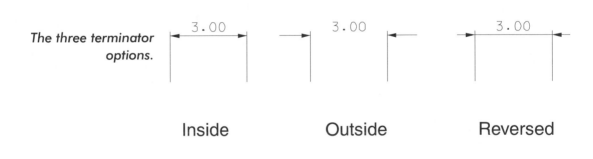

The one parameter you will probably find yourself adjusting on this settings box is the Arrowhead field. The default terminator used with MicroStation is a simple open linestring; in reality, you have three choices for arrowheads. The Closed selection simply closes the open end of the linestring arrow. The Filled selection creates a closed and filled shape for each terminator. Be sure to turn the Fill display on (**Settings ➡ View Attributes ➡ Fill**) for your views to see this.

> **TIP:** *Most CAD products still do not create good-looking arrowheads. However, by selecting the Filled Arrowhead option and adjusting the width-to-height ratio in the Geometry section, MicroStation gives you some of the best-looking arrows available in any CAD program.*

Using the Color, Style, and Weight fields in the Attributes section, you can even control the symbology of the terminators independently of the other dimension components.

Terminator Symbols

Although MicroStation supports a variety of simple terminators, you can replace them with one of your own design or one of a variety found in a font library. The Terminator Symbols category allows you to selectively replace the Arrow, Stroke, Origin, or Dot dimension graphic with either a symbol from a font or a shared cell. Symbol font 102, a font delivered with MicroStation, contains a number of arrowheads perfect for use with custom terminators.

The Terminator Symbols category on the Dimension Settings box.

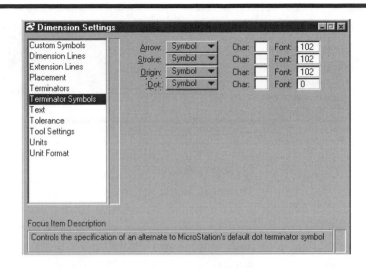

The terminators found in font 102 are designed for use with the Terminator Symbols settings box. Note that all of these symbols are uppercase.

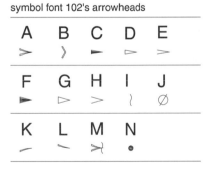

symbol font 102's arrowheads

Text

This category controls both the attributes and placement options for dimension text. If you need to specify that text symbology in a dimension take on different settings than dimension or extension lines, or to set the size of text different from the active text size, this is where you do it.

The Text category controls the attributes and placement parameters of dimension text.

Orientation

This option gives you three choices: Above, In Line, and Horizontal. Above places the dimension text above the dimension line, In Line breaks the dimension line and places the text midstream, and Horizontal breaks the line, but also forces the text in all cases to appear horizontal to the screen.

The results of each dimension text orientation setting.

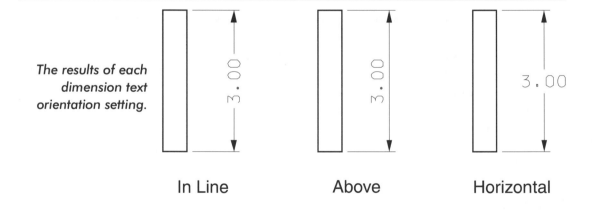

In Line   Above   Horizontal

Justification

Justification controls where the text appears in relation to the dimension line. The default, *Center,* places the text in the center of the line. The Right and Left options place it to either side of the line midpoint. You usually use the latter two settings when stacking dimensions and staggering the text for better appearance.

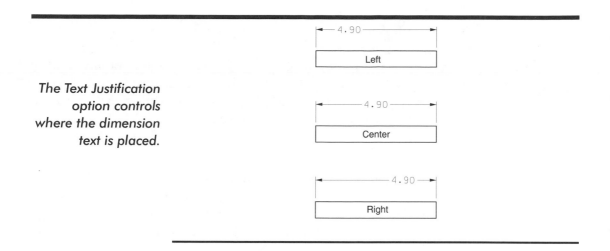

The Text Justification option controls where the dimension text is placed.

Text Frame

The Text Frame option controls the addition of graphic elements around the dimension text. The text frame default, None, represents normal text, the most common form of the dimension element. The other two selections, Box and Capsule, provide a graphic box or capsule-like construct around the dimension. These are usually associated with reference or quality control dimensions.

Margin

The Margin field sets the space between the leader line and the dimension text. The unit of measure is relative to the dimension text height, which as a default is the active text height. Thus, the default value of 0.5 means that the space between the dimension text and the leader line is half the dimension text height.

Underline Text (NTS)

The Underline Text checkbox controls the placement of a line underneath the dimension text. This is normally used to indicate a dimension is "not to scale" (NTS).

Attributes

The Attributes section in the Text category of the Dimension Settings box offers checkboxes to control the color and weight of the dimension text. Also, if you need to use for dimension text a font or size different from the active text setting, you have the font, height, and width checkboxes.

Tolerance

In mechanical design it is common to find tolerances defined with various dimensions on a drawing. MicroStation supports this capability through the use of the Tolerance dimension setting category. By selecting the Tolerance Generation checkbox, all dimensions placed from this point on will include the tolerance configuration established using the rest of this setting category.

The Tolerance dimension setting category controls all aspects of the tolerance function. Selecting the Tolerance Generation checkbox activates the use of tolerance values with your current Place Dimension *tools.*

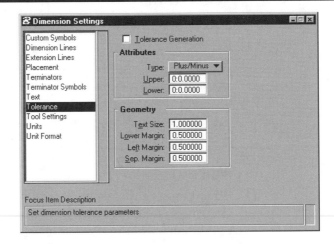

The Type field provides you with two options: Plus/Minus and Limit. The default shows the tolerance as a plus and minus text string appended to the dimension text. Limit is a minimum/maximum configuration where the dimension is two lines of text, the top being the maximum dimension allowed and the bottom the minimum dimension allowed.

Both of these tolerance types use the Upper and Lower field for calculating the tolerances. The Text Size option in the Geometry section of the setting box is used with the Limits option to set the height of the two strings of text. The default of 1 means the text is the full height of the current dimension text value.

 NOTE: *Tolerance can only be used with the mechanical format dimensions.*

The three fields for the Lower, Left and Sep. margins set the space between the dimension line and the bottom of the dimension text, the horizontal space between the dimension text and the tolerance text, and the vertical space between the tolerance values. Again, the unit of measure of the margins is a ratio of the dimension text.

Tool Settings

The dimension tools' parameters are controlled via the Tool Settings category on the Dimension Settings box (**Element ➡ Dimensions ➡ Tool Settings).**

When you choose Tool Settings from the settings box, you are initially presented with the default tool, *Size Arrow*. This name is the shortened version of the actual tool name, *Dimension Size with Arrows* (more on this tool later). If you select the *Size Arrow* text or the icon next to the Tool label, you will bring up a list of all tools Tool Settings supports.

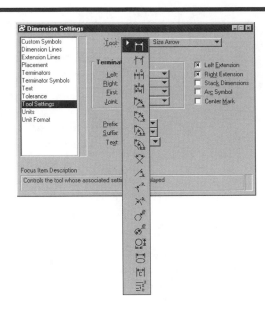

Selecting the tool icon presents you with the entire list of tools for use with the Tool Settings box.

You may recall that we had discussed the Extension Lines category to control the display of a dimension's extension lines. This global setting affects both of the extension lines associated with most tools. However, there are times when you will want finer control over the display and control of the extension lines or even the terminators themselves. That's the purpose of the next section.

Terminators

Under the Terminators section you select the type of terminator used by the dimension tool. You have independent control over each terminator associated with the current tool. In each case you select from the option field the type of terminator you wish to use.

There are four fields listed under the Terminators section. The Left and Right fields are self-explanatory; however, the First and Joint fields need a short explanation. When you put in a string of dimensions with certain dimension tools such as *Single Location,* the first terminator used is very different from the rest. (In this case, a dot signifies a single datum.) This is known as the First terminator. The Joint terminator is used at the shared junction between two dimensions. This occurs when there are two or more dimensioned distances in the same dimension string.

Prefix and Suffix

Although similar to the global custom symbols discussion, the prefix and suffix used here are more specific and are used with each tool. For instance, the prefix for the *Diameter Extended* tool consists of the diameter symbol.

The settings associated with the Diameter Extended tool include the diameter symbol as its prefix. Note the use of special terminators with this tool.

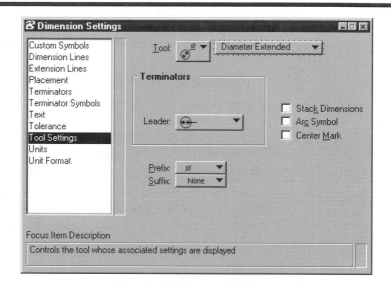

Text

This field controls the orientation of the text with respect to your dimension line. In most cases you will leave it at the Standard setting; however, there may be occasions when you may want to change this.

The Text option controls the orientation of the text with respect to the dimension line, not the drawing.

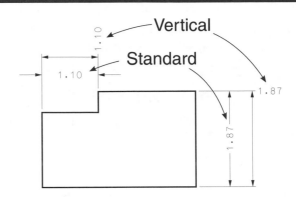

The Mixed option will normally place the text in standard mode. However, in cases where the text doesn't fit the space (i.e., small dimensions), this option allows MicroStation to place the text in the vertical format.

Extensions

There are two checkboxes that control the creation of extension lines. The Left and Right Extension boxes can be selectively turned on and off while you are placing dimensions. This is one of the most used options on this settings box.

Stack Dimensions

This checkbox option controls the placement of multiple options. If selected, the result is a series of stacked dimensions. Normally this option is already selected for the appropriate dimension tool; *Dimension Location (Stacked),* for instance.

Arc Symbol

This checkbox option controls the placement of an arc symbol above arc dimensions.

Center Mark

This checkbox option controls the placement of a center mark graphic at the center of a radial dimension. The size of this center mark is controlled by the Center Size field in the Placement category on the settings box.

Units

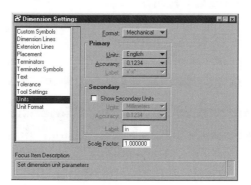

When it comes time to dimension your drawing, you must choose whether you will be using a mechanical or architectural dimension style. This is usually an easy decision to make. You normally know whether you are a mechanical designer or an architectural designer.

Examples of mechanical (top) and AEC (bottom) dimensioning styles.

However, just for the record, the difference between the AEC dimensioning format and the mechanical format is AEC's use of master units and subunits versus mechanical's use of master units only. Formatting the feet and inches with the appropriate "gingerbread" (ft-in or ft′ in″, and so on) used with AEC dimensions is the other main distinction.

The Format Field

The Format field in the Dimension Units settings box gives you the two dimensioning options just described, AEC or Mechanical. When you select AEC format, the Labels field for both the primary and secondary dimension sections are activated.

Primary and Secondary Dimension Control

MicroStation's dimensioning system supports dual dimension standards. This means you can simultaneously display a dimension in both English and metric units, either singularly or combined. This is controlled via the primary and secondary dimension sections of this settings box.

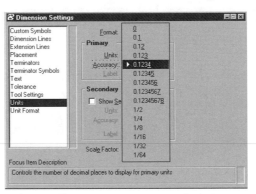

In addition to the units of measure, you control the amount of accuracy for each dimension via the Accuracy field. Note how you can set the accuracy for the secondary dimension independent of that of the primary dimension. Clicking on either will present an array of options, ranging from eight decimal places of accuracy to half a unit or a whole unit.

Scale Factor

The Scale Factor field allows you to enter a multiplier that is applied to all linear dimension values prior to their placement in the drawing. This is handy if you want to enlarge a detail on a drawing, but want the dimension to still read true value. For instance, if a detail is drawn at twice the scale of the design file, setting this value to 0.5 (or 1/2) results in the correct dimension text.

Unit Format

The Unit Format category on the Dimension Settings box controls the format for angular and metric units, and whether or not to display leading/trailing zeros for primary or secondary units.

Angle Format

The other major unit of measure you use in dimensioning your drawing is the Angle format. These settings are used with the *Angular Dimension* tools. MicroStation gives you control over how the angular information is displayed.

Angle Parameters		
Angle Parameter	**Values**	**Description**
Units	Length	Measured distance along the arc curve
Degrees	Sweep of the angle measured in degrees	
Accuracy	0 through 0.0000	Degree of accuracy to display for each angular value
Display	Decimal degrees	Degrees shown in decimal format
	DD^MM'SS"	Degrees shown in degrees/minutes/seconds format

NOTE: *The Dimension Settings box associated with dimensioning can stay active during the entire design process. This allows you to select the various options during the placement of the actual dimension. Thus, you can control the accuracy and the selective display of witness lines and arrowheads while creating the dimension.*

Metric Format

Although the metric system is in use worldwide, the character used as a decimal separator is not the same everywhere. Whereas Europe uses the comma, Asia uses the period. Also, it is the convention in many parts of the world to use a space after the thousand and million places.

Use Comma for Decimal

This option swaps the period that is used as a decimal separator in the USA, Asia, and other regions with the comma that is common in Europe.

Unit Separation

This option, when enabled, leaves a space after the million and thousand places in a number.

Additional Options

In addition to the options just discussed, there are a number of common checkbox options found on Unit Format. Each controls the display of specific dimension text features related to units. These features are applicable to both primary and secondary units.

Show Leading Zero

When a dimension is less than one unit, selecting this option results in a zero being placed in front of the decimal point of the dimension.

Show Trailing Zeros

When selected, this option pads the dimension value with zeroes out to the number of places set by the accuracy value for the Primary and/or Secondary dimension field. For example, if a dimensioned distance is 1.5 and the accuracy is set to 0.12345678, the resulting dimension text will be 1.50000000.

The Dimensioning Tools

"With all of the setting up involved with dimensions, there had better be a rich selection of dimensioning tools." Yes, there is a wide variety of dimensioning tools. In fact, there are no fewer than 33 different dimensioning tools at your disposal.

MicroStation's Dimension toolbox.

The dimensioning tools are accessed from the *Dimension* toolbox (**Tools ➡ Main ➡ Dimension**). All dimensioning tools—whether linear, angular, or radial—are found on this toolbox. Even tools to update dimensions, or to place geometric tolerancing symbols can be found here. Although there appear to be only 16 icons on the toolbox, the options many of them implement in the Tool Settings window are the key to the flexibility of MicroStation's dimensioning tools.

The Linear Dimensioning Tools

Linear dimensioning is usually the first type of dimensioning you try. Simply put, the linear dimension measures the straight-line distance between two given points. Such linear dimensions are among the most common in design.

MicroStation supports normal, stacked, ordinate, and datum methods of linear dimensioning. Depending on your design discipline, you will use the appropriate method.

The Dimension Size Tools

Measuring a distance between two points and creating a dimension is the most common dimensioning style used. MicroStation calls this the *size* method of dimensioning. When you use the *Dimension Size* tools, you get two witness lines, a dimension line, a text string showing the measured distance, and two arrowheads or slashes. The type of terminator generated depends on which of the two tools you selected.

 Dimension Size with Arrows

 Dimension Size with Strokes

These tools operate in exactly the same manner. The only difference is their terminators. Depending on the dimension control settings, some or all of the bits and pieces of the dimension may be suppressed or automatically created.

The simplest of the dimension commands, the Dimension Size with Arrows or Slashes tool gives you straight-line dimensioning between two points.

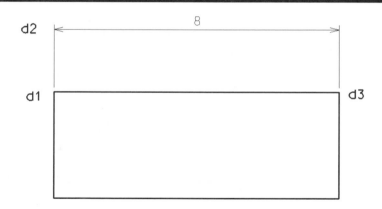

The *Dimension Size* tools can also create a string of dimensions with the end of one dimension serving as the beginning point of the next dimension. Two Resets will start a new chain of dimensions. One Reset tells MicroStation of a new location for the next dimension string. This is helpful when you want to turn a corner and dimension a second side of an object, as shown in the following illustration.

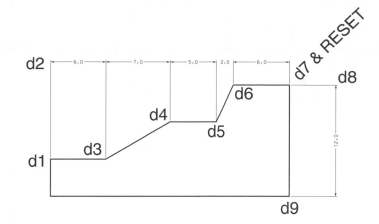

Dimensioning with a continuous chain of dimensions. Note that when you turn the corner for the second string of dimensions, this becomes a separate dimension.

The Dimension Location Tools

 Dimension Location

 Dimension Location (Stacked)

The other common linear dimension used extensively in mechanical design is the datum, or location, dimension. This dimensioning method uses a common starting point, or datum, from which all dimensions are referenced. MicroStation provides two tools for performing this type of dimension: *Dimension Location* and *Dimension Location (Stacked)*.

The *Dimension Location* tool creates one linear dimension line containing dimensions for each datapoint entered. The *Dimension Location (Stacked)* tool, on the other hand, creates a new dimension line and text for each additional datapoint. The next diagram shows the operation of each tool.

The results of the Dimension Location tools. Note the different appearances between the stacked version and the normal version of this tool.

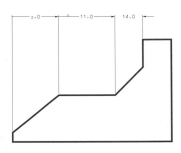

Dimension Location

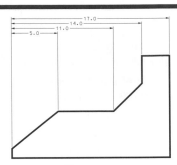

Dimension Location (Stacked)

Before proceeding with the rest of the dimensioning tools, try your hand at dimensioning a drawing. In this example you will be using the widget drawing you created in a previous chapter. This time, however, you will document it with dimensions. At the conclusion of this exercise and the ones that follow, you will soon find out if your previous work was accurate.

Editing a Dimension's Text

When you place a dimension, you have the option to modify the text string associated with it. This is done just after you have established the endpoint of the dimension. If you look at the status bar after picking the endpoint of a dimension, you will notice the words "Press Return to edit dimension text."

After hitting return (just make sure the focus is on the Key-in window when you hit return), you are presented with a dialog box where you can change the values of the text or add to them as needed. Why would you want to do this? The answer is simple. In many instances you will want to add suffixes such as "REF" or "TYP." This feature allows you to do this without compromising the measurement text of the dimension.

Hitting the Enter or Return key at the right time in the dimensioning process will bring up this dialog box. Here you can append to or change the text of the dimension. The asterisk represents the dimension value.

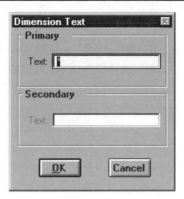

NOTE: *The Key-in window must be the active window for this feature to work. If the Tool Settings window is active, the result will be the selection of one of its options. Use the Utilities menu to open the Key-in window. If the Tool Settings window has the focus, and the Key-in window is open, hitting the Escape key makes the Key-in window active.*

Exercise: Linear Dimensioning a Mechanical Part

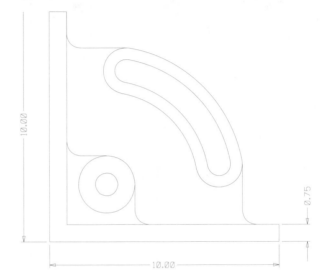

1. Open the design file BRACKET.DGN. To get started we need to select the default dimensioning parameters. From the Element menu, select the Dimensions option to open the *Dimension Settings* box. Select the options on the settings box to match the following figure.

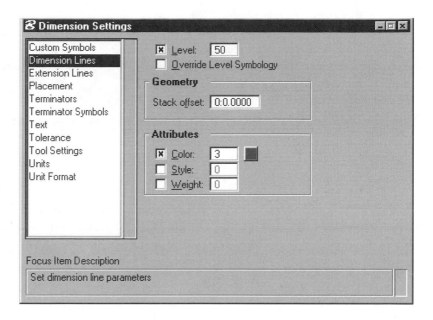

The values just entered are self-explanatory. You have selected the Mechanical dimensioning method to two decimal places of accuracy with trailing zeroes. You have also selected the dimensions as RED and on level 50.

> **2.** Activate the *Dimension Size with Arrows* tool *(Tools ➡ Main ➡ Dimension ➡ Dimension Size with Arrows)*.

> Because dimensioning tools have specific steps to follow, you should pay close attention to the prompts in the status bar. At this point the status bar should be prompting you to "Select start of dimension."

> **3.** You will be placing the horizontal 10″ dimension along the bottom edge of the bracket.

4. The first step is to tie down the starting point of the dimension. Select the lower right corner of the bracket with a Tentative Point/Datapoint sequence. The status bar will now prompt with, "Define length of extension line."

5. You must select where the dimension string will appear. This would be where the 10″ dimension's rightmost arrowhead is located. This location does not need to be precise. To avoid confusing the dimension command as to which direction your dimension string is going to face, always pick the point in line with the starting point of the dimension. Click a datapoint below the bracket's lower right corner.

6. A dynamic display of the dimension should now appear. All that remains is to provide the tentative point/datapoint sequence at the lower left corner of the bracket's base. The status bar should now be prompting you to "Select dimension endpoint."

7. The *Dimension Size* tool will prompt you to place more dimensions along the same line. However, you need to turn the corner to dimension the left edge of the bracket. Hit Reset once.

8. Retaining the last endpoint as the starting point for a new string of dimensions, MicroStation prompts you for a new witness line location. Click a datapoint just left of the vertical face of the bracket at the location you want the vertical dimension line to run. To finish the second dimension, use the tentative point/datapoint sequence at the top left corner of the bracket.

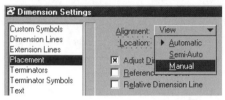

9. To control where MicroStation places the next dimension's text, we need to turn Dimension Text Location to Manual. This is done via the Text category on the Dimension Settings box (**Element ➡ Dimensions ➡ Text**). Set the Location option to Manual.

10. To start a completely new set of dimensions, you must reset to the top of the *Dimension Size* tool. To do this, hit Reset twice. The status bar will prompt you to "Select start of dimension."

Next, we'll place the 0.75″ dimension on the base of the bracket by again selecting its base at the lower right corner with a tentative point/datapoint sequence.

11. Now define the extension line. Click a datapoint just to the right of the point just selected. Remember, this step sets how far away from your design the dimension string will appear. Define the endpoint for the dimension by selecting the opposite edge of the bracket base.

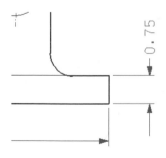

Now you have to select the location of the text along the dimension string. Note how MicroStation already sets the arrowheads and leader lines as outside. To complete the dimension, click a datapoint either above or below the dynamic dimension. You won't have room between the extension lines, so pick a point outside the dimension. Hit Reset twice to complete the dimension placement.

This rather simple exercise shows how you string the dimensions around your drawing. As you can see, you do need to be aware of how the various dimension options are set. If your results weren't precisely the same as shown, it is probably due to an incorrect setting of these values. You might want to try some variations to the values in the Dimension Settings box and see how they affect your dimension placement commands.

Using the Association Lock

You may have noticed the presence of a checkbox option on the Tool Settings window called Association Lock. Although simply a checkbox, it is a powerful option. In essence, this lock creates a connection between your newly placed dimension and the object in your design file it dimensions.

With the Association Lock enabled, a tentative point/datapoint sequence attaches the dimension to whatever element was highlighted as part of the tentative point. If, in the future, this element is moved, or the selected point is modified, the dimension associated with the point will be automatically updated.

The Association Lock adds a degree of intelligence to a dimension by establishing a link between it and a specific design element. In this example the Modify Element was used to stretch the tip of this shape, resulting in the dimension change.

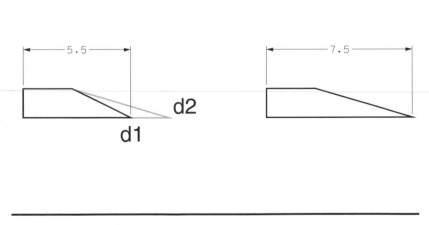

NOTE: *If you opt to use associative dimensioning, use it throughout your design. You will come to rely on the dimensions as being associative, and if you place some of them without association you may be in for a rude surprise.*

The Angular Dimension Tools

In addition to the linear dimensions just described, MicroStation supports angular dimensions. As a companion function to the various arc and circle construction tools, these dimensioning tools document the one unique property every arc has: sweep.

Angular Dimensioning Setup

As with linear dimensioning, you need to set up some parameters before you can begin using the angular dimensioning tools. The first decision you must make is how the angle readout should be formatted.

You have two options: decimal degrees, or degrees, minutes, and seconds. The latter is useful in survey and mapping projects. You set which readout is used in the Unit Format category on the Dimension Settings box under the Angle Format section.

The angle format used with the angular dimensioning tools is controlled via the Dimension Settings box. You select both the format and measurement technique (degrees or arc length).

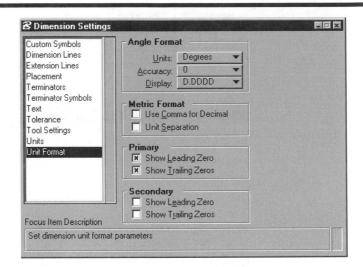

MicroStation also lets you specify the number of places to display after the decimal point. You can set between zero and four decimal places. Both the Show Leading Zero and Show Trailing Zeros checkboxes also affect the appearance of angular dimensions.

Dimension Angle Size

 Similar in function to its linear cousin, this tool prompts you for a starting point, the extension line location, the center point for the angle, and the endpoint of the angle.

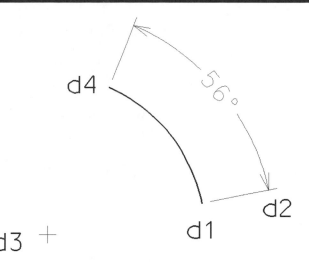

The sequence of datapoints required by the Dimension Angle Size *tool.*

 NOTE: *First-time users of* Dimension Angle *tools are confused by the order in which they are prompted for the locations of various points. This sometimes results in unexpected results (usually a large, circular dimension). Keep an eye on the prompts in the status bar and follow them. If you get confused, just hit Reset several times and start over.*

Dimension Angle Location

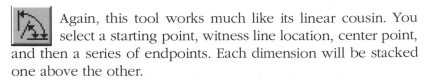 Again, this tool works much like its linear cousin. You select a starting point, witness line location, center point, and then a series of endpoints. Each dimension will be stacked one above the other.

Dimension Angle Between Lines

This tool takes some of the drudgery out of dimensioning angles. By selecting the two elements between which you want a dimension, MicroStation skips the requests for center point and starting/ending points. All you have to do is supply the location of the dimension.

Dimension Angle from X-Axis

Dimension Angle from Y-Axis

The Dimension from axes tools are a slight modification of the previous *Angle Between Lines* tool. Instead of selecting two elements, you identify only one. MicroStation then calculates the angle from that line to the axis you specified by the specific tool you selected.

The Dimension Radial Tool

Angles and arc lengths aren't the only dimensions of interest when detailing arcs and circles on a drawing. Many times you need to provide hole diameters and radius information. MicroStation does this with the *Dimension Radial* tool. As with most other tools, the various options implemented by the tool are available on the Tool Settings window.

The Mode option button lets you select a radial dimensioning option.

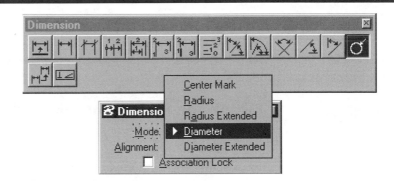

Dimension Diameter and Dimension Diameter (Extended Leader)

These two tools provide a means for dimensioning circles by their diameter. By selecting the target circle, you are prompted for the final location of the dimension text. Depending on the Location setting on the Text category in the Dimension Settings box, this may take one or more datapoints. A final reset creates the dimension. By default, the dimension text includes the diameter symbol Ø.

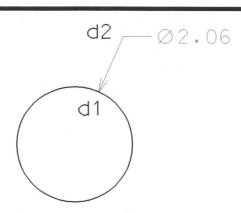

The Dimension Diameter *tool in action.* By setting the Text Orientation to Horizontal in the Dimension Placement settings box, the resulting dimension always appears level.

Dimension Radius and Dimension Radius (Extended)

By selecting a circle or arc, MicroStation generates the appropriate dimension. The *Dimension Radius* tool gives you a leader line, with text denoting the radius of the arc or circle selected. The *Dimension Radius (Extended)* tool gives you the same leader and text, except that it also extends the leader to the center of the arc or circle.

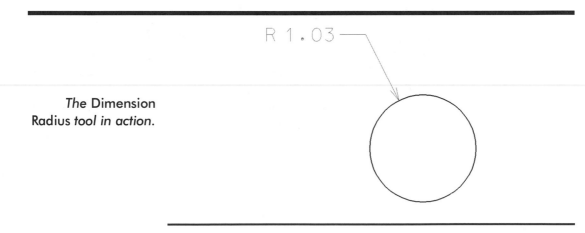

The Dimension Radius *tool in action.*

Place Center Mark

The *Place Center Mark* tool prompts you to select an arc or circle and proceeds to place a center mark at the center of the selected element. The Center Size field on the Tool Settings window lets you control the size of the center mark placed by the tool.

Exercise: Dimensioning the Bracket Drawing, Continued

Let's add some radial and angular dimensions to the bracket.

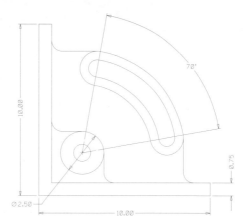

1. Select the angle format from Unit Format on the Dimension Settings box, and set the options as shown in the following illustration.

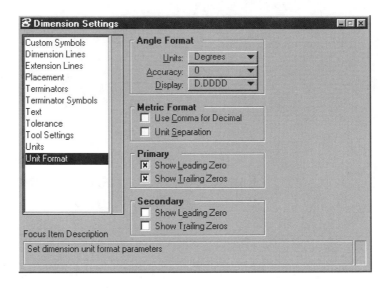

2. Next, select the *Dimension Angle Size* tool from the Dimension toolbox.

3. Select the lower right end of the 70-degree arc and use the tentative point/datapoint sequence. MicroStation prompts you with "Select start of dimension."

4. Select a point outside the arcs where you wish to place the dimension line and click a datapoint. MicroStation prompts you in the status bar with "Define length of extension line."

5. Select the center point of the angle (the pivot point of the bracket) with a tentative point/datapoint sequence. You are prompted with "Enter point on Axis."

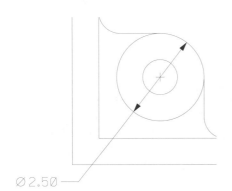

∅ 2.50

6. The angular dimension should now appear in dynamic mode. All that is needed is the final endpoint to tie the dimension down. Select the other end of the arc angle with a tentative point/datapoint click sequence.

7. Next, let's label the diameter of the larger circle of the bracket's pivot point. Select the Diameter Extended option under Mode on the Tool Settings window for the *Dimension Radial* tool.

8. Select the larger of the two concentric circles with a datapoint. MicroStation prompts you to identify the element.

9. Click a datapoint just to the left of the vertical plate. The dimension will be placed with the diameter symbol. You can continue to use the other dimensioning tools just discussed to further annotate this drawing.

Additional Dimensioning Tools

In addition to the three categories of dimensions just discussed, MicroStation includes several other tools. The most important of these is the *Dimension Element* tool.

Dimension Element

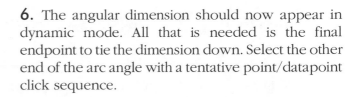

One of the more pleasant dimensioning tools, *Dimension Element* prompts you to select an element for dimensioning. Once an element has been selected, you have the option to choose the type of dimension you want generated. This is done by selecting the Next button, or by hitting either the Enter key or the space bar on your keyboard. *Dimension Element* will step through the types of dimensions available for the element chosen.

Dimension Element Selections

Linear Elements	Circular Elements
Dimension Size with Arrow	Dimension Diameter
Dimension Size with Stroke	Dimension Diameter (Extended Leader)
Label Line	Dimension Radius
Dimension Size Perpendicular to Line	Dimension Radius (Extended Leader)
Dimension Diameter Parallel	

Dimension Ordinates

An alternative to the linear dimensions discussed, the *Dimension Ordinates* tool labels distances as numbers and a line along a specified axis. The result is a simple annotation of distances from a fixed point. This is quite effective in some design disciplines where the drawing would otherwise be overwhelmed with dimensions.

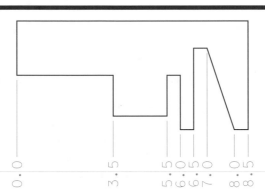

An example of the ordinate dimensioning system.

Geometric Tolerance

Although not actually used with any of the dimension tools, this tool belongs to the Dimension toolbox nonetheless. By combining the various graphic symbols found on the settings box that pops up, while using the *Place Note* and *Place Text* tools, the result is a label used in specifying various geometric tolerances in a mechanical drawing. You string together the symbols found on the Geometric Tolerance box in combination with other text to form the final feature control box.

Using feature control symbols in MicroStation is simply a matter of choosing the appropriate symbols from the Geometric Tolerance box.

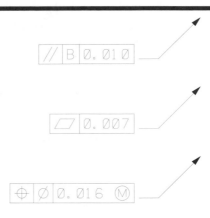

MicroStation provides two text fonts specifically for use with the Geometric Tolerance function just described. They are:

Font 100   Standard geometric tolerance symbols, including the enclosing box that normally surrounds this type of annotation

Font 101   Standard ANSI symbols

 NOTE: *When using Geometric Tolerances with the* Place Note *tool, make sure to turn off the Dimension Text Font override on the Dimension Attributes settings box. If you don't, the override text will take precedence over your geometric tolerance font.*

Label Line

A simple dimensioning tool, *Label Line* is available either as a key-in or as one of the *Next* options described in the table under the description for the *Dimension Element* tool. It is particularly useful to civil engineers who need to work with bearings and lengths of lines. On keying in `Label Line` in the Key-in window, MicroStation prompts you to select a line. Once selected, two lines of text are displayed along it—the text above the line representing its length, and the text below the line representing its angle. You must accept this dynamic display with a datapoint to place the label for the line. If Dimension Text Location is set to Manual, you must provide an additional datapoint to locate the position of the text.

Modifying Dimensions

Once you've placed your dimensions, you may need to modify them. As mentioned earlier, MicroStation treats dimensions as a fundamental, or primitive, element. This means the various tools provided to modify such elements work as well on dimension elements. The secret to their use is where you select the dimension for modification. Let's look at some of these tools and situations.

Modify Element

Used to change the vertices of lines and the diameters of circles, the *Modify Element* tool can be used to change key features of a previously placed dimension.

The Effect of Selecting Specific Parts of a Dimension with the Modify Element	
DIMENSION SELECTED	**MODIFY ELEMENT'S EFFECT**
Extension Line	Modifies the endpoint of the dimension.
Dimension Line	Repositions the dimension line and text without affecting the endpoints.
Dimension Text	Repositions the text along the dimension line.

Insert Vertex

Selecting an extension line of a dimension with *Insert Vertex* results in a dimension being appended to the dimension string. Selecting a dimension along its dimension line results in the dimension being divided into two separate segments. In either case, your second datapoint defines the location of the new extension line.

Delete Vertex

The inverse of the *Insert Vertex* tool, *Delete Vertex* removes an internal dimension of a dimension string and recreates a single dimension of the combined values. It should be noted that both vertex modification tools work even if the chosen dimension was placed with the association lock turned on.

Changing a Dimension's Settings

As with other elements in MicroStation, dimensions may need to have their parameters adjusted after they have been placed in the design. Fortunately there are two tools to help accomplish this.

Match Dimension Settings

Due to the wealth of options associated with each dimension, when you are ready to change a dimension's parameters it is best to set the current dimension settings to the target dimension first. In this way, you can change only those parameters you need without affecting other settings. To do this use the *Match Dimension Settings* tool (**Tools** ➡ **Match** ➡ **Match Dimension**). This sets the current dimension settings to match that of the chosen element. Through its *SmartMatch* tool on the Change Attributes toolbox, MicroStation 95 offers yet another way to match these settings.

Change Dimension to Active Settings

 Once you've adjusted the parameters to the way you want them, you use the *Change Dimension to Active Settings* tool (**Tools ➡ Main ➡ Dimension ➡ Change Dimension to Active Settings**) to identify those dimension elements you want updated to the current dimension settings.

Saving Your Dimension Settings

There is no question that MicroStation's dimensioning system requires close watch of many parameters. It gets even more difficult when you try to maintain uniformity across multiple drawings. Some would say it is impossible. Fortunately, there is a way to save your dimension settings and use them in this and other design files.

Part of the Settings Manager, the dimension settings can be extracted from your active design file and stored in a special file. Conversely, you can open one of these settings files and import the settings found there into your active design file. This is done using the Manage option on the Settings menu.

 NOTE: *The Settings Manager and its functions are not for the faint of heart. Designed to be used as a standardization tool, the manager supports more than just dimensioning parameters. As a result, the procedure for using it can be somewhat confusing. However, if you keep in mind that you are only using one small part of this facility, you should be able to comprehend its functions.*

Accessing Settings Groups

To access an external settings file, you need to bring up the Select Settings settings box. (Talk about a tongue twister!) This is done from the Settings pull-down menu (**Settings ➡ Manage**). The name of the current settings file is displayed in the Select Settings title bar. If you are using the default workspace (chances are good you are), the name of this file is STYLES.STG.

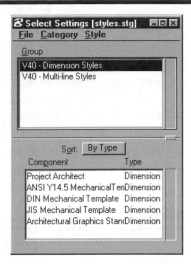

The default settings called up with the Settings Manage command.

Looking at the settings box, you will see two major sections: Group and Component. You can see that there are two distinct groups whose contents are readily identified by their names: dimensions and multi-lines. As you may remember, multi-lines also suffer from too many parameters to manipulate, and are thus good candidates for the settings file.

With the V40 Dimension Styles group selected, you will see a number of items listed in the Component section of the settings box. These components are a variety of dimension settings that have been saved under descriptive names for recall at a later time. Here you can see there are dimension settings for ANSI Y14.5, DIN, JIS, and Architectural. To set your active dimension settings to any one of these, all you have to do is click on the one of interest, but not just yet.

Creating Your Own Dimension Component

Instead of selecting one of these "store-bought" components, let's see how you would go about storing one of your own. From the menu bar in the Select Settings box activate the Edit Settings box

(**Select Settings ➡ File ➡ Edit**). Again, you will see the same Groups and Components as before; however, this time you will be able to add your own settings to the STYLES.STG file.

Selecting the Create Component Dimension command (**Edit Settings ➡ Edit ➡ Create ➡ Dimension**), you will insert an unnamed component in the Component section of the settings box. To change this name to something you recognize, go to the bottom of the settings box, select the Unnamed text with your cursor, and type in a new name (try INSIDE MS for starters). This changes the default Unnamed component's name to INSIDE MS. Double-clicking on this new component brings up the Modify dialog box.

The Modify dialog box is used to set the parameters in the new settings component.

Although there are a number of settings associated with this dialog box, the one most important to you is the Match button. Selecting this collects the settings from your active design file into the component definition. You are prompted for a name and description, sort of like that of a cell. Once you've acknowledged the update to the new component, all that remains is to exit the Edit Settings box.

Your new dimension component is now ready for use in any number of design files. Use the Select Settings command to access this new settings component. You can store any number of settings within your active settings file (patterns, cells, dimensions, text, and multi-lines, to name a few). In addition, you can set your working units and plot scales from this facility.

 NOTE: *If you have the Dimension Settings box active at the time you select settings components, the current parameters in Dimension Settings will update dynamically as you select components from Select Settings.*

Compatibility with Previous Versions

One aspect of much of this added functionality in MicroStation is its effect on compatibility with older versions of MicroStation and IGDS. Element types such as multi-lines and dimension elements are not found in these older programs. What do you do?

If your design is intended to be IGDS-compatible, you may have to give up the dimension element and its associative nature. This is accomplished via the Preferences dialog box (**Workspace ➡ Preferences...**). The Compatibility can be set to the version of MicroStation with which you need to maintain compatibility (5.0+, 4.x, or 3.x). As you select each, you will see the appropriate checkboxes deselect as you choose older versions. Keep in mind that IGDS is the same as version 3.x of MicroStation, which means that hardly any of the new features will be allowed in your design file.

Setting compatibility to 3.x ensures your design will be 100% compatible with older versions of MicroStation and the VAX-based IGDS systems. This is done at the expense of the newer features of MicroStation. (Note the dimmed-out options.)

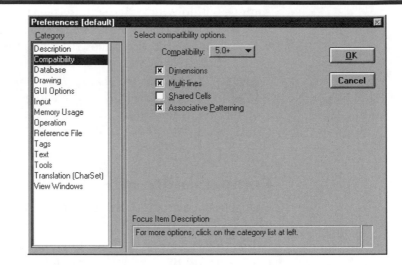

When you select one of these older versions for compatibility, you force MicroStation to create your dimensions, for instance, out of more primitive elements. Dimensions created this way cannot be modified quite as easily as their 5.0 counterparts. Each dimension, however, does share its own graphic group number, so you can still manipulate 3.x dimensions as one unit with the Graphic Group lock on.

Freezing and Thawing: A Temporary Bridge

If you need to temporarily send a design file to IGDS or 3.x MicroStation, you can set specific dimension elements to a pseudocompatible form. This is done with the Freeze command, which can be keyed in at the Key-in window. Identifying a dimension with this command will mask it, while providing the more familiar lines and text for display purposes. Use the key-in command Thaw to reverse the process.

NOTE: *If you delete individual elements of the frozen dimension under 4.x or 3.x, the changes will be lost when the dimension is ultimately thawed. You should use the Freeze / Thaw for display compatibility purposes only.*

Patterning Tools

How to Fine-tune the Look of Your Drawing

Besides dimensioning, the other major detailing operation you perform is that of *patterning*. This is the act of adding texture to your drawing's appearance to better convey the purpose of various features. For instance, in a wall section detail, you invariably show insulation batts as curves, a marsh line in a map with grassy details, and a cross section of a machined part with some sort of hatch pattern. All of these are pattern operations.

Typical example of a detail drawing with patterns.

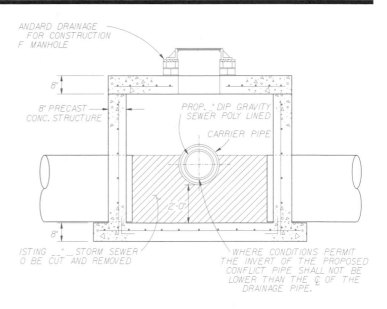

Area and Linear Patterning: The Old Days

Before version 5 of MicroStation, patterning was the only practical method for giving your drawing a little extra style. Unless you did some fairly extensive modification to the plotter configuration files, you were stuck with MicroStation's seven basic line codes.

Here's where patterning came in. By creating a custom cell containing the repeatable pattern of elements you wanted to use instead of MicroStation's line styles, you could mask an element's appearance with this pattern. This also applied to filling vast areas of the drawing. In fact, you could make very complex patterns, and many users did.

"...And They Lived Happily Ever After"

Not exactly. The downside of all this patterning was twofold. First, the space required to store elaborately patterned design files grew at an incredible rate. This was due to MicroStation's technique of storing all those little lines and arcs as individual elements. (Later on, this was somewhat reduced with shared cells.) Remember, no matter how long or short a line is, it still takes up the same space in the computer file. The second problem with patterning was editability. Once an element was patterned, it was difficult to edit. Modify Element had to be used with care. Many times, a seemingly simple edit to a drawing could end up as a nightmare of cleaning up patterns.

With version 5, when MicroStation implemented Custom Line Styles and associative area patterning, these problems with patterning were all but eliminated. A word of warning, however: although these new capabilities are cool and great, many companies have yet to convert to them. This means for compatibility's sake, you may have to deal with the old way of patterning for a while. The good news is that the new methods are so compelling in their efficiencies that no CAD administrator in his or her right mind would stick with the old way of doing things. With that said, let's look at the patterning operation.

Overview of the Area Patterning Process

One of the major areas (pardon the pun) where patterns are used is area fills. Anyone who has drawn cross-section diagrams can attest to the sheer boredom of drawing hundreds of lines, whether it's steel, concrete, or earth. This is where MicroStation's area patterning tool comes to the rescue.

Simply put, area patterning takes a selected cell (or hatch pattern) and repeatedly copies it into an identified area. By trimming off those parts of the cell that lie outside the boundary (sort of like a Fence Clip command) and repeating the process row after row, the final effect is an area filled with texture.

Such patterning does require additional parameters and a specific type of target element. Typically, an area pattern candidate should be a closed element. This means it must be either a circle, shape, ellipse, or complex shape. There are other methods for specifying the area to be patterned with datapoints or even a fence; however, the majority of patterning is done with a closed element.

Patterning Parameters

Patterning by its very nature involves the repetitive copying of a small pattern into a larger area. Unless you really only want a large copy of the pattern placed across the entire pattern area, you have to provide additional information for controlling the patterning process.

Using a row and column arrangement, the patterning process takes the cell or line you've specified and repeats it at a given distance and in a given direction. When it hits one of the edges of the pattern area, it offsets by the provided spacing and repeats the process. By specifying the orientation of the pattern itself and this offset distance, you control the final density of the pattern.

The parameters that most affect the outcome of the patterning process are Pattern Spacing and Pattern Angle. In the previous illustration, you can see how the patterning process repeats over and over in a specific direction. When the pattern process encounters an obstacle (the edge of the pattern element), it clips the current pattern occurrence and resets back and up the pattern spacing distance, and starts the entire process over.

Each of the patterning tools provides a data field in the Tool Settings window for entering these critical patterning parameters. The patterning settings follow.

Patterning Tool Settings	
Setting	**Description**
Pattern Cell	The name of the cell to be used as the pattern
Scale	The scale to apply to the pattern cell during the pattern process
Row Spacing	The distance between each row of pattern cells (same as Spacing)
Column Spacing	The distance between each cell along a row
Angle	The angle of the pattern rows or hatch lines
Tolerance	How close to a curved element a pattern is calculated
Spacing	The distance between each hatch line

The Row and Column Spacing settings control how far apart each cell is placed with respect to each row and column. By controlling this inter-cell spacing you can generate dense or sparse area fills with relatively simple patterns.

The distance between the cells is expressed in the actual distance between one cell's *extents* (the area of the design file it occupies) and the next cell's extents. In this way, you do not need to know how "fat" a cell is to specify the spacing.

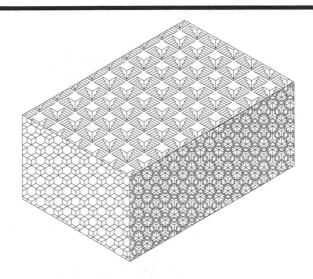

The Pattern Area command is a time-consuming process, especially if the pattern cell is complicated. The cell used in this example is from the GEOMPAT.CEL cell library.

The Tolerance setting may be a bit confusing. What it refers to is a mathematical dilemma. Because a curved element's (circle, arc, curve) edge is an approximation (due to that irrational number pi), you must tell MicroStation how fine to calculate the cutoff point for the pattern. The finer the tolerance, the longer it takes to complete the pattern.

Associative Pattern

One of the significant enhancements to version 5 of MicroStation was the ability to create associative patterns. Remember the discussion about the difficulty in modifying elements after they had been patterned? Well, no more! With pattern association turned on, you can easily modify patterned elements without a second thought. Because MicroStation stores the pattern with intelligence, any changes to the underlying master element will result in a recomputation of the pattern. Associative patterns also take up much less space. When selected, an associated pattern is nothing more than a description stored within an element's definition.

When you modify an element with associative patterning, the pattern takes care of itself.

Snappable Pattern

Another feature of patterns is *snappability*. This refers to the ability to use the tentative point snap with a pattern. If selected at the time you pattern an element, MicroStation will allow future tentative points to find the pattern elements.

On the face of it, this sounds good. However, there are many times you do *not* want to snap to a pattern. In fact, if there are small elements within the pattern close to a desired vertex, the result may be an inadvertent snap to said pattern components. This option should be used with great care.

Pattern Methods

In MicroStation you are not limited to just patterning a closed element or shape; you can use Boolean operations on closed elements to define a virtual area that should be patterned.

Patterning Methods	
Setting	**Description**
Element	Pattern a selected closed element
Fence	Pattern the current fence
Intersection	Pattern the intersection area of two or more closed elements
Union	Pattern the combined area to selected closed elements
Difference	Pattern area of element 1 less area of element 2
Flood	Find an area enclosed by elements
Points	Pattern area enclosed by a series of user-entered datapoints

If these methods sound familiar, it is probably because they are the same ones used in automatically creating a complex shape. If you think about it, this makes sense. After all, patterning requires a closed shape, even a complex one, to work. So, why not combine the function of making the shape with the patterning process? That is precisely what's going on here.

Area Patterning Tools

MicroStation's patterning tools are accessed from the Patterns toolbox that can also be torn away from the Main toolbox (**Tools ➡ Main ➡ Patterns**). Let's take a look at the tools you use to create patterns.

Recognizing that a majority of area fill is in the Crosshatch category, MicroStation supports tools for performing this simplest of area fills. Instead of using a user-defined cell, a simple line is used at the specified angle and offset to fill an area. The two tools that perform this function are *Hatch Area* and *Crosshatch Area*.

Hatch Area

 Hatch Area requires you to enter a spacing and angle in order to perform its function. In most instances, you will want to select Associative Pattern.

Setting the angle to 45 degrees results in the hatched pattern shown.

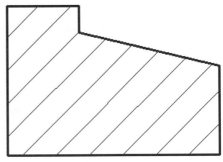

Crosshatch Area

The major difference between this tool and the *Hatch Area* tool is the addition of the second Spacing and Angle fields. This is necessary to set the angle of the second set of hatch lines. If you leave the second fields blank, MicroStation defaults to a right-angle pattern to the first angle at the same spacing.

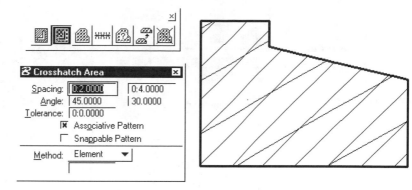

Varying the value of the two hatches can give you surprising results.

NOTE: *If you repattern an element that already contains an associated pattern, the new pattern replaces the previous one. This is handy when experimenting with the settings.*

Pattern Area

The workhorse area-patterning tool, *Pattern Area* uses a shared cell as its pattern element. Using the Scale, Angle, Row, and Column spacing, the *Pattern Area* tool computes a final pattern shape based on the method chosen.

Definitely a "cruncher," the Pattern Area tool can create simple to complex patterns.

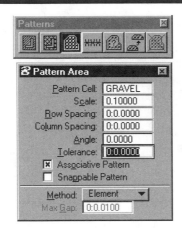

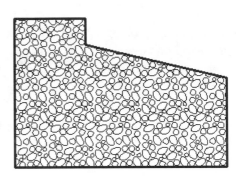

Punching Holes in a Pattern

One of the typical situations that arises with patterning is the creation of voids within the pattern's field. Take a plate, for instance, drilled with holes. How do you pattern the plate but leave the holes clear?

There are two methods for performing this feat. In both cases, however, the result is a static pattern (one that is not easily edited). This harks back to the bad old days of patterning (version 3.x and IGDS).

First Method: Patterning by Difference

The first method involves the Difference method. With this method chosen, select the main element in which the holes are "drilled."

❑ Select the *Pattern Area* tool and set Method to Difference.

❑ Identify the main object with a datapoint.

❑ Identify each element representing a hole in the main object.

❑ Datapoint once, clear of any element.

❑ Reset once to create the pattern.

If you take a close look at the result, you may be surprised by what you find. Your original outline is still a separate entity, but all of the elements you chose as holes, a copy of the outline element, and the pattern itself have been turned into a single orphan cell. This happens regardless of the alignment setting.

Second Method: Create a Group Hole Cell

This act of creating an orphan cell is similar to the other method for patterning with voids. Found under the Groups toolbox, the *Group Hole* tool lets you manually create the orphan cell before patterning it.

❑ Select the *Group Hole* tool (**Tools ➡ Main ➡ Groups ➡ Group Hole**).

❑ Identify the main object with a datapoint.

❑ Identify each element representing a hole in the main object.

❑ Datapoint once, clear of any element.

❑ Reset once to create the orphan cell.

❑ Select the appropriate *Patterning* tool and use the Element method to select the freshly created cell.

Line Patterning Versus Custom Line Styles

Before we begin the discussion of linear patterning, some differences between linear patterning and custom line styles should be discussed. Prior to version 5 of MicroStation, linear patterning was the only tool available for creating a custom line style beyond the eight standard line styles (LC=0-7). With the advent of custom line styles this is no longer true. You can create and use complex custom line styles. Although the process of creating such line styles is a little tricky, their use is not.

By selecting a line style from the Line Styles settings box (**Primary Toolbox** ➡ **Line Style** ➡ **Custom**) at the time you place the original element, you do not need to go back and pattern it. Because these custom line styles are stored external to your design file, it also provides greater consistency between drawings than with linear patterning.

However, due to historical reasons (custom line styles were implemented for the first time in version 5), you may still encounter in your day-to-day operations files that use linear patterning. For this reason, you should be familiar with this tool.

Linear Patterning

Linear patterning is the function performed when a cell is placed repetitively along a linear element. First, the target element of the patterning process is converted into a special class of elements called the "linear patterned element." This allows you to selectively display those elements initially used for patterning.

As an element is patterned, the shared pattern cell is repeatedly copied and modified as necessary to create the pattern for the target element. The components of the pattern cell are specially modified to allow for selective display control of the overall pattern. That way, if you have a complicated pattern that takes time to update, you can opt to turn it off. Then only the original element is displayed. This display option is controlled by the view-dependent key-in Set Pattern On/Off, or from the View Attributes command on the Settings menu.

In other words, the linear patterning process continually copies the selected cell over and over until it reaches the end of the selected element. Linear patterning can be performed on both individual and complex elements, such as connected strings or shapes. As an aid to manipulating a patterned element, the original element and its pattern components are placed into a graphic group.

There are four variants, or *cycles,* associated with the linear pattern tool. All four operate in essentially the same manner, the difference being in how the pattern is applied to the source element. The linear pattern tools are:

Linear Patterning Cycle Options	
Setting	**Description**
Truncated	Pattern is applied with active pattern scale. If the last element does not fit, it is truncated.
Complete	Scale of pattern is slightly adjusted so pattern ends with complete pattern cell.
Single*	Pattern cell is stretched to fit each segment of the selected element.
Multiple*	Scale of pattern is slightly adjusted so pattern ends with complete pattern cell on *each* segment.

* If a segment falls below 80% of the patterning cell's length, a line segment will be substituted instead of the pattern on this one segment. This avoids confusing patterns along short segments on the patterned element.

Examples of each linear pattern cycle and their results.

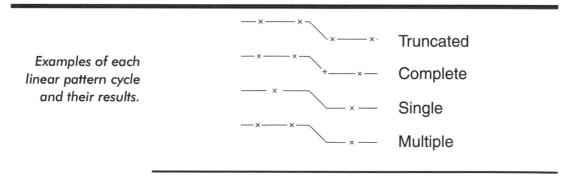

Truncated

Complete

Single

Multiple

Linear Pattern

 As with the area patterning tools, there are a number of parameters you must provide prior to actually patterning an element.

❑ Cycle (described previously)

❑ Pattern cell

❑ Scale

❑ Tolerance

With the exception of the Cycle parameter, these are the same options used with the area patterning tools, and they perform the same functions. After selecting the pattern cell, the other major parameter that must be considered is the pattern cell's scale. Because the cell may have been created under different working units, this is critical.

> **TIP:** *Try placing a potential pattern cell as a normal* (AC=) *cell and adjust the active scale appropriately until you get the desired results. To set the pattern scale, use the* ACTIVE PATTERN SCALE *key-in (or* PS= *) and set it equal to the final value of the active scale.*

To pattern an element, invoke the appropriate tool, select the element to be patterned, define a direction, and wait for the patterning process to complete.

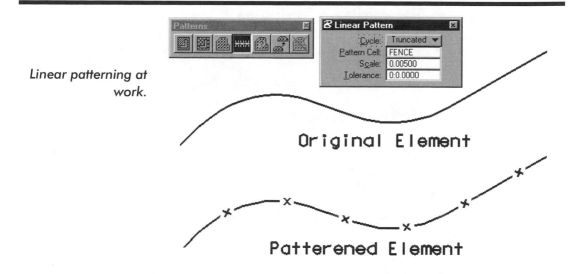

Linear patterning at work.

Defining a direction is necessary if your cell has a discernible direction such as an arrowhead. The wait is necessary because the patterning process can take a fair amount of time. Once finished, the results appear on the screen.

Turning the Pattern Display On and Off

As mentioned earlier, the patterning elements include a special marker that allows selective display. Referring to the cells delivered with MicroStation, you can see that some of them are rather complicated.

Imagine having a large number of patterns all turned on, and zooming in and out. You could wait a considerable amount of time between tools. Use the Set Pattern command to toggle the display of patterns in each view.

Other Pattern Tools and Functions

Basically, that is all there is to patterning. However, recognizing the complex nature of the patterning function, MicroStation is equipped with a set of helpful tools and commands that make working with patterns a little easier.

Show Pattern Attributes

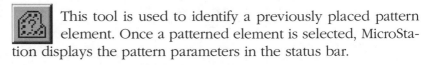 This tool is used to identify a previously placed pattern element. Once a patterned element is selected, MicroStation displays the pattern parameters in the status bar.

Match Pattern Attributes

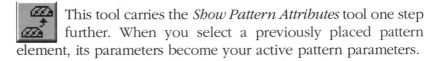 This tool carries the *Show Pattern Attributes* tool one step further. When you select a previously placed pattern element, its parameters become your active pattern parameters.

Delete Pattern

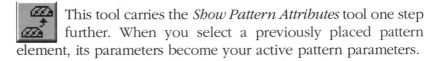 This tool removes a previously placed pattern. In the case of grouped holes, however, it does not release the orphan cell. That requires the use of the *Drop Complex Status* tool.

Conclusion

With the dimensioning and patterning facilities just described, you can detail just about any drawing imaginable. There is a lot to these two facilities, and it will take time to sort them out. However, you can begin simply and work through these tools and procedures.

Even if you haven't mastered the dimensioning package, you can begin using portions of it to modify your design. The key here is to keep trying the commands. Eventually you will master the various complexities and become adept at their use.

Three-dimensional Design

Modeling the Real World

MicroStation is without a doubt an excellent 2D design tool. Its construction tools allow you to develop just about any drawing imaginable. Well, surprise! In addition to being a good 2D tool, it is also one of the best 3D design programs.

In this chapter you'll get a good overview of many of Micro-Station's 3D capabilities. Because 3D is a subject worthy of an entire book, this discussion is not an in-depth coverage of MicroStation's entire 3D capabilities. However, at the conclusion of this chapter you'll have gained a good understanding of how MicroStation can be used to create 3D models. This chapter concludes with instructions on where to go for more information on MicroStation's 3D operations.

Video Display Limitations

There is one inherent limitation in creating 3D designs on a video display that is basically a 2D tool. Until someone develops a holographic display system, you must contend with manipulating your 3D model through the flat plane of the video monitor.

This restriction may not seem like a problem now, but after a time you will begin to appreciate what this 2D conversion of a 3D construct does to your mind—sort of like stereo in the brain.

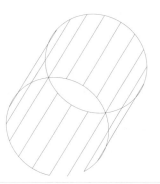

Take, for instance, this diagram. It is obviously a 3D cylinder. But is it an open tube with its opening facing up, or facing down? M.C. Escher became famous by exploiting the limitations of presenting 3D perspectives in a 2D medium. The point here is that 3D construction is an acquired skill that may take awhile to master.

There are times when working with three dimensions is appropriate. Emphasizing the modeling concept, you can create highly accurate designs of the physical world using MicroStation's 3D capabilities. You perform this task by using a combination of tools you've already mastered with 3D-specific tools and techniques.

Patience

Don't get frustrated the first time you try something and it does not turn out the way you had hoped. Instead, learn from each situation, and be prepared to correct your technique to improve your skills. Three-dimensional design, especially in free space, is difficult at best. So, now let's look at the 3D environment.

MicroStation 3D

Creating 3D Design Files

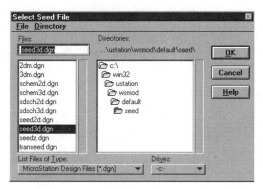

When you created your first 2D design file, you may have remembered the seed file named SEED2D.DGN. If you choose the Select button in the Seed File section on the Create Design File dialog box, you are presented with a number of additional seed files for your selection. You'll note a common theme with the names of the seed files. Almost all of them come in 2D and 3D versions. If you select one of the 3D seed files, the result is a 3D design file.

Why does MicroStation supply two separate versions of seed files, one for 2D and another for 3D? Because 3D is intrinsically more difficult than 2D. That darned Z axis is always getting in the way. If you don't need it, why carry it along?

The Design Cube

In 3D design, the already familiar design plane takes on a new dimension. By adding a direction perpendicular to the X and Y axes, you create a design cube.

The idea of perpendicular in this situation is appropriate. Because you are viewing this design cube through the video screen, the information presented to you is perpendicular to your line of sight. In essence you are sighting down this third axis all the time, piercing the design at the plane of the screen.

The design plane takes on a new dimension when you work in 3D.

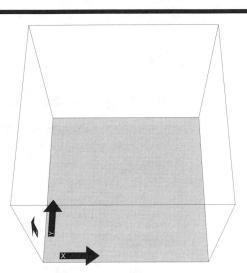

Those elements you see on the screen are projected on the video screen's plane. Even when you rotate the various drawing axes, the physical plane of the video monitor stays intact. (It would be difficult to get the video monitor to change its shape.)

In 3D, the third axis points toward you. In the default Top view this axis is the Z axis.

Instead of being a hindrance, this video plane is used with great success by MicroStation and is referred to as the *view plane*. Because the user can count on it always staying put, it is often the point of reference used to develop the 3D objects.

MicroStation maintains two fixed frames of reference for creating your 3D image: the *view plane* and the *drawing plane*. The drawing plane refers to the absolute design cube consisting of the X, Y, and Z directions in which the 3D object is oriented.

As you rotate your vantage point to peer at your object, the XYZ coordinates of the 3D object remain rooted to the drawing cube, whereas the apparent position of the individual elements moves with respect to the view plane.

You begin by maintaining the normal orientation of the three axes while creating your design. In fact, in some applications you may never deviate far from this "top-down" view of 3D.

Digital terrain modeling (DTM) always maintains a more or less 2D planar reference, treating the Z direction as a terrain elevation. A numeric control programmer or mechanical engineer, by contrast, will change the view plane quite often. This is to better orient it to the portion of the model under construction.

A digital terrain model treats the third dimension as an elevation.

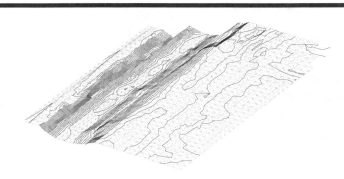

From this view the digital terrain model appears flat. The contour lines shown simulate those found on USGS maps.

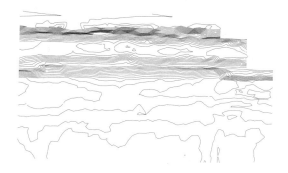

Drawing Coordinates

Even when twisting and turning the view plane, the coordinates stored are always in drawing coordinates. No matter how you rotate your view of the design, or whether you placed your design elements using the view coordinates or auxiliary coordinates, the results will be converted and stored in the standard XYZ coordinates of the design file.

If, during the course of design, you get turned around and place some elements along the wrong axis, corrective action is relatively easy. At worst it will require you to rotate a fence full of elements about one or two axes to orient the design elements the right way.

The Right-hand Rule

With all this talk of angles sweeping this way and that, it is easy to get lost. Even selecting view parameters in a 3D design file can be frustrating if you can't keep your bearings straight.

As an aid to navigation and element placement, the *right-hand rule* was developed. This rule states that all angles sweep in a direction counterclockwise around the positive direction of an axis.

Strangely enough, your right hand follows this rule. If you assume that your thumb is pointing in the positive direction of an axis, your fingers curl in the positive direction of the angle. Let's test this with what you know of 2D motions.

In 2D you will remember that all angles are specified in a counterclockwise direction. Now, assuming your thumb is pointed along the positive direction of the Z axis, which would be directly at your face, and you curl your fingers, guess what? They curl counterclockwise. Looked at this way, using counterclockwise angles no longer seems arbitrary.

The right-hand rule is derived from the action of your fingers on your right hand. The thumb represents the positive direction of the Z axis.

All of the MicroStation axes, whether cylindrical, spherical, or rectangular, exhibit this trait. The key is to remember which direction is positive along any given axis.

Rotating Your Views

To help you maintain your orientation within the design cube, MicroStation includes a set of standard views. These views match the standard orthographic views you would work with in manual drafting.

❑ Top

❑ Bottom

❑ Right

❑ Left

❑ Front

❑ Back

❑ Iso

There are several ways you can invoke these views. First, there is the Rotation command (**Tools ➡ 3D ➡ 3D View Control**). Selecting this brings up the 3D View Control toolbox containing an icon for Change View Rotation. Clicking this icon brings up the View Rotation settings box that offers these standard views for your selection. You can also select a standard view with the View (VI=) key-in command. Typing in VI=FRONT and selecting a view will set that view to the Front standard view.

Top-down Design

Back when you were using 2D, all of your element placements were done in a top-down view. Think of how you look down on your drawing when it is on the drafting board. This top-down approach is maintained in 3D. The X axis points positively to the right, and the Y axis points positively up. This is easy to grasp because it matches how you view your typical drawing.

Analogous to a box, each view is "hinged" off specific views. Starting with the top view, the front view is hinged from the bottom edge of the top view. The back view is hinged from the top edge of the top view. Confused? That's okay, you are allowed.

To help clear up the relationships of the various views, take a look at the next figure. It shows how the views are related to one another.

The first six named views and their relationship to one another.

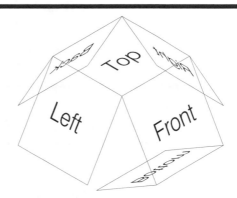

As just mentioned, you can use the VI= key-in with the appropriate view name. The VI= key-in is the same one you use to retrieve user-saved view parameters. If you think about it, these standard views are only X, Y, and Z rotations with respect to the design plane.

View Rotation Settings Box

In addition to selecting the standard views, the View Rotation settings box lets you rotate the view along all three drawing axes. This is done in the right half of the settings box. By clicking on the plus or minus sign along the appropriate axis, you affect the cube's orientation in the left half of the settings box. Selecting the appropriate view and hitting the Apply button updates that view.

The View Rotation settings box presents you with an effective method of rotating any view.

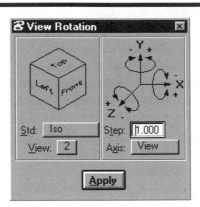

An option associated with this settings box is the Axis option. Normally, you rotate a view with respect to the view's own axes. There are times, however, when you will want to orient the view precisely along the drawing's axes. By selecting Axis/Drawing, all rotations are done around the drawing's axes.

For instance, to illustrate the fact that the Z axis pierces the Top view, selecting the Drawing axis followed by a rotation about the Z axis, + or –, results in the cube rotating about the Top view. Holding down the mouse button makes the cube spin about the top view.

One of the more unique tools found in any CAD package, the View Rotation settings box has been known to provide an entertainment break during intense design sessions. More than any other tool, *View Rotation* also brings home the action of the Z axis as it relates to the plane of the video monitor.

Exercise: View Rotation Along the Z Axis

1. Activate the CUBE3D.DGN design file.

2. Invoke the View Rotation settings box (**Tools ➡ 3D ➡ 3D View Control ➡ Change View Rotation**).

3. Select the Iso view in the "Std:" view field. Make sure the Axis field is set to View.

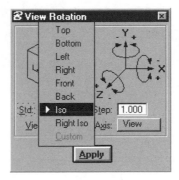

4. The View box should now be tilted, with the Top, Left, and Front views shown.

5. Click on the positive Z axis arrow and hold down the mouse button. The cube should now be spinning in a counterclockwise direction.

This short exercise illustrates how the Z axis always faces out of the video screen when the Axis is set to View. Just like the fingers on your right hand, the direction of rotation sweeps to the left. Now, what happens if you select one of the other axes?

Exercise: Rotating Along the X Axis

1. Continuing with the View Rotation settings box, select the Top view from the Std. view selection box.

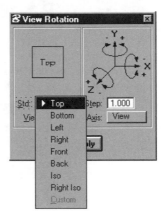

2. The view cube should now show only the Top view. Now, briefly click on the positive X rotation arrow.

3. Note how the Back view slowly emerges from the top of the cube.

4. Click briefly on the positive Y axis. Another view, the Left one, comes into view.

5. Try rotating the various axes back using the negative direction. Remember, you must select the rotation in the reverse order in which you originally rotated the view cube. This is because the XYZ axes are oriented with respect to the view itself, *not* the view cube.

This exercise showed you how easy it is to move your perspective around within the design file. However, it's one thing to rotate a view, and quite another to place elements in this 3D space. To do this, you must begin to associate the standard views and their relationship to one another.

Using Adjacent Views

Because you must keep your orientation with respect to the design plane straight in your head at all times, a good habit to get into now is to always display at least one additional view that is *adjacent* to your working view. Adjacent, in this case, means a view that is from a right angle to your working view. With the standard views, this means that if you are working in the Top view, your adjacent views would be Left, Right, Front, and Back. Any of these views can be used to specify a depth with respect to the Top view.

By keeping a view oriented in the general direction you are working, you stand a better chance of maintaining your bearings within the design cube. As you place an element, the element's planar view (in other words, a straight line) should appear. This little visual cue will go a long way toward keeping you sane with 3D.

 TIP: *Start developing standard view combinations you can relate to. For instance, when working in the Top view, you should have the Right view active as well. To make sure they are both looking at the same part of the design, use the Copy View command (***Tools** ➡ **View Control** ➡ **Copy View icon***) to copy one view's orientation into another view. Next, use the view rotation, or* VI= *key-in, to select the adjacent view. This way, the levels that are echoed on, the zoom scale, and so on are all set the same.*

Setting Your Active Depth

So, how do you control where MicroStation places elements along this third axis? By setting a view's active depth.

Not to be confused with active level, the active depth sets the position on a view's perpendicular axis where your elements are going to appear when you click in the view. Again, referring back to the cube, you know that the Top view's perpendicular axis is the Z axis. If you were to set your view's active depth to 5 master units, all elements placed from this point on would be at 5 units from the global origin.

The 3D Tool Frame

Although you can key in your active depth and select your view, most users will prefer to use the *Set Active Depth* tool. This tool, and many of the 3D-specific tools, can be found on its own tool frame, the 3D tool frame (**Tools ➡ 3D ➡ 3D**). This tool frame contains six related toolboxes organized by function.

As you can see, the diminutive 3D tool frame contains six toolboxes that access some of the more complicated tools found in MicroStation.

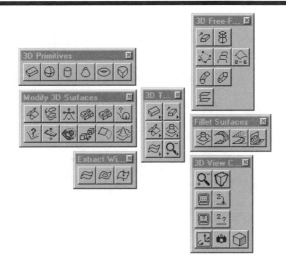

The 3D Primitives toolbox contains tools for creating 3D elements of various types. The four surface-related toolboxes contain tools for creating, manipulating, and extracting MicroStation's surface element type. Finally, the 3D View Control toolbox of interest in this discussion contains tools for controlling various 3D aspects of your views.

Set Active Depth

This tool allows you to visually set a view's active depth. By selecting the view, a dynamic plane appears in adjacent views, allowing you to identify with a datapoint the depth at which you want planar elements to be placed in the chosen view.

Display Active Depth

The complement to the *Set Active Depth* is the *Display Active Depth* tool. Selecting a view with this tool results in the active depth value being displayed in the status bar.

The following exercise shows you how to set your active depth in a view. Try your hand at placing elements at a given active depth.

Exercise: Setting Your Active Depth

1. Open the design file CUBE3D.DGN. When you bring up this file, note the standard four views and their orientation. If yours does not match this, use the V I = key-in with the appropriate standard view names to set the view orientation.

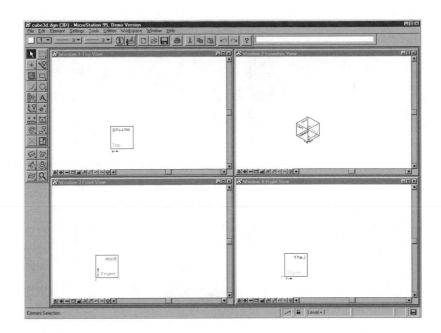

2. Let's initially set the active depth in the Front view (View 3). Select the *Set Active Depth* tool from the 3D View Control toolbox (**Tools ➡ 3D ➡ 3D View Control**).

MicroStation prompts you to select a view. Click a datapoint anywhere in the view window labeled Window 3-Front View.

3. A dynamic dashed box should now appear in all four views. This box represents the display cube associated with the Front view. The Iso view really shows the relationship of the Front view to this cube. Compare the relationship of the word *Front* in the Window 3-Front View with that of Window 2-Isometric View.

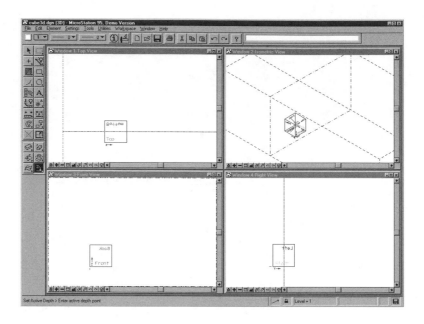

4. Look at the status bar. MicroStation is now prompting you to "Enter active depth point." Click a datapoint in the center of the 3D box in Window 4-Right View.

5. With the active depth set, let's place a circle in the Front view. Activate the *Place Circle by Center* tool.

MicroStation will prompt you to identify the center of the circle. Click a datapoint in the Window 3-Front View, just to the right of the box.

6. A dynamic circle should appear in all four views. Note its orientation in each view. In the top and right views it appears as a line. This indicates that both of these views are adjacent to the Front view. Also, note how the position of the circle in the Right view is exactly where you clicked when setting the active depth a moment ago. Click again to set the circle's diameter.

7. Of interest is the orientation of the circle in the Isometric view. It appears as an ellipse in this view, which is precisely how you would expect a circle to appear in a view 60 degrees off the Front view. Now place a circle in the Isometric view. Click a datapoint once in the Isometric view at the corner of the box.

8. Note how the resulting circle appears exactly the same in the three opposing views. This is, of course, because of the Isometric view's 60-degree orientation to the Front, Top, and Right views.

Active Depth Key-in

In addition to selecting your active depth with a datapoint, you can use a key-in, AZ=, to specify it. This depth is always set with respect to the global origin, X=0, Y=0, Z=0. If you have moved the global origin using the GO= key-in, AZ= will be in reference to this new location.

View Depth

One other wrinkle that makes itself apparent when you begin working with 3D is the transparency of your design. As you construct your wireframe design, you fill your design file with all sorts of elements turned at all sorts of angles.

Unlike the real world, where details become fuzzy or disappear altogether with distance, the design plane's elements remain sharp and in focus at all times. What happens then is that when you are trying to work inside a relatively complex 3D construct you begin to get interference from the elements placed earlier.

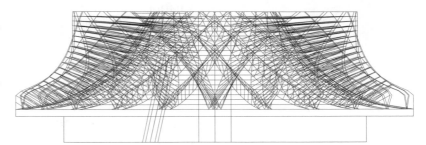

Without control of your display depth, you would not be able to find your way around a complex design.

Because these elements are all over your design file, you cannot avoid selecting one if it crosses your view no matter how far down the perpendicular axis it is placed. Recognizing this problem, MicroStation provides a mechanism to clip out a section of the perpendicular axis and display only a portion of your design file that lies within the bounds of the display depth.

Set Display Depth

This is done either directly, using the `DP=min, max` key-in, or by interactively defining the required depth in an adjacent view with the *Set Display Depth* tool (on the 3D View Control toolbox). By selecting two points in an adjacent view you tell MicroStation which portion of the design cube you wish to see. Let's try it.

Exercise: Setting Your Display Depth

1. Using the design file from the last exercise, let's set the display depth in the Front view. Select the *Set Display Depth* tool from the 3D View Control toolbox.

2. MicroStation prompts you with "Select view for display depth." Click anywhere in Window 3-Front View to identify it as the view you wish to operate on.

3. The dashed box delineating the display depth for the Front view will appear in all views. You must identify the front and back clipping planes in proper order. MicroStation prompts you to define the front clipping plane.

4. Click a datapoint just to the left of the Right text string in Window 4-Right View. Much like the previous exercise, in which MicroStation displayed in dynamics a plane that identified the active depth plane, it displays a plane identifying the front clipping plane and prompts you to define the back clipping plane.

5. Click a datapoint just to the right of the Left text string in Window 4-Right View.

6. The words *Front* and *Back* will disappear from the Window 3-Front View, along with the squares representing the front and back planes. These two elements are now outside the display depth you selected for the Front view. To get a better idea of what just happened, with the Set Display Depth command active, click in Window 2-Isometric View and define the depth in the Top view around the top right corner of the cube by first clicking inside the cube and then outside.

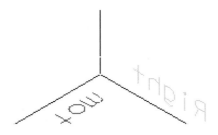

7. Whoa! Wait a minute. What happened to the view? Instead of a slice of the box being shown, you get what appears to be a corner of the box. Because the display depth is calculated with respect to the view, and *not* the drawing, the "slice" you defined with your datapoints cuts through the heart of the box. This leads to only a portion of the box being displayed.

8. Display depth can be restored with a key-in. Use the Set DDepth Absolute or DD= key-in to add or subtract the display depth. This command is cumulative and is easier to remember as "delta depth," referring to the difference between what you see and what you want to see.

DD=-60,60

Click a datapoint in Window 2-Isometric View.

9. The view should now be returned to its original state. The distances provided with the DD= command were added to the display depth you defined earlier. The –60 was added to the backside of the display depth, and the +60 was added to the front.

Starting Out Simple

When you first start out with 3D design, the best bet is to stick with a single view plane and use the Active Depth, or AZ=, command to control how your elements get placed with respect to the Z axis. It is also a good idea to start at a known XYZ location on the design plane. In this way, if you get all turned around, all you have to do to return to a known state is specify a view and XYZ locations.

Working in 3D

Using Datapoints

3D datapoint operation works similarly to that of 2D.

Boresite Lock

When using tools such as *Change Element Attributes* or *Delete Element*, you may want to grab only those elements at the active depth of your view. This way, other elements that may be present on the view, but not at your active depth, will not be highlighted when you click near them.

This is in marked contrast to the fence commands that will affect any element visible and within the fence. To turn Boresite off (thus restricting element selection to your active depth), key in LOCK BORESITE OFF↵ or select the option from the Locks submenu under the Settings menu.

Using Tentative Points

As mentioned before, all MicroStation element placement and modification tools function properly in the 3D environment. As you adjust your Active Depth and place elements, you begin to feel confident with working in 3D—that is, until you try using the tentative point. Using the tentative point does require some forethought and understanding of how it treats your design cube.

When you click a tentative point near an object, the resulting datapoint takes on not only the X and Y values of the "snapped to" object, but also its Z depth. Thus, if you were to place a circle by diameter by snapping to two lines at different depths, the resulting circle would be skewed between the two lines. (See the next figure.)

This circle is perfectly round. (Note view 4.) Because it was placed using a tentative point between two lines at different depths, it looks distorted in the other three views.

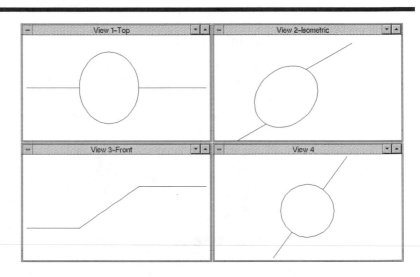

For this reason, when you use the tentative point you should use one of the passive measurement commands associated with the tentative point, SET TPMODE VDELTA. When you click a tentative point between two elements, the delta difference between the points will be displayed. (See the next figure.)

The resulting readout from setting TPMODE to VDELTA. Note the Z value.

2.9565, -2.8796, 0.8750

The 3D Tentative Point and 3D Datapoint

No matter how often you rotate views and select active depths, there are times when you just want to select a point in space. Fortunately, MicroStation provides this capability in the form of 3D tentative and datapoint. These are accessed with a combination of the Alt key and the appropriate mouse button.

3D Mouse Button Assignments	
Function	**Default Assignment**
3D Datapoint	Alt - Mouse Button 1
3D Tentative Point	Alt - Mouse Button 2

If you hold down the Alt key on the keyboard while hitting either datapoint or tentative point, a dashed bore line will appear in the views adjacent to the one in which you clicked a data/tentative point. Clicking the 3D datapoint or 3D tentative point again, but this time in an adjacent view, results in a datapoint or tentative point at the intersection of your first data/tentative point and the second one.

The 3D datapoint can be used to select a point in free space. Note how the cursor in the Front view is lined up with the bore line on the Top and Right views.

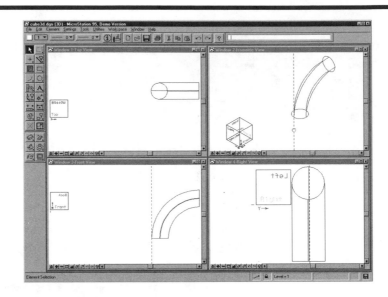

Using the Fit View Command

One last note about view control. When you have gotten really lost in your design cube, as a last resort you can invoke the Fit command. In 3D this command looks for the extents of your elements in all three directions and sets the chosen view to display them. It also resets your active depth for that view to the center of the display depth. In this way, you have a starting point from which to rotate.

Using Everyday Tools in 3D

Placing Elements in 3D

MicroStation 3D allows you to place elements in much the same way as you did in 2D. Most element types are *planar* by nature. Thus, in 3D they still exhibit the same characteristics as they did in 2D.

For instance, when you place a circle in a 3D file, it appears like an ordinary circle. However, by definition a circle must be planar. When you *Place Circle* in a 3D design file, its orientation is to the view in which you placed it. This means that if you are working in the Right view, you will see a circle in that view. However, if you were to view it in an adjacent view—say, the Front view—the circle would appear as a line, its planar surface being along your line of sight.

Fence Operations

There will be times when you will need to use a fence operation in 3D. When you do, there is a simple rule. What you see is what you affect. In other words, if your display depth is set to display only a portion of the design, your fence manipulation command will only operate on those elements present.

You still need to be aware of the Fence Lock condition, as this is still active. Fence Clip Lock will cut those displayed partial elements that fall within the fence.

3D Construction Tools

There are a number of special-element placement tools unique to the 3D environment. In most cases, these tools generate some sort of projected or extruded element such as a cylinder or cone. In addition, you can extrude your own elements using the *Construct Surface of Projection* tool.

Construct Surface of Projection

In its simplest form, the *Construct Surface of Projection* tool creates a complex 3D shape of your selected element by pushing or pulling that element along the perpendicular view axis. To get predictable results with this tool, you need to understand how it works.

When you select a shape for projection, the direction of the projection must be supplied. Remembering that datapoints always drop your element at the chosen active depth, an element already at this depth will create a flattened projection. The easiest way to see this is to place a shape, project it, and then rotate the view.

Exercise: Projecting a Shape

1. Using the CUBE3D.DGN as before, start by setting the active depth in the Window 3-Front View. Next, place a block on this view away from the display cube using the *Place Block* tool.

2. Next, invoke the *Construct Surface of Projection* tool. Set the options of this tool to match those shown in the following illustration; that is, ensure that Orthogonal is off.

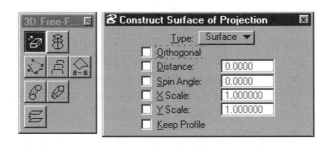

3. Select the block you placed in step 1 in Window 3-Front View. Click a datapoint again just to the right of the block in the same view when prompted to define height.

4. If your Isometric view is zoomed out enough, you should see your projection just to the side of the view cube. If the view doesn't show your projection, use the *Fit View* tool to recalculate the extents of the view. The result is probably not what you expected. Instead of a nice 3D box, you have a skewed, flattened object. Because the starting and ending depths for the projection are the same, you have created a flattened projection that goes sideways instead of down.

This points out an important aspect of the project tool. It takes your input literally and stretches your surface from the source element to your datapoint no matter which direction you go. So, how do you control the projection tool? With precision key-ins or by selecting the Orthogonal option.

5. To remove this misshapen projected shape, use the Undo function (**Edit ➡ Undo…**). This returns your block to its original shape. Of course, you could also type UNDO in the Key-in window.

6. Reselect the *Construct Surface of Projection* tool, but this time select the Orthogonal option. Select the shape in Window 3 again.

7. This time, move your cursor over one of the adjacent views or the Isometric one and see what happens. Instead of a skewed box, you have a perfectly orthogonal block. A datapoint in any view results in a 3D box.

8. As an alternative to entering the second datapoint, you can project the box along your view's axis by keying in DX=0,0,-50. This results in a box that extends 50 units into your View screen. Remember that the positive direction of the perpendicular axis of a view always points out of the video screen.

The other options associated with the *Construct Surface of Projection* tool control the scale and "twist" of the resulting image. This comes in handy in some cases. The rotation always occurs along the perpendicular axis, thus twisting the projection. The scale causes the projection to shrink or expand from one end to the other.

Try the previous exercise using various scales and angles, but keep using the same DX= key-in or the Orthogonal option. If you use an extremely small scale value, say 0.1, the resulting projection looks almost like a pyramid.

Surface of Revolution

The other major type of surface creation you will use is *Construct Surface of Revolution*. This tool takes an object and sweeps it through space at a specified angle, and around a specified point. Sort of like a supercharged version of the *Place Arc* tool, this function is extremely useful when constructing pipe elbows and circular extrusions.

Creating an elbow with the Surface Revolution command.

Working with Area

Both construction tools create complex elements. Each surface of revolution or surface of projection uses linestrings and arcs as part of the complex element used to create the finished 3D object. In addition, all such constructs also have an area property.

When rendering 3D objects, the area of each surface is used to define how an object would appear if it were a solid. The area property is the same as that exhibited by traditional 2D elements, such as circles or shapes. However, when you create a 3D surface, you may or may not want the ends of it capped with an area.

Capping a Surface

You may have noticed the Type field associated with the two construction tools just discussed. The option of selecting a solid or a surface refers to what the tool does to the open end of the complex element it creates as a result of its operation.

With Type:Solid selected, the project or revolution tool will finish the construction with a shape or circle closing the end of the new surface. You can create either open pipes or closed cylinders by setting this parameter. Many of the *3D Primitive* tools support this option.

The effect of Surface selected as type of construct is shown on the left, and the effect of Solid on the right.

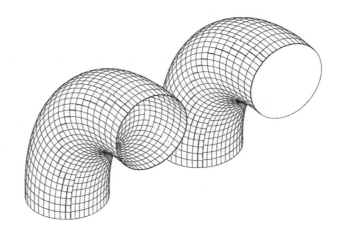

3D-specific Elements

There is a class of elements available for creating specific 3D objects commonly used in design. Known as *truncated cylinders* and *cones,* they are similar in appearance and action to projected circles.

3D Primitive Element Tools

Toolname	Description
Place Slab	Places a 3D rectangular shape
Place Sphere	Places a circular volume of revolution
Place Cylinder	Places a cylindrical surface or shape
Place Cone	Places a cone-shaped object
Place Torus	Places a donut or toroidal shape
Place Wedge	Places a pie-shaped projection

A short description of a couple of these tools follows.

Place Slab

Recognizing that many element projections performed in a design session result in orthogonal shapes (i.e., cubes and boxes), MicroStation provides the *Place Slab* tool. By defining three corners of a rectangle and a depth using an adjacent view, you can create such boxes in a hurry. The advantage of this tool is that you don't have to deal with active scales, active angles, or even active depths.

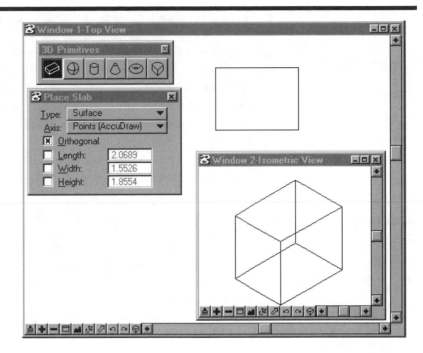

A simplified version of the Surface Projection tool, the Place Slab tool makes it easy to create perfect boxes every time.

The Axis option allows you to pre-orient the slab to one of the major axes, either the drawing X, Y, or Z, or the View X, Y, or Z. As with many of the *Place Element* tools, the size of the resulting object can be predetermined. Using Length, Width, and Height options accomplishes this.

Place Sphere

Used to place a sphere in your design, the *Place Sphere* tool offers the same axes options as the *Place Slab* tool. In addition, you can select Radius to predefine the size of the sphere.

Introduction to Image Rendering

Most readers of this book will have undoubtedly seen some of the 3D illustrations that grace the sales literature for MicroStation. All of these images were created using MicroStation 3D tools and rendering capabilities. In the previous section we discussed the basics of creating a 3D model. In this section we look at MicroStation's rendering capabilities.

Rendering or performing a hidden line process on a MicroStation system is useful for more than just pretty pictures. When you are dealing with extremely complicated models, blatant spatial errors are not apparent until you perform a rendering of the design.

In the following wireframe images, the multitude of objects makes it difficult to identify potential problems in the design. In situations such as these, there is a real hazard of pipes interfering with one another and the surrounding structure. By performing a rendering operation on this image, you can see that there is an unintentional intersection between a pipe and a wall.

The wireframe image of a model doesn't reveal an interference problem...

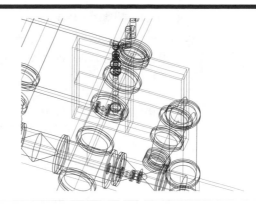

...whereas the hidden line view of this model shows the problem with the pipe and wall. (Image courtesy of CH2M Hill.)

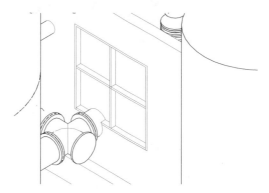

Some of MicroStation's Advanced Rendering Features

MicroStation has had rendering capabilities since its inception. Version 3 implemented rendering by spawning a separate application that processed a 3D design file. Version 4 tightly integrated rendering in its environment. Version 5 saw the implementation of significant rendering enhancements. MicroStation now offers rendering capabilities that easily surpass those found in competing packages. The following are some of these advanced features.

Pattern Mapping

MicroStation supports the use of pattern mapping. Once the exclusive domain of dedicated modeling products such as ModelView or 3D Studio, this capability brings a level of realism to MicroStation that must be seen to be believed. In essence, pattern mapping takes a raster bit map image and drapes it over the surface of the elements being rendered.

For instance, to simulate a brick facade on a building, all you have to do is assign a brick pattern to the elements that make up that facade. When rendered, the colors of the elements are replaced by the assigned brick pattern. The result is a very realistic-appearing image. Pattern and bump maps are part of MicroStation's material definition and assignment facility.

Bump Maps

In conjunction with pattern mapping, MicroStation supports an additional texture enhancement. In the previous example the brick appears a little "flat." This is due to the 2D nature of the brick pattern. Using an additional bit map that highlights the mortar portion of the brick image, MicroStation can darken this region, which results in a more realistic 3D image.

Casting Shadows

Shadows can provide a dramatic effect in Phong shading for spot, distance, or solar lights. Used with solar light, shadows can help architects create more effective client presentations and solar studies.

Transparency

Elements can be assigned transparency. Objects behind such transparent elements will be visible depending on the amount of transparency assigned to the intervening element. This is controlled by the material definition and assignment settings.

Anti-aliasing

This feature reduces the jagged edges (jaggies) that are particularly noticeable on low-resolution displays. This is done by blending sharp edges of an object into the background color. This feature is only available as an enhancement to the Phong rendering function.

Setting Up the Rendering Process

Rendering-related features in MicroStation can be found under either the Settings menu or the Utilities menu. After a fair amount of setup, you render a view with one of several rendering methods. True, you can render any view at any time. However, to improve the quality of the rendering process, Micro-Station provides a number of rendering settings and options. These are accessed via the Settings menu (**Settings ➡ Rendering**).

General Rendering Settings

The Rendering Settings box is the first place you start when fine-tuning your rendered image output.

The first of the rendering settings boxes is where you set the more advanced features of the rendering process. The most notable option found here is the set of Distance Cueing values. These are used to simulate the effect of atmosphere on your rendered image. You can adjust the distance cueing from none, such as a clear day with zero humidity, to a foggy San Francisco morning. In addition, you can select the color of the fog itself (maybe a brownish color to simulate smog?).

Rendering View Attributes

The Rendering View Attributes box is important for turning on fundamental rendering attributes for each view. Note, especially, the Pattern/Bump Maps, Shadows, and Transparency options.

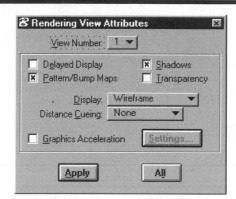

Used to set specific view attributes related to rendering, these options have a profound effect on your rendered image's appearance. Three options found here are of the most interest. The Pattern/Bump Maps option activates the use of MicroStation's advanced rendering capability, the ability to use pattern maps to add texture to your rendered objects.

Shadows turns on MicroStation's shadow casting simulator used with the high-end rendering methods. You can get reasonably good shadows, useful in adding an extra level of realism, to any rendered image. Transparency allows you to see through specific objects, such as windows or glass vases.

The Display field controls whether you want to enable real-time rendering on a specific view. Normally set to Wireframe, you can elect to have a view always shown as a rendered image. This is great when you have a simple image with some confusing 3D features. However, the tradeoff is the increased time it takes for MicroStation to keep this view updated. Distance Cueing enables the atmospheric effect previously described.

Finally, there is a checkbox to enable graphics acceleration. This option is helpful only if your computer is equipped with an OpenGL accelerator video adapter, such as those from Intergraph, Accel Graphics, and others. To support these high-end video adapters that embed the 3D OpenGL specification to accelerate rendering and other 3D operations, MicroStation supplies the "msopengl" application that must be loaded with the `MDL LOAD MSOPENGL` key-in to exploit the features in the hardware.

Global Lighting

Many of the rendering methods perform not only a hidden line function but calculate the brightness of the various surfaces within your design. How bright an object appears depends on a number of variables. The most important aspect is the object's angle to the light source.

When you select any of the shading options with the default lighting source, MicroStation sets the light source as that of the viewer. This would be as if you were shining a flashlight at the view. And just as with a flashlight, the image does not quite look real. Think of how things look in the headlights of a car. To better control the look of a shaded image, MicroStation provides a number of lighting options.

Controlling the Lighting

Selecting the Rendering Settings box from the Settings pull-down menu presents you with a number of lighting options. You have three choices: Ambient, Flashbulb, and Solar. Although you can turn all three on, this diminishes the effect of the individual lighting options.

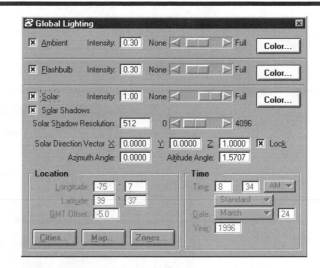

The Global Lighting settings box is used to set all of the parameters related to lighting your design.

Ambient Lighting

An artificial light source, the Ambient option controls the uniform illumination surrounding your rendering. Similar to general office lighting, ambient lighting is good for highlighting model details that would otherwise be too dark to see. The default value of 0.10 (i.e., 10%) is a good value. Anything over 0.4 will wash out the colors of your rendering.

Flashbulb

The default lighting source, the Flashbulb option is the light that is "shined" on the elements from your viewing perspective. This can be adjusted from 0.0 to 1.0 (100%). Lower values darken the colors used to shade the surfaces.

Solar Light

A very interesting option, the Solar light source simulates the direction and intensity of light as it would appear coming from the sun. By setting the latitude and longitude, date and time, you can approximate how your project would appear on a given day.

This is most appropriate for architectural renderings, but can be applied to any project. You could enter this information via the fields provided. However, a fun alternative is to call up the map with the Map... button and directly select your location.

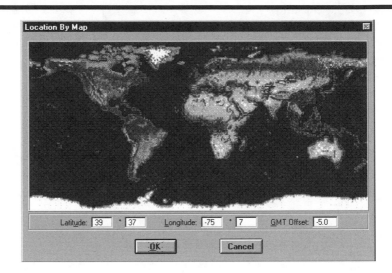

The Location by Map option allows you to select your project's location from a world map.

You can also choose your location from a list of cities of which MicroStation knows the whereabouts. However, this is not as much fun as the "You Are Here" selection from the world map.

You can also specify whether you want solar shadows. This option is only applicable to the Phong rendering method, and the Shadows option must be enabled in the Rendering View Attributes settings box as well.

Source Lighting

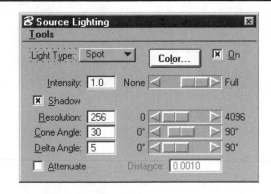

The Source Lighting settings box is crucial in placing light sources within your drawing. It includes both settings for the light sources and the commands for placing the lights themselves.

In addition to the global lighting just described, MicroStation supports fully customizable source lighting. This refers to the ability to place lighting sources within your design that can, in turn, cast light upon, and around, your model.

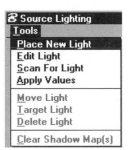

The Source Lighting settings box assists you in the placement and configuration of these sources, providing you with quite a few options. MicroStation uses specialized cells to simulate these light sources. The Tools pull-down menu gives you a number of commands for the placement and editing of these light sources.

Rendering a View

Selecting Render from the Utilities pull-down menu presents you with a set of rendering options. From top to bottom, they go from the simplest to the most computationally intense rendering options.

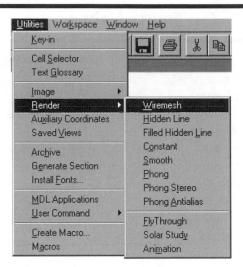

The rendering technique is chosen from the Render option's submenu.

Wireframe, the default, is what you have been looking at while creating 3D images. In this mode, a view shows you all of the elements in your design. An element's area has no effect on this view mode. This is the mode that MicroStation returns to anytime you update a view. This means that if you were to perform one of the more computationally intensive rendering functions—say, Phong Shading (the most difficult)—and immediately update the view, the Phong results would be lost. To set a view permanently to one of the rendering methods, select the Display option button in the Rendering View Attributes settings box, which is opened from the Settings pull-down menu.

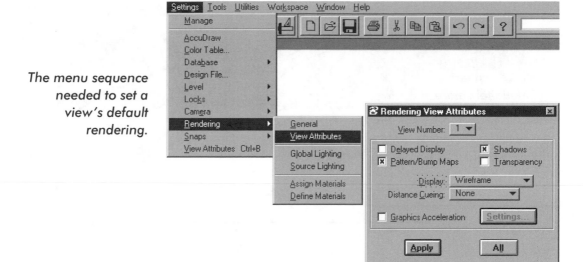

The menu sequence needed to set a view's default rendering.

Although you can set a view to use a rendering method for display, many of the options will greatly reduce the display performance in most activities. However, when working with curved surfaces (i.e., spheres, cones, and cylinders), it may be advantageous to use the Wire Mesh option.

Wire Mesh

This rendering option affects only curved surfaces. By laying a wire mesh over these surfaces, you can better see their relationship to other objects and elements. The Wire Mesh option does not require intense calculations, so it is a good alternative to wireframe when working in 3D (as opposed to one of the rendering options).

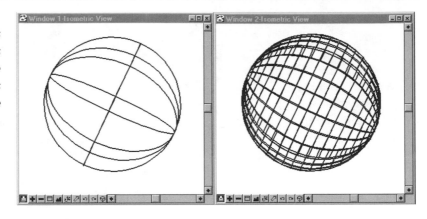

View 1 shows wireframe, whereas view 2 shows wire mesh. The sphere is definitely more obvious in view 2.

Hidden Line

One of the most useful of the day-to-day rendering techniques, one that you will use during the design process, is Hidden Line. Effective on monochrome displays as well as color, Hidden Line treats all element surfaces as opaque in nature. Calculating which surfaces and elements are closer to the viewer (i.e., you), those elements partially or completely obscured will be modified appropriately. The effect is a line drawing reminiscent of an illustration.

A Hidden Line rendering of a 3D object.

Filled Hidden Line

A modification of the hidden line technique, the Filled Hidden Line option fills each element polygon with its color. The edges are then highlighted with white. This gives an almost cartoon-like appearance.

The same object rendered with Filled Hidden Line.

Constant Shading

By far the simplest form of shaded rendering, the Constant Shading option breaks curved surfaces into a series of facets. Each facet is in turn colored with a solid color calculated with a flat face at an angle to the various (or one) light sources. The result is a rough, computer-looking image.

The roughest of the three shading techniques, Constant Shading works best with noncurved objects. It is good for quick results.

Smooth Shading

The next best shading method is Smooth. Again using a faceted approach to breaking down a curved surface, the difference is in how these individual facets are treated. The shading algorithm includes an operation that averages the shading from one facet to adjacent ones. Sort of like blurring the image, the result is a smoother appearance.

The Smooth Shading option gives you a more realistic appearance. The look of the image still appears computer-generated.

Phong Shading

The most computationally intense of the three shading options, Phong calculates the shading value at each pixel location. This means that if you are shading a VGA screen, the calculation for shading is done at each dot along each column, row by row. This would result in a calculation of 307,200 pixels. This can take some time.

Now, if you are using a higher resolution monitor of say, 1,280 by 1,024 pixels, the number of calculations would jump to 1,310,720. Obviously, this number of calculations means you should save this type of rendering for the final product, using the Smooth and Constant options for testing.

The Phong shading option is the most computationally intensive of the renderings functions. The results are excellent if used with displays capable of displaying 256 colors or more.

Defining and Assigning Materials to Your Design

Rather than limiting your rendering capabilities to the use of color and some minor texture control, MicroStation gives you truly sophisticated tools that allow you fascinating control over the appearance of the final rendered image. Although you can still render images using the basic colors of the elements themselves, with the use of material assignments and pattern/bump maps, you can create images that are almost impossible to distinguish from normal photographs. Called Photo-rendering, the use of scanned-in samples of real-world textures means you can take your model and apply the stucco, shingles, and other features just as you would a physical model of a project.

Overview of Material Assignment and Definition

On the surface, this process may look rather magical, and it can be somewhat intimidating. However, if you look at how the system works, it becomes obvious that it is really rather simple. The following is a list of the steps involved:

❑ Define material palettes.

❑ Assign pattern maps to specific material definitions.

❑ Assign materials to specific parts of your design.

❑ Select rendering options.

❑ Render your view.

Material Definition Files

To start this process, you need to have material definitions ready. MicroStation comes with a series of predefined materials for use in your design. However, there is nothing stopping you from creating your own or modifying existing definitions. The hierarchy of the various files associated with materials follows.

Relationship of files related to material definitions and assignments

A road map of the relationship among the various file types associated with the material definitions and their assignment to your active design file.

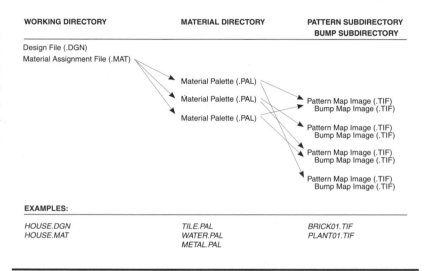

WORKING DIRECTORY	MATERIAL DIRECTORY	PATTERN SUBDIRECTORY BUMP SUBDIRECTORY
Design File (.DGN) Material Assignment File (.MAT)	Material Palette (.PAL) Material Palette (.PAL) Material Palette (.PAL)	Pattern Map Image (.TIF) Bump Map Image (.TIF) Pattern Map Image (.TIF) Bump Map Image (.TIF) Pattern Map Image (.TIF) Bump Map Image (.TIF) Pattern Map Image (.TIF) Bump Map Image (.TIF)

EXAMPLES:

HOUSE.DGN	TILE.PAL	BRICK01.TIF
HOUSE.MAT	WATER.PAL	PLANT01.TIF
	METAL.PAL	

As you can see, material assignments are made in a separate file using the .MAT extension. Essentially a text file, the material assignment file contains a list of which material palettes to use, and what specific materials to map to which object.

Materials are mapped to a combination of levels and colors. In other words, each level can have up to 256 materials assigned to it (one for each color). This works out to 16,128 distinct materials, more than you'll ever use.

Material Palettes

Sort of like an artist's palette, a *material palette* file contains definitions for individual materials, including their various parameters and, most importantly, the names of the pattern maps associated with them. As you can see in the preceding diagram, a palette can point to many different pattern map files, but each material found in the palette can have only one pattern map.

MicroStation is delivered with a number of predefined palettes. The palettes (found under the USTATION directory in the MATERIALS subdirectory) are organized along the type of material definitions they contain.

Material Palettes Delivered with MicroStation

Filename	Description
BACKDROP.PAL	Various backdrops useful as active backgrounds
BACKYARD.PAL	Fences, mulch
BRAKE.PAL	Used by the brake design file in the default workspace
CARPET.PAL	Samples of carpeting material
DOOR_WIN.PAL	Samples of doors and windows for mapping to rectangular objects
FABRIC.PAL	Fabric samples
FINISH.PAL	Variety of material finishes
FLORA.PAL	Trees and bushes and other plant life
GLASS.PAL	Samples of glass showing transparencies
GRANITE.PAL	Samples of granite patterns
HOMEOFIC.PAL	Book covers, computer fronts, clocks
KITCHEN.PAL	Typical kitchen appliances
MARBLE.PAL	Samples of various marble patterns
MASONRY.PAL	Various masonry patterns
METAL.PAL	Definitions of metallic materials
PEOPLE.PAL	Examples of people for use with block elements (this is also where the author can be found)
RUG.PAL	Samples of rugs

SURFACE.PAL	Miscellaneous samples of surface treatments
TILE.PAL	Examples of various tiles
TOWER.PAL	Used by the tower design file in the learning workspace
VEHICLE.PAL	Examples of automobiles and a Jeep
WATER.PAL	Examples of water (no, really!)
WOOD.PAL	Wood varieties

As you can see, these files contain a wide array of material definitions. In most but not all cases, a pattern and even a bump map file are associated with each material sample.

The Define Materials Settings Box

All of the material definitions were created via the Define Materials settings box (**Settings ➡ Rendering ➡ Define Materials**). You can, of course, create or modify each material definition if you desire. However, before you go out and wholesale change the world, it is highly recommended that you back up the palettes delivered with MicroStation, or create your own material palettes.

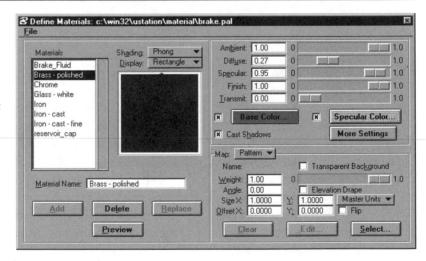

The Define Materials settings box.

The Define Materials settings box is used to create and edit individual material definitions. A bit map image in any of the supported formats—such as TIF and JPG—can be assigned to a material. Note the various settings associated with each material definition.

As you can see, there are numerous settings associated with each material; more than can be covered in an overview. However, you should note the use of the Map Pattern section to designate the .TIF image file to be used with the material name.

The Assign Materials Settings Box

After you've decided which materials you want to use, you must assign the chosen materials to your design file. This is done using the Assign Materials settings box (**Settings ➡ Rendering ➡ Assign Materials**).

The Assign Materials settings box is the main tool for assigning individual levels and colors to specific materials.

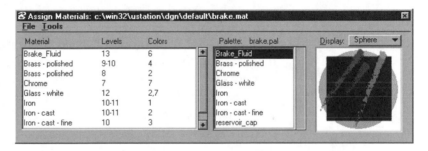

A distinctly visual settings box, Assign Materials provides you with a preview of the material you are currently working with. To assign a specific material, the steps are as follows:

❑ Open the desired material palette (**Assign Materials ➡ File ➡ Open Palette...**).

❑ Select the desired material from the Palette listing (middle column).

❑ Assign the material to a specific level/color (**Assign Materials ➡ Tools ➡ Assign or Assign by Selection**).

The Assign command requires you to enter the level and color for the assignment. An alternative is the Assign by Selection command. This command allows you to click on an element to which you wish to explicitly assign a material definition. This overrides the normal level/color assignment and is good for exceptions. However, as a general rule you should use the level/color assignment, as this allows you to assign a material to related elements (a brick facade for the front of a building, for instance).

Saving Rendered Images

Until now, you've been able to render individual views using MicroStation's rich set of rendering tools. What do you do when it is time to create a hard copy of such renderings? You could use MicroStation's built-in screen capture command (**Utilities ➡ Image ➡ Capture**) to save a rendered view to disk. This, however, limits the final resolution of the image to that of your video screen.

Most color-capable output devices print at a higher resolution than most video monitors. Your video display is usually limited to between 72 and 90 dots per inch. Color hard copy devices (laser printers, dye sublimation printers, and thermal printers) can print anywhere from 200 to 400 DPI. When you print your screen-captured image at these resolutions, the result is either an image that is a fraction of the page size or very blocky-looking hard copy.

To get around this, MicroStation provides a mechanism to render images to any size. Called Save Image, this feature is found on the Utility pulldown menu. Invoking this command results in the Save Image dialog box. Here you select the various options associated with this rendering process.

The Save Image dialog box provides the mechanism to create larger-than-life (view) images from your design file model.

Although the Shading option may appear to be your most important consideration, other key decisions are also made here. For the process to work at all, you need to prepare a view with all of the parameters necessary to orient your view. This includes lighting, camera parameters, levels, and so on.

Next most important is the format of the resulting image file. Because different printers and graphics programs require different data formats (Tell me about it. This book required the use of no less than three different formats!), you must select the appropriate file format.

❑ Img

❑ Img (24 Bit)

❑ Ingr COT

❑ Ingr RGB

❑ Ingr RLE

❑ JPEG (JFIF)

❑ PCX

❑ PICT

❑ PostScript

❑ Sun Raster

❑ Targa

❑ TIFF (Compressed)

❑ TIFF (Uncompressed)

❑ Windows BMP

❑ WordPerfect (WPG)

As you can see, MicroStation supports quite a variety of formats. Choosing the one right for you is beyond the scope of this book. However, it is safe to say that with a little research and trial-and-error, you will find the image type most suited to your needs.

The Compression field is used with only a couple of the formats, most notably the JPEG format. By controlling the amount of signal loss, you can balance the space the image takes on your hard drive against the quality of the image. This can be a real consideration when generating large, 24-bit (16.7 million possible colors) images, where a single file can run into the multimegabyte range!

The Mode field allows you to adjust the color depth generated in the final image. As just mentioned, MicroStation supports millions of colors. However, if your final output is a black-and-white document (like this book), there is no sense in generating a 16.7-million-color image just to crunch it back into a gray-scale image. It also reduces the time it takes to generate the image.

The Shading field gives you the same basic rendering types as the View Rendering functions. The Resolution fields are the real reason you selected the Save Image dialog box in the first place. This is where you can set the exact size of the final image. By keying in a number in the X or the Y field, you set that aspect of the final image. One point to note is that the ratio of X to Y is set by the view you've selected in the View field, so you will want to make sure it is adjusted to the correct X-to-Y ratio.

Gamma Correction is a little-understood adjustment field. When printed, most screen-shot images appear very dark. This is due to the difference in how colors are created. Without going into a long dissertation on transmissive versus reflective colors, this difference requires you to do some "tuning" of the output. This is the purpose of the Gamma field. It allows you to bring up the middle tones of your image without lightening true black or darkening true white regions. A higher number results in a lighter and better printed image.

Selecting the Save... button starts the rendering process. You should be warned that selecting a large image size, Phong, and 24-bit color will result in a *long* computation session. It could be hours or even a day before MicroStation returns from this process. You should plan such a session at the conclusion of your work day, or prepare yourself for a boring couple of hours.

For More Information...

Rendering and 3D construction are subjects in and of themselves. It would be an injustice to say that what has been discussed here is anything more than an introduction to them. For more in-depth coverage of these subjects, a companion book is available covering 3D construction and final rendering. Titled *Adventures in MicroStation 3D,* it will take you from this introduction through the various ways to bring it all together for complete 3D project construction.

Plotting, the Final Frontier

Putting Your Design on Paper

All the effort you put into your design file is for naught if you can't create plotted drawings. MicroStation gives you the ability to plot your hard work on any number of output or hard copy devices.

Pen Plotters

The most common type of hard copy device in use with CAD today is the pen plotter. Essentially a robotic draftsperson, this device uses a modified technical pen or felt-tip pen to generate drawings on paper.

Using motions similar to a draftsperson, the pen plotter moves the pen over the surface of the paper and draws your design as a series of lines and arcs. When the plotter is finished drawing, the result is an original plot of your computerized drawing.

With this more traditional drawing, you can now reproduce the drawing using standard blueprint equipment. Most pen plotters can also create master Mylar prints plotted on polyester film material for durable originals.

Raster Plotters

Another type of plotter in common use today is the raster plotter. These plotters use a technology similar to that of your photocopier, and they come in a variety of sizes. Ranging in capacity from A-size (8-1/2 x 11") to J-size (36–43 x 20+ feet!), raster-type plotters are capable of generating incredible drawings, both in quantity and quality. The advent of ink-jet technology now brings the speed associated with raster plotters to even the smallest professional office because of their extremely competitive price.

A Word About "Original" Drawings

But is it really an original? The term *original* was always applied to the master hand-drawn design, produced on the most durable drawing medium (typically Mylar, Vellum, or linen). This was done to ensure the drawing's survival during the project life cycle, with its innumerable updates and constant erasures and changes.

This fact is brought up because with CAD, the actual original print is stored electronically on the disk of the computer. MicroStation can create, on demand, a new original drawing via the plotter. For this reason, durability and the ability to withstand alterations to the final plot have become less important.

In fact, you may actually want the final plot to be fragile to modification. This way, all changes that occur to the plot will be readily apparent and can be incorporated back into the computer file from which it came. Many times last-minute manual updates to a final plotted drawing are not incorporated in the CAD file. A year or two later, when it becomes necessary to update the drawing, the changes are missed. In many cases, this has led to embarrassment or more serious problems, even litigation.

To keep the lawyers at bay, you and/or your CAD administrator should set a policy within your design department to maintain a "To-do List" of updated prints for slow days. The key point here is to *always keep your computer CAD files current*.

Plotting Options

MicroStation comes equipped with the ability to generate plots directly from within the graphics environment. In addition, there are a number of products designed to offload this sometimes time-consuming process and allow you to continue with design work. Currently there are at least three ways to get a plot of your design:

❏ MicroStation's native plotting facility

❏ Intergraph's Interplot network plotting product

❏ Byers Plot Station network plotting product

Each method has its strengths and weaknesses. Determining which one is right for your operation is well beyond the scope of this book. However, because many companies are using one or more of these plotting solutions, a brief overview of Interplot and Plot Station is included later in this chapter. Regardless of whether you have one of these enhancements or another product for generating plots, you should be familiar with MicroStation's built-in plotting facility.

MicroStation's Plotting Facility

MicroStation's built-in plotting system is very flexible and thorough in its ability to create final plots. In fact, the plotting process is where you finally get to see what all of those funny line weights and styles really look like in the real world.

The plotting process is also where you must set the relationship between the modeling world (the design file) and the real world (the plotter). This is done by equating the design file's units with the plotter's measuring or *resolution* units. In addition to knowing your design file's working units, you need to know what units your plotter uses. In most cases it is either fractions of an inch or millimeters. These data and other plotter-specific information are stored in your plotter's *driver file*. This file is discussed in greater detail later in this chapter.

Plotting Your Drawing

MicroStation's plotting process is very straightforward. There are four steps involved in generating your final drawing:

❑ Identify the portion of your design file to be plotted.

❑ Select the appropriate plotter driver file.

❑ Generate plotter-ready data and store it in a plotter spool file.

❑ Transmit the spool file data to the plotter.

MicroStation manages the first three steps from within your active design file. Depending on your company's CAD operation, the last step may require further attention. In many instances, the operation of "dumping" the data to the plotter is automated and requires minimal attention by the user. In other cases, you may have to physically connect a plotter to your workstation and perform the data transmission yourself (more on this later).

TIMEOUT: *There are many pen plotters out there with worn-out casters, and many company hallways with dings and scrapes, all from wheeling plotters from department to department. However, with the advent of inexpensive network solutions, plotters can stay in one physical location. Now the user is the one banging into the walls!*

Before You Plot

Before actually generating the plotter spool file, you need to identify the area of the design file you wish to see on your plotted drawing. This is typically performed using one of two methods:

❑ Plot by View

❑ Plot by Fence

The most common of these two methods is Plot by Fence. You identify the area to be plotted by placing a fence around it.

Once you have either your views or a fence placed, select the conditions of the various display attributes. In most but not all cases the plotting process uses the current values of View Attributes for either the target view you are going to plot or the view within which you placed the fence.

NOTE: *If you use a fence for selection, make sure the view in which you placed the fence has the attributes you desire for your plot. More ruined plots are created by forgetting to check the fence's source view than almost any other mistake.*

Invoking the Plot Command

Starting the plot process couldn't be easier. Simply key in PLOT or PRINT at the key-in window, press the Ctrl+P accelerator key, or select the Print/Plot command from the File pull-down menu. In either case, you are presented with the Plot window. Through this window, you control the creation of the plotter data spool file.

The Plot window is where you control the entire plotting process.

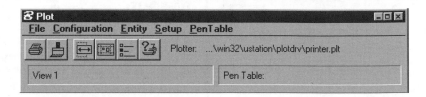

As you can see from the size of the menu bar on this window, along with the five icons there are quite a few options associated with this dialog box. This is appropriate, as there are many options to the plotting process. We'll look at each in turn, starting with the most important parameter, the target plotter.

Verifying the Plotter Model and Driver File

Once you've started the plotting process, the first order of business is to verify the output plotter type and driver. To the right of the icons, in the Plot window, you will see words something like:

```
Plotter: ...\ustation\plotdrv\printer.plt
```

This piece of information is important. Here, MicroStation is displaying the name of the plotter driver file, *printer.plt*, it will use to generate the plot. All plot operations start with this plotter driver file, which controls almost the entire plotting operation. This is why it is a good idea to verify that you are plotting to the correct type of plotter.

"But what if I don't have the right plotter chosen?"

This is not an uncommon situation. Many companies have more than one type of plotter. For this reason, you may not have the correct driver file chosen for your particular plotter. Choosing the correct one is just a button push away. Clicking the Plotter Driver button, the rightmost icon, brings up the Select Plotter Driver File dialog box.

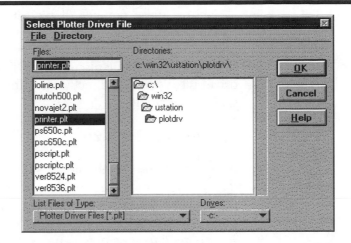

Invoked by selecting the Plotter Driver icon, the Select Plotter Driver File dialog box allows you to select the target plotter for your plotter spool data file.

MicroStation supports practically all modern plotters. By scrolling through the various files found here, you can see this. Just for the record, the following is an overview list of the plotting families supported by MicroStation.

Plotters Supported by MicroStation	
Plotter Language	**Description**
Calcomp 906	Calcomp's pen plotting language.
Calcomp 907	Calcomp's second-generation plotting language. Used by many electrostatic plotters
Calcomp 960	Calcomp's older pen plotting language. Used with Calcomp's 960 family of pen plotters.
DM/PL	Developed by Houston Instruments.
ESC/P	Epson dot matrix printer support.
HP-GL	Includes most of Hewlett Packard's plotting family.
HP-GL/2	Includes HP's LaserJet laser printers and newer plotters.
PCL	HP's older LaserJet laser printer format.
PostScript	Support for most PostScript devices. Can be used to create EPS files. Includes support for color PostScript.

Each of these families of plotters consists of many separate plotter driver files. Each named file is customized to the particular plotter model. This is necessary owing to the variety of plotter sizes and individual plotter capabilities. By selecting a plotter driver file, you are indirectly selecting the size of the plot you are going to generate.

Specifying Plot Size

With the correct plotter selected, the next step is to verify the size of the plot. As just mentioned, the plotter driver file contains definitions for the page size supported by the chosen plotter. However, many plotters support more than one page size, so you need to specify which one you want. This is done via the Page Setup icon on the Plot dialog box. Selecting the Page Setup button brings up the Page Setup dialog box. In the example shown in the following illustration, you see a page size option of 42 inches by 32 inches, and a Page Size of E. This corresponds to the largest of the standard sheet sizes used by most companies.

The Page Setup dialog box is used to select a page size for the final plot output. Its look may vary with the plotter driver you select.

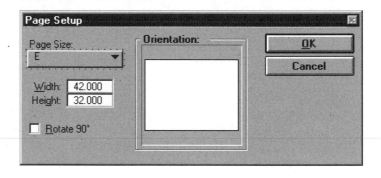

The Page Size field allows you to select your plot output size. Selecting one of these page sizes results in the adjustment of the other fields in this dialog box. For instance, selecting the A page name results in a page size of 8.5 x 11 inches. Selecting the OK button changes the page size; selecting Cancel ignores your selection and reverts back to the previously set page size.

Selecting What to Plot

In the Plot dialog box you specify the area to plot in the Entity menu. If there is a fence active at the time the Plot dialog box opens, the Fence option on the Entity menu is automatically selected; namely, an arrowhead appears to the left of the Fence option. If you decide not to use the fence, you can deselect it from the menu.

If there is no fence when you select Print/Plot from MicroStation's File menu, the Fence option on the Entity menu is dimmed. If you place a fence around the area you wish to plot after you invoke the plot command, you can switch to using the fence by selecting the Fence option on the Entity menu and selecting an available view from the View submenu.

Drawing Settings and Scale

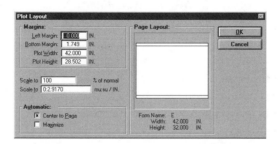

When you select the appropriate sheet size, you are also telling MicroStation the limits of the plotter. This will be important as you set your scale.

The scale factor is the next question to be answered. You have two different ways to set this. You can key in the master units to plotter units directly, or key in the size as a percentage of normal and let MicroStation calculate the scale.

The scale is defined as the ratio of design file units to plotter units. Depending on the target scale of your drawing, this can be any positive number. Keep in mind, however, that this is the ratio of design file master units to plotting units. This means that if you are plotting a drawing done in feet, and the scale is 4 feet per inch, this results in a final ratio of 48:1 (48 inches, the drawing subunit, to 1 inch of paper).

The Scale factor and the four fields in the Margins section of the Plot Layout dialog box are interlinked. When you change one, the other values update to reflect the change. You click on the field you wish to change and enter the new value. In this way you can keep selecting values until you get the plot size or scale desired.

Remember it was mentioned that MicroStation uses the sheet sizes to identify the limits of the plot area? If you key in a scale or a size larger than the sheet size specified, MicroStation beeps to warn you that an invalid size was supplied.

 NOTE: *Many users place a block or lines representing the outside edge of the plotted page and attempt to use this block as the plot fence. This does not always work. Most plotters are incapable of plotting to the extreme edge of the paper. Instead, a small portion of the paper's edge is reserved for plotter use (pinch rollers, alignment marks, and so on). It is better to place tick marks at the plot origin point and at the maximum page area just inside the plottable area. In this way, you can enter the correct plot scale and not exceed the limits of the page size.*

Maximizing a Plot

Sometimes you may want to plot the contents of a fence or a view at the maximum size of the plotter's chosen page size. Instead of adjusting the plot layout accordingly, you can enable the Maximize checkbox. This results in the chosen area of your drawing being plotted to the extents of the plotter's page size. This is also the default condition when you first enter the Plot dialog box.

Centering a Plot

If you haven't selected the Maximize option, you may opt to use the Center to Page checkbox. This option shifts the entire plotted area to the center of the chosen page size. This is noted by a box drawn on the plot layout frame. In many cases the plot area you have selected doesn't use the same height-to-width ratio as the page size. Using the Center to Page option makes the final plot look more like a finished drawing and may eliminate the need to trim the paper plot after the fact.

TIP: *Use the Center to Page option when plotting to A- and B-size plotters, such as a laser printer. In this way, the final result will look more professional.*

Rotate 90

The Rotate 90 Degrees option on the Page Setup dialog box is similar to a portrait/landscape option on printer drivers. Many times your design will fit more economically on a sheet of paper if you rotate it 90 degrees. This is especially true of some of the electrostatic plotters that have a fixed width of paper (usually 36 inches) that can accommodate C-size drawings lengthwise.

Plot Origin

Each plotter supports a point on the drawing page known as the *plot origin*. With pen plotters, this is typically the point at which the plotter's X0Y0 location can be found. In some cases, this plot origin is manually identified on the plot for alignment with preprinted format paper. Such operations are specific to each company and are beyond the scope of this discussion.

Plot Options

The Plot Options icon brings up a list of additional options for plotting your drawing. If the entity to plot is a view or a fence, which will almost always be the case, the bulk of the options on the Plot Options dialog box will be dimmed. These are displayed on the dialog box for information. However, if you need to modify any of them, you will need to control those options in the View Attributes dialog box (**Settings ➡ View Attributes**).

The Plot Options
dialog box.

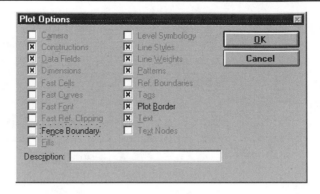

The Draw Border option results in a box drawn around the extents of the plot. This is useful for trimming a drawing to its finished size. Select this option as you need it.

The Description field allows you to enter a message (50 characters or fewer) that is plotted just outside the border. This field is very helpful for date stamping or otherwise identifying the resulting plot. If you decide not to use this feature, just hit Return. The support for this field depends on options set in the plotter driver file, so you may not have access to it.

Previewing Your Drawing Plot

Before actually generating your plot, you have the option to preview its appearance right in the Plot window. This is done via the Preview Refresh icon. When selected, MicroStation actually generates a plot of your drawing, but instead of directing it to the plotter device, it uses the options you have selected along with specific plotter driver data to generate a "thumbnail" view of the plot. This is very helpful for seeing the effect of line weight definitions within the plot driver file and other key data. For instance, if you are using a single-color output, and your plot driver file has been set up, the result of this should be a black-and-white-only image of your plot.

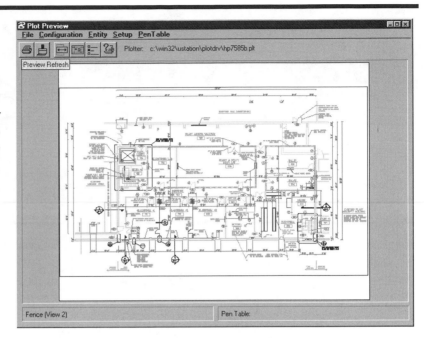

The Preview Refresh button results in a "heads up" preview of your plot prior to actually creating your plot file.

Creating the Plot Data File

When you have selected all of your plotting parameters and are ready to go, click on the Plot icon. This action launches the plot data generation. You are prompted for the filename into which the plot data will be placed.

The Save Plot As dialog box allows you to change the name and location of the output spool file. The default directory is controlled by the MS_PLTFILES configuration variable.

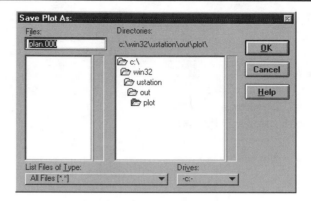

By default, the filename's extension is .000. In some operations, you will need to change this to .HPG or .PLT for automated network software to work. This is not critical at this time; however, it is something to be aware of.

MicroStation doesn't actually start using the plotter at this point. Instead, it creates what amounts to a plot instruction data file for processing by the plotter later. In the case of the Hewlett Packard plotters, this is one gigantic text file describing a series of pen up and pen down commands. Calcomp plotters, on the other hand, use a machine-readable file format that takes up less space on your hard drive, but gives you fewer options for sending the plot data to the plotter.

Did we mention disk space? That's right, the resulting plotter file created as a result of this process can be *huge*. Whereas MicroStation efficiently stores your design file in a compact format on your computer's hard drive, the resulting plot file can be many times larger. This is why you will want to know where these files are and delete them when your plots are completed.

NOTE: *The plotter driver file "printer.plt" on the Windows platform refers to the system printer or plotter. If your system printer is set up to directly plot to a local port or a network printer or plotter, selecting the Plot button sends the plot directly to the printer, without first prompting you for a filename.*

Plotting Data

"How do I plot thee? Let me count the ways…"

The most common method for transferring plot data to the plotter is to use MicroStation's PlotFile batch program. This is available on both the PC and the Mac. MicroStation 32 uses a separate MDL program (mplot) to accomplish this. In all cases, the purpose of this program is the care and feeding of the plotter using the plot file just generated.

From the PC

From the DOS prompt (or DOS session in Windows NT) key in P L O T F I L E *filename* ↵, or just P L O T F I L E ↵. In the latter example the program will prompt you for the filename.

This batch program sets some key system variables (MS_PLTFILES, MS_PLTR), then invokes the actual plot transfer program, PLOTUTIL. If the spool file exists, the program will begin sending the data to the plotter connected to your computer via the I/O port specified in your plotter driver file. While transmitting your plot file to the plotter, your computer will not be available for other work. It will, however, give you a progress report until completion.

An alternative is available for directing plot output to the plotter. By using the DOS PRINT utility, you can spool the output of the plot file directly to the plotter in a background mode, thus allowing you to go back to work…theoretically.

However, the overhead involved in running MicroStation causes such erratic operation of the pen plotter that such activity usually leads to poor plot quality or plotter time-outs. If you need this capability you must do the following.

Add the following two lines to your AUTOEXEC.BAT file:

```
mode com1,96,n,8,1,P
print/d:com1/q:32
```

To actually plot the file, use:

```
c:\print\plotfile directory\plotfile name.ext ↵
```

If available, another method can be used by setting up a PC XT or AT dedicated to plot control. By using "sneakernet" (copying a file from system to system using a diskette), you can continue to use the main system for design. The two alternatives just discussed cannot be used with Calcomp-type plotters due to the binary nature of their plot files.

If your plotter is connected to one of the PC's parallel ports, you can also use the DOS copy command with a command such as `copy /b \directory\ plotfilename.000 lpt1`. The `/b` modifier is needed if the data is in one of the binary formats (PCL or ESC/P). Finally, if a parallel port is used, you can plot directly from the plot dialog by changing the name in the Save Plot As dialog box to the device name (e.g., lpt1). (Do not add the colon (:) character to the end of the device name.)

From the Interpro

Unlike the PC, the Interpro is a multitasking computer, meaning it can do many things at once. MSPLOT takes advantage of this and can be invoked even while in MicroStation. Again, you specify the filename to be plotted and MSPLOT does the rest.

From the Macintosh

In a manner similar to the PC, you launch the PlotFile application, whereupon you select a valid file to plot. However, due to the Mac's unique use of its serial ports for networking, you may have to turn off the AppleTalk network via the Chooser desk accessory prior to starting your plot. If, however, you have selected the Laserwriter, an 8.5 x 11 network printer, as your plotter, the Appletalk network *must* be selected.

Advanced Plotting Topics

As mentioned earlier, when MicroStation is installed on your computer, there are a number of special files delivered to the *plotdrv* directory (usually MicroStation root directory\plotdrv\). These .PLT files are text files that contain a number of parameters to control your plotter.

The Plotter Driver File

Up until version 5, these files were called plotter configuration files, but are now called plotter driver files. The name change was necessary due to the introduction of plot "configuration" files that can store design-file-specific information for quickly recreating a plot. You should consider the supplied plotter driver files as working samples. You are encouraged to modify them to suit your needs. In fact, savvy users can fine-tune plotter driver files to greatly enhance the final output of their projects.

Let's take a look at how the plotter driver file controls plotting. The first thing the driver file does is set the size of each sheet of paper that can be used in the plotter. Usually these are the standard A through E sheet sizes traditionally used in drafting. However, you can specify other sizes. The most important part of this section is the *offsets* specified with each sheet size.

Because some of the popular plotters used today (i.e., HPGL) specify the origin point at the center of the media, while your drawing really starts at the lower left corner of the video screen, you have to calculate the offsets from this center location to the real location of the drawing.

Style Control

The style(n)= and pen(n)= parameters are the important link between your design file's logical weights and styles, and what the pen plotter actually generates. The style(n)= parameter sets the line lengths and gaps for each of the line styles. As delivered, these are set to approximately match what you see on the video screen.

The pen(n)= command assigns which pen in the pen plotter's carousel is used to plot which weight. For instance, if you use a 0.25-mm technical pen in carousel position 1 and want to use this to plot weight 0 elements, the line in the PLTCFG file would be:

```
pen(1)=(0)
```

Another parameter that controls the line quality of your drawing is WEIGHT_STROKES=(0,1,2...). This command tells the plotter how many times to run the pen back and forth over the linework. Each position in the parentheses represents each line weight, starting with 0. An example of this command is:

```
WEIGHT_STROKES = (1,2,2,3,4)
```

In this example, line weight 2 is drawn once, whereas weights 1 and 2 are drawn twice, weight 3 is drawn 3 times, and so on. If your pen plotter is prone to pen skipping, usually something that happens with fine-tipped pens, it's a good idea to increase the number of strokes to ensure complete coverage of the line. This can add appreciable time to the plotting function, but it is better than a drawing of questionable quality.

Documenting Your Plot

There are a number of ways to document your plot. One feature you can choose to activate is the time and filename stamp. Part of the border directive in the plotting driver file (.PLT), this feature can help keep track of when and how a plot was generated.

```
border/pen=2/filename/time/nooutline
```

The last option, nooutline, eliminates drawing a box around your entire plot. The filename and time options are not supported by all plotter types, so try it out first.

Plotting Raster Files

MicroStation allows you to attach raster files, also know as bit-mapped files, as references to your design file. For this purpose, its plotting facility supports the ability to plot raster files.

Hard copy devices fall under two categories: vector and raster. No matter which category your printer or plotter falls under, MicroStation can plot raster reference files on it. Of course, you will get the best results when using supported raster hard copy devices such as PostScript or Versatec electrostatic plotters.

The HARDWARE_RASTER, or the equivalent SOFTWARE_RASTER record in the plotter driver file, tells MicroStation whether the hard copy device is capable of directly handling raster images.

NOTE: *When plotting raster reference files, keep in mind that the raster image is sent first and the vector data is plotted on top of it.*

Documenting Level Usage

One method of documenting which levels were plotted is to incorporate a level coupon in the drawing. A simple matrix of lines and numbers, this aid is easy enough to draw. By placing a hash line on each level, the result will be a hard copy of the displayed levels.

When developing your own coupon, it is a good idea to optimize the plotter's motion by drawing the lines and numbers in a serpentine fashion. It is also a good idea to keep this coupon as simple as possible to minimize plotting time spent drawing it. Don't forget to set aside one level (for instance, level 63) for the coupon's skeleton.

TIP: *Using a diagonal line on each level usually results in faster plotting of the coupon. Most pen plotters draw their fastest at a 45-degree angle.*

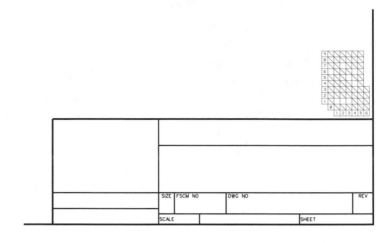

An example of a simple level coupon, showing the levels associated with the plotted drawing. This coupon can be found on the companion disk.

Plot Configuration Files

When you create a design file, more likely than not, you will revise it and have a need to recreate plots of the revised design. Usually, all the plot parameters you used the first time will still be valid for plots you create later. It is for such plot recreation that MicroStation supports plot configuration files. These files are stored as "ini" files for reuse later.

The Configuration menu item on the Plot dialog box offers options to create new plot configuration files, open existing plot configurations, and save edits to previously created configuration files. To create a new plot configuration file, you would use the buttons on the Plot dialog box to set up your plotting environment as desired and choose New from the Configuration menu. In the Create Plot Configuration dialog box that comes up, you would simply key in the filename in the Files field, and hit the OK button. The following is a list of the plot parameters a plot configuration file saves:

❑ Information about the plotted area

❑ Attributes of the view window being plotted

❑ Location of the fence in the design file

❑ Display status of levels in the view window being plotted

❑ Page setup information, such as size, margins, and scale

❑ Pen table information, if used

Yet another benefit of plot configuration files is to bypass the Plot dialog box altogether. To entirely bypass the plot dialog box, you can type in the following at the Key-in window:

```
PLOT configuration_filename plot_filename
```

In this case, MicroStation uses the configuration file specified and directly generates the plot file specified.

Pen Tables

High-end plot servers have long provided the ability to "resymbolize" hard copy output. MicroStation now supports that capability through its Pen Tables facility. Resymbolization refers to the process of modifying the appearance of plotted drawings without having to actually edit the design file itself. For instance, an architect may want to use a heavier line weight for windows on a building elevation plot, but an engineer may want to keep it a lighter weight. Both needs can be accommodated through the use of pen tables without actually editing the design file.

Pen tables are stored as external files and consist of a variety of sections that define resymbolization parameters. When a pen table is used to generate a plot, these sections are compared against each element in the design file and the plot data is resymbolized accordingly. It is important to keep in mind that the design file elements are not edited in any way; only the generated plot data incorporates the changes. With pen tables you can:

❑ Alter the plotted appearance of elements

❑ Control the sequence in which the active design file is plotted in relation to its attached reference files

❑ Include text substitution and MicroStation BASIC macros as part of pen table sections that define resymbolization

A detailed discussion of pen tables is beyond the scope of this book. Suffice it to say that when you need this capability it is there.

Other Alternatives to Plotting

The plotting support discussed thus far is native to MicroStation. Third-party developers offer plotting alternatives geared toward network operation and additional capabilities.

Many MicroStation and AutoCAD users are members of design groups within larger organizations, all needing both check and final plots as their projects progress. Each of these design groups may have a system administrator who keeps the networks up and running and the network plotting tools producing check plots. From the first day of any project, the need for closer coordination between the design groups becomes necessary. In the case of a hospital being designed, for example, the HVAC, electrical, and plumbing groups need to work with one another, sharing information to ensure each of their respective subsystems work as designed. How does network plotting make a contribution to this project? Why is network plotting important?

Why Use Network Plotting?

What are the benefits of using a network plotting system? In the instance of hospital design teams, a network plotting system makes it possible to generate a high volume of plots very quickly. If each group were expected to create its own set of final plots, the designer's workstations would be tied up processing plotting tasks instead of furthering the design efforts of the group. With a network plotting system, the plotting requests can be forwarded to the plot server for processing, alleviating any delay the designer encounters from plotting locally.

A network plotting system uses a common file format type for transferring files from client design systems to plot servers. The plotting systems on the market today all have their specific names for this file. Intergraph's InterPlot system calls this file a metafile. In conjunction with pen tables, which are used for specifying the relative line weights and area fills of plots, the network plotting system offers the hospital's design group a series of tools for resymbolizing their data. Parameter files are also archivable; they serve to preserve the drawings generated by each of the development groups.

Another key benefit of a network plotting system is the increased availability of printers and plotters on the network. By using network-based plot queuing capabilities, a network-based plotting system gives each of the design groups equal access to the printers, plotters, and film recorders available to the entire design team. Having these devices available to all design groups ensures that the final plots given to the customer are consistent from one group to the next.

Intergraph's InterPlot Product

Intergraph's Network Plotting System InterPlot is a comprehensive series of plotting tools that include metafile interpreters, device drivers for plotting to hundreds of devices, and client interfaces for submitting plots from distributed network locations. How does InterPlot work?

When using InterPlot for MicroStation-based plotting, the most relevant products are IPLOT 7.0, NQS, IPLOT Serve, and the device drivers used for creating hard copy. The following figure shows how these components work together. As the metafile interpreter is performing the plot processing, information about a specific device's attributes are needed so that the plot data generated by the metafile is usable by the target device.

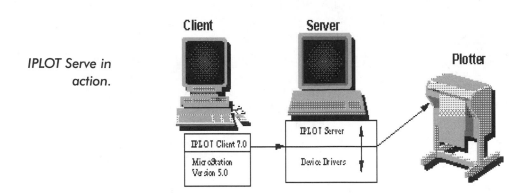

IPLOT Serve in action.

Putting this in terms of the hospital example, the designer would submit a check or final plot to the server using IPLOT. Within a few minutes, the designer's workstation could be freed up, making it possible for work to continue on the hospital's design.

InterPlot Complements MicroStation Plotting

MicroStation includes advanced plotting features not found in earlier versions. Included in this release are plot previewing capability, enhanced support for vector plotters, pen tables, and more expanded support for PostScript printers. These are but a few of the new benefits to MicroStation plotting. With all these new plotting features in MicroStation, how does InterPlot continue to add extra value to MicroStation customers? By providing the following benefits:

❏ InterPlot offloads plot processing from Intergraph Clipper CLIX workstations, MS-DOS based PCs, Sun OS SPARC workstations, and Microsoft Windows NT clients to an Intergraph Clipper-based workstation or server running CLIX, or an Intel-based system running Microsoft Windows NT.

❏ IPLOT provides support for both raster- and vector-based devices. Hundreds of devices are supported within the InterPlot Plotting System.

❏ InterPlot provides extensive control over how a plot looks. This is called resymbolization and is accomplished using pen tables and resource files for defining how a final plot appears.

❏ InterPlot supports hybrid raster-vector plotting as long as Intergraph's IRAS/B or IRAS/C is installed on the client node.

❏ InterPlot saves plot parameters for future use. Called an *IPARM*, this file contains a description of the plot's size, orientation, queue being submitted to, and many other factors customizable through the use of the IPLOT 7.0 interface or by using the IPLOT command line interface.

Using IPLOT 7.0 for MicroStation NetworkPlotting

In the case of a hospital's design team working with MicroStation, using IPLOT 7.0 makes it possible to submit check plots and continue working. The IPLOT 7.0 interface works on Intergraph, PC, Sun, and Microsoft Windows NT workstations, and is used for submitting the plot request from the client to the server. The designers could use either a command line interface, which resides outside MicroStation, or the graphical interface equivalent. Both are equally versatile at creating, generating, and submitting plot files. If the designer is working on the electrical lines for a specific floor, a check plot could be generated from within MicroStation by using the IPLOT 7.0 GUI. For final plots, the designer can either forward the IPARMS to the CAD administrator, or plot them directly using the IPLOT 7.0 interfaces' options. The IPLOT 7.0 GUI is shown in the following illustration.

IPLOT 7.0 Graphical User Interface.

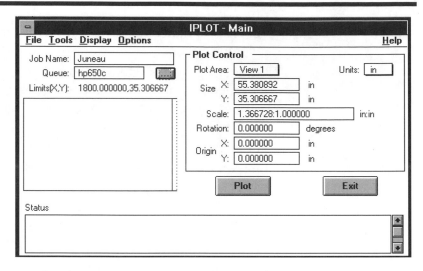

After completing a check plot to a local laser printer, the designer decides to change the design and add more emphasis to the main electrical lines using pen tables. A pen table is a series of if-then-else statements within an ASCII file, which when applied to the metafile generates a desired effect. This is called *resymbolization,* where the plot description located in a metafile is changed through the use of a pen table to create enhanced plots. In the case of a designer working in the electrical group, pen tables that adhere to a common series of standards could already exist. Choosing Select Plotting Files… from the File menu provides the designer with an option to specify which pen table to use when plotting the design. The next figure shows an example of the Select Plotting Files dialog box. Other designers on the project also have developed color tables, feature tables, and rendering attribute files for various aspects of the hospital's design. The Select Plotting Files dialog box is used for associating the design file being plotted with these other color and pen tables and rendering attributes files.

IPLOT's Select Plotting Files dialog box.

IPLOT - Select Plotting Files

Color Table:	bigdog.ctb
Pen Table	NONE
Rendering Attributes:	NONE

Next, the designer could use the commands found in the Tools pull-down menu for further customizing the plot. For instance, the plot could be centered, maximized, mirrored, or scaled using options in this menu. If the designer wants to change the disproportionate scaling of a check plot, selecting Scaling... from the Tools menu provides selections for specifying size of the plot in X and Y coordinates, and the rescaling of data and plot areas. These options are included in the IPLOT Disproportionate Scaling dialog box shown in the next figure.

IPLOT 7.0's Disproportionate Scaling dialog box.

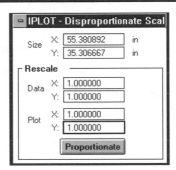

After completing another check plot, the designer discusses the wiring diagram with others in the group. It's decided that the design will be more effective with the line styles, area fills, and patterns enabled. Using the IPLOT Set Attributes menu, these changes are made before submitting the design for plotting again. The next figure shows an example of the IPLOT Set Attributes dialog box.

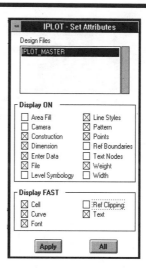

The IPLOT Set Attributes dialog box.

With the electrical aspects of the hospital's design nearing completion, the work group decides to view the entire series of drawings with both the 120- and 220-volt lines for the floor being designed. Using the IPLOT Set Levels dialog box in IPLOT, the designer can toggle on or off any of the active levels with the design without leaving the IPLOT 7.0 interface. The next figure shows an example of the IPLOT Set Levels menu.

*IPLOT's Set Levels
dialog box.*

The designer could use this dialog box for turning on all levels of the main design files that had included 120- or 220-volt wiring. This dialog box could also be used for providing the architects with a complete reference to the hospital's design, floor by floor. Each floor of the design could correspond to a level.

If the designer decides that the settings specified in the series of dialog boxes shown here will be needed for each plot, a Settings file can be created. A Settings file acts like a macro, where settings available in IPLOT 7.0 can be saved and used with each plot or series of plots produced.

InterPlot's Command Line Interface

After the design teams have completed their work on the hospital, the CAD system administrator for the project is responsible for streamlining how plots are generated and for producing plots that will be delivered to the customer. This entails being able to reliably produce a high volume of plots on a regular basis. Using the InterPlot parameter files (IPARMS) generated during plotting sessions initiated by the design teams, the CAD administrator can accomplish the task of generating a high volume of plots with little advance notice. The command line interface included with

IPLOT 7.0 includes a comprehensive series of options used for creating, modifying, showing, generating, and submitting revised IPARM files. Instead of having to redisplay each design file, then change the plot parameters for a specific plot, the CAD administrator need only use the command line options for changing the plot's characteristics. The IPLOT 7.0 command line interface includes five commands that streamline production plotting. These commands are:

❏ Create

❏ Modify

❏ Show

❏ Generate

❏ Submit

The command line syntax for using any of these five commands is:

```
$iplot and qualifiers iparm_name
```

Using the combination of commands and qualifiers available within the command-line interface, the CAD administrator has just as much flexibility as the designer in changing the appearance of a single plot, or a series of plots. The iparm_name is the file that contains all necessary plotting parameters for a single plot. The IPARM is modified instead of the original design file, giving the user flexibility in creating customized plots, without having to redisplay the original design file.

In terms of the hospital design example, the contractors need to get plots on B-size sheets, so they can carry the electrical wiring diagrams with them as they walk through the site. The CAD administrator can use the Modify command to change all IPARMS that apply to the electrical wiring designs so that they will print on the Intergraph Model 2217 B-size laser printer. The command for changing the queue and scale of the electrical wiring diagram would be:

```
$iplot modify -queue=ilp2217 -scale=100:1 electric
```

This command line scales the plot, then submits it to the ILP2217 queue. Next, the IPARM is submitted for plotting, using this command line:

```
$iplot submit -copies=25 electric
```

This command accomplishes the same result as the GUI the designers used during MicroStation plotting sessions. The Submit command initiates the plot request, sending the IPARM file to the ILP 2217 queue, requesting 25 copies be made.

InterPlot Summary

MicroStation includes many advanced plotting features, making the task of generating output easier than before. In addition, MicroStation now includes enhanced support for vector plotters and PostScript printers. The IPLOT Client 7.0 client interface is a useful tool for those MicroStation users requiring production plotting capability along with the benefits of plot file resymbolization without redisplaying the original design file. In addition, the IPLOT 7.0 interface makes distributed plotting possible by giving each MicroStation user on a network the option of plotting to any Intergraph-supported printer, plotter, or film recorder. The IPLOT 7.0 plotting interface includes both a GUI for plotting design files directly from MicroStation and a command line interface. The GUI is an effective tool for getting a "snapshot" or check plot of a drawing or design in process. The command line interface is equally useful for modifying IPARMS and achieving a high level of efficiency during production plotting. Using the command line interface, you can create, modify, show, generate, and submit IPARMS for plotting. There are a wide variety of options available within the command line interface as well, with over 30 options available for the Create command alone.

For more information about Intergraph's plotting products, contact the Intergraph Plotting Group, Intergraph Corporation, Huntsville, AL 35894-0001, (205) 730-2000.

Byers Plot Station

Byers Plot Station is a client/server-based plotting management application for MicroStation. (It also supports AutoCAD.) All plot generation activities are offloaded from the user's workstation to a PC-based plot server. Plot Station can interface with LAN-(Novell, NFS, LAN Manager, and so on), XNS-, and DECnet-based networks.

Few MicroStation users actually come into direct contact with Byers Plot Station. Instead, most are more familiar with the Byers PRF Generator, an MDL-based application used to submit drawings for plotting from MicroStation. To plot, the user creates a Plot Request File (PRF) by selecting the ByersPRF option on the menu. This calls up a dialog box that the user fills in with the appropriate information for creating the plot.

Byers' PRF Generator dialog box.

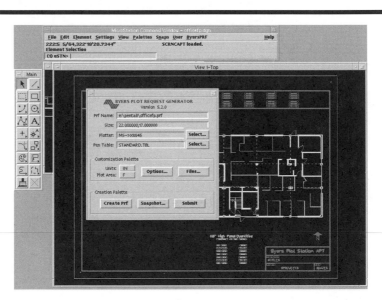

Users have the option to plot a file, fence, or named view and select from dozens of logical plotter configurations. A pen table can also be selected to resymbolize drawing appearance at plot time for line thickness, area fills, and halftone screening.

Plot Station Supports Pen Tables

Pen tables also allow prioritization of elements, levels, and reference files. Other options include specification of units of measure, scale, rotation, number of copies, reference file selection, and font library selection. The following is a portion of a typical Plot Station pen table. You can develop very complex tables to do such functions as halftone selected elements, change the size of text, eliminate specific elements from the plot, and so forth.

```
/* Plot Station pen table example code */
/* start file processing section */
by_file
/* perform setup actions based on file type */
switch ( FILE )
   0:/* DGN file */
/* force all thickness to 0.0150 (3 raster
lines) */
DEF_THICKNESS(0-31) = 0.0150
   1:/* Ref 1 file */
/* force all styles to small dot, thickness to
0.0050 */
DEF_STYLE(9)     = ( 0.01, 0.02 )
MAP_STYLE(0-15)  = 9
DEF_THICKNESS(0-31) = 0.0050
end_switch
/* then set MAP_COLOR() from file type */
MAP_COLOR(0-255) = FILE+1
end_by
```

A unique feature of PRF Generator is its Snapshot... option. It allows users to create a single new design file from several design and reference files. This creates a valid design file that can be brought up from within MicroStation. The condensed snapshot file and the PRF are the only files needed to produce a plot. Because a snapshot file is typically much smaller than its parent design and reference files, plot processing is greatly accelerated.

To create the new PRF, the user selects Create PRF and then Submit. This copies the text-based PRF file to a queue on the network file server. Plot Station, running on the network plot server, is continually polling for PRFs or plot files on the plot queue directories of the network file server. When it locates a PRF, it reads the necessary information (design and reference files, font libraries, pen tables, scale, rotation, and so on) and processes the plot. Once processing is finished, the plot is spooled directly to any plotter connected directly to Plot Station or spooled to a network print queue. Once processing is completed, the files are deleted from the plot server and an entry is placed in Plot Station's plot accounting log. Plot Station then begins processing the next PRF.

One of the other key benefits of PRFs is that they allow batch plotting. PRFs once created can be reused multiple times, even if changes have been made to the design or reference files. Many users store all of their PRFs in a project directory with their design files, making it simple to batch-submit drawings using the DOS Copy command. For more information on Byers Plot Station, contact Byers CADNET, Atlanta, GA (800) 800-PLOT.

Plotting: The End of the Line?

Quite often, when a CAD system is installed in a company, the "technowizardry" of the workstations overshadows the need for high-quality output. Like buying $30 speakers for a $1,000 stereo, it is all too easy to cut corners on what is probably the most abused part of the overall system.

When you look at the cost of the complete system, it is sometimes difficult to justify purchasing a plotter that can cost as much as *two* PC stations. However, keep in mind that most engineering firms, regardless of the design discipline, really only deliver one thing to the client—paper. How this paper looks is quite often as important as what's on it. Take the time to fine-tune the plotting system to get the best results.

PART THREE

3

BEYOND BASIC DESIGN
Advanced concepts for a productive design environment

Understanding and Using AccuDraw

The Intelligent Alternative to Keying Coordinates and Keeping Your Bearings Straight

In the world of CAD, precision in placement of graphical elements is the name of the game. While drawing most elements, except annotation text and symbols such as a North arrow, where you place them in relation to other elements in the drawing is of vital importance.

When you create a building plan, the location of the door with relation to the building walls must be precisely drawn. When you model a mechanical assembly, its interconnecting components must be precisely drawn. In fact, if precision were not important to your drawing needs, you would not even choose a CAD software.

Throughout this book, whenever the need arose to supply MicroStation with the exact coordinates of a point, we used precision key-ins, such as XY= and DL=, at the Key-in Window. This chapter introduces you to AccuDraw, an alternative to precision key-ins.

To say that AccuDraw is helpful only in situations when you need to key in coordinates would be doing injustice to this marvelous tool. It is designed to help you create precise geometry while operating in a freehand sketching mode. In addition to coordinate input, it significantly reduces the need to switch back and forth between axis lock and free cursor modes, and generally helps speed up most drafting operations. The following list summarizes the most important features of AccuDraw:

❏ Simplifies coordinate key-in by sensing the direction of cursor movement and moving the input focus to the appropriate data field

❏ Aligns with element axes during their placement to simplify the creation of orthogonal shapes

❏ Aligns with view axes to simplify placing datapoints horizontal or vertical in relation to the previous datapoint

❏ Constrains datapoints to lie along a particular axis

❏ Speeds up drafting by letting you operate in a freehand sketching mode while maintaining precision

❏ Reduces the need to invoke snap modes

❑ Provides visual feedback on what it intends to do for improved usability

❑ Simplifies placement of equal-length line segments

❑ Modifies its behavior based on feedback from element placement commands that are designed to exploit it

❑ Greatly simplifies the creation of 3D models by locking cursor movement along desired axes

❑ Implements a host of shortcut keys for added functionality

In this chapter you will learn how to invoke AccuDraw, the options it makes available to you, and how you would use it in normal drafting operations. This chapter is divided into two sections:

❑ Using AccuDraw shows you how to start AccuDraw, explains its behavior, and walks through an example of how to use it.

❑ AccuDraw Settings discusses the AccuDraw Settings dialog box and explains what the available options mean.

Using AccuDraw

As you may have guessed, AccuDraw is a very flexible tool. It is designed to aid virtually all aspects of drafting. Whether you need to draw new elements, or manipulate existing elements, you will appreciate the help it offers by way of dynamic feedback.

The key to understanding AccuDraw's nature is its presumptive behavior. It presumes that most drafting tasks require you to draw elements perpendicular to previous segments or parallel to view axes and thus cues you to these constraints as you come within its target range.

Activating and Quitting AccuDraw

When you start MicroStation, by default, AccuDraw is not active. To activate AccuDraw, click the Start AccuDraw icon in the Primary tool bar located under the menu bar. The AccuDraw window opens up.

Click the Start AccuDraw icon on the Primary tool bar to activate the AccuDraw window.

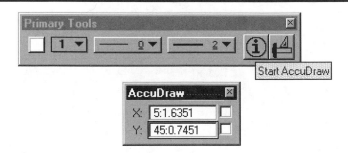

The AccuDraw window is deliberately small and unobtrusive. It only shows the X and Y coordinate input fields and checkboxes next to it. You can dock it along either the top or the bottom edge of your screen, but not along the left or right edges. Like toolboxes, to dock the AccuDraw window, drag it with the mouse along the top or bottom edge of the MicroStation application window.

Once you get to know AccuDraw, you will want it most of the time by your side. However, there are times you might find its presumptive behavior obtrusive to an operation you wish to complete. It is at times like this you will want to turn AccuDraw off.

To turn off AccuDraw, with the focus in the AccuDraw window, press the Q key. If you are running MicroStation under Windows 95, or Windows NT version 4, you can also click the "x" icon to the right of its title bar to close AccuDraw.

 TIP: *If the active focus is not on the AccuDraw window, use the function key F6 to cycle the focus.*

The AccuDraw Compass

In addition to the AccuDraw window that opens up when you click the Start AccuDraw icon, the other significant component of the tool is its "compass." The compass is inactive until you click a datapoint after selecting a tool.

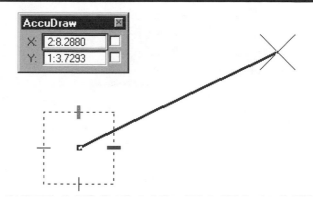

Clicking a datapoint after selecting a tool activates the AccuDraw compass.

The center of the compass is known as its origin point. This origin point is used by AccuDraw to determine how and when to cue you for your next datapoint as your cursor moves in relation to it. When AccuDraw cues you for an orthogonal line, it will pass through this origin point.

As you continue to click additional datapoints, the AccuDraw compass moves behind you. Unless you modify its setting, or use one of its shortcut keys to relocate it, the compass will be located at the datapoint you entered last.

The compass origin point is surrounded by a dashed rectangle, or a dashed circle if you are in polar coordinate mode. This dashed rectangle, or circle, is known as the "drawing plane indicator." It indicates the drawing plane AccuDraw will operate in. Its function is not as obvious in a 2D design file because it is limited to a single plane. However, if you work in 3D design files, you will notice that its orientation can change to lie in any plane.

The dashed rectangle surrounding the compass origin indicates the plane AccuDraw will operate in.

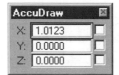

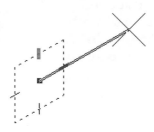

As noted earlier, the dashed shape surrounding the origin point can either be a rectangle or a circle. If the shape is a dashed rectangle, the rectangular coordinate system, which accepts X, Y, and Z coordinates, is active. If the shape is a dashed circle, the polar coordinate system, which accepts a radial distance and an angle, is in effect. You can toggle between the rectangular and polar coordinates by pressing the space bar on your keyboard with the focus in the AccuDraw window.

With the focus in the AccuDraw window, pressing the space bar toggles between rectangular and polar coordinates.

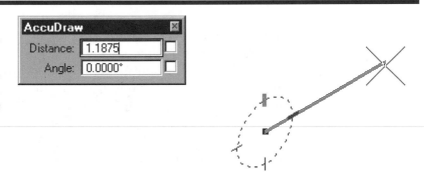

In addition to the origin point and the drawing plane indicator, the AccuDraw compass includes four tick marks oriented at right angles to one another. Two of these tick marks are color coded to indicate their positive direction. Furthermore, each axis has a different color. As a default, AccuDraw displays the positive X axis as red, and the positive Y axis as green. We will later see how to change these colors using the AccuDraw Settings box.

Using AccuDraw

Depending on the tool you use with AccuDraw, its behavior can change slightly. For instance, when you activate the *Place Line* tool, you must enter a datapoint before the compass will appear. However, if you were to select the *Place Text* or *Place Cell* tool, both of which display dynamics prior to entering a datapoint, the compass would appear at your last datapoint location. This modification in behavior can be helpful if you need to place the text or cell in relation to the last datapoint.

Yet another way AccuDraw affects text and cell placement is how it orients them in a view. When placing them without AccuDraw, they orient themselves to the view. In other words, text placed in the top view will orient to the top plane. But if AccuDraw is active, and its drawing plane indicator is oriented to the front plane, no matter which view you are in, the text or cell will be placed in the front plane. Of course, you can change the drawing plane orientation at any time to suit your needs.

There are times when you need to click datapoints without regard to their relationship with the last datapoint. Such is the case when selecting objects, placing a fence, or dimensioning. Under such circumstances, AccuDraw automatically disables its compass.

Enough introductions! Let's now move on to using AccuDraw to create a simple widget. This exercise has been specially chosen to highlight many of AccuDraw's features you are likely to use in your day-to-day operations.

Exercise: Drawing a Widget with AccuDraw Active

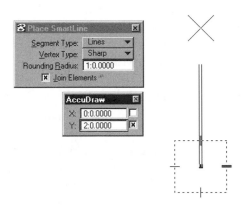

1. If not already on, invoke AccuDraw by clicking the Start AccuDraw icon on the Primary tool bar in a blank 2D design file. Select the *Place SmartLine* tool and click a datapoint somewhere along the lower left corner of a view window. The compass should appear at the point you just clicked. Now move the cursor vertically above the last datapoint. Notice how MicroStation indexes along the Y axis and the focus in the AccuDraw window moves to the Y data field. Simply key in the number 2 and click a datapoint while the cursor still indexes to the Y axis. You just placed with a minimum of keystrokes a 2-unit-long vertical line segment without using axis lock.

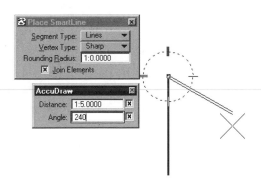

2. Now you want to place a line 1.5 units long to the right and inclined 30 degrees downward. Press the space bar to switch to the polar coordinate system. In the Distance field, key in 1.5, press the tab key to move to the Angle field, and key in 240 (the angle is measured from the direction of the previous vector; i.e., vertically up). Click a datapoint to place the desired line segment.

3. Next, you wish to place a line segment of the same length as the previous one, but perpendicular to it. Simply move the cursor in the general direction shown in the figure at left until the line indexes to the drawing plane axis and shows a tick at its end. The appearance of a tick at the end of a line segment is a cue from AccuDraw that the length of this segment is identical to that of the previous segment. By clicking a datapoint you will have placed a precisely aligned line segment of a precise length without having keyed in any number.

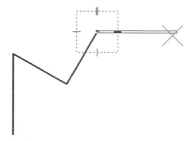

4. Let's now place a 2-unit-long horizontal line. Switch to the rectangular coordinate system by pressing the space bar. Note that the compass is oriented to the angle of the last line segment. Because you wish to place a horizontal line, you need to rotate the compass to follow the view axes. To achieve this press the V key. Now move the cursor to the right so the cursor indexes to the horizontal axis. The focus in the AccuDraw window will automatically be in the X data field where you can key in 2 and click a datapoint to place your line.

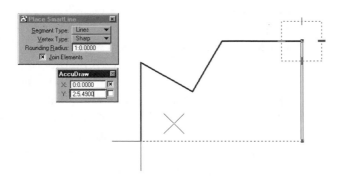

5. Now, to place a vertical line that is in line with the point you started the widget from, you will need to lock the cursor to the vertical axis. Thus far we have been keeping our cursor within the target range of an axis to stay indexed to it. But now we wish to index to the vertical axis while straying away from its target range to click a tentative point. For this you will use the Enter key. Move the cursor vertically down so it indexes to the vertical axis and press the Enter key. This enables the checkbox next to the X data field and constrains the cursor to move only along the vertical axis no matter where your cursor strays. Now you can click a tentative point as shown and accept it with a datapoint to place the desired vertical line.

6. All that remains now to complete the widget is to close the shape. Click a tentative point to the start point and accept it with a datapoint. SmartLine automatically closes the shape.

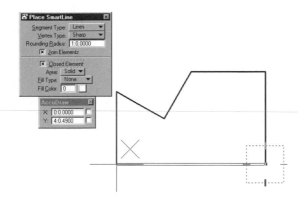

This exercise showcased the usefulness of AccuDraw and how it simplifies the task of keying in coordinate data and aligning a new line segment to the last segment. There will be times when you want to use the precision key-ins used in the previous chapters. AccuDraw helps you get to them via the "P" and "M" key-ins. When you press P with focus on the AccuDraw window, the Data Point Keyin window opens to accept a single value. Once you press the Enter key to execute the keyed-in value, the window automatically closes. Pressing the M key opens the same window, but remains open for the entry of multiple datapoints.

As you begin to use AccuDraw, you will find its dynamic preview and datapoint constraining behavior helpful in tasks such as placing and editing elements. However, when you wish to move an element just a tiny bit from its existing location, you will find AccuDraw gets in the way as it clings to the old location if the distance you wish to move is less than the target range (a default of 10 pixels). To resolve this, you could turn off AccuDraw by pressing Q, but there is another way.

Temporarily relocate the compass away from your work area by using the shortcut O key. To move an object very close to its present location while keeping AccuDraw active, activate the *Move* tool and identify the element to move. When the compass appears, move the cursor away from your work area and press the O shortcut keystroke to relocate the origin point. Now you can go back to the work area and AccuDraw will not get in the way.

As you've noticed, there are quite a few keyboard shortcuts AccuDraw responds to. In addition to the Q, V, O, Enter, and the space bar we have discussed, there are many others. To get a complete list of available shortcuts, press the "?" key.

Pressing the "?" key displays a list of shortcut keys supported by AccuDraw.

To get context-sensitive help on how to use AccuDraw and its various components, simply press the function key F1 when the item you wish to get help on has the focus.

Pressing the F1 function key when the AccuDraw window has the focus displays system help on the tool.

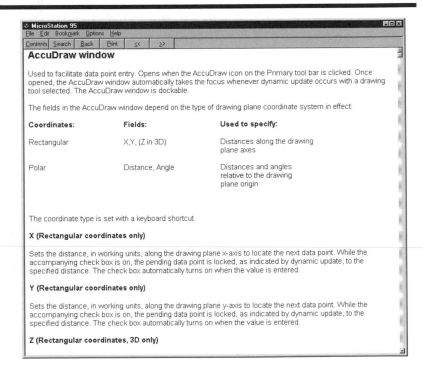

AccuDraw Settings

Many aspects of the behavior of AccuDraw are controlled from the AccuDraw Settings box. To activate the settings box, select AccuDraw from the Settings menu.

Select AccuDraw from the Settings menu to activate the AccuDraw Settings box.

This settings box provides options in four different categories: Unit Round-off, Coordinate System, Operation, and Display. Let's take a look at each of these.

Unit Round-off

Similar to the MicroStation grid when the grid lock is enabled, you can constrain AccuDraw to move the cursor in increments of the value you supply in the *Distance* round-off field. The number you supply should be in working units. You can override this round-off at any time by keying in a value in the AccuDraw window.

You might find the angle round-off handy when drawing an isometric view of an object. By using a value of 30 in the *Angle* field, you lock cursor movement along the normal isometric axes.

Again, you can override this round-off by keying in a value in the AccuDraw window. To turn off the unit round-off function, simply clear the checkbox next to the appropriate field.

Coordinate System

This section of the settings box lets you control the orientation of the drawing plane. The Rotation option button gives you a choice of Top, Front, Side, View, Auxiliary, and Context. The first four let you rotate the drawing plane to any of the standard planes: top, front, side, or view axes. The Auxiliary option lets you align to the active ACS axis, and Context lets you interactively rotate the plane for the duration of a single command. The Type option button gives you the choice of a rectangular or polar coordinate system, similar to the space bar shortcut discussed earlier in the chapter.

Operation

This category offers four checkboxes to control the way AccuDraw constrains the cursor movement.

❑ If the Floating Origin checkbox is on, the compass origin point moves to the last datapoint you click. This is the default behavior.

❑ If the Context Sensitivity checkbox is enabled, AccuDraw adjusts the compass rotation based on feedback it gets from tools written to exploit it. For instance, when you draw an inclined line with the *Place SmartLine* tool, the compass rotates to the line segment's inclination. This is the default behavior.

❑ If the Smart Key-ins checkbox is enabled, a number in the AccuDraw window is interpreted as positive or negative, depending on the location of the cursor with respect to the compass. Additionally, when in the rectangular coordinate system, the focus moves to the X or the Y data field, depending on the position of the cursor. This is the default behavior.

❑ If the Auto Point Placement checkbox is enabled, a datapoint is automatically placed when the cursor position is fully constrained. If off, you must click the data button to place a datapoint. The checkbox is off as a default.

Display

This section of the AccuDraw Settings box contains buttons to control its display-related characteristics. The X Axis and Y Axis buttons open up the Axis Color dialog box that lets you select the color for the axis tick marks on the drawing plane indicator (the dashed rectangle or circle).

The Coordinate Readout button invokes a dialog box to let you set the format and display accuracy of distances and angles. This is the same as the Coordinate Readout category in the Design File Settings box and affects coordinate display in all of MicroStation.

The Shortcut Key-ins button opens up the same window you get by pressing the "?" key with focus in the AccuDraw window. A list of all available key-ins is displayed. You also have options to create new shortcuts or edit existing ones.

The External Connection

Interfacing MicroStation with Other Applications

By now you probably realize that MicroStation provides a uniquely powerful blend of CAD functionality. Realizing that design work does not happen in isolation, MicroStation includes the ability to interact with other software at many levels.

For instance, you may have a need to supply design files, in a computer-readable format, to others who use a different software. Or, you may need to import existing drawings, not in MicroStation format, supplied by a client. To address this need, MicroStation provides a full complement of import/export filters.

Geographic information systems (GIS) and facilities management (FM) tasks are not your traditional engineering design disciplines. These require the ability to link nongraphic information maintained in external databases to a design file, and MicroStation, with its ability to link to Xbase, ODBC-compliant applications, Ingress, Oracle, and other databases, depending on platform, is particularly well suited to addressing these needs.

Another area of importance, especially to users of Microsoft Windows and Windows NT, is MicroStation's support for the Windows Clipboard, its interapplication protocol called dynamic data exchange (DDE), and OLE Automation. Using the Windows Clipboard you can have a piece of text dynamically change in MicroStation if it is updated in the word processor in which it was created. Using DDE, you can have a spreadsheet macro pass key-ins to MicroStation to create a drawing from data and calculations maintained in the spreadsheet. Using OLE Automation, you can even have custom applications built with popular tools, such as Visual Basic, work with MicroStation at a much more intimate level that involves executing built-in MicroStation functions previously available only to MDL (MicroStation Development Language) developers.

Finally, there is the add-on application that customizes MicroStation to make it more useful to a particular market segment, such as architectural, civil, electrical, mechanical, plant design, or other. This chapter, divided into the following four sections, further explores interface issues.

❑ Dealing with Various File Formats is a discussion of vector and raster formats supported by MicroStation. This section shows where import/export commands are located on the menu, how to access translation settings, and the tools available for viewing and plotting raster image files. It also contains an example of embedding MicroStation key-ins to control settings in a text file being imported.

❑ Dealing with Databases discusses the issues involved in linking graphic data in MicroStation to external relational databases.

❑ MicroStation Under Windows introduces you to the terms and concepts needed to understand what Windows Clipboard support, DDE, and OLE Automation are all about. An exercise walks you through the creation of a simple spreadsheet macro that passes key-ins to MicroStation for Windows.

❑ Adding Applications to MicroStation introduces you to the world of add-on applications. There are several hundred such applications, which run the gamut from useful drafting utilities to full-fledged engineering design applications.

Dealing with Various File Formats

Besides reading its own native DGN file format, MicroStation can read and write to several popular vector formats, such as IGES, CGM, GRD, DXF, and DWG. MicroStation design files can also incorporate bit-map images in any of a dozen file formats. Such flexibility makes it easy to integrate MicroStation in any office setting, whether you are new to MicroStation or an experienced user of another CADD software.

Most of the tools for different file formats are located under the Import and Export options of the File menu, and the Image submenu of the Utilities menu. Some of the image utilities available include screen capture, file format conversion, and animation playback.

Vector Formats

Most CADD software store drawing files in a proprietary binary format. There probably are as many file formats as there are CADD packages. To make it possible to exchange drawings among different systems, the Initial Graphics Exchange Specification

(IGES) was developed and became popular among vendors of mainframe and minicomputer-based packages. Support for the IGES file format is an integral part of the base MicroStation package.

There are two ways of importing drawings that are in an alien file format into MicroStation. The first method is to select the drawing from MicroStation Manager, the startup application that lets you choose an existing file or create a new one. Although this is a straightforward procedure, it uses default import settings, and lacks the control offered by the second method.

The List Files of Type option button on the MicroStation Manager startup application lets you import, with default settings, any of several supported vector file formats.

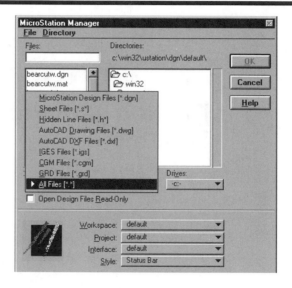

The second method involves importing the drawing into either an existing design file or a new one. With a design file open, you select the Import option under the File menu and select the desired file type. This opens up a file navigation dialog box to let you pick the desired file. When a file is imported this way, the File Import settings box opens that displays status information about the file selected for import, and provides two menu options: File and Settings. The File menu lets you save or retrieve settings, and the Settings menu lets you adjust import settings before importing the file. As you build experience with different settings while importing drawings, you may want to use the File menu in the Import File window to save settings for later use.

When importing a drawing with the File → Import menu option, the Settings menu on the Import File window lets you adjust font, level, line style, and other settings before clicking the Open button.

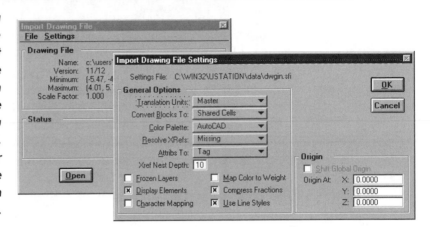

TIP: *While importing DWG files created with AutoCAD's Architectural or Engineering units, set your MicroStation master and subunits to Feet and Inches, respectively, and map AutoCAD units to MicroStation subunits. By the same token, when importing DWG files created with AutoCAD's decimal units, map AutoCAD units to MicroStation master units.*

No matter which method you use to import a drawing, the original copy of the drawing is left intact. The file is translated into MicroStation's native DGN file format on the fly to let you edit it.

In addition to importing IGES, CGM, GRD, DXF, and DWG files, you can also export to these formats. The **File → Export** menu selection lets you access this function.

Raster Formats

All CADD packages store graphic elements in their drawing file as a set of coordinates that define their location in space, along with other attribute information (such as color, weight, and style). This is known as the vector file format. In contrast, most "paint" programs, such as Paintbrush, store an image as a sequence of individual pixels, a term for picture elements.

Whereas you can edit a line drawn in a vector-based drawing program as an individual entity, a line drawn in a bit-map paint program is really a collection of individual dots lying next to one another. To edit the line, each pixel must be individually manipulated. A bit-map image is also known as a raster image. A scanned image or a screen shot is the most common source of raster files you will need to deal with.

MicroStation can include in its design file most of the common types of raster images you are likely to encounter. Raster images attached to a design file cannot be edited within MicroStation. You can display and plot these images as a part of your design file. You can delete the images or resize them, but you cannot edit their contents. The raster file formats supported by MicroStation follow.

❑ CALS (Type 1)

❑ CompuServe GIF

❑ IMG (8- and 24-bit)

❑ Intergraph's BUMP, COT, TG4, RGB, Raster and RLE formats

❑ JFIF's JPEG

❑ PCX

❑ Sun Raster

❑ Targa

❑ TIFF

❑ Windows BMP

To import a raster image into the design file, choose **File ➡ Import ➡ Image**. This opens up the Select Image File dialog box to let you choose the desired file type and file name.

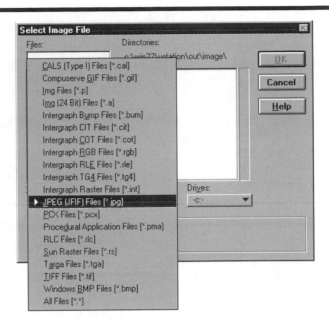

The List Files of Type option button in the Select Image File dialog box lists the raster file formats supported by MicroStation.

NOTE: *You can also key in* MDL LOAD PLAIMAGE *to bring up the Select Image File dialog box.*

Importing raster images into a design file is only one aspect of MicroStation's support for them. The software's sophisticated rendering capabilities enable it to create photorealistic screen images from your 3D models. MicroStation also lets you save these rendered images as raster files. To save a rendered view as a raster image, choose **Utilities** ➡ **Image** ➡ **Save** to bring up the Save Image dialog box.

The Save Image dialog box lets you save rendered views as raster files in resolutions exceeding those supported by the computer they are generated on.

The *Save Image* tool, in addition to the file formats listed previously for the import image tool, supports three more file formats:

❑ PostScript

❑ Macintosh PICT

❑ WordPerfect WPG

Take a close look at the previous figure. Notice that the Save Image dialog box has a field labeled Resolution. By simply changing the value for resolution in this field, you can generate high-quality image files even on computers equipped with inexpensive display adapters and monitors. Thus, an image file fit for processing through a typesetting machine can be generated from a computer equipped with a plain VGA display.

Several other tools worth mentioning in this discussion of raster file format support in MicroStation are:

❑ A raster file conversion utility (**Utilities** ➡ **Image** ➡ **Convert**) that converts raster files from one format to another.

❑ A slide show utility invoked by keying in `MDL LOAD SLIDESHW`. It lets you arrange previously saved raster images into a sequence for display one after another.

❑ A screen capture utility (**Utilities** ➡ **Image** ➡ **Capture**). Once this utility is loaded, you can capture the entire screen, a rectangular area on screen, a palette, a dialog box, a view window, and so on by keying in any of its supported commands: `CAPTURE DIALOG`, `CAPTURE FOCUS`, `CAPTURE PALETTE`, `CAPTURE RECTANGLE`, `CAPTURE SCREEN`, `CAPTURE VIEW CONTENTS`, and `CAPTURE VIEW WINDOW`.

❑ An animation display utility (**Utilities** ➡ **Image** ➡ **Movies**). It lets you display an animated sequence of images in FLI, FLC, and other raster formats. It can display the fly-through you create with the FlyThrough utility (MDL LOAD FLYTHRU) from your 3D models.

Text Files

Placing text in a design file is an integral part of the drawing process. We have already discussed in an earlier chapter the tools available in MicroStation to let you interactively place text, edit it, and control various settings such as text height, justification, line spacing, weight, color, and level. Here we look at the **File** ➡ **Import** ➡ **Text** option in MicroStation and see why it is preferred by power users when dealing with large amounts of text.

To place text in your design file from an external text file, use the FileImportText option on the menu.

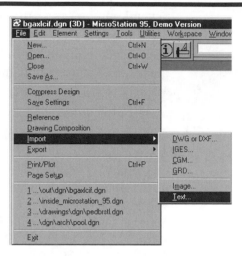

TIP: *If you already know the name of the text file to import, rather than picking it from the file list box, you will save time by keying in the* INCLUDE <filename> *command at the command prompt in the Key-in window.*

Embedding Text Setting Commands in a Text File

The power of "including" a text file becomes obvious when you realize that in addition to text, you can embed any command in it. If you wish to place the first line in the text file with a different text height, color, and weight than the remainder of the lines, you can embed commands before the first line to change settings, and embed additional commands after it to restore settings for the remainder of the text.

To make effective use of MicroStation's text import option, you should know the key-ins that control its settings. Some of the important key-ins, mentioned throughout this book, are summarized here for convenience.

Text Height	TH=value
Text Width	TW=value

Text Size	`TX=value (same as TX and TW set to the same value)`
Line Spacing	`LS=value`
Text Justification to Left Bottom	`ACTIVE TXJ LB`
Active Font	`FT=value`
Active Color	`CO=value`
Active Weight	`WT=value`
Active Level	`LV=value`

The syntax for embedding commands in a text file is simple. Place one command at a time on a line by itself and precede each command by a single "dot" to identify it as a command and not a part of the text in the file. The following is a sample "include" file.

```
.TX=0:2
.LS=0:1
.LV=6
.CO=3
NOTES
.CO=2
.NEWGG
1. All steel to conform to ASTM A-36 specifications.
2. Timber to be Douglas Fir or equal.
```

This file, when imported into MicroStation, first sets the text size and line spacing to 2 and 1 subunits, respectively. Then it sets the active level to 6, the active color to 3, and places the text "NOTES." Finally, it changes the active color to 2, starts a new graphic group, and places the remaining two lines.

 NOTE: *Large blocks of text from an include file are placed as a single group. If you wish to separate sections of the text into different groups, embed the NEWGG command to start a new graphic group.*

Dealing with Databases

The term *intelligent drawing* refers to a drawing that maintains links to nongraphic data. When you link an office inventory database with the graphic representation of the equipment in a design file, or link a street address database with the street map in MicroStation, you gain additional power in being able to query and report on the graphic data in your design file.

Many will find the element data tagging capability integrated within MicroStation adequate for their nongraphic data management needs. But if your needs call for capabilities offered by relational databases, you will need to explore MicroStation's sophisticated data-linking tools. In addition to providing support for Oracle, Xbase (a term that includes all databases that support the dBase file format), and INFORMIX, MicroStation also supports Intergraph's Relational Interface System (RIS). The first three are relational database systems; RIS is an interface to access SQL databases.

While installing MicroStation, when you choose to copy the files associated with its support for external databases, several configuration variables, including MS_DBASE and MS_LINKTYPE get defined. If an Xbase database is selected, the former points to the directory where DBF files are located. The latter specifies the type of link, whether Xbase or another database, you wish to work with.

Before you can do any linking, you must create a database file with a supported database software. In addition to the fields you need for your application, a numeric field MSLINK with a width 10 and no decimal must be included in your database's structure definition.

Once the structure of the database you wish to link with your design file is ready, you will want to populate it with data. The data you enter will be specific to your application. However, the numeric data in the field MSLINK must be unique for each record. You will also need to create index files for the key fields you wish to query the database on, along with one for the MSLINK field.

There are other preliminaries, such as the creation of a control database file (MSCATALOG) and a screen format file, that must be attended to before you can key in SET DATABASE to specify the name and link to the database file, its index files, and the screen format file from within MicroStation. With the link established, you activate a record in the database with fi=database:field=value and then use the *Attach Active Element* tool from the Database palette to attach the record to any graphic element in the design file. The Database palette also provides tools to review the contents of the database record attached to a graphic element.

NOTE: *No screen form is necessary before using SET DATABASE. It is only required that you have an mscatalog table.*

The Database option under the Tools menu invokes the Database toolbox that gives you access to data linkage, attachment, review, and reporting tools.

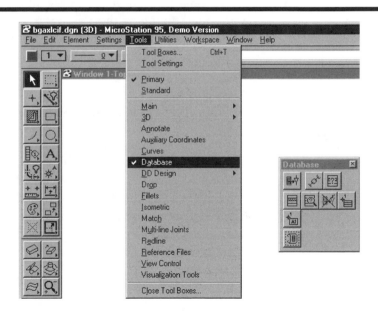

MicroStation Under Windows

Although MicroStation provides the same interface on all platforms it runs under, it provides special support for Windows. It supports the Windows system Clipboard and the inter-application communication Dynamic Data Exchange (DDE) protocol. New to MicroStation 95 is its status as an OLE Automation server.

Thus you can paste or embed text or other objects in your design file from other Windows applications using the Clipboard. You can also use the macro language in a spreadsheet software to create graphics in MicroStation using DDE. And if you use application development tools such as Visual Basic, you can also invoke internal MicroStation commands from your custom application using its OLE Automation support.

To paste a line of linked text from Microsoft Word for Windows that automatically updates in MicroStation when it is changed in Word, first highlight the text in Word, and then copy it to the Clipboard with the **Edit ➡ Copy** command.

If you are using Word version 6 or higher, you will need the USTNDDE.DOT document template included on the diskette accompanying this book. This file is necessary because Microsoft changed the way Word sends text to the Clipboard. For the newer versions of Word, after highlighting the text in the word processor, you will need to run the "UstnCopyLinkedText" macro in the document template to send the text to the Clipboard in a linkable format.

Once the text is in the Clipboard, MicroStation is ready to paste it. Select Paste Special from the File menu (**Edit ➡ Paste Special...**) to display available options. Selecting the Linked Text to Design File option retains the link with text in Word, thus updating the text in your design file if the source changes.

MicroStation's Edit ➡ Paste Special command displays text-related options that let you paste the text in the design file while retaining its link to the creating application.

In addition to supporting the placement of text, bit-map, and vector graphic elements through the Clipboard, MicroStation also supports sound objects. You can thus annotate critical areas of a design file with recorded sound so that when a user double-clicks on the sound object embedded in the design file the Windows Sound Recorder (an accessory application that is bundled with Windows) plays back the message. Of course, you need a supported sound card and a microphone to create sound files.

Dynamic Data Exchange Basics

Having taken a quick look at MicroStation's support for the Windows Clipboard, let's move on to examine the more sophisticated type of interapplication link, DDE. Windows supports three types of DDE links: hot, warm, and cold. With a hot link in place between applications, when data changes in the originating application, it is automatically transferred to the receiving application. A warm link means that when data changes, a message, but not the data, is sent to the receiving application. A cold link means that the receiving application is not informed when data changes and must poll the originating application to find out its status. Thus, the link established with Word, shown in the previous figure, is a hot link because when you edit the text in Word it is automatically updated in MicroStation.

Other than establishing interapplication links manually through the Clipboard using the **Edit ➡ Copy** and **Edit ➡ Paste** commands, DDE links are typically initiated through the macro language of an application. As in any interaction, one application initiates the link and the other responds. An application that initiates a link is called a *DDE client,* and an application that responds is called a *DDE server.* Because MicroStation is designed to respond to commands that originate in another application, it is a DDE server.

When a DDE client wants to initiate a remote link, it broadcasts a message identifying the *application* it seeks to communicate with, along with the *topic* in the application it needs to link to. Windows intercepts this message and routes it to the application, which in turn responds to the remote application's requests. Windows does not restrict applications to a single link. Because several simultaneous DDE links are possible, each link must have a unique identification. The unique thread of communication assigned to a DDE link by Windows is an integer number and is called a *channel.* There are three steps involved in getting two applications to talk to each other.

1. *Initiation:* The client application, such as Lotus 1-2-3 for Windows, through its macro language function, requests a link with MicroStation. The name of the function that initiates a DDE link differs from application to application. Lotus 1-2-3 for Windows uses the statement {DDE-OPEN "APPLICATION","TOPIC"}, and Microsoft Excel uses the statement =INITIATE("APPLICA-TION","TOPIC"). MicroStation's application name is USTN, and its topic name is KEYIN. So, to initiate a link from Lotus 1-2-3 or Excel, one would use the macro statements {DDE-OPEN "USTN","KEYIN"} or =INITIATE("USTN","KEYIN"), respectively. Visual Basic for Excel uses the statement *Application.DDEInitiate("Ustn", "Keyin").* Executing this macro statement returns a number identifying the channel of communication. This channel

number uniquely identifies the link and is used by subsequent data exchange functions.

2. *Data Exchange:* Once again, the names of data exchange functions in client applications vary. There are several such functions, but only the DDE Execute function is supported by MicroStation. So, to remotely pass the Place Line command to MicroStation from Lotus 1-2-3 or Excel, one would use the macro statement {DDE-EXECUTE "PLACE LINE"} or =EXECUTE(CHANNEL,"PLACE LINE"), respectively. Visual Basic for Excel uses the statement *Application.DDEExecute channel, "PLACE LINE"*. By using a sequence of data-exchange commands in a macro file, you can do virtually anything in MicroStation remotely that can be done by key-ins.

3. *Termination:* After completing the data exchange process, when the dynamic link is no longer needed, it is wise to terminate the link to free system resources. This is typically done through the client application's TERMINATE command. In 1-2-3 and Excel, the syntax for termination is {DDE-CLOSE} and =TERMINATE(CHANNEL), respectively. Visual Basic for Excel uses the statement *Application.DDETerminate channel*. The use of the channel ID in 1-2-3 is optional if a single DDE link is opened from the spreadsheet.

The following section presents a complete working example of a DDE application that uses Lotus 1-2-3 for Windows to initiate a link with MicroStation for Windows NT to draw a gridline typically used for laying out building plans.

A Dynamic Data Exchange Exercise

The purpose behind getting an application to talk to MicroStation is to either better integrate the design process with drafting or to customize the CAD environment. Spreadsheet software, such as 1-2-3 for Windows, excels in interactive number crunching tasks, and many engineers use it for their design problems. As will be demonstrated in this exercise, your knowledge of the 1-2-3 macro language is a potent tool for customizing MicroStation.

To follow through this exercise, you will need Lotus 1-2-3 for Windows (Release 1.1, Release 4, or Release 5) already installed on your system, along with MicroStation running under Windows 3.1, Windows 95, or Windows NT. You must have a working knowledge of how spreadsheets work and how to create a spreadsheet macro. If you use Microsoft Excel or Corel Quatro Pro instead, by reading through these pages, you should be able to recreate an equivalent macro sheet that performs essentially the same task.

Our exercise calls for the creation of a front end to the process of generating in MicroStation regularly spaced gridlines with "bubbles" at their ends. Such an application is useful when drawing office building floor plans that build on regularly spaced columns. The worksheet we create will assume that the design file will be set up to use feet as master units and inches as subunits.

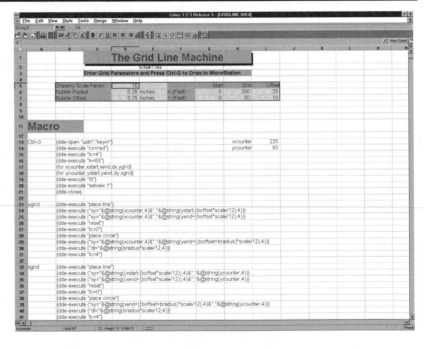

A bird's-eye view of the Lotus 1-2-3 for Windows spreadsheet that draws gridlines in MicroStation using DDE links.

Without much ado, the following is the complete listing of the spreadsheet shown in the previous figure.

 NOTE: *This spreadsheet application, written by the author, first appeared in the December 1992 issue of* MicroStation Manager *magazine.*

In Lotus 1-2-3, you will first need to create range names for the cells shown in the following table.

Cell	Range Name	Description
D5	SCALE	Drawing scale factor for placing bubbles
D6	BRADIUS	Bubble radius as measured on plotted drawing
D7	BOFFSET	Bubble offset as measured on plotted drawing
G6	XSTART	Absolute X coordinate for start of grid
G7	YSTART	Absolute Y coordinate for start of grid
H6	XEND	Absolute X coordinate for end of grid
H7	YEND	Absolute Y coordinate for end of grid
I6	DX	X distance between gridlines
I7	DY	Y distance between gridlines
I13	XCOUNTER	Used by the "Ctrl-G" macro for loop control
I14	YCOUNTER	Used by the "Ctrl-G" macro for loop control
B13	\G	Start of the "Ctrl-G" macro
B23	YGRID	Start of the "ygrid" subroutine
B33	XGRID	Start of the "xgrid" subroutine

The foregoing table sums up all important cell addresses used in the worksheet. All but the last three cells are used for data or variables used by the macro code. The last three cells refer to the starting location of the main macro and its two subroutines. The Ctrl-G macro lies in the cell range B13 to B21 and uses the subroutines in cell ranges B23 to B31 and B33 to B41. The macro listing follows.

Cell	Contents
B13	`{dde-open "ustn","keyin"}`
B14	`{dde-execute "co=red"}`
B15	`{dde-execute "lc=4"}`
B16	`{dde-execute "lv=63"}`
B17	`{for xcounter ,xstart,xend,dx,ygrid}`
B18	`{for ycounter,ystart ,yend,dy,xgrid}`
B19	`{dde-execute "fit"}`
B20	`{dde-execute "selview 1"}`
B21	`{dde-close}`
B23	`{dde-execute "place line"}`
B24	`{dde-execute ("xy="&@string(xcoun-ter,4)&","&@string(y start-(boff-set*scale/12),4))}`
B25	`{dde-execute ("xy="&@string(xcoun-ter,4)&","&@string(yend+( boffset*scale/12),4))}`
B26	`{dde-execute "reset"}`
B27	`{dde-execute "lc=0"}`
B28	`{dde-execute "place cir-cle"}`
B29	`{dde-execute ("xy="&@string(xcoun-ter,4)&","&string(yend+(( boffset+bradius) *scale/12),4))}`
B30	`{dde-execute ("dl="&@string(bradius*sc ale/12,4))}`
B31	`{dde-execute "lc=4"}`

B33	```{dde-execute "place line"}```
B34	```{dde-execute ("xy="&@string((xstart-(boffset*scale/12)),4) &","&@string(ycounter,4))}```
B35	```{dde-execute ("xy="&@string((xend+(boffset*scale/12)),4) & "," & @string(ycounter,4))}```
B36	```{dde-execute "reset"}```
B37	```{dde-execute "lc=0"}```
B38	```{dde-execute "place circle"}```
B39	```{dde-execute ("xy="&@string(xend+((boffset+bradius)*scale/12),4) & "," & @string(ycounter,4))}```
B40	```{dde-execute ("dl="&@string(bradius*scale/12,4))}```
B41	```{dde-execute "lc=4"}```

The use of range names, in lieu of cell addresses, in macro functions is highly recommended. This way, even if you change the location of the input cells, the macro does not have to be revised to reflect the new cell addresses. Cell D5 is used as an input field for the drawing scale factor used in computing the actual size of the bubbles to be drawn. Thus, if the plot scale is $1/8'' = 1'\text{-}0''$, the drawing scale factor would be 96 (= 12 x 8/1). A bubble with a radius of $0.25''$ on the plotted drawing would need to be drawn with an actual radius of $24''$ (= 96 x 0.25) in the design file. (See the macro code in cells B30 and B40.) The bubble offset refers to the length of projection of the gridlines beyond the grid start and end coordinates.

The macro starts by establishing a link to MicroStation by passing the "ustn" application name and the "keyin" topic name as parameters to the {dde-open} macro function in Lotus 1-2-3.

Once the channel of communication is open between Lotus 1-2-3 and MicroStation, the {dde-execute} macro command is used to pass key-ins to MicroStation. The contents of cells B14 through B16 set the active color to red, the line code to centerline, and the active level to 63.

Next, the subroutines YGRID and XGRID are called in cells B17 and B18 by the loop control function {for}. The loops start with a value of XSTART (and YSTART), are incremented by the DX (and DY) values, and end on reaching XEND (and YEND) values.

The subroutines YGRID and XGRID place the vertical and horizontal gridlines, respectively, with bubbles at their ends. Because the {dde-execute} macro function accepts a string variable as its parameter, the numerical data in the input cells are converted to string type through the use of the @string() function.

Once your worksheet is ready, you will find it convenient to tile Lotus 1-2-3 for Windows and MicroStation as shown in the following figure. This will enable you to see the macro in action.

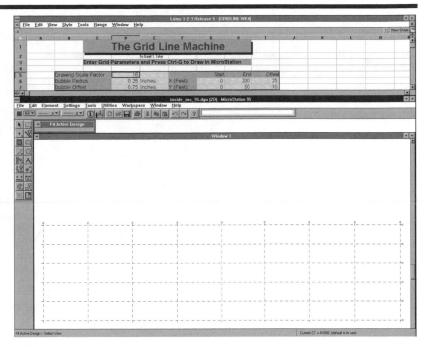

Tile Lotus 1-2-3 and MicroStation as shown. Make Lotus 1-2-3 active, key in desired values for data fields that define the grid layout, and press Ctrl-G to have 1-2-3 draw the gridlines in MicroStation.

The spreadsheet application discussed previously is a mere glimpse, much like the proverbial tip of the iceberg, of what can be done with DDE links. By using a spreadsheet for numerical analysis of your engineering problems and MicroStation to receive the results via DDE key-ins, the variety of custom applications that can be created is boundless.

One important class of problems the spreadsheet is useful for is that of parametric shape creation. Virtually all disciplines need it. For instance, the American Institute of Steel Construction table of standard steel shapes, used by structural engineers while designing steel structures, contains hundreds of sections with a similar shape but varying dimensions. By storing the shape dimension database in a spreadsheet and using its powerful data query capability, the implementation of on-the-fly shape creation is far more efficient than keeping the entire shape collection individually drawn in a cell library. Besides the enormous savings in disk space requirements, parametric shape creation allows you to use the same database for generating not only a section view but plan and elevation views.

OLE Automation

Besides Dynamic Data Exchange, Windows provides yet another means of sharing data between applications: Object Linking and Embedding, or OLE for short. As we saw earlier in this chapter, you can use the Clipboard to paste data from one application to another. If you paste data between OLE-compliant applications, the pasted data knows about the application it originated from. Thus if you were to double-click an embedded object in a document, the source application would be launched with the object loaded.

The OLE 2 specification extended the original specification to provide in-place editing of an embedded object. Thus if you double-clicked an embedded object in a document, the menus of the target application would change to reflect object editing commands from the source application. In addition to in-place editing, at the programming level, OLE 2 provides guidelines on how an application can expose its functionality for use by other applications.

MicroStation for Windows is designed to be an OLE automation server. What that means is it opens up its graphics engine for use by other Windows programs to control MicroStation. Programs that can access the functionality of OLE automation servers are referred to as OLE automation controllers.

There is a significant parallel between MicroStation Basic and MicroStation's OLE automation implementation. However, let's first outline the difference. Applications you write in MicroStation Basic can exist only within the MicroStation environment. But, OLE automation controller applications that you create using tools such as Visual Basic 4 (Visual Basic 3 cannot build OLE automation controller applications) are executables that can exist outside, but interact with, MicroStation. Another point to keep in mind is that OLE automation is supported only on the 32-bit implementations of Windows; namely, Windows 95 and Windows NT.

The parallel is in the MicroStation-specific functions each can access. Virtually all functions available to a MicroStation Basic application are also available to OLE automation controllers. Each can query a design file to determine active symbology settings, or ask MicroStation to perform a fence operation, or any other task you might have used the C-based MDL (MicroStation Development Language) for.

If you intend to create OLE automation controllers that exploit MicroStation, you will want to get intimately familiar with MicroStation Basic. A tutorial on MicroStation Basic is beyond the scope of this book. Suffice it to say that the concepts of objects and methods you learn in MicroStation Basic are directly applicable to OLE automation.

Adding Applications to MicroStation

MicroStation is one of the most adaptable CAD packages on the market. Its rich set of element types, coupled with a variety of manipulation tools, enables MicroStation to meet the CAD needs of just about every design discipline.

That's not to say it can't be extended to address vertical market needs. On the contrary, when it comes to addressing the needs of a particular engineering field, MicroStation lends itself to an incredible level of customization. Of course, you could take matters into your own hands and customize MicroStation by writing user commands, creating special menus, and even getting involved with MicroStation Basic, MDL, and MicroCSL, but before you go to all that trouble, there *are* alternatives.

MicroStation has its own cottage industry of third-party vendors, also known as independent software developers (ISDs), specializing in products that enhance MicroStation. Today there are hundreds of add-on applications, which run the gamut from simple utilities, to engineering design packages, to sophisticated photorealistic rendering and animation products.

What follows is a broad, and not necessarily complete, overview of the types of third-party products available. For a more complete listing of such products, see the *MicroStation Solutions Catalog* or the *MicroStation Buyer's Guide*. Both are available free to registered MicroStation users from Bentley. Or, you may browse them electronically on Bentley's home page, *http://www.bentley.com.*

❑ Architectural Design

❑ Cell Libraries

❑ Design File Repair Utilities

❑ Drawing and Document Management

❑ Earth Sciences and Environmental Management

❑ Electrical and Lighting

❑ Facilities Management and Space Planning

❑ Hydraulics and Hydrology

❑ Imaging and Photogrammetry

❑ Infrastructure and Utilities Management

❑ Landscape Design

❑ Mapping and GIS

❑ Mechanical Engineering

❑ Mining

❑ Piping

❑ Plotting Utilities

❑ Plumbing and HVAC

❑ Rendering and Animation

❑ Structural Engineering

❑ Surveying and Civil Engineering

❑ Translation

Where to Go from Here

As with life, you never stop learning MicroStation. To assist you in this task there are a number of additional books to aid you on the way to mastery of this very powerful tool. Other OnWord Press books are listed at the back of this book.

Electronic Bulletin Boards

Another source of utility software as well as a source of help are the electronic bulletin boards (BBSs) that focus on MicroStation.

CompuServe and America On Line: MicroStation Forum

In late 1993 MicroStation began hosting a separate forum on CompuServe. You can access it with the keyword GO MSTATION. The keyword for the MicroStation Forum on America On Line is also MSTATION. With access to CompuServe or AOL you now have access to all of the library files once found only on Intergraph's BBS or Bentley's BBS. These forums are an excellent place to discuss ideas, identify problems, and review the latest shareware and sample design files.

Bentley Home Page

In 1995, Bentley set up a home page on the World Wide Web. The URL for the site is *http://www.bentley.com*. This is the ultimate on-line resource for MicroStation users. Here you will find late-breaking MicroStation-related news and press releases, information on the ongoing MicroStation FORUM and Exhibitions around the country, freeware and shareware utilities, demos of products, and other exciting stuff.

TMC and MicroStation Manager Magazine

MicroStation Manager magazine is published by The MicroStation Community, or TMC for short. TMC is a MicroStation user group recently formed with Bentley's blessing. Its purpose is to disseminate information about MicroStation and to be a forum for the exchange of ideas between MicroStation users and Bentley. The popular MicroStation FORUM and Exhibition events now being held around the world are organized by TMC. The Community also recently purchased *MicroStation Manager* magazine to further its goal of reaching a much larger audience. The magazine circulates monthly to paid readers and contains up-to-date information about all aspects of MicroStation, including associated software and hardware designed to get the most performance from MicroStation. Regular monthly columns include four different levels of how-to, from very basic up to programmer/developer levels. Site profiles discuss how other companies are using MicroStation to increase profits and efficiencies. Every article is written from a technical viewpoint and contains immediately useful information. TMC may be reached on the World Wide Web at *www.tmc.org*.

Customizing
MicroStation

Becoming a Power User

A knowledge of the basic commands in MicroStation is essential to creating any design drawing with the software. To get any useful work done, you must know how to create a new design file, place primitive graphic elements, manipulate your views, and snap to existing elements. This chapter assumes you are already familiar with these concepts. But even a good working knowledge of the drawing and editing commands does not a power user make.

There is much more to MicroStation than just the flexibility of its basic drafting tools. Understanding why the tools take on the default settings they do, where to change the defaults so MicroStation works the way you prefer, and how several commands can be grouped together to act like a new single command are just the first steps to taking control of MicroStation's design environment and command set.

There is a belief that customizing MicroStation requires programming skills. On the contrary, there is an entire set of interactive, dialog-box-driven tools that enable you to mold MicroStation to your company, discipline, project, or user needs without such skills. Customizing MicroStation can be thought of as the task of changing its default behavior. To be sure, MicroStation provides a few sophisticated programming environments, but an enormous amount of customization can be done without even venturing there. The focus of this chapter is the exploration of end-user customization tools. In addition, we will briefly discuss the programming interfaces in MicroStation.

 TIP: *Although the demanding nature of a production CAD environment in a design office leaves little time for exploring MicroStation customization, it offers an ideal opportunity to identify processes that do not seem to work the way you want. Always keep a "wish list" notebook handy, and when you find yourself repeating the same sequence of commands or inadvertently making the same mistake over and over, jot it down. Going through your notes later, when you have time to customize MicroStation, you will find a treasure chest of ideas to implement as custom tools.*

This chapter is divided in two parts. The first is titled "Sorry, But I Don't Program," and introduces you to the easy-to-use, interactive customization tools in MicroStation. As you will find, the scope of this section is extensive. Here you will learn about:

❏ Preferences

❏ Workspaces

❏ Settings Manager

❑ Function keys

❑ Custom line styles

❑ Glossary

The second part in this chapter is titled "Programming Micro-Station," and highlights the more involved methods of customizing MicroStation that require some background in programming. We will not cover these aspects in much detail here. However, after reading this part you will at least understand how MicroStation can be programmed, and the level of effort needed to tackle the task. In this section you learn about:

❑ User commands

❑ MicroStation Basic

❑ MicroStation Development Environment

❑ MicroCSL

Sorry, But I Don't Program

Even if you have never written a MicroStation user command, an MDL program, or any other program, you can still customize MicroStation. Many data files and configuration settings used for items such as level names and function key assignments are controlled via dialog and settings boxes.

In fact, even many of the sophisticated capabilities implemented by other CAD systems as difficult-to-master command line utilities are made accessible in MicroStation through interactive tools. The Settings Manager and the Line Style Editor are such examples.

All customizable options described in this section require no programming. Whether you wish to establish CAD standards at your office with the Settings Manager, modify configuration variables so that different projects have easy access to cell libraries specially made for them, or create custom line styles, these tasks can be easily accomplished within MicroStation by any end user. For some tasks, however, such as creating user and project configuration files, you may want to take the faster approach of copying existing configuration files and modifying them with a text editor.

Preferences

The Preferences dialog box is the control center for modifying all user preferences. It is invoked from the Workspace menu (**Workspace ➡ Preferences**). The dialog box is split into two panes. The left pane displays various preference categories, and the right pane lists the items under the category selected in the left pane. Some common preference items you may wish to change are:

❑ The size of font used by menus and dialog boxes

❑ The look of MicroStation's dialog boxes, whether Motif or Windows

❑ Reference file settings

❑ Text display options

❑ The behavior of tool palettes

❑ Line weight display settings for the screen

The Preferences dialog box displays user preference categories on the left side and preference options from the selected category on the right side.

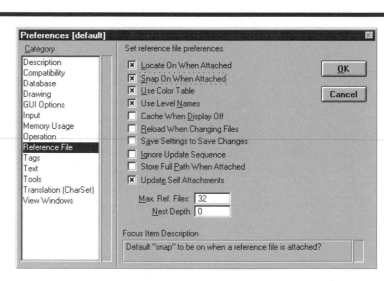

There really is nothing to changing preference settings. You simply highlight the appropriate category in the left pane of the Preferences dialog box and edit the desired preference field in the right pane. The real issue is understanding what each of the preference settings does. To help you understand the implication of each preference, MicroStation implements a Help pane along the bottom of the Preferences dialog box. If you are unsure of what a preference setting does, simply highlight it and read the description in the Help or the Focus Item Description pane.

You are not restricted to a single preference setting for a given computer. The implementation of workspaces in MicroStation enables you to maintain a different preference setting for a different workspace. Thus, different users can have their own workspaces with their own preference settings, or a single user can maintain multiple workspaces for different projects. The following section delves a little deeper into this.

Workspaces

Depending on what you use MicroStation for, the collection of files you need, such as cell libraries, seed files, and symbology resources (font and line styles), are different from the set of files another user may need. Thus, if you are working on a mapping project, the working units in your seed files would be different than if you were working on a commercial building project. Similarly, if your project calls for a frequent interface with an AutoCAD user, the default set of fonts and line styles you use is likely to be different from someone using MicroStation exclusively.

The collection of data files—cell libraries, fonts, seed files, dimension styles, multi-line definitions, named levels, and the like—is referred to as a workspace module. MicroStation comes with several workspace modules ready for you to use and customize. In keeping with the modular nature of a workspace, MicroStation uses a structured directory hierarchy to store these files.

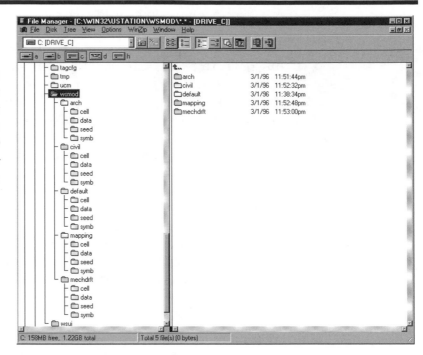

MicroStation organizes workspace modules as subdirectories in the WSMOD subdirectory under its base directory.

A MicroStation workspace is a custom environment designed for easy access to interface components and workspace modules for a particular task or user. MicroStation uses configuration variables to define a workspace. For a default Windows NT installation, the various subdirectories, where project and user configuration files are stored, are located under the directory:

`C:\WIN32APP\USTATION\CONFIG.`

NOTE: *MicroStation supports five types of configuration files: System, Application, Site, Project, and User.*

> **TIP:** *The Project and User configuration files have the PCF and UCF filename extensions, respectively. These are plain text files, and you can learn a great deal about creating your own workspaces by examining them closely.*

When you start MicroStation as installed, with no command line parameters, you are automatically using the default workspace and its associated modules. Notice that the design files MicroStation brings up in the MicroStation Manager at startup are in the C:\USTATION\DGN\DEFAULT directory. To use the sample civil workspace, at your operating system's command line, or at the system prompt, key in:

```
USTATION -wuCIVIL
```

You will notice that the design files listed in MicroStation Manager, when the Civil workspace is active, are from the C:\USTATION\DGN\CIVIL directory. The command line switch -wu shown above stands for workspace user, and it must precede the name of the user configuration file you wish to use. A configuration file predominantly defines the search path for various data files.

Another method of selecting a new workspace is from the MicroStation Manager dialog box at startup. The Workspace option button on this dialog box lists all user configuration files installed on your system.

The Workspace option button on the MicroStation Manger dialog box makes it easy to select the workspace for your session.

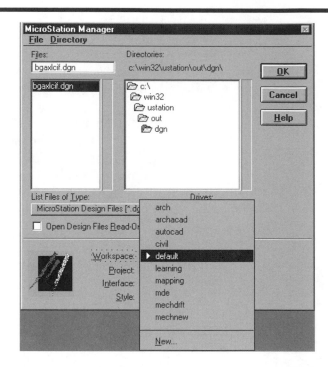

Here is a look at the partial contents of the sample ARCH.PCF file supplied with MicroStation:

```
_USTN_PROJECTDESCR= Architecture Example
_USTN_ARCHDIR= $(_USTN_WSMOD)arch/
#  Set architecture search paths/data.
MS_DEF < $(MSLOCAL)dgn/arch/
MS_CELL < $(_USTN_ARCHDIR)cell/
MS_CELLLIST= $(_USTN_ARCHDIR)cell/*.cel
MS_CELLSEED= $(_USTN_WSMOD)default/cell/seed2d.cel
#----- set architecture seed file as default #
MS_DESIGNSEED= archseed.dgn
#----- architecture level names -----#
MS_LEVELNAMES= $(_USTN_ARCHDIR)data/
#----- architecture glossary terms -----#
MS_GLOSSARY < $(_USTN_ARCHDIR)data/*.gls
#----- architecture function key menu -----#
MS_FKEYMNU= $(_USTN_ARCH DIR)data/archfkey.mnu
#----- architecture symbology resources ----  -#
MS_SYMBRSRC= $(_USTN_ARCHDIR)symb/*.rsc
#----- find the architecture settings resources -----#
MS_SETTINGSDIR= $(_USTN_ARCHDIR)data/
```

The lines in the foregoing listing that have the # as the first character are comments. The variables in parentheses preceded by the $ symbol are configuration variables that expand to their directory path value when used in an assignment statement. Look at the definition for the MS_DEF variable in the listing. (MicroStation looks for design files in the directory defined by the MS_DEF variable.) The default design file directory for the ARCH workspace user is $(MSLOCAL)DGN/ARCH/, which expands to C:\USTATION\DGN\ARCH\ on a DOS platform, because the variable $(MSLOCAL) has a value of C:\USTATION\, the local MicroStation directory.

NOTE: *Although an experienced user may find it more convenient to use a text editor to directly modify and create configuration files, there is a more convenient method of dealing with them. The Configuration option under the Workspace menu invokes a dialog box to let you create and edit User configuration files.*

The Workspace menu offers items to edit the workspace User configuration file, work with the Preferences dialog box, and customize the MicroStation interface.

In addition to the configuration files, a workspace also includes user preferences and a user interface resource. It is worth noting that each workspace User configuration file has a corresponding User preference file, so that each workspace user can maintain his or her own preference environment.

Let's move on to the user interface. The user interface of a workspace consists of icons and menus the user interacts with to invoke commands. All of these interface elements can be modified with the help of the interactive Customize dialog box. The interface elements you can customize with it follow.

❑ *Toolboxes:* You can modify any of the native MicroStation toolboxes with Customize, or you create your own toolboxes. Custom toolboxes can borrow native MicroStation icons, or you can create your own icons and assign them a key-in.

❑ *Tool Frames:* Tool frames look like toolboxes, but they are of a fixed size and are a repository for toolboxes. You can modify any of MicroStation's native tool frames, or you can create your own with the Customize dialog box.

❑ *Menu Bar:* The pull-down menu bar along the top edge of the MicroStation application window is also customizable. Because an application has only one menu, the Customize dialog box lets you edit the existing menu bar, not create a new one.

❑ *View Border:* You can modify the view toolbox that graces the left side of the horizontal scroll bar on a view window. However, you are allowed to only place view control commands on it.

Any of the items you choose to modify with Customize, whether a menu option or a command icon, can be assigned a command key-in or a sequence of commands strung together and separated by semicolons. To invoke the Customize dialog box, select **Workspace ➡ Customize** from the menu bar. This opens a dialog box with a few option buttons, command buttons, and item lists.

The upper left option button in the Customize dialog box lets you choose any of the four item types listed above to customize. Depending on which option you select, the list box on the left displays all available tools or menus. The list box to the right displays available tools in a specific toolbox or menu you select from the option button just above it.

The Copy button between the two list boxes lets you copy an available tool or menu from the list of available items on the left to the items list you are editing on the right. Double-clicking an item in the right list opens that item's properties for you to edit.

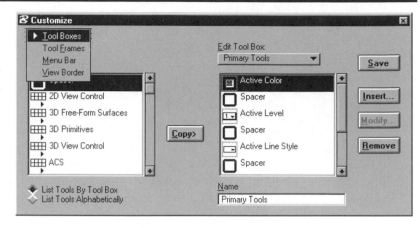

*Double-click an item
in the list on the
right of the
Customize dialog
box to edit its
properties.*

Several sample customized interfaces are supplied with Micro-Station and are invoked when you log on with one of the sample workspaces. For instance, the Arch workspace includes a new Architecture item under the Tools menu to open a custom tool frame. Additionally, the AutoCAD workspace includes a redesigned menu where several items display their AutoCAD equivalent terminology in parentheses next to MicroStation's commands.

TIP: *To display the user, project, interface, and preferences files your current session is using, select the About Workspace option from the Workspace menu.*

Settings Manager

The Settings Manager should perhaps be called the symbology manager, as most users are likely to use it in that capacity. Then again, perhaps the term *Settings Manager* is the more appropriate name, because you can also control other settings with it in addition to active symbology, such as dimension styles, multi-line element definitions, text settings, and drawing scales.

Of what use is the Setting Manager, given that the active color (CO=), weight (WT=), line style (LC=), and level (LV=) can be easily changed at any time? The answer lies in examining how design offices have standardized their use of symbology. This is done for creating drawings that are consistent and easier to manage from project to project.

Most engineering drawings are produced on a monochrome plotter, and so the element color and level play no role insofar as the hard copy is concerned. Thus, most beginners tend to draw virtually everything on the same level with the same color, only taking care to set element weights and line styles to correspond to project standards. Of course, paying attention to the colors and the levels on which elements are placed helps you create more flexible drawings. Just think of the *Select By* tool for element selection by color, and of the need to turn off the levels containing text and dimensions prior to plotting, as illustrations of the flexibility offered by standardizing all symbology components for your drawings.

Considering the differences in drafting requirements for different departments within a company, most CAD standards are discipline-specific, and they share some elements among them. The following table illustrates in concept what most standards offer as guidelines. The table has deliberately been kept small for simplicity.

Drafting Standards for Civil Drawings				
Item	**Level**	**Color**	**Weight**	**Line Style**
Border	50	4	2	0
Roads	6	3	1	0
Storm Sewer	21	5	2	0
Tree Line	6	2	1	Tree Line

Let's see how such a standard can be implemented with the help of the Settings Manager. You use the Edit Settings window to create settings groups, and you use the Select Settings window to activate them. To invoke the Edit Settings window, select **Settings ➡ Manage** to bring up the Select Settings window, and then choose Edit from the Select Setting window's File menu.

The Edit Settings window lets you create a group and associated settings entries.

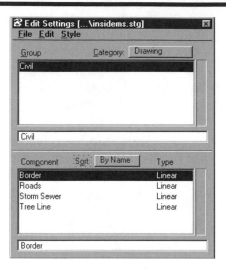

Exercise: Creating a New Settings Group

The following are the steps you will take to create a new settings group called "Civil" in an existing settings file or in a new one:

1. Select **Edit ➡ Create ➡ Group** from the menu in the Edit Settings window. This creates an un-named group, whose name can be edited to read Civil in the Edit field under the Group list window.

2. With the Civil group highlighted, select **Edit ➡ Create ➡ Linear** to create an unnamed item associated with the Civil group. Repeat this command three more times to create a total of four items for this exercise.

3. One by one, highlight each of the four unnamed items in the lower list box and edit their names in the Edit field below to read Border, Roads, Storm Sewer, and Tree Line, respectively.

4. All that remains now is the task of assigning settings to each of these items. Double-click a settings item to invoke the Modify window that lets you assign various settings, such as color, weight, line style, and level. Use the table titled Drafting Standards for Civil Drawings introduced earlier in this section to assign settings for each of the four items.

The Modify window is invoked by double-clicking a settings item. It lets you assign various settings to the selected item.

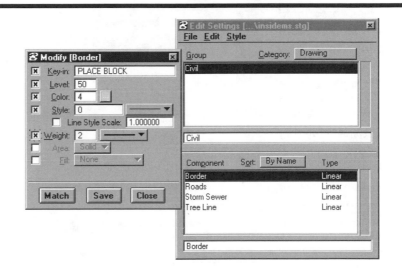

As you can see, creating a settings group is not at all difficult. Such settings groups, once created, are put to use by the *Select Settings* tool. You invoke the Select Settings window by selecting **Settings** ➡ **Manage**. The Select Settings window probably opened up with your recently created settings group already loaded. If not, you can use the **File ➡ Open** command from the Select Settings window to open your settings group. The following figure illustrates the use of this command.

NOTE: *Settings group files have the .STG filename extension, and, for the default workspace, they are stored in the C:\USTATION\WSMOD\DEFAULT\DATA directory.*

Highlight a group in the top pane to display the settings items associated with it in the bottom pane. Notice how clicking on the settings items in the bottom pane changes the symbology and issues a command making the implementation of company standards a simple task.

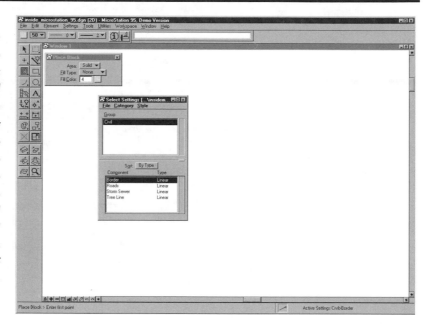

Whereas the traditional method of creating sidebar menus for implementing company standards was a little tedious to write, and only larger companies with development resources usually ventured into creating them, Settings Manager lets you manage settings down to the smallest office by making the task so simple. Even novice users will have no trouble conforming to project standards.

Function Keys

Of all the types of menus MicroStation supports—pull-down, digitizer, sidebar, tutorial, and function key—the function key menu is the easiest to customize. The function key menu is really just a text file that contains command key-ins for all the ways a function key can be used. Thus, on a personal computer with an enhanced keyboard, this means a total of 96 keystroke combinations: F1 through F12 when pressed alone, or when pressed in conjunction with either the Shift, Control, or Alt, or any combination of these keys, including Shift+Control+Alt+F1.

The format of the function key menu file is simple. Every line in the file has two fields separated by a comma. The first field identifies the keystroke, and the second field lists the command key-in to be assigned to it. Keystroke identifiers you enter in the first field have a length of three or four characters. The rightmost digit of the identifier is a number from 1 (for F1) to 9 (for F9), *a* (for F10), *b* (for F11), or *c* (for F12). The left two or three digits are codes identifying which other qualifier keys the function key is pressed with. The line `1305, Window Area` in the function key menu file means that the key Shift+F5 is defined as the Window Area command. The following list shows the codes for the function key qualifiers.

30	Function key alone
130	Shift+Function key
70	Alt+Function key
b0	Ctrl+Function key
f0	Ctrl+Alt+Function key
1b0	Shift+Ctrl+Function key
170	Shift+Alt+Function key
1f0	Shift+Ctrl+Alt+Function key

The function key menu file is a part of the workspace module and is stored in the C:\USTATION\WSMOD\DEFAULT\DATA directory for the default workspace user. The function key menu file can have any name, and a few workspace-specific function key menus are supplied with MicroStation.

Of course, if you prefer the dialog box approach, MicroStation also provides an interactive tool to create and modify these files (**Workspace ➡ Function Keys...**). The dialog box has a File menu to let you open existing function key menu files for modification. Modified files can be saved to replace the original file, or saved in another file to preserve the original one.

Function keys are easy to program. Here, F5 is being reprogrammed as Update View, followed by a datapoint in view 1. Notice how commands can be concatenated with a semicolon separating them.

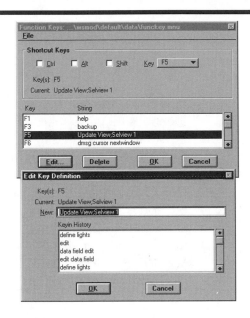

Programming your new function key menu is just a matter of selecting the appropriate function key and clicking Edit to invoke an edit field to supply the command text. The command text can be any valid MicroStation key-in. You can also combine several commands on a single line by separating them with a semicolon. Function key menu command text also supports the same syntax as that used in other types of menus, such as paper menus.

Custom Line Styles

MicroStation provides eight built-in line styles and support for an unlimited number of custom line styles stored in an external resource file. The term *external* refers to the fact that the dash-dot pattern that defines custom line styles is maintained in a file external to MicroStation. If others are to use line styles you create, the resource file must be made available to them. For a default MicroStation installation, the external line style resource file is located in:

```
C:\USTATION\WSMOD\DEFAULT\SYMB\LSTYLE.RSC
```

Custom line styles are used like the built-in line styles. Virtually all graphical elements that can be drawn with a built-in line style can also be drawn with custom line styles. In fact, the shortcut method of invoking both types of line styles is the same. You key in LC=name, where "name" is a number from 0 to 7 for the built-in line styles or the alphanumeric name of a custom line style. Another way of activating custom line styles is by selecting Custom from the Line Style option button (third from left) on the Primary toolbox located under the menu bar.

Double-clicking a custom line style name in this settings box activates it.

Custom line styles offer an immense amount of flexibility. Not only can they consist of a stroke pattern, they can incorporate symbols in their definitions. Additionally, the same line style definition can be placed in your design file with different scale, shift, or width settings.

 NOTE: *Clicking the Show Details checkbox in the Line Styles settings box expands the window to provide access to the three custom line style placement parameters: scale, width, and shift.*

Being able to scale a custom line style before placing it in a design file means that you can scale up or down the stroke, or dash-dot pattern, for a single instance without modifying the line style definition. Similarly, being able to shift it or change its width means that the defined origin of the style can be shifted or its width can be changed. Custom line styles can also have varying widths.

Using custom line styles is a trivial matter. However, deciding on the line styles to create, and actually creating them, takes some advance preparation. Several sample custom line styles are provided with MicroStation and include tree line, railroad track, earth line, and telephone line.

A custom line style can be defined in terms of three components: a stroke pattern, a point symbol, or a compound definition that combines stroke patterns and point symbols. You define line styles by using the Line Style Editor invoked by selecting Edit from the Line Style option button in the Primary toolbox.

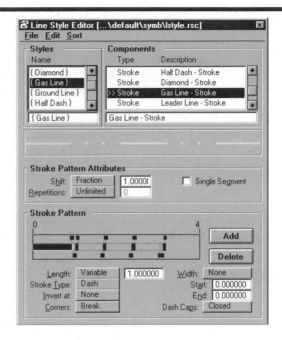

The Line Style Editor invoked from the Element menu lets you create new or edit existing custom line styles.

The process of creating custom line styles is like that described for the Settings Manager. You must first open an existing line style resource file, or create a new one using the File menu in the Line Style Editor window. The following steps outline the process of creating a line style with a stroke pattern component.

1. Create an unnamed line style by using the **Edit ➡ Create Name** menu option, and edit its name in the Edit field under the Styles list box.

2. Create an unnamed line style stroke component by using the **Edit ➡ Create Stroke Pattern** menu option. Again, you'll want to edit the unnamed component's name to be more descriptive.

3. Link the newly defined style name with the stroke component by highlighting both and selecting **Edit ➡ Link** from the menu.

4. Add the necessary number of stroke patterns (dash and gap sequence) to the stroke component created in step 2. To do this, highlight the stroke component and click the Add button in the Line Style Editor's lower half section titled Stroke Pattern.

5. Edit each of the stroke patterns created by first highlighting it and then selecting appropriate values for its length, type, and width. This completes the line style definition, and you can now save the line style resource file.

The procedure for creating line styles based on a point symbol component or a compound component is similar except for the specific attributes that define it.

 NOTE: *To create your own point symbol for use in line styles, draw it using primitive elements such as lines and arcs, place a fence around it, define an origin for it just as you would for a cell definition, and finally key in* CREATE SYMBOL <symbol_name>. *This adds the symbol to the active line style resource file, making it available for inclusion in line style definitions.*

Text Glossary

Glossary is a helpful text placement utility used to place standard text expressions in the design file by clicking on their abbreviation from a customizable list displayed in a dialog box interface. You can use this tool to maintain a list of commonly used text expressions so you do not have to key them in when needed.

You invoke Glossary by either selecting **Utilities ➡ Text Glossary** or by keying in MDL LOAD GLOSSARY at the Key-in window prompt. The following illustration shows the Glossary utility.

Below the list of abbreviations in the Glossary utility are two panes. The top pane displays the full text expression corresponding to the selected abbreviation, and the bottom pane displays the text expression built so far, prior to placement in the design file.

To place text in your design file from the glossary file, highlight the abbreviation for the expression desired, click the Build button, and place a datapoint at the desired location. The sample glossary file supplied with MicroStation is named EXAMPLE.GLS and is located in the C:\USTATION\WSMOD\DEFAULT\DATA directory.

TIP: *The glossary file is workspace-specific and pointed to by the configuration variable MS_GLOSSARY. To edit configuration variables, select* **Workspace** ➡ **Configuration.**

A glossary file is a plain text file with a simple structure. A # character in the first column of a line starts a comment. $date and $time are special variables that represent system date and time. A set of two lines constitutes a glossary entry. The first line contains an abbreviation for the glossary entry and the second line contains the expanded text expression corresponding to the abbreviation. The following is a sample Glossary file:

```
STEEL
All structural steel to conform to ASTM A-36 specifications.
CONC
All concrete to have 4,000 psi 28-day compressive strength.
TIMBER
All timber to be Douglas Fir or equal.
DATE
Today's date is: $date.
TIME
The current time is: $time.
```

Programming MicroStation

As you have seen thus far, a great deal of customization of the design environment is possible. Nevertheless, there are times when you may want to roll up your sleeves and delve into the world of programming MicroStation.

The most powerful way of taking control of command input and of integrating drawings to design calculations is through the use of MicroStation's programming interfaces. Each of the three ways of programming MicroStation is introduced here. This section serves merely to introduce you to the tools. No attempt is made to teach the terminology, language, or its syntax. However, if you wish to find out what it takes to program MicroStation, and which interface will be the more appropriate one for you, read on.

User Commands

The simplest way to program MicroStation is through the use of its User Command (UCM) language. All you need is your favorite text editor, a knowledge of MicroStation's key-ins, rudimentary programming skills, and an interest in creating custom functions. With user commands you can concatenate several primitive commands, query the user for input, display feedback to the user in the Status Bar, perform calculations, and even invoke MDL programs.

Several useful UCMs come with MicroStation in the C:\USTA-TION\UCM directory. You can learn a great deal by examining these files. In essence, a UCM consists of several lines, where each line has the format:

```
label: operator, operand, operand,...
```

The label is optional and serves to identify the location of a statement in a program so that the GO (an unconditional branching operator) or TST (a branching operator that tests for the truth of a condition) operator can be used to transfer program control to a given statement. All user commands must end with the END operator.

UCMs support several types of operators. To query the user, there is the GET operator; to display messages in the status bar, there is the MSG operator; to send a datapoint or a reset, there are the PNT and RST operators; to calculate, there are standard mathematical and matrix operators; and to key in a command at the command line, there is the KEY operator. Dozens of others exist. To store numbers and character strings, UCMs provide several registers, similar to memory registers in a calculator.

The following is the listing for a trivial user command you may enter in a file named TAIL.UCM:

```
key 'CO=3;LV=6;WT=2'
key 'PLACE LINE'
key 'DL=0,0'
key 'DL=5,0'
rst
end
```

This UCM changes your active symbology and invokes the Place Line command to add a horizontal line five units long, starting at the last datapoint entered. To invoke the UCM simply key in UC=TAIL at the command line.

 NOTE: *Be sure to save your UCMs in a directory pointed to by the configuration variable MS_UCM so that MicroStation can find them.*

MicroStation Basic

MicroStation's user command language is akin to a programmable calculator's language. Although still supported for the sake of compatibility with prior MicroStation and IGDS versions, it is not being enhanced, nor is it the recommended method for creating macros. MicroStation Basic is a much more powerful and complete programming environment.

The purpose of a macro is to automate the repetitive sequence of commands you use frequently. This sequence may consist of any of MicroStation's drawing, editing, or view control tools; changes to active settings; or other MicroStation operations. To help you get started, MicroStation comes with a bevy of useful macros located in the C:\USTATION\MACROS directory. The Basic language source files have the extension BAS and are plain text files.

If you have written programs in the Basic language, MicroStation Basic will be immediately familiar to you. The syntax of MicroStation Basic is closely patterned after Microsoft's Visual

Basic. In addition to the standard set of language keywords, MicroStation Basic extends the language with hundreds of MicroStation-specific functions, all of which have the "mbe" prefix.

The simplest way to get started writing a macro is to record it. You start the macro recorder by choosing *Create Macro...* from the Utilities menu. This opens up the Create Macro dialog box, where you supply a name for your macro and, optionally, a description of what the macro does.

Click the OK button after supplying a macro name in the Create Macro dialog box to start your macro recording session.

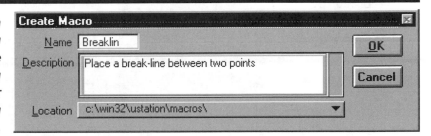

Upon clicking the OK button, your macro session starts and VCR style Play, Pause, and End buttons appear in a small dialog box as a reminder that your macro recording session is in effect. The Play button should be depressed at this time, indicating that all of your interactive actions in MicroStation will be recorded. If you wish to temporarily pause the recording of your actions, you would click the Pause button. The End button closes the dialog box and writes your actions to the file you had initially specified for the macro.

After you have recorded your macro, you will typically want to review and edit the source generated. This is done through the Macro Editor. To load and edit a BAS file, choose *Macros* from the Utilities menu, select the desired macro file, and click the Edit... button.

At this point you will want to enhance the code by replacing with variables the hard-coded numerical values representing coordinates of locations you had clicked while recording the macro. You will also want to add other standard Basic function to make the program interactive and functional. MicroStation Basic allows you to create dialog boxes for this purpose.

Use the Macro Editor to edit the recorded code to make it interactive and more useful.

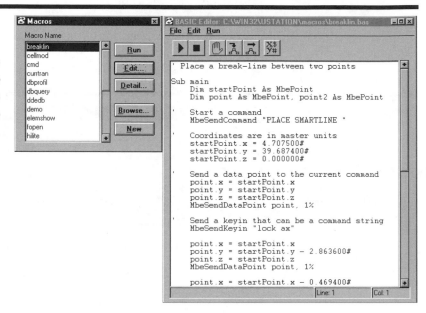

Macros you create with MicroStation Basic are procedural, meaning they follow a top-down sequence of operation. Any interactive dialog boxes you create for your macros will be modal.

The fact that macros are simple to get started does not mean you cannot create sophisticated applications with it. On the contrary, MicroStation Basic provides functions to deal with all element types and to query environment settings; even to work with reference files. You are encouraged to explore the supplied examples and use the on-line Help to get familiar with the vast functionality of the macro language.

MicroStation Development Environment

With the introduction of MicroStation version 4 came the powerful MicroStation Development Language (MDL) for the ultimate in creating MicroStation add-on applications. MDL is an implementation of the C programming language designed specifically to run under MicroStation. Applications written in MDL can have an interface indistinguishable from MicroStation's own interface. In fact, many of MicroStation's commands and tools, such as the multi-line joint tool, are implemented in MDL.

Later, the MDL product was enhanced by bundling it with the MicroStation Development Environment (MDE), a programming environment that now includes interactive resource building tools. The simplest way to access the MDE tools is to invoke the MDE workspace. Start MicroStation with the "-wuMDE" command line switch:

```
ustation -wuMDE
```

Programming an MDL application is much like developing a C language program for any GUI. Interface components of an application, such as dialog boxes and icons, are referred to as *resources*. MDE provides easy access to the four resource editors: Command Table Editor, Dialog Box Builder, Icon Editor, and String List Editor. MDE also includes a debugger and a "make" utility. If your application needs these resources, and you have built them with the appropriate editor, you can invoke the Resource Source Generator from within MDE to create source files for your application's resources. In addition to the resource files, you must also create MDL source files to impart functionality to your application.

Once all resource and source files have been created, you invoke the Resource Compiler, RCOMP.EXE, to process the resource files and create compiled resources. At this stage, you also process the MDL source files through the Source Compiler, MCOMP.EXE, to generate an object module, followed by the linker, MLINK.EXE, to generate files that are ready to be combined with your program's resources. The resource librarian, RLIB.EXE, accepts compiled resources and source files to generate the final MDL application that has the .MA extension.

Even though MDL applications are compiled into a binary format, they are not truly executable files. These binaries are interpreted by MicroStation as they execute. The MDL functions that call upon built-in MicroStation graphical commands execute at full speed, but computational functions execute relatively slowly because they are interpreted.

MDL applications you create are easily portable to other platforms. The MDL source from one platform usually requires a simple recompile to get it running in the host environment. MDL applications you create are invoked from within MicroStation by issuing the `MDL LOAD filename` command, where *filename* is the name of your .MA application.

As you have seen in this brief discussion of MDL programming, creating MDL programs requires an understanding of programming concepts in general, and the C language in particular. If you are serious about creating powerful MDL applications, the investment in learning C will pay itself back in the professional quality of your add-on applications.

MicroCSL

MicroCSL stands for MicroStation Customer Support Library. As the name suggests, it is an object library for the development of MicroStation add-on applications. This object library is not a part of MicroStation and must be acquired separately from Intergraph at additional cost. You must already have a supported C or FORTRAN language compiler to develop applications with this library.

When Bentley's IGDS used to run on DEC VAX/VMS minicomputers, the FORTRAN compiler was a standard part of the operating system supplied with the computers. This heritage is the reason for the support of FORTRAN as a third-party development language. However, C is by far the more popular language.

Whereas MDL applications are integrated to MicroStation and cannot be executed outside the CAD software, MicroCSL-based applications can be either integrated or stand-alone. All MicroCSL applications must be compiled, and so are fast in execution speed. For applications that must perform extensive calculations, be stand-alone, or be compatible with IGDS, MicroCSL development makes sense.

The major disadvantage of MicroCSL is its limited user interface interaction with MicroStation; information can be requested from, and output to, the status bar only. Therefore, the suggested method for developing compute-intensive applications is to program the interface in MDL, and call auxiliary MicroCSL programs from it to handle the computations.

Where to Go from Here

If any of these advanced programming topics interest you, several additional books from OnWord Press are available to extend your knowledge in these areas. For learning how to program UCMs you may wish to consider *MicroStation Productivity Book, Programming with User Commands,* and *101 User Commands.* For MDL programming, you may wish to consider *Programming with MDL* and *101 MDL Commands.* If you prefer classroom instruction in programming, you can obtain training from Bentley authorized training centers, from Bentley directly, and from Intergraph.

Index

A

G

H

I

U

More OnWord Press Titles

Pro/ENGINEER and Pro/JR. Books

INSIDE Pro/ENGINEER, 2E
Book $49.95 Includes Disk

Pro/ENGINEER Quick Reference, 2E
Book $24.95

Pro/ENGINEER Exercise Book, 2E
Book $39.95 Includes Disk

Thinking Pro/ENGINEER
Book $49.95

Pro/ENGINEER Tips and Techniques
Book $59.95

INSIDE Pro/JR.
Book $49.95

MicroStation Books

INSIDE MicroStation 5X, 3d ed.
Book $34.95 Includes Disk

INSIDE MicroStation 95, 4E
Book $39.95 Includes Disk

MicroStation Reference Guide 5.X
Book $18.95

MicroStation 95 Quick Reference
Book $24.95

MicroStation 95 Productivity Book
Book $49.95

MicroStation Exercise Book 5.X
Book $34.95 Includes Disk
Optional Instructor's Guide $14.95

MicroStation 95 Exercise Book
Book $35.95 Includes Disk
Optional Instructor's Guide $14.95

MicroStation for AutoCAD Users, 2E
Book $34.95

Adventures in MicroStation 3D
Book $49.95 Includes CD-ROM

Build Cell for 5.X
Software $69.95

101 MDL Commands (5.X and 95)
Optional Executable Disk $101.00
Optional Source Disks (6) $259.95

Windows NT

Windows NT for the Technical Professional
Book $39.95

SunSoft Solaris Series

SunSoft Solaris 2.* User's Guide
Book $29.95 Includes Disk

SunSoft Solaris 2. for Managers and
Administrators*
Book $34.95

SunSoft Solaris 2.* Quick Reference
Book $18.95

Five Steps to SunSoft Solaris 2.*
Book $24.95 Includes Disk

SunSoft Solaris 2.* for Windows Users
Book $24.95

The Hewlett Packard HP-UX Series

HP-UX User's Guide
Book $29.95 Includes Disk

HP-UX Quick Reference
Book $18.95

Five Steps to HP-UX
Book $24.95 Includes Disk

Softdesk

*Softdesk Architecture 1 Certified
Courseware*
Book $34.95 Includes CD-ROM

*Softdesk Architecture 2 Certified
Courseware*
Book $34.95 Includes CD-ROM

ISoftdesk Civil 1 Certified Courseware
Book $34.95 Includes CD-ROM

Softdesk Civil 2 Certified Courseware
Book $34.95 Includes CD-ROM

NSIDE Softdesk Architectural
Book $49.95 Includes Disk

INSIDE Softdesk Civil
Book $49.95 Includes Disk

Other CAD

*Manager's Guide to Computer-Aided
Engineering*
Book $49.95

*Fallingwater in 3D Studio: A Case Study
and Tutorial*
Book $39.95 Includes Disk

Geographic Information Systems (GIS)

INSIDE ARC/INFO
Book $74.95 Includes CD-ROM

ARC/INFO Quick Reference
Book $24.95

INSIDE ArcView
Book $39.95 Includes CD-ROM

ArcView Developer's Guide
Book $49.95

ArcView/Avenue Programmer's Reference
Book $49.95

101 ArcView/Avenue Scripts: The Disk
Disk $101.00

ArcView Exercise Book
Book $49.95 Includes CD-ROM

INSIDE ArcCAD
Book $39.95 Includes Disk

The GIS Book, 3d ed.
Book $34.95

INSIDE MapInfo Professional
Book $49.95

Raster Imagery in Geographic Information Systems
Book $59.95

GIS: A Visual Approach
Book $39.95

Interleaf Books

INSIDE Interleaf (v. 6)
Book $49.95 Includes Disk

Adventurer's Guide to Interleaf Lisp
Book $49.95 Includes Disk

Interleaf Exercise Book
Book $39.95 Includes Disk

Interleaf Quick Reference (v. 6)
Book $24.95

Interleaf Tips and Tricks
Book $49.95 Includes Disk

OnWord Press Distribution

End Users/User Groups/Corporate Sales

OnWord Press books are available worldwide to end users, user groups, and corporate accounts from your local bookseller or computer/software dealer, or from Softstore/CADNEWS Bookstore: call 1-800-CADNEWS (1-800-223-6397) or 505-474-5120; fax 505-474-5020; write to CADNEWS Bookstore, 2530 Camino Entrada, Santa Fe, NM 87505-4835, or e-mail ORDERS@HMP.COM. CADNEWS Bookstore is a division of SoftStore, Inc., a High Mountain Press Company.

Wholesale, Including Overseas Distribution

High Mountain Press distributes OnWord Press books internationally. For terms call 1-800-4-ONWORD (1-800-466-9673) or 505-474-5130; fax to 505-474-5030; e-mail ORDERS@HMP.COM, or write to High Mountain Press, 2530 Camino Entrada, Santa Fe, NM 87505-4835, USA. Outside North America, call 505-474-5130.

On the Internet: http://www.hmp.com

OnWord Press 2530 Camino Entrada, Santa Fe, NM 87505-4835 USA